The Browns of California

The Browns of California

The Family Dynasty That Transformed a State and Shaped a Nation

MIRIAM PAWEL

BLOOMSBURY PUBLISHING
NEW YORK · LONDON · OXFORD · NEW DELHI · SYDNEY

BLOOMSBURY PUBLISHING
Bloomsbury Publishing Inc.
1385 Broadway, New York, NY 10018, USA

BLOOMSBURY, BLOOMSBURY PUBLISHING, and the Diana logo are
trademarks of Bloomsbury Publishing Plc

First published in the United States 2018

ISBN: HB: 978-1-63286-733-9; eBook: 978-1-63286-735-3

LIBRARY OF CONGRESS CATALOGING-IN-PUBLICATION DATA IS AVAILABLE

2 4 6 8 10 9 7 5 3 1

Typeset by Westchester Publishing Services
Printed and bound in the U.S.A. by Berryville Graphics Inc., Berryville, Virginia

To find out more about our authors and books visit www.bloomsbury.com
and sign up for our newsletters.

Bloomsbury books may be purchased for business or promotional use.
For information on bulk purchases please contact Macmillan Corporate
and Premium Sales Department at specialmarkets@macmillan.com.

For those who believe in the geography of hope

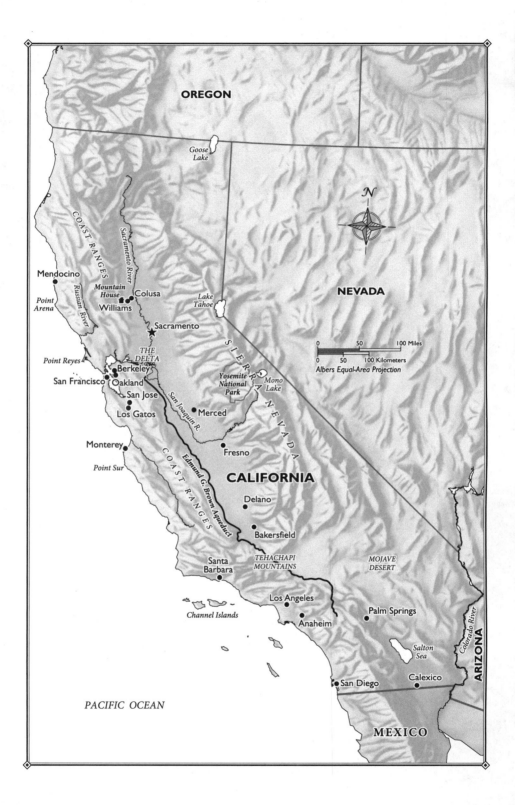

Contents

Preface

The genesis of this book was a conversation several years ago, on an isolated ranch in Northern California, with Jerry Brown. The governor had talked in recent speeches about this land, settled by his great-grandfather soon after the Gold Rush and still in the family four generations later. I was curious to see the homestead and understand what had drawn the last heir of California's storied political dynasty to spend his weekends in a small cabin with no running water, off the grid.

Amid the rolling hills dotted with oaks, Jerry Brown talked about "reinhabitation." He explained his desire to return to his ancestral home, his quest to research every aspect of the land, and his effort to trace his family roots. It is a history worth studying, he said, because history offers anchors in time of disruption and helps us understand how to respond to change.

The same could be said, of course, about the history of California. I came away from that conversation struck by the parallel arcs of the Browns and California. Jerry Brown traced a family history that spanned the life of the state he and his father had governed. I thought the story of four generations might offer a lens through which to tell a unique history of the thirty-first state.

It is, by definition, a selective history, shaped by the paths of the extended family. It is more Northern California than Southern, more modern than early, more political than cultural. Yet, because the family is so intertwined with California, the Browns' story illuminates core values, concepts, places, and events that have molded the world's fifth-largest economy. There is arguably no family more passionate about California, more closely identified with the Golden State, or more influential in determining its fate. The heart of this book is the story of two men who collectively governed California for almost a quarter century—an ebullient, beloved, old-style politician and his cerebral, skeptical, visionary son.

The book is first and foremost a family saga, a narrative history built around collective lives and actions—from far-reaching policy decisions to private, personal choices. My goal is to convey through that tapestry a sense of the sweep and spirit of California, to highlight that which has stayed the same over time and that which has changed. I leave it to future historians to pass judgment on the Brown legacy, which will become clearer with distance.

Given that the two principal protagonists have the same name, and many other characters share the same surname, I refer to the various Browns by their first names. I did this for clarity and readability; it is also true that for many Californians, the state's two longest-serving Democratic governors are known simply as Pat and Jerry.

The Mansion

The corner of Sixteenth and H was just a vacant lot when August Schuckman reached Sacramento in 1852, a square of frontier dirt awaiting its destiny.

August drove a stagecoach, peddled fruit, and dreamed big. The German immigrant had come west seeking land, not gold. Within a decade, he staked his claim to a ranch sixty miles north of the state capital in Colusa County. August's daughter Ida was born there in 1878, the same year a prosperous Sacramento merchant moved into a majestic Victorian mansion he had built at Sixteenth and H. The empty lot had become the most elegant house in town: Seven fireplaces of Italian marble. Elaborate bronze hinges and doorknobs engraved with hummingbirds. Intricate wood inlay on the ballroom floor.

By the turn of the century, more than a million people had been lured to California by visions of gold, land, and sun. Sacramento needed a residence suitable for its governors. In 1903, the state bought the wedding-cake house at Sixteenth and H for $32,500. Two years later, August's daughter Ida gave birth to her first son, Edmund Gerald Brown. He would grow up to be the twelfth governor to live in the Mansion.

Sixteenth and H would become the coordinates where the history of the Golden State intersected with the destiny of August Schuckman's descendants. A family shaped by California would grow into a dynasty that transformed the state, with ambition and audacity to match the grandeur of the towering, turreted Mansion.

Edmund Brown, known to all but his mother as Pat, loved his life in the Mansion, where he seamlessly blended work and family. Most days began with meetings in the breakfast room. That's where Senator John Kennedy asked Pat for support in 1959, and where Pat took a congratulatory call from President Kennedy three years later after defeating Richard Nixon in the governor's race. Most nights, Pat stayed up late reading files from his overstuffed briefcase in the mustard-colored easy chair in the living room or the upstairs office with the special panic button hidden in a drawer. Weekends brought grandchildren splashing in the kidney-shaped pool and sliding down the curved mahogany banister. Pat's sister might arrive with Ida to find Frank Sinatra at dinner. Adlai Stevenson stayed overnight, and Earl Warren often stopped by his old home.

Each Thanksgiving and Christmas, four generations of Browns gathered in the Mansion. News photographers snapped photos of Pat with the turkey, fresh out of the oven. At Christmastime, the Browns chartered a bus to bring San Francisco friends to the Mansion, decorated with lights on the turrets and towers, with 14-foot Christmas trees in the parlor and hall and smaller trees in almost every room.

First lady Bernice Brown oversaw the formal entertainment, dozens of dinners for legislators and lobbyists that eased partisan divides and

Pat Brown was the twelfth governor to live in the Mansion, originally the home of a wealthy hardware merchant. More than four decades later, Jerry Brown became the thirteenth. (Library of Congress, Prints & Photographs Division, HABS Cal,34-SAC,19-1)

smoothed important deals. Visitors knew to check for the small black ceramic cat on the table in the entryway; as long as the sleeping cat was on display, conversations were off the record.

Only the Browns' youngest child grew up in the Mansion. As a teenager, Kathy painted red nail polish on the toes of the clawfoot tub, held slumber parties in the old ballroom, and sought privacy by using the telephone hidden in the music room closet. One Halloween, she climbed the two flights of walnut spiral stairs to the gaslit cupola and dropped water balloons out the porthole window on trick-or-treaters six stories below.

Her older brother, Jerry, lived in the Mansion only briefly, just long enough for the house to hold sway. Jerry first visited the day his father took office in 1959, a young Jesuit seminarian in cassock and collar posing stiffly next to Grandma Ida at a celebratory dinner. Within a year he was in college, then law school. In 1965, Jerry studied for the bar in his father's office on the third floor of the Mansion. He found the lessons tiresome. Wandering out onto the stair landing one day, he heard his father in heated conversation with the Assembly Speaker over which man would run for governor the following year. The debate was as exciting as the studies were tedious. At that moment, Jerry decided that he would be governor, too.

When Pat Brown was voted out of office, the Mansion became another California boom-and-bust tale. Governor Ronald Reagan moved to a classic estate in the Fabulous Forties neighborhood, shunning the house his wife called a "firetrap." The Mansion, eulogized by Sacramento native Joan Didion as "an extremely individual house," perhaps her favorite in the world, became a museum. Visitors toured rooms full of relics a dozen families had left behind: The 1902 Steinway piano from George Pardee, the first governor to live in the Mansion. The plum velvet sofa and matching chairs selected by Mrs. Hiram Johnson. Hand-knotted Persian carpets from the Warren era. Bernice Brown's self-cleaning oven. In the upstairs bedroom, her inaugural gown.

In 1975, a decade after his epiphany on the Mansion stairs, Edmund G. Brown Jr. became the youngest California governor in modern times. He preached "small is beautiful" and spurned the sixteen-room suburban residence that Reagan had commissioned, opting for a spartan apartment near the capitol. He soon became the state's most popular governor, and just as quickly among those held in lowest esteem.

In the land of reinvention, both the man and the Mansion would have a triumphant second act. In 2010, decades after he had left Sacramento, written off as a political has-been, Jerry Brown was elected governor once again. One of the first things he did was bring his wife to see the house at Sixteenth and H.

The state finally began a renovation. Craftsmen restored the original Victorian details while they discreetly added modern plumbing, appliances, and solar panels. Jerry invited relatives to lunch at the Mansion to celebrate his seventy-sixth birthday. On November 4, 2014, he hosted a dinner for staff on the evening he was elected to a historic fourth term. He claimed victory on the Mansion steps.

One year later, the Browns moved in, just in time to celebrate Christmas. The family gathered once more in the elegant house at Sixteenth and H. They posed for pictures. A news photographer watched the governor inspect the turkey. The children who had learned to swim in the kidney-shaped pool showed their children the secret places in the special house.

A photo of August Schuckman sat on the fireplace mantel in the old music room. Jerry called his new home a spiritual place. On a fall afternoon, he recalled the moment he had decided he would be governor. He gestured toward the bottom of the grand staircase a few feet away.

"Every day I come down the stairs, my whole life is unfolding."

1

The Pioneer

Long before the discovery of gold conferred upon the state its universal, enduring epithet, the land imbued California with its seductive, lyrical promise.

Its name was bestowed by early Spaniards, in homage to a popular sixteenth-century romance novel about an island paradise ruled by Queen Califia. In the centuries that followed, explorers discovered the wonders of Yosemite, the fertile valleys, natural ports, blooming deserts, and breathtaking coastline.

Then came the Gold Rush, catapulting California forward with the warp speed that would become one of the state's defining characteristics.

In the spring of 1848, the population of San Francisco was 575 men, 177 women, and 60 children. Within a year, the city had close to twenty-five thousand inhabitants. Doctors and lawyers abandoned practices; tradesmen, laborers, and professionals from around the world arrived in California by boat and stagecoach. In the early days, the mines yielded as much as $50,000 a day in gold (more than $1.5 million in 2016 dollars), money that fueled the region's explosive growth. First the pioneers sought fortunes in gold, then they created the infrastructure and provided the services demanded by this brave new world. An American frontier that had been gradually inching westward suddenly leapfrogged across the country. Californians improvised, unburdened by tradition, open to experimentation. They devised routines, invented machines, and established lifestyles that suited their needs. They could not wait for supplies and knowledge to migrate from the East. They had neither time nor inclination to adopt the staid wisdom or customs of the Eastern establishment.

California was a land "now engrossing the attention of the civilized world with its future importance," Polish immigrant Felix Wierzbicki wrote in *California As It Is, and As It May Be*, the first book published in English in California. The 1849 guidebook foresaw transcontinental railroads, millions of residents, trade with China, and a booming agricultural economy. "It is not necessary to be gifted with an extraordinary foresight to predict that as soon as the industry and enterprise of the Americans take a fair footing on this soil, the commerce of the country will grow daily."

The carpenter John Marshall had first spotted gold in early 1848, just as officials were signing the Treaty of Guadalupe Hidalgo, which ended the Mexican-American War and ceded California to the United States. When the Gold Rush began, California had only a makeshift government. Suddenly, the need for laws became urgent. Congress proposed that California skip territorial status and move directly to statehood. But lawmakers deadlocked for months over whether to allow slavery, a decision that could upset the fragile compromise that had been crafted to hold the Union together. In a pattern destined to be repeated, Californians took matters into their own hands. They called a convention and adopted a constitution that banned slavery, on pragmatic rather than moral grounds. Delegates argued that the nature of work in California was unsuitable for slavery; left unsaid was the fear that large slaveholders could have posed unwelcome competition. The free state of California joined the union on September 9, 1850, which would become an official holiday, Admission Day.

The story of those early years, wrote California's first great philosopher, Josiah Royce, was the story of how "a new and great community first came to a true consciousness of itself." Writers like Royce witnessed that evolution and penned words that shaped lasting visions of California: A land of immigrants. A place of reinvention. A spirit of openness. An incubator of innovation.

That was the world that drew a young German named Simon August Schuckman.

The boy known as August was the second son of Friedrich Kixmöller Schuckman and his wife, Caroline Wilhelmine Luise. Because the Schuckmans had property but no male heirs, Friedrich's father had taken his bride's surname, Schuckman, when they married. Friedrich and Caroline had eight children; five boys and one girl lived into adulthood.

Born July 10, 1827, August grew up in Wüsten, a tiny town in the principality of Lippe-Detmold, in the middle of what was then Prussia. His father operated an inn. August's older brother stood to inherit the family business, leaving the younger son an uncertain future. As revolution spread across Europe in 1848, August, believing he would soon be drafted, made his way north to Hamburg and used savings to book passage to a new life. Two months shy of his twenty-second birthday, August Schuckman arrived in New York on May 8, 1849, on the ship the *Perseverance*.

He was among almost one million Germans who emigrated to the United States in the decade that followed, driven by political and economic upheaval. By 1855, German immigrants were outnumbered only by those from Great Britain. Many had read about California, both at home and once they arrived in the new land. They had heard about the exploits of John Sutter, a Swiss German (né Johan August Suter) who founded, with his son, the city that became Sacramento; gold was discovered at Sutter's Mill. *The Emigrants' Guide to California*, published in St. Louis in 1849, was quickly translated into German, the first of numerous guidebooks that outlined ways to reach the new frontier. Travel "around the Horn" could take nine months and cost $600; cutting across Panama saved time but entailed a dangerous, disease-ridden land crossing; the overland route from Missouri cost as little as $55, the most popular option.

By the time August Schuckman headed for California, the perilous trip had become increasingly routine. Maps laid out detailed routes; books offered guidance on where to find water and grass for cattle; and additional ferries expedited the river crossings. A journey first made almost exclusively by men now included women and children. By 1852, an overland trip that had taken an average of 136 days could be completed in fewer than 90, though many took longer.

August was part of a record number of pioneers who crossed the Plains in 1852, following the Oregon Trail to one of the branches that headed southwest into California. More than fifty thousand people and a hundred thousand cattle and sheep crossed that summer, according to estimates, most in ordinary farm wagons drawn by oxen. They left behind ruts that lasted into the twenty-first century. Dysentery and cholera were common, and letter writers told of graves dug before travelers were even dead. They also wrote of the camaraderie. Women took care of other women's children; men warned other travelers of hostile Indians and dangerous river crossings; families cared for one another's sick and shared food and water when supplies dwindled.

August was vague in his accounts of his first few years in the United States, during which he worked as a hired hand on boats on various rivers and the Great Lakes. But he kept a diary when he joined a party that set out from St. Louis on March 10, 1852.

Six foot one, blue-eyed, sandy-haired, and strong, he hired on with a captain shepherding a group of fifty-three pioneers. They traveled up the Missouri River to Jefferson, where the captain stopped to buy seventy-two oxen and cows he planned to sell in California. Then they headed to St. Joseph, Missouri, their progress slowed as men on horseback chased after oxen that strayed into nearby forests. A month into the journey, on Easter Monday, they reached St. Joseph, minus three cows and two oxen.

The captain bought nine more oxen and eight horses and collected provisions that had been shipped up the river by steamer, and they set off. After six miles they reached the first mountains, where they stopped for six days to rest the cattle, which had walked more than two hundred miles. They set out again on April 24: nine wagons, eighty-one oxen, and eighteen horses. They traveled between eight and twelve miles a day, and by the fifth day, water and wood ran short and tempers flared. They stopped cooking with water and rationed it out to drink.

Two months and three hundred miles into the trip, they reached Fort Kearney in Nebraska, low on provisions and in revolt against their captain, who had been skimping on food. The officer in charge of Fort Kearney listened to their grievances—and their threats to shoot the captain—and told the travelers all he could offer was return passage to St. Joseph. Eager to reach California, the emigrants made peace and pushed on along the well-worn trail.

On May 13, they reached the Platte River, which August described as three times wider than the Weser, the river that bordered his Prussian hometown. He marveled at the herds of pronghorn antelope, which he thought at first were a type of deer. They saw occasional herds of buffalo. But the most common animals were wolves, which circled the camp at night and howled.

A week later they crossed the Platte by ferry, taking two hours to get everyone across. Out of wood to cook by fire, they ate zwieback and ham.

On May 26, they passed what August described as "a clot of earth straight up about 300 feet," later known as Chimney Rock.

Five days later, they reached Fort Laramie in the Wyoming Territory, a major trading post in the land of the Sioux. August was intrigued by their customs. "These Indians do not bury their dead," he wrote. "They weave baskets and put their dead into them and stand them in the tops of trees."

The travelers forged ahead on the dusty, crowded trail and on June 8 reached the head of the Platte River in Casper, Wyoming. More than a hundred wagons waited to cross, a boon for ferry operators who charged $3 per wagon and $1 per animal. By noon the next day, August's party had safely made it to the other side, swimming the animals to the far shore to save money.

Within a week, the party confronted their captain again and threatened to leave him behind. They demanded he provide two and a half pounds of food per day, which would last forty days, and promise to buy any food needed after. He counteroffered: If they would stretch the food for six more days, he promised milk for coffee. Fourteen men accepted that deal, while the rest insisted on their original terms.

On June 18, they saw snow-covered mountains of the Wind River Range in the distance as they approached a juncture known as "the parting of the ways." They took the more difficult Sublette Cutoff, which shaved four days off the trip, and began a forty-one-mile trek across a desert described in guidebooks as "the dry Sandy." They traveled mainly at night to avoid the extreme heat.

On July 26, they reached "the big Sandy," also known as the Forty-Mile Desert, a tough stretch in Nevada. They traveled again at night. "Here the measure of water cost 1 dollar," August wrote. "Here we lost 7 oxen who died of thirst. We also had to leave a wagon here. Here thousands of cows, horses, mules were lying about dead . . . the discarded wagons by the hundreds were driven together and burned. Here we saw wagons standing that would never be taken out again, and more than 1,000 guns that had been broken up. Here on this 40 miles are treasures that can never be taken out again."

On September 1, they reached the eastern foothills of the Sierra Nevada and camped for several days before starting the ascent. "After 15 days of crossing these mountains, letting our wagons down by rope and tying trees behind the wagon, we came to a little mining town called

Hangtown," August wrote. "Very bad town. Close to where gold was discovered. Here I will go work for a while."

Six months after leaving St. Louis, the twenty-five-year-old immigrant had reached his new home in California—Hangtown, later renamed Placerville.

Practical and frugal, August stayed away from the frenetic, speculative life of the mines. Instead, he found steady work making money off those who came to get rich quick. Hangtown, about eight miles south of Coloma, where gold had first been discovered, was a hub for the mining community. Within a few weeks, August had a job driving a freight wagon from Coloma to Sutter's Fort, on the outskirts of Sacramento, about forty miles south.

August became friendly with John Sutter and began to venture farther afield. He took supplies by boat from Sacramento up the Feather River to Marysville, a German settlement where Sutter owned a cattle and hog farm. By the spring of 1853, August was still driving a stagecoach and scouting options to settle down and farm. "I will go up in this fruitful valley and get myself a large tract of land," he wrote. "I have gone up this river which has been named the Sacramento river to a little settlement named Colusa."

Colusa was a small town in a county of the same name, roughly sixty miles long and fifty miles wide, bordered on the east by the Sacramento River and on the west by the Coast Range. The name came from the local Indian tribe. The mines were on the other side of the river, so Colusa developed slowly; in 1850 there were only 115 residents. But as gold grew scarcer and pioneers became discouraged, they fanned out, settled land, and started businesses. At first the land was used mainly to graze livestock. Then Colusa farmers found they could make more money growing barley and wheat, which they sold as feed for horses that drew the wagons that resupplied the mining camps. By spring 1852, three steamboats—the *Jenny Lind*, *Captain Sutter*, and *Orient*—offered regular service up the river from Sacramento, a ninety-mile trip that took eighteen hours. The river traffic turned Colusa into a boomtown, with two hotels, a bakery, three blacksmith and wagon-making shops, a soda fountain, a vegetable depot, and a doctor. The 1852 census reported a population of 620—400 white men, 63 white women, 5 "negroes," 3 "mulattoes," 66 Indians, and 21 foreign residents. Soon hotels opened along the main routes, providing rest and food for travelers and their horses. There were hotels every few miles, their names reflecting the distance from Colusa: Five Mile House, Seven Mile House, Nine Mile House, Ten Mile House, Eleven Mile House, Sixteen Mile House, Seventeen Mile House, Nineteen Mile House, and Twenty Mile House.

Wary of the river, which often overflowed and swept away livestock on low-lying ground, August chose his first ranch land carefully and staked his claim. "I have taken up land 15 miles west of Colusa, on high land and very fine land near to a large range of mountains called the Coast Range," he wrote in 1854. "They are a great range which lies between the Pacific Ocean and the Sacramento Valley—that is what this valley is called now."

A remote county with cool winters, blazing hot summers, and lots of rattlesnakes, Colusa was not for everyone. But pioneers drawn to the sparsely settled farmland embraced the quiet, provincial lifestyle and put down roots that lasted generations. With little fanfare or effort to lure settlers, the low-key town grew to about forty-five hundred residents by 1862. "Those who came here came to stay," wrote local historian Justus Rogers a few decades later. "They remained, and the generation that succeeded them, inspired with the same love for their environments, knew no other and sought no other region to be dedicated with that sweet, endearing, soul-satisfying word, 'home.'"

Home for August by 1860 was a house next door to two of Colusa's leading citizens, fifth-generation American Will Green and his uncle Charles Semple. Charles's brother Robert Semple had been an early pioneer, cofounded the first newspaper, the Monterey *Californian*, presided over the constitutional convention in 1849, and then founded the city of Benicia. Inspired by his success, Charles and Will left their Kentucky home and headed for California. Charles scouted land where he, too, might found a city, and settled on Colusa. His nephew became editor of the *Colusa Sun* and author of the first history of Colusa County, one of about 150 history books about California counties published in the nineteenth century.

Like Green and Semple, most Colusa residents had come from the South. The county was politically conservative and known for its secessionist sentiment. During the Civil War, politicians gathered at the Copperhead Saloon, where they served "Habeas Corpus Juleps." When President Abraham Lincoln was assassinated, the flags at half-staff were mysteriously raised on the day of the funeral. Several citizens were arrested for unpatriotic celebrations, including the district attorney, the deputy assessor, and the justice of the peace.

The settlers of Colusa had a reputation for respecting property rights and generally maintaining law and order without resorting to the lynch law that prevailed nearby. In 1854, they built a small, temporary courthouse. By 1860, the county had outgrown the makeshift structure and commissioned a white stone building in the Classical Revival style, its columns and portico familiar to the residents with Southern roots.

August Schuckman had become a naturalized citizen on May 24, 1859, and registered to vote. But his focus was on business, not politics. As a citizen, he could obtain federal patents to land and register deeds. He purchased an eighty-acre parcel from the heirs of a Revolutionary War veteran who had been granted title under a government bounty program that offered free land as an incentive for soldiers to enlist. August paid the government rate, $1.25 per acre, and filed his claim on April 22, 1862. Having secured his farm, he temporarily stepped away. Knowing full well the travails of the trip, August set out to retrace his route—all the way back to Germany. Thirteen years after he had arrived in America, he was ready to start a family, and he went home to find a bride.

Progress and August's financial stability gave him more options on his trip back east. He chose the quickest route—south from San Francisco by ship to Panama and then across the isthmus on the recently opened Panama Railroad. In the Panama port of Colón, he boarded the *North Star*, and on May 23, 1862, he arrived in New York Harbor. The same day, he applied for a United States passport.

He sailed back to Germany and found his bride in the town of Soest, about sixty miles from his hometown. Augusta Sophie Fiedler was twenty-seven years old when she met August, who was thirty-five. She was the youngest of seven siblings, all but one of them girls. Her father, Max Mathias Fiedler, had been a captain and then a noncommissioned officer in the army and worked for the local tax authority. The Fiedlers were a well-educated middle-class family. If August and Augusta ever told their descendants the story of how they met, the tale was lost to subsequent generations. Whether motivated by love, adventure, or dim prospects at home, Augusta embarked on a journey to a radically different life.

August and Augusta married in the Lutheran church in Wüsten on May 1, 1863, across the street from the Schuckman family tavern. They set off immediately, boarding the SS *Hansa* in Bremen. Most of the 546 passengers traveled in steerage; the Schuckmans were in first class, lower saloon, one step down from the best berths. They arrived in New York on May 26, then boarded another ship to travel around the Horn to San Francisco, and finally journeyed up the Sacramento River to Colusa. August had been gone from the farm for more than a year.

Augusta had found the trip arduous and looked forward to reaching her new home. Yet Colusa proved small comfort. Augusta was educated, enjoyed playing the piano and was accustomed to a refined life. She spoke no English and found herself lonely and isolated in a primitive farming community—not at all the life she had likely imagined. She had but a few possessions from Germany to remind her of home: clothes, a white china teapot. August bought her an elegant parlor organ from the Estey company in Vermont, the finest on the market.

In 1863 August Schuckman brought his bride, Augusta, from a cultured German city to an isolated Colusa ranch. They posed for a charcoal portrait. (Courtesy of Brown family)

On April 21, 1865, the day that Lincoln's funeral cortege left Washington, D.C., the Schuckmans' first son was born. They named him August, and he was known as Gus. He would live the rest of his life on Colusa farms. Gus was followed by Charles in the fall of 1866 and Frank in the spring of 1868.

August continued to prosper, both as a farmer and as a land speculator. He raised cattle, hogs, and chickens and doubled the size of his farm, paying the federal government rate of $1.25 per acre. He profited handsomely from his $200 investment: On May 7, 1869, he sold his 160-acre ranch for $3,000. Ten days later, August bought the 800-acre Lett Ranch for $4,000 and settled in the northern end of the county, on rich soil nourished by Stoney Creek. By 1870, his farm produced 500 bushels of winter wheat, 100 bushels of barley, and 10 tons of hay. He owned livestock worth $1,200—three horses, three milk cows, nine other cattle, 290 sheep, and nine swine, some of which he slaughtered and sold for $450. The total estimated value of his farm's produce was $1,050, and he estimated his personal wealth to be $3,950.

The shrewd businessman took no chances. In a wild West where patent claims took months to travel back and forth to Washington, D.C., and ownership rights were often fuzzy, August filed a homestead claim in 1873 on the land he had been farming for four years. Once the paperwork came through, he was ready for his next deal. In the fall of 1874, he sold the ranch for $5,000, banked half the money, and spent the rest on the Twenty Mile House, a small inn and saloon.

Augusta gave birth to two more sons, Louis and Will, then two girls, Minnie and Emma. The Schuckmans' eighth and final child was born January 11, 1878. They named her Ida.

Six months after Ida's birth, August engineered a business coup. The Twenty Mile House included a parcel that one of the county's largest landowners needed to cross in order to graze his herds. August agreed to trade the Twenty Mile House for a property just a few miles away but far more valuable—a well-known inn and tavern called the Mountain House. August wanted to be an innkeeper, like his father.

August moved his family to the nearby city called Central, just as the town that was little more than a crossroads began to grow. The railroad had reached Colusa County.

On a smaller scale, the railroad brought to Colusa the same dramatic change that the arrival of the first cross-country trains had brought to

California a decade earlier. Once the first trains reached Oakland in 1869, a trip to New York took only a few days. Such easy access would enhance California, but also spur greater inequality, warned bestselling author Henry George in a well-read, prescient essay, "What the Railroad Will Bring Us." As George predicted, land escalated in value, which was a boon for existing owners but a bar for newcomers. More people meant more competition for jobs, which lowered wages. The railroad centralized wealth and created a class of tycoons whose power would soon have profound implications for California.

In Central, an enterprising builder named W. H. Williams had bought up land and laid out a grid in anticipation of the railroad terminus. Once trains began to run in 1876, goods could be shipped south to Sacramento by rail, and proximity to the terminal trumped access to the river. Williams resold land, Central boomed, and the city was renamed in his honor.

While goods went south, people came north. The trains facilitated travel to several hot springs that were a day's journey west of Williams by stagecoach. Renowned for their healing powers, Bartlett, Allen, and Wilbur Springs attracted hundreds of visitors a year from as far as San Francisco. Many were Germans, who compared the baths to those of Baden Baden. Advertisements and history books cited testimonials to the waters' ability to cure rheumatism, liver and kidney ailments, fever, and asthma. Strategically located along the route from Williams to the springs sat August Schuckman's inn.

The Mountain House, built in 1855 at a fork in the road twelve miles west of Williams, became a popular stopping place to feed or change horses and to enjoy a drink, a meal, or an overnight rest. The inn had twelve bedrooms—one of them large enough to bunk ten single men—a long bar, a large sitting room, two dining rooms, a kitchen, and a pantry. Meals cost a quarter, and whiskey was ten cents a shot or a dollar a quart. To board a horse overnight cost fifty cents.

Stagecoaches could carry more than a dozen passengers from Williams west to the Mountain House. There the coaches divided, some heading to the hot springs while others veered off to the mining community at Sulphur Creek. Mineral waters from the springs were bottled and sold as a tonic for ailments. Mule-drawn wagons hauled the bottled water from the springs to the Williams railroad station for shipping to San Francisco and points east. They, too, stopped at the Mountain House.

Like many locals, the Schuckmans sometimes spent a day or a week at the springs to escape the brutal summer heat. Photographs show August, his bearing erect, his sandy hair now gray, his face covered with a long beard, with his three daughters—Minnie and Ida rail-thin, Emma heavyset.

The older Schuckman boys grew up and found work, two as telegraph operators for the railroad, one as an innkeeper in another county, one as a hired hand. William died in a farming accident at twenty-nine; Louis and his wife died of tuberculosis in their early thirties.

A decade younger than their siblings and just two years apart in age, Ida and Emma were very close. German was their first language, and neither of their parents ever mastered English. When Ida was nine years old, her mother suddenly fell ill just before her fifty-second birthday. Augusta Schuckman, who had never embraced her life in California, died in the doctor's office on May 22, 1887. She was buried in the Williams cemetery with a simple headstone that read OUR MOTHER, and a short verse, "A precious one from us has gone, a voice we loved is stilled. A place is vacant in our home which never can be filled."

A few years later, August and his daughters moved to the Mountain House. There they grew grains and vegetables and raised cattle, hogs, and chickens, selling whatever they didn't eat or use at the hotel. They stored food in two large rooms under the house, covered with wet sacks to keep it fresh, until they acquired the luxury of an icebox. Gus, the eldest son, was an avid newspaper reader and self-taught animal expert, content to work on the farm. Frank had inherited his father's financial acumen and helped run the business.

Still mourning their mother's early death, Ida and Emma watched as their older sister Minnie began to waste away. She suffered from a stomach ailment that went undiagnosed, and she died on March 25, 1892. She was buried near her mother, MINNIE carved into the top of the stone and the inscription reading M. SCHUCKMAN, AGED 18YS 7MS 9DS.

Soon after, Emma married and moved to a nearby farm. Teenaged Ida was on her own in the rugged and relatively isolated world of the Mountain House. She and Emma would remain close the rest of their lives, though their personalities differed markedly. Content to raise a family in the small world of Colusa, Emma never yearned for anything more. Ida found her hometown stifling and longed for adventure. She would later tell her grandson that the Mountain House was "wonderful"; yet in a photograph of herself with her sister, brother, and father outside the inn, fifteen-year-old Ida scratched out her face. She told her family she wanted to erase any association with the place.

Other families with children lived on farms scattered five to ten miles apart in Venado, the name of the area around the Mountain House. Ida's close friends were two sisters, Millie and Lu Clark. Ida finished eighth grade at the one-room Williams schoolhouse, riding a buckboard to and from school. She liked her studies well enough to keep her English grammar book, which included a chapter on letter writing. The subject was not taught until high school rhetoric class, but "very few of the pupils of the grammar schools will ever attend any school of a higher grade," the textbook noted. "Their equipment for the duties of life, so far as given in a school education, must be completed here. As all persons find occasion to write letters, it seems desirable that some specific instruction should be given in this important subject."

Letters soon became a source of entertainment for Ida. Her father had scored another business coup by winning a post office for the Mountain House, a patronage plum that provided additional income. Ida worked as the Venado postmistress. Out of boredom and inquisitiveness, she clandestinely steamed open letters to read them before they were delivered. Then the Clark girls moved to San Francisco, and Ida went to visit.

2

The Paris of America

Turn-of-the-century San Francisco called itself "the Paris of America," a cosmopolitan city that reveled in its public life, entertainment, and culture.

"There is in the whole world no city—not even Constantinople, New Orleans, or Panama—which possesses equal advantages," Henry George wrote in San Francisco's first literary journal, *Overland Monthly*. "She will be not merely the metropolis of the Western front of the United States, as New York is the metropolis of the Eastern front, but *the city*, the sole great city."

A remote outpost just a few decades earlier, San Francisco had become the ninth-largest city in the United States and a major tourist destination. Visitors and locals alike flocked to the Palace Hotel and the Opera House, grand buildings that were emblematic of the city's vitality and ambition. Renowned architects were drawing up plans for the thousand-acre parcel the city had set aside for recreation, which would eventually become Golden Gate Park. A Midwest transplant named Hubert Howe Bancroft had opened the largest bookstore west of Chicago. Frank Norris, a recent graduate of the new University of California, wrote features about San Francisco culture for *The Wave*, a magazine that had been started by the Southern Pacific Railroad to promote tourism and morphed into a journal for the sophisticated literary set.

Artists and writers presented in public venues and celebrated in private at the Bohemian Club, the male-only bastion that would later host presidents and counted among its early members Mark Twain, Bret Harte, Ambrose Bierce, and John Muir. To emphasize the premium placed on enjoying leisure free from business pursuits, the Bohemians adopted their distinctive motto: "Weaving spiders come not here." Summer outings into the redwoods north of the city grew into longer encampments on the Russian River.

San Francisco was less than 150 miles from Venado, but a world apart. While the rest of the Schuckmans were content with the Colusa lifestyle, eighteen-year-old Ida had other plans. After she visited her friends in San Francisco in 1896, Ida never returned to the Mountain House. San Francisco became her classroom, and Ida embraced with delight and curiosity the city she would call home for more than seven decades. "There were suddenly all these opportunities," she would later say.

Soon after Ida arrived in San Francisco, friends introduced her to Ed Brown. She was eighteen; he was eight years older, five feet seven and three quarters inches tall, green-eyed, fair-haired, full of energy and big dreams.

Ida Schuckman was still a teenager when she left the family ranch in Colusa for turn-of-the-century San Francisco, a city she loved. (Courtesy of Karin Surber)

Ed was born to Irish immigrants who had fled the oppression and misery of the potato famine. His father, Joseph Brown, was born August 14, 1829, the youngest of five, all baptized in the Catholic parish of Tipperary. Joseph had a typical Irish childhood, growing up in a mud house on an estate owned by a large landowner in the town of Spring-house. Later the family moved up the hill to a coveted spot above the stables, an indication that they had skills valued by the land barons. After potato blight destroyed the principal source of food and income for Irish peasants, Tipperary lost a quarter of its population to death and departures. Between 1847 and 1854, more than one million Irish men and women emigrated to the United States. Joseph joined the exodus, arriving in Boston Harbor on November 25, 1850, on the clipper ship *Anglo American*. He settled in Framingham, midway between Boston and Worcester, a rural town more than two centuries old.

Sixteen-year-old Bridget Burke had also fled Tipperary for the United States at almost the same time. With her parents and three sisters, she had sailed from Liverpool with more than four hundred other passengers aboard the *Aeolius*, landing in New York on June 26, 1850. By fall, the Burkes had settled in Framingham, where Bridget met Joseph Brown. They were married on January 26, 1857. He was twenty-seven; she was twenty-two.

Joseph worked on a farm. The Browns started a family and lived in a neighborhood called Saxonville, named after the Saxon Factory mills that produced carpets and woolen blankets. Many of the Browns' neighbors were scions of long-established families, like the blacksmith Joseph Angier, whose roots in America went back nine generations.

Sometime around the end of the Civil War, the Browns decided to move west. Like many cities in the East, Framingham had offered the Irish an escape from the famine that wreaked havoc in their homeland, but not from the oppression or stigma of their roots and religion. Ed Brown would grow up hating the English for how they had treated his parents, in both the old country and the new.

Being Irish in San Francisco was different. Catholicism was the dominant religion, despite the best efforts of Protestant churches in the East, which had dispatched emissaries after the Gold Rush to try to save the souls of the new state. San Francisco acquired fine churches and prominent ministers, but the strong Catholic presence easily withstood the proselytizing. Catholics built community around schools, orphanages, and hospitals. In 1851, the Jesuits opened Santa Clara, a preparatory school south of San Francisco, which became the first college in California. The Catholic presence in the Bay Area attracted Irish immigrants, who in turn strengthened the state's Catholic roots. That circumstance, coupled with the lack of an established elite, made California a place where the Irish could aspire to greater prosperity, dignity, and even political power.

By 1866, Joseph Brown was a registered voter in the Twelfth Ward of San Francisco. Edmund Joseph Brown was born on October 12, 1870, the fourth of five children. They grew up on North Point Street, a block from the bay and the Pioneer Woolen Mills, where their father worked as a teamster and the older girls worked in the mills, until the building was taken over by the Ghirardelli Chocolate Company (later to become Ghirardelli Square). Ed's father worked grading streets and then for more than two decades as a gardener helping with the construction of Golden Gate Park.

Ed went to Spring Valley School, one of the earliest public schools in the city, which earned notoriety around the time he graduated as a test case in San Francisco's discrimination against the Chinese. The racial prejudice that had led to the national Chinese Exclusion Act of 1882 was particularly prevalent in San Francisco, where Chinese made up almost 10 percent of the city's population. Tens of thousands of Chinese had been hired to build the transcontinental railroads; when that work ended, many settled in what became the country's first Chinatown. In 1884, eight-year-old Mamie Tape was denied admission to Spring Valley School, though she lived a block away. Her Chinese immigrant parents sued to force admission and won. Rather than integrate, the city set up a separate school for Chinese pupils.

When Ed Brown met Ida, he was living with his parents on Shotwell Street in the Mission District and working for the nearby La Grande and White Laundry Company. He collected dirty clothes from customers on his route, delivered them to the laundry to be washed and ironed, and returned the clean clothing.

On Monday, August 16, 1897, Ida and Ed took a ferry across the bay, the only way to reach Oakland, and were married by a justice of the peace.

They moved frequently in the early years of their marriage—156 Seventh Street, 613 Larkin, 201 Turk, 1408 Divisadero. Ed hustled enough capital to open a cigar store on Turk Street, then added a nearby penny arcade. When he was in the money, he bought Ida the fine clothes, furs, and jewelry that she enjoyed. Ed was often out at night, leaving Ida on her own to explore the city. She attended talks by writers and became an avid reader and frequent patron of the library, which already had half a dozen branches.

Ida was so thin that she padded her clothes. She likely suffered from anemia, which may have contributed to her infertility. The Browns had almost given up hope of having a family. Then, seven years after her marriage, Ida became pregnant. Edmund Gerald Brown was born April 21, 1905, at Children's Hospital and baptized two months later in St. Agnes Church. His parents doted on the boy and outfitted him for photographs in the style of the day—dresses and patent leather shoes with pink tops, which Ida kept long after her son outgrew them.

In the early hours of April 18, 1906, three days before Edmund's first birthday, the great earthquake struck San Francisco, triggering one of the country's greatest natural disasters. The Richter scale had not been invented, but the best estimates place the strength of the quake at magnitude 7.8. Several thousand died and most of the city was leveled. Damage from the tremors was compounded by dozens of fires that erupted during the confused response. People poured into the streets, uncertain what to do or where was safe. Ed sent Ida and the baby to stay with her sister in Colusa. Then he went up into the hills and watched the city burn.

The visit would have been one of the last times that Ida saw her father. By the fall, she was pregnant again and stayed close to home, giving birth to Harold Clinton Brown on July 19, 1907. August Schuckman died two weeks later. He had just turned eighty. The German immigrant and his family had become fixtures in the community, and his passing merited a lengthy write-up in the *Colusa Sun* about "the Pioneer of Venado." August left the bulk of his $1,200 estate to his nine grandchildren, including Edmund, who each received $75. The remainder, after expenses, was split among the surviving children—$7.47 apiece.

August had sold the Mountain House to his son Frank in 1894 for $1,500, and Frank proved to have the frugal Schuckman business genes. He rebuilt the inn. As cars replaced stagecoaches and business dropped off, he bought adjoining parcels to expand the size of the ranch to more than two thousand acres. Frank became a moneylender and a civic pillar of the nearby city of Williams. He put up money to finance bonds to build the first City Hall, set up telephone lines from Williams west to Venado, and then sold the lines to the phone company. He was a Mason of such long standing that the secret society eventually waived his annual dues.

During the summers, Ida would bring Edmund and Harold to stay with her sister for several weeks. The trip took a full day. Ed accompanied them on the ferry to Oakland and then saw them off at the Fourteenth Street train station. Like Ida and Emma, Edmund and Harold were two years apart, so close that their mother swore that they talked to each other in their sleep. Edmund was dark and Harold was blond, and Ida perceived that her husband favored Edmund, so she compensated by paying special attention to Harold. In Colusa, the boys played with their older cousins. They collected eggs, pestered the chickens, roamed the ranches, and absorbed a sense of how their mother had grown up, in an isolated house with no indoor plumbing.

San Francisco, the city that had sprung up overnight during the Gold Rush, rose quickly yet again after the earthquake. Officials rejected plans to redesign the city as a grand metropolis with wide European-like boulevards and opted instead to recreate familiar streets and buildings. Spirited and defiant in the face of natural and man-made calamities, San Francisco returned to business and prepared to welcome tourists again by hosting the World's Fair in 1915.

Like the city, Ed Brown was resilient. He had an eye for the next big thing and rode each wave of civic reinvention with great gusto. Henry George might have been writing about Ed when he described the special sense of hope and self-reliance among Californians that dated back to the Gold Rush days, "the latent feeling of every one that he might 'make a strike,' and certainly could not be kept down long." Being broke was not a cause for embarrassment or hopelessness; everyone had been there. "The wheel of fortune had been constantly revolving with a rapidity in other places unknown, social lines could not be sharply drawn, nor a reverse dispirit. There was something in the great possibilities of the country."

For a while, Ed marketed Dr. Rowell's Fire of Life, a muscle liniment that promised to cure asthma, rheumatism, cancer, and colds. In the back of his cigar store, Ed started a betting operation. He had an aptitude for math, which may have contributed to the success of his lucrative sideline as a bookie. For ten dollars, Ed bought a lot in the Western Addition, a neighborhood sprouting on the outskirts of the city. Ida took the money her husband had made from gambling and invested in the construction of a three-story flat. She later regretted allowing the architect to persuade her to omit a garage. He argued that cars were a passing fad.

The house at 1572 Grove Street had one large apartment on each floor. The Browns lived on the second floor and rented out the other two. There was a bedroom over the stairs, a kitchen, a dining room, washtubs, bins for wood and coal, then a long hall that led to a half bath, full bathroom, and two bedrooms in the back. The fireplace in the front room was the primary source of heat, which they supplemented with small round stoves fueled by coal and oil and carried from room to room.

The Panhandle, two blocks away, became the children's backyard, first as babies in strollers and toddlers on swings, then as youngsters playing soccer and baseball. Dunes began only a few blocks from the house, nothing but sand all the way to Ocean Beach, where the boys swam in the summer. The boundaries of their neighborhood encompassed nine square blocks, from Fillmore west to Masonic, from Haight north to Turk. They attended Fremont Grammar School, two blocks from the house, which drew about four hundred students from a six-block radius, including several dozen from the nearby Pacific Hebrew Orphan Asylum.

The Browns' tenants at 1572 Grove were Jewish. They brought the Browns gefilte fish and matzo on Passover and asked the boys to light their gas on High Holy Days. The neighbors were German, Italian, Russian, Mexican, Jewish, Irish, and English. Ida shopped at the neighborhood butcher, the corner grocery, bakery, creamery, vegetable market, and delicatessen. There was a drugstore, a barber, and a tailor. Stores delivered goods by horse and buggy. For a nickel, you could get downtown in about twenty minutes on the No. 5 McAllister cable car, which stopped two blocks from the house, or the No. 21 Hayes line, which stopped even closer. In good times, Ed would take the family out to dinner once a week at a popular restaurant like the German House or the Heidelberg Inn.

Ed put his sons to work at an early age, giving them late edition papers to hawk in the street and Christmas cards to peddle. He took the boys to fights and to minor league baseball games where they cheered for the San Francisco Seals. Ed loved poetry and recited reams of poems by heart; he had Edmund read speeches aloud to coach him on delivery. Ida focused on the content of the speeches and instilled a love of learning. She read so much that Edmund and Harold mimicked her by starting their own lending library.

In 1912, the Browns' daughter, Constance Augusta, was born. Four years later Ida gave birth to their youngest, Franklin Marshall. Nine-year-old Harold wrote his mother a letter while she was in the hospital, which she kept for the rest of her life: "We are all anxious about you. Pa told us that we got a little baby boy . . . Edmund is writing a composition on Carbon tonight . . Papa said we couldn't come over to see you because we were not of age. We have a little canary bird. Papa bought it a couple of days ago. We all send our love."

The house at 1572 Grove gave the Browns a permanent home as well as a source of steady income from the rental apartments. That financial security helped offset the frequent ups and downs of Ed's entrepreneurial pursuits.

After the cigar store, Ed moved into the entertainment business. He nabbed one of the last vacant storefronts on the south side of Market Street and opened a penny arcade in the building that housed the Portola, an eleven-hundred-seat theater that was one of the first to open after the earthquake. Then he opened his own small theater in a store-front on Fillmore Street. Musee Moving Pictures was a nickelodeon, one of the increasingly popular entertainment venues where a nickel bought admission to watch a combination of short silent movies and live vaudeville acts.

Nickelodeons popularized movies as entertainment, and soon feature films that required large theaters put the smaller storefronts out of business. By 1912, Ed moved up to operating a real theater, the Liberty, on Broadway in North Beach. For several years, business was good. Ed took the boys to the movies once a week, walking through Chinatown to the theater. Then the theater across the street was renovated into a modern movie house that sapped the Liberty's business. Ed fired the stagehands to save money. They picketed, and he came home ranting about unions. Labor unionists, he told his children, were bad people—just like the English.

Forced to reinvent himself again, Ed jumped on the next hot trend: quick-finish photo studios. A quarter bought three pictures, developed and printed in ten minutes. Ed opened a novelty store on Market and Fourth with a photo studio in the back. The pennants and souvenirs sold well during the Panama-Pacific International Exposition, and the photos proved even more popular. Ed expanded the photo booths to several more locations on Market Street. He was able to offer enough money to lure photographers away from more prestigious jobs. As he explained to one photographer who was reluctant to leave a classier job at the upscale Gump's department store: When you take your girl to the Palace Hotel, she won't ask where you made the money.

Ed and Ida were sharp dressers, he in three-piece suits and a gold watch and chain, she in elaborate dresses and feather hats. The photo studios featured picturesque backdrops of arbors and bridges, and Ed often posed his family on the faux park bench or motorcar. Edmund was about twelve when he began working for his father after school and on weekends, helping develop and enlarge pictures. Business boomed when the United States entered the Great War in 1917. Soldiers wanted photos before they shipped out or when they came back on leave. Ed doubled the price to fifty cents and added several more photo booths.

In a significant historical footnote, the United States declaration of war against Germany also affected the Brown family legacy.

Within weeks of entering the war in April 1917, the United States issued Liberty Bonds to underwrite the military campaign. The first sale of $5 billion worth of bonds at 3.5 percent interest met with a tepid response from large investors. Before the second bond sale in the fall, the Treasury Department launched a public relations campaign to promote the sale of bonds to individuals, a relatively new concept. By marketing bonds as a patriotic act, the government hoped to raise cash and build support, after voters had just reelected President Woodrow Wilson on the slogan "He kept us out of the war."

UNCLE SAM NEEDS MONEY AS WELL AS MEN, read Liberty Bond posters. BECOME AN INVESTOR AND HELP YOUR COUNTRY FIGHT! Movie stars like Al Jolson, Mary Pickford, Douglas Fairbanks, and Charlie Chaplin appeared at rallies to help sell Liberty Bonds. Chaplin made and starred in a short film, "The Bond," which moved from the bond of friendship to the bond of marriage to Liberty Bonds and ended with Chaplin using a Liberty Bond to knock out the German kaiser.

The Federal Reserve coordinated contests tied to another public relations effort of the Wilson administration, the "Four-Minute Men." Tens of thousands of men, women, and children were recruited to proselytize for the war bonds in speeches that lasted exactly four minutes—the time it took to change reels at a movie theater. While the speaker delivered the four-minute pitch, volunteers went through the theater aisles selling Liberty Bonds.

Edmund Brown was in seventh grade in the fall of 1917 when he entered a school contest to compose and deliver one of the four-minute speeches. He won. The prize was an opportunity to give the speech at the Fox Theater. Edmund wound up his speech by quoting Patrick Henry: "Give me liberty or give me death." Edmund's friends began to good-naturedly kid him and call him Pat. The nickname stuck. From then on, only his family called him Edmund. To the rest of the world, he was Pat Brown.

3

The Yell Leader

In high school, Pat Brown said, only half-jokingly, he ran for president of every club even if he was not a member.

Because the Browns lived two blocks away, Pat attended Lowell, one of the oldest public high schools west of the Mississippi and one of the most prestigious. The school's opening in 1856 augured the state's extraordinary commitment to accessible higher education and was celebrated as a milestone in the quest to build a democracy around an educated populace. "The citizens of San Francisco have, with their accustomed liberality, cheerfully devoted their means and influence in planting upon these Pacific shores the seeds of virtue and knowledge, which, if properly nourished and guarded, will soon ripen into a rich harvest of intelligent citizens," the city school superintendent said at the opening celebration. Sixty years later, the interest in higher education had spawned multiple high schools in San Francisco, but Lowell remained the most renowned. Its focus on college preparation attracted high-achieving students from wealthy families around the city.

Pat was a member of the debating society, the rowing team, and the camera club, and at various times president of all three. He was the shortest boy at Mrs. Chase's dance school, but his stature did not deter him from joining as many sports teams as possible. He competed in broad jump for the track team and played on the basketball team for those weighing less than a hundred pounds—until he skipped practice to be in the soccer team picture and the basketball coach threw him off.

As a junior, Pat ran for yell leader, defeated the incumbent, and took to the field decked out in white flannel trousers and a red jersey emblazoned with white megaphones. The next year he was elected class secretary after shying away from the office he really wanted, student body president, to avoid competing with the captain of the football team. He never enjoyed being secretary and later said he took from the experience a determination not to avoid a campaign solely for fear of losing.

Pat was both popular and an outsider. The wealthier boys hung out at the Bonbonniere candy store across the street; Pat went home for lunch fixed by his mother. He was invited to join a fraternity but spurned the offer when they wouldn't accept his good friend Arnold Schiller because he was Jewish. Outraged, Pat started an ecumenical fraternity, the Nocturnes, later renamed Sigma Delta Kappa. His popularity confounded the better-dressed students from upper-class families who looked down on the short kid in corduroys. But Pat's decency, drive, and moral convictions won him lifelong friends. His exuberance compensated for any lack of polish.

In history class his junior year, the yell leader launched another determined quest. Pat began to court Bernice Layne, the precocious daughter of a police captain. He walked her home sometimes, almost two miles to the house at the corner of Seventeenth and Shrader. When Pat asked her out on a date, Bernice accepted, then backed out at the last minute without explanation. She was embarrassed to tell him her mother wouldn't allow her to date. She was only thirteen.

Bernice's mother had seen that her daughter was bored as soon as she entered grammar school and enrolled her in a small experimental school for training teachers. Students progressed at their own pace. Bernice completed eight grades in three and a half years. Math was her favorite subject. Accumulating points for every book read, she plowed through Horatio Alger, the Rover Boys, and *Little Women*. After school, she learned to sew, making dresses for Belgian babies in a program set up by the Red Cross to help with the war effort. She was still ten when she finished all the coursework necessary to enter high school, so she spent six months working in the school library and the cooking classroom. She turned eleven and entered Lowell High School at the start of 1920.

Like Pat, she was the child of a mixed marriage. Arthur Layne, a well-known police captain in the toughest precinct in the city, traced his Protestant roots back several generations in Texas and the South, where his ancestors had been strong supporters of the Confederacy. Captain

Layne's reputation for honesty in a department known for corruption was bolstered during a year-long graft investigation. His testimony helped get five of nine captains fired.

On her mother's side, Bernice was a mix of French, Italian, and Irish Catholic, harking back to the polyglot community formed around the California gold mines. Bernice's great-grandmother Zelia Rouhaud had emigrated from France in 1854 to keep house for her brother, a French diplomat. The French played a big role in the early mining days, but their dominance faded because, unlike Spain, France did not allow dual citizenship and the United States did not allow noncitizens to acquire property. While taking care of her brother, Zelia met and married an Italian merchant, Giovanni Baptiste Cuneo. Their first child, named Hippolyte after her brother, grew up to be an ironworker and labor activist in San Francisco, serving as secretary of the Iron Moulders' Union. Hippolyte married Julia Roche, a Californian of Irish descent. Their oldest daughter was Alice Cuneo. She married Arthur Layne in 1904.

Bernice was born to the couple four years later. She and her four siblings were raised as Episcopalians. When she was thirteen, Bernice was allowed to attend Friday night dances that her mother helped organize at All Saints Episcopal Church. Pat began to show up at the dances.

Although he was not religious, Ed Brown wanted his children raised Catholic. Ida acquiesced and sent the boys off to church on Sundays. When he was twelve, Pat skipped his own confirmation and stopped attending services. His mother, initially indifferent, grew increasingly skeptical of the Catholic Church and then openly hostile. Several things sparked Ida's strong and vocal rejection of the Church. She bristled at derogatory remarks that Ed's sisters made about Ida's insistence on sending her children to public school. Her reading caused her to question some Catholic dogma. And a priest tried to harangue her into conversion, warning that her children were bastards until she was married in the Church. For the strong-willed Ida, such admonishments backfired.

Ida's antipathy to the Catholic Church did not stem from lack of faith or spirituality, which were integral to her character. She studied the Bible and read Bible stories to her children before bed. So Ida set out, in her methodical fashion, to find a satisfactory place to worship. She auditioned religious leaders in visits to church services around the city. In the end, she chose the First Unitarian Church of San Francisco, an institution with a reputation for social justice and a storied past.

The First Unitarian Church had risen to prominence during the Civil War under the leadership of Thomas Starr King, who came west with some reluctance in 1860 and died four years later as a state hero. The story of the young minister who rose from relative poverty based solely on his talent became an important brick in the California legend. King embraced his adopted state and wrote extensively about its natural beauty, particularly the Yosemite Valley. His writings, published in the East, were credited with helping naturalist John Muir in his crusade to establish Yosemite as the first national park. During the Civil War, King delivered so many passionate speeches around the state urging support for Lincoln that he became known as "the man who kept California in the Union." King was thirty-nine years old when he died from pneumonia and diphtheria; twenty thousand people lined his funeral route.

When Ida joined the Unitarian Church, Dr. Caleb S. S. Dutton, known as Sam, was preaching inspired sermons in the lilting accent of his native Britain. Dutton had come to San Francisco from Brooklyn, where he helped found the National Association for the Advancement of Colored People. In his first sermon in San Francisco in 1913, he laid out his vision for the congregation: "To identify ourselves with social causes wherever apparent and bring them to their full, complete fruition in all just expression, to stand for that complete democracy which is the demand of idealism, to fight as champions of the God of Righteousness every form of oppression—economic, social or political—and consecrate ourselves to that form of spiritual religion."

This was a vision Ida could embrace. The Unitarians' Channing Auxiliary, a pioneering women's group, offered a range of literary and cultural programs. The church had a relationship with Temple Emanu-El that dated back to Thomas Starr King and included a joint Thanksgiving service. Ida brought her children to debates between reform and orthodox Jews. She enrolled in a course about the Old Testament and took Pat to a synagogue. One of her favorite quotes, recited often to her family, was from the Book of Micah: "What doth the Lord require of thee but to do justly and to love mercy and to walk humbly with thy God?" If people lived like that, Ida told her offspring, there wouldn't need to be any laws.

Through church and civic activities, Ida immersed herself in a circle of educated and intellectually engaged friends. Dutton held Thursday evening book club discussions. Once or twice a week Ida attended lectures, the principal form of intellectual entertainment in the era before radio became popular. She took Pat to hear politicians like Hiram Johnson, the Progressive ex-governor who was running for Senate. Lectures sent her back to the library in search of books to decipher or deepen her knowledge of what she had heard. A reference to something she did not understand—"Trojan horse," for example—became an excuse to further her self-education. She read voraciously and eclectically; Jack London and Robert Louis Stevenson were favorites, as were Mark Twain and Robert Ingersoll. She read Hubert Howe Bancroft on California history and William James on religion and psychology. For several years, she taught Sunday school at the Unitarian church.

She passed along to her children the value of learning and also her condemnation of bigotry. She believed fervently in civil rights, religious tolerance, and the need to crusade for equal rights for blacks. By nature and by nurture, her children grew up with the moral certainty that prejudice was wrong and must be fought. She conveyed her spirit of independence through actions as well as words. "To thine own self be true," she would often cite.

Increasingly, that advice took her further away from Ed. They pursued parallel lives and had less and less to do with each other. At home, the tension increased. Frank, the youngest child, would sit at breakfast hoping that his father would find the two-minute soft-boiled eggs satisfactory; if not, Ed threw them out the window. Ed slept in the front bedroom, Ida slept in the back, Pat and Harold shared the third bedroom, and Connie and Frank slept in the dining room. Eventually, Ed moved into an apartment downtown. Though they had little use for each other, neither parent denigrated the other to their children, rather praising each other for working hard to provide and care for the family.

After the end of World War I, business slowed down at the photo studios. Ed hired a barker in top hat and cane who stood in front and tried to drum up business. Then he fired two employees and replaced them with Pat and Harold. Both boys found additional work at the city's four competing newspapers. Harold put together inserts for the Sunday edition of the *Examiner*, earning fifty cents an hour for twelve-hour shifts that started Friday afternoon. Pat had a newspaper route for the *Call-Bulletin* and then the *Chronicle*.

On weekends, Pat took the ferry across the bay with friends to attend home games of the Golden Bears, the football "Wonder Team" at the University of California that was in the midst of a fifty-game unbeaten streak. The university charged no tuition and only a token student fee, and most of Pat's high school classmates expected to end up on the Berkeley campus, known as Cal. Some preferred rival Stanford, which also charged minimal tuition and fashioned itself as an entry point for working-class Californians. "In no other state is the path from the farmhouse to the college so well trodden as here," boasted Stanford's first president, David Starr Jordan (who had taken Starr as his middle name in honor of the Unitarian tradition of public service and the man who "saved California for the Union," Thomas Starr King). Ida later traced her love of literature to a talk that Jordan had delivered at the Unitarian church.

Pat seemed likely to head to Cal, closest to home. But as high school graduation approached, the eighteen-year-old made a major decision: He scrapped plans for college. His friend Arnold Schiller's brother had gone directly from high school to night law school, and Pat saw that path as both financially and politically expedient. College was not automatic for many people, and attending Cal would have required a lengthy commute to Berkeley—streetcar to ferry to another streetcar on the other side, about a three-hour round trip. By attending night law school, Pat could earn money during the day and also fast-track his career. He was always in a hurry to get where he was going; he had no use for men who smoked pipes, because he felt it slowed them down.

Pat entered San Francisco Law School in 1923. Adjusting to the work meant average grades the first few semesters. By the third year, he hit his stride, and by the fourth and final year he was first in his class. Just as at Lowell, Pat also excelled at extracurricular activities. He started a student organization, a law journal, and an affiliate for a legal fraternity—and headed all three.

The part-time class schedule—three to four nights a week and summer courses—gave Pat plenty of time to work. For the first two years he worked for his father, who ran a quasilegal poker club. Poker was legal only if played at a private club. Pat's job was to guard the door to give the operation a veneer of exclusivity, though in reality anyone could play. He earned $150 a month sitting outside the Railroad Men's Social Club, then made another $150 to $200 running his own dice game. He often ended up giving much of that to his father, who was perennially broke.

In his third year, Pat accepted a job with a well-known lawyer, Milton Schmitt, who had lost his sight and needed an assistant. The switch meant a pay cut, but it netted Pat experience in a law office and in the courts.

During his two-year apprenticeship, he made connections and became familiar with the milieu.

Schmitt was a conservative Republican who had served four terms in the state Assembly, and he discouraged Pat when he talked about running for office. But the twenty-three-year-old was in a hurry. One year out of law school, Pat challenged an incumbent assemblyman in a Republican primary, campaigning with the indisputable slogan "23 years in the district." Some of his fraternity brothers helped, and Bernice rang doorbells on one side of the street while Pat went down the other, up and down hills on Castro Street. She told people she was his sister. He spent about $500 and fell far short, winning only about five hundred votes.

Each summer, Pat took two weeks off and went with his brother Harold and three friends on a pilgrimage to Yosemite, a place both familiar and wild, a touchstone of the outdoor world he loved. They hiked during the day and danced at night. Pat and Harold scaled summits and posed for photos on high ledges. Pat was thin, 140 pounds on his five-foot-ten-inch frame, and he smoked. On one trip, Pat met Tom Lynch, who would become one of his closest, lifelong friends. Lynch was also San Francisco Irish. Orphaned at a young age, he attended Jesuit schools until he had to drop out and work, then enrolled in night law school. Lynch and Pat bonded over a shared fondness for the Red Nichols and His Five Pennies jazz band and the *American Mercury,* a review founded by H. L. Mencken. Pat introduced Lynch to his future wife, a sorority girl from Cal who had registered at the Yosemite hotel under an assumed name she took from an old Jeanette MacDonald movie.

Hiking, camping, and outdoor excursions were essential parts of the California lifestyle from the state's earliest days. All over the vast state, mountains and valleys were covered with trails, and tens of thousands took advantage of the mild weather to hike during much of the year. In addition to visiting Yosemite and the Sierra Nevada range, the Browns made short jaunts to the nearby Russian River, where groups had gone for vacation and summer encampments since the 1860s, a tradition called the *paseár.*

The stunning beauty of Yosemite drew Pat back year after year. From 1864, when President Lincoln made Yosemite the first nationally protected wilderness area, the valley attracted thousands of tourists by train, stagecoach, and horseback. Yosemite was painted, photographed, and written about so much that it became a symbol of California to the rest of the

In 1926, twenty-one-year-old Pat Brown (seated in front) and his brother Harold (squatting) climbed Half Dome with three friends on their annual summer vacation in Yosemite. (Courtesy of Karin Surber)

world and a symbol of their identity to Californians—a scene of immense natural beauty, an outdoor playground, and an environmental battle-field. The fights over the destruction and degradation of the pristine wilderness led John Muir to found the Sierra Club in San Francisco in 1892. Charter members included academics and outdoor enthusiasts who became the vanguard of the conservation movement.

During the school year, Pat used his free time to court Bernice, who was a student at Cal. On Saturdays, his only day off, Pat dressed in his best suit and told the family he had to see a client. They all knew he was going to see Bern. During the week, Pat collected nickels and called her from the pay phone in the Palace Hotel near the law school. He wrote her letters on any paper handy—a pad swiped from the Hotel Whitcomb or stationery from Yosemite's Camp Curry cabins.

Always a strong student, Bernice enjoyed college, particularly language classes. She studied Spanish and French and joined the French club. Her only poor grade was an E in archery. Students were required to go outside to the field when it rained and be marked present, even though class was canceled. She viewed this as a waste of time and refused. Bernice commuted from home to school her first three years and then shared an apartment with a friend who worked part time as a secretary for Senator Hiram Johnson. She finished the necessary credits to graduate in December 1927; just as in grammar school, she was told to stay for another six months because she was only nineteen.

Bernice's options after college were limited to the traditional paths for women—teaching, secretarial work, or marriage. She pursued a teaching credential, worked as a substitute teacher during the day, and taught naturalization classes at night. By 1930 she had become a probationary teacher. One of the conditions of her job was that she remain unmarried.

On the evening of October 30, 1930, a telegram arrived from Reno, Nevada, at the Browns' house at 1572 Grove Street: "Married this morning at Trinity Cathedral. Now staying at Riverside Hotel." Pat's fourteen-year-old brother Frank was awakened by the news, and shrugged. The timing may have been a surprise, but the outcome had long been expected. The elopement was typical of Pat. Like the decision to skip college, eloping was efficient and financially expedient. As it was, Bernice had to buy her own wedding ring. (It would be six years before Pat's finances allowed him to buy her an engagement ring.) Bernice would later regret the timing of their wedding, because October 30 always fell the week before Election Day.

Bernice had hoped the marriage would stay secret, but she was front page news in the *Examiner* and the *Chronicle*: POLICE CAPTAIN'S

BERNICE E. LAYNE   San Francisco
Letters and Science—Philosophy Club (1); L'Alliance Française (1); Education Club (3); Costume Staff, Little Theatre (3); Crop and Saddle (4); Senior Formal Committee (4).

A precocious student, Bernice Layne was only fifteen when she entered the University of California. She graduated in 1928.

DAUGHTER ELOPES WITH ATTORNEY. She lost her job. At first the newly-
weds lived in the basement of the Gaylord Hotel; the $45-a-month rent
was all they could afford. Bernice was not enamored of the window-
less apartment, although the twelve-story Spanish Colonial Revival
building, open only two years, was in an up-and-coming neighborhood.
The Gaylord had been built at the end of a housing boom on the south
slope of Nob Hill, an area leveled by the 1906 earthquake. More than three
hundred multistory residential buildings were erected in a three-by-five-
block area adjacent to the Tenderloin, stucco-and-brick structures with
cornices and bay windows, attractive for their design and proximity to
the business districts.

San Francisco had been known since the Gold Rush as a town of hotel
dwellers, with accommodations that spanned bare-bones to luxury.
Transients needed cheap lodging, while many who could afford fancier
homes preferred the convenience of full-service accommodations. The
1929 Blue Book, the social register, listed permanent residents for half the
rooms at the elegant Fairmont Hotel. Apartment hotels like the Gaylord
were a transitional hybrid during a period when apartment buildings
started to edge out residential hotels as multifamily housing.

On the second Saturday in January 1931, Pat sat on their new sofa in
the basement apartment late at night. The radio played music. He had
given up trying to read his book, *Mixed Marriages*. Several drinks of
moonshine emboldened Pat to write down his thoughts. He wanted to
preserve the moment. He was feeling overwhelmed. He had been married
for just two and a half months, and he had learned he was going to be a
father.

> I have a peculiar, lackadaisical somewhat remote feeling. Diffi-
> cult to understand, more difficult to write. I just feel the urge to
> jot it down . . . I feel that genius lurks somewhere in my system.
> I am not thinking. I am writing just as the thought enters my
> head. The liquor (if it can be dignified by calling it liquor) has
> permeated my system until my surroundings seem strange,
> unreal and not true.
>
> I meditate. I am a young lawyer, recently married. I doubt my
> own ability but will to push it forward with bromides I read.
>
> It is an interesting evening—a Saturday night which used to
> be depressing unless I did something. Now I am married. In a

nineteen-year-old critiqued Stanford for not providing real-world experience and community interaction, recommendations met with silence and then rebuke.

Three years at Harvard Law School solidified Tobriner's conviction that labor unions were essential to equalize opportunities for workers. He didn't know any labor lawyers, or whether such a specialty existed, but returned to California to find out. In 1933, he started his own practice on the twelfth floor of the Russ Building, where he and Pat Brown, who knew a great deal about working people, had long conversations about how to change the world.

Both had grown up in Republican families, imbued with a sense that Democrats were not respectable. They were also not in power. The Depression changed both the reputation and the reality. Pat listened to President Roosevelt's Fireside Chats and discussed them with Tobriner. They watched the Socialist and prominent novelist Upton Sinclair run for governor as a Democrat in 1934 on the platform of End Poverty in California (EPIC), promising guaranteed work and pay for all. Sinclair lost, his populist campaign defeated in large measure through the work of the original political consultants, Clem Whitaker and Leone Baxter, who combed through everything Sinclair had written, pulled incendiary quotes from fictional characters, and fed them to the Los Angeles Times. The newspaper ran a daily front page box that attributed the quotes to the candidate. Whitaker and Baxter would go on to national prominence, popularizing the tactics and dirty tricks they had pioneered in California.

Despite his admiration for Roosevelt, Pat viewed the idea of changing parties as a leap akin to changing religions. He had campaigned for Republican Herbert Hoover, the orphan who graduated from Stanford and became the first president born west of the Mississippi. Pat's father had been friends with San Francisco's Republican boss, Tom Finn, since they were classmates in grammar school. But when Tobriner began to consider changing parties, his persuasive arguments influenced his friend. Tobriner delighted in recalling their final conversation on the subject, which took place over adjoining urinals in 1936. Tobriner told Pat he was heading to the registrar's office to become a Democrat and vote for Roosevelt; Pat, typically impulsive, said he would go along and switch, too. Notwithstanding the impetuous decision, he fundamentally embraced the Democrats' vision of a government that helped people, a concept that would be central to the rest of his career.

In California, Democrats had for many years offered largely token opposition, and Republicans had controlled state government in Sacramento since 1898. In part, this was a function of migration; many new arrivals came from Republican-leaning states. The constant influx of newcomers and transients offered little opportunity to build loyalty to a political machine and made East Coast–style ward politics impractical. California's unusual system of allowing candidates to run simultaneously in Democratic and Republican primaries, without indication of party affiliation, also undercut attempts to develop party loyalty. Often an incumbent lawmaker won both Democratic and Republican primaries and ran unopposed in the general election.

The cross-filing system had been the idea of Governor Hiram Johnson, though it was neither his most significant nor his longest-lasting political initiative. Johnson had been elected in 1910 on the strength of his promise to take on the so-called third party in California, the Southern Pacific Railroad. He promised to act to dilute the railroad's power, and the changes that ensued during the Progressive Era had a profound impact on California. Direct democracy enabled voters to make laws, repeal laws, or amend the constitution at the ballot box. Citizens could place initiatives and referenda on the ballot by collecting petitions with a requisite number of voters' signatures. Propositions that passed could be changed only by another popular vote. Californians could ever after bypass the legislature and governor to enact laws that affected everything from taxation to immigration. And they did. Used sparingly at first, the initiative and referendum measures grew to become a common way of budgeting as well as legislating social policy.

Pat Brown would soon witness that firsthand, but in his early days in politics, the impact of cross-filing was a more immediate concern. His initial foray into electoral politics had shown Pat the difficulty of challenging an entrenched incumbent. To groom candidates and build a base outside the party structure, Pat and a few friends formed a group called the New Order of Cincinnatus. Modeled after a nonpartisan group in Seattle, Cincinnatus took aim at government corruption and championed politicians who worked for the public good rather than their own private benefit. Members had to be under forty. Most were under thirty-five. They were a mix of Republicans and Democrats, many recruited by Pat through two other groups he had founded for young professionals, the Barristers Club and the Contact Club.

Each Cincinnatus member signed a pledge not to dispense favors to fellow members of the organization nor to request special treatment from friends who might end up in office. Honesty and idealism were the watchwords, and their attacks on the well-known graft in city government soon attracted attention. Cincinnatus nominated four candidates for the San Francisco Board of Supervisors in the 1935 election. Members chipped in to rent a small headquarters office. One member with journalism experience put together a newspaper that they published a week before the election. Cincinnatus members gathered at the Ferry Building, parceled out bundles of papers, and streamed into the streets handing them to streetcar commuters. "Our New San Francisco Requires New Methods and New Men," was the Cincinnatus motto. One of the four candidates won.

Pat juggled his political ambitions with his law practice, making a living during the Depression mainly with bill collection work. Small businesses like J. J. Dinneen Groceries and Progress Fruit Market gave him names, addresses, and amounts owed by customers—as much as a few hundred dollars, as little as three dollars. Pat's commission was 40 percent. Through a friend of Bernice, Pat picked up a big client, a lumber company that placed liens on construction materials. The uncertainty of the Depression left many projects in limbo, and the lumber company would have a claim to the unfinished construction. Pat also handled bankruptcy cases, along with a scattering of probates and divorces.

He ended 1938 with $120 in the bank, net income for the year of $4,932.67, and the prospect of a state job that would bring political cachet as well as financial security. He was confident that Culbert Olson, the first Democrat elected governor in more than forty years, would recognize Pat for the campaign work he had done with his friend down the hall, Mat Tobriner. Tobriner had written much of the candidate's platform. Pat helped raise money and headed the Northern California speakers bureau, which arranged for surrogates to address various groups. The two lawyers roomed together at the state party convention in Sacramento—Tobriner holed up in the hotel room writing while Pat worked the convention floor. At the end of the weekend, none of the delegates knew Mat Tobriner. Everyone knew Pat Brown.

Both men were disappointed when the Olson administration declined to reward their efforts. Pat asked for an appointment to a municipal court. He inquired, several times, about a vacancy on the State Board of Prison Directors. He tried for a week to arrange a meeting but couldn't get past Olson's secretary. "I have been using all of the pressure that I can think of to bring my abilities to the attention of the Governor, but whether it will suffice or not, I do not know," Pat wrote to friends in July 1939. With no appointment forthcoming, he asked for legal work on bank liquidations. "I cannot understand why my name should be cast aside without any consideration unless someone has told you that I was not one of your supporters during the past campaign," he wrote Olson, recalling how he had raised money and organized speeches. Though he felt he had been treated "shabbily . . . I was, and am now, and have been since January of 1938, an Olson man."

Privately, Pat blamed his treatment on anti-Catholic bias. Pat had had little to do with the Church for years, but that changed in 1939. A friend he had met during the Olson campaign invited Pat to a weekend retreat at El Retiro, a Jesuit center in Los Altos, just south of San Francisco. The experience had a profound and unexpected impact.

During the retreat, Pat wandered the acres of winding paths in the hills that overlooked the Santa Clara Valley, the rich farmland and apricot groves known as the Valley of Heart's Delight. From Thursday night until Monday morning, he followed the strict schedule: early morning prayers, breakfast, spiritual exercise, five lectures a day about different aspects of faith. He walked the Stations of the Cross and maintained the vow of silence, except for thirty minutes during dinner. The retreat was led by Father Harold Ring, who presented a vision of Catholicism starkly different from what Pat had been exposed to as a child. Rather than hell and brimstone, Ring emphasized an intellectual vision of Catholicism based on love of God, not fear. Pat found himself intensely interested and surprisingly moved. Back home, he read books on Catholic philosophy, *The Preface to Morals* by Walter Lippmann and *The Spirit of Catholicism* by the German theologian Karl Adam. Then he went to confession at St. Ignatius Church, for the first time in twenty years. Pat embraced Christianity anew, and he determined to raise and educate his children as practicing Catholics. He asked Bernice to marry him in the church. They obtained a dispensation for the mixed marriage and exchanged vows on May 27, 1940, at St. Agnes, the Jesuit church where Pat had been baptized. Three days later, he returned to El Retiro for the second of what would become annual retreats.

Bernice, a nonobservant Protestant, resisted Pat's religious prose-lytizing, but she acceded to the political—in 1938, she, too, became a Democrat. She served briefly as executive vice president of the League of Women Voters, with duties that included monitoring county Board of Supervisors meetings. When Pat picked up legal work representing the union of county employees, he felt that her presence at meetings posed a conflict. She resigned with regret.

Her focus became her growing household. The Browns' first child, Barbara, was born in the summer of 1931. Cynthia followed two years later. The family moved several times, living on Fillmore Street, then Chestnut, then Clarendon, where they leased furniture for $20 a month. Then Bernice's mother died, and they moved into the Layne house to help take care of Captain Layne. Pat became a ready audience for his voluble father-in-law's stories, while the family saved on housing costs.

On April 7, 1938, the Browns' son was born. Pat was adamant that they name him Edmund Gerald Brown Jr. Bernice disliked the nickname Ed, so they called him Jerry.

Ida still lived at 1572 Grove and often babysat her grandchildren. In a safe city and a family that valued independence, the children navigated the streets alone at an early age. By the time she was seven, Barbara walked by herself to catechism class at St. Agnes, then crossed the Panhandle to visit her grandmother. Ida took the children to movies, read them "The Tin Soldier," and recited poetry by the light of the fire as they huddled in her bed. Her sister Emma came to visit for a month each summer from Colusa, with her granddaughter Pat, whom she was raising. Emma was as much a homebody as Ida was independent. Emma told her grand-daughters to be content with what they had; Ida told them to always strive for more. She set the table with white linen and napkins and talked about the Unitarian vision of Jesus as a great man and teacher. She was not argumentative, but strong in her opinions and sure of her judgment in ways that influenced and impressed the young women. She gave them the confidence, her daughter Connie later said, that they could solve their own problems.

Connie, long the only girl at 1572 Grove, had been thrilled when Bernice joined the family. Now she welcomed her nieces, Barbara and Cynthia, who would remain close to their aunt her entire life. Like her mother and her older brother, Connie was a voracious reader. Back when Pat still lived at home, he had bought small dime books that explained the great philosophers. Connie searched for them in his jacket pockets and read them all. When Pat bought a set of the Harvard Classics, Connie was the one who read them first, cutting the pristine pages. Connie was a strong student who had followed her brothers to Lowell and then enrolled at the University of California, over the protest of her parents. Tuition at Cal was free, and all she had to pay were the costs of commuting. But her family had little understanding of university life and traditional expectations of their only daughter. When her mother was sick the day of a final exam, Connie was expected to stay home. She took the final instead. Only a lengthy illness after her first two years threw her off stride. She dropped out and took a job as a stenographer.

Although they were a generation younger, Barbara and Cynthia Brown grew up with many of the same limited expectations as their aunt Connie. They would get married, perhaps work as teachers or secretaries, but only until their husbands finished graduate school. Ida, the woman who had left home as a teenager, delivered minimal advice to her children and grandchildren: Work hard. Be a go-getter. She imparted far more by example as a self-reliant woman who had raised children as a de facto single mother. She cherished her independence. She had wanted her daughter to forgo college for secretarial school not because she devalued learning but so that Connie would have a trade to fall back on.

The boys, of course, were different. Harold had graduated from Lowell, spent two years in college, then gone to law school, apprenticed with his brother, and joined his office. Frank attended the University of California for two years, paying the $26-a-semester student fee and living in a boarding house for $25 a month, which he earned by washing dishes. Then he followed his brothers to law school and worked for them after school, serving and filing papers for $5 a week. They both cosigned his checks, only after he provided a detailed accounting of his work, which he resented. He stopped by the office at lunchtime hoping they would talk to him about law, but they were usually too busy.

San Francisco did not suffer the same degree of relentless poverty and "Hoovervilles" that plagued the state's vast agricultural valleys during the Depression, the plight of Dust Bowl migrants popularized by John Steinbeck's novel *The Grapes of Wrath*. Yet the geography of the city changed during the 1930s, driven by dozens of federally funded New Deal projects. New parks, schools, sculptures, sidewalks, and playgrounds provided short-term employment and long-term recreation and culture. Inside Coit Tower, a signature landmark on Telegraph Hill, artists painted magnificent murals depicting struggling workers, a project financed through the New Deal's public art program. And in the midst of the Depression, California commenced two colossal public works projects, the Bay Bridge and the Golden Gate Bridge. One would serve as a vital link between San Francisco and the East Bay; the other would become a symbol of the city.

Construction began in 1933 on the bridges needed to provide better access to San Francisco, the tip of the thumb of land that jutted out into the Pacific. Both projects, debated for decades, posed major financial and engineering challenges, requiring cantilever and suspension spans of record lengths, anchored in deep and turbulent waters. President Hoover, a Stanford graduate and engineer, approved a $72 million loan to finance the Bay Bridge, which would largely replace the ferries that shuttled millions of passengers a year between Oakland and San Francisco. When the span opened on November 12, 1936, the trip became a routine drive. The iconic Golden Gate Bridge, which connected the northern tip of the city to Marin County, was financed through the Bank of America and its founder, A. P. Giannini, who had pioneered the concept of branch banks and provided critical support for the agricultural and motion picture industries. When the Golden Gate Bridge opened on May 27, 1937, for "Pedestrian Day," an estimated eighteen thousand people gathered before dawn, ready to walk across the span in their Sunday best. Among the crowd of more than two hundred thousand that strolled the bridge from sunup to sundown was Pat Brown, holding the hands of his five- and three-year-old daughters, Barbara and Cynthia.

As the prospect of U.S. involvement in the European war grew more likely, Pat read up on the conflict, filling in gaps in his education from the stack of newspapers and books always piled by his bed. "I do not see how anything but a German 'blitz' leading to an immediate defeat of England can . . . prevent us from getting into the war. We are a cinch to send our men and boats over there within the year," Pat wrote on February 7, 1941, to a friend who had moved to Hawaii. "I am terribly afraid this time that they will not repeat 1917 and that there is nothing that we can do other than to prolong the war."

A few weeks later, he wrote again, more pessimistic and uncertain:

I personally find it difficult to determine which side is right or wrong. This is particularly true after finishing *The Road to War 1914–1917* by Walter Miller. It is very enlightening and permits you to understand some of the present day propaganda a whole lot more. I do not believe that I am a fifth columnist, but cannot justify some of the British imperialistic policies. I feel that if they would make a grand gesture to give up some of the things that they have acquired by banditry, that it might cause Hitler to call it quits. This may be wishful thinking, but I believe that something revolutionary must be done.

When the Japanese attacked Pearl Harbor on December 7, 1941, overnight the war went from far-off conflict to imminent danger for California, the nearest mainland state. Pat's close friend Tom Lynch was an assistant U.S. attorney; he drove to the office that morning and didn't leave for five days. Someone brought in mattresses and they slept on the floor, anticipating an attack. Newspapers fanned fears of the "Yellow Peril" and suggested Japan might invade California via Mexico. The coast became part of the theater of war, and nighttime blackouts were mandatory. ENEMY PLANES SIGHTED OVER CALIFORNIA COAST screamed a banner headline in the *Los Angeles Times* on December 9, 1941. Even inland in Colusa, Emma Schuckman's granddaughters joined volunteers around the state who scanned the skies and reported the shapes of planes overhead.

Pat was determined to find a way to help his country. Days after Pearl Harbor, he requested an application to be a special agent of the FBI, though at thirty-six he was too old to qualify. "My practice now returns to me a salary larger than I expect to receive from the bureau, but it is my desire to serve in some capacity during the period of the emergency," he wrote. The next day, he asked for an application to be an investigator in the Air Force. He appealed to friends with political connections, only to learn he would have to provide evidence of support for his family before he would even be considered, a decision Pat protested to California's senator, Sheridan Downey: "I would prefer something wherein I would be making a real contribution to government."

When the civil service commission told him he lacked the educational credentials to be a war department investigator, Pat shot back: "I sometimes think that the Civil Service Commission does not know that there is a war going on because if you did, you certainly would not have rejected the applications without examination of some of the splendid young lawyers with vast investigation experience who have applied for this position."

His brothers, with no children to support, joined the Navy. When Harold's application to serve in the Intelligence Department was rejected because of his German ancestry, Pat was incensed. "You can have no conception of the feeling of alienage that has been created by such advice," Pat wrote U.S. Navy secretary Frank Knox. "If there is any disunity in this country, such silly rules as this are the cause of it."

Pat settled for experiencing military life vicariously. Harold wrote home with detailed accounts from the Rhode Island barracks where he trained to become a lieutenant. Hanson Baldwin, military affairs reporter for the *New York Times*, provided a briefing that "gave us the far eastern picture from his personal observation." Harold's most interesting course was on how to identify ships and planes in one twenty-fifth of a second; he took tests called "peep show quizzes" in which he looked through a small hole in "a box-like affair much like the machines we used to have in father's penny arcade."

Frank was an ensign training in San Diego, a city rapidly becoming a major military hub. His wife was pregnant. "I know that you probably feel that it is kind of tough that you have to be away at the present time but I sincerely envy you and I am looking at all times for something that might permit me to broaden my view by travel or other change in life," Pat wrote to his younger brother. "I am not dissatisfied but I am not completely satisfied." By the spring of 1943, Pat's envy had been tempered by the reality of war. "I felt very sorry to see the young lawyer just about to commence his career halted and ordered off to kill whenever necessary," Pat wrote to Harold after taking his daughter Barbara to watch Frank's ship set off for parts unknown. "This is particularly true because to him the reason for such conduct on his part is not quite clear to him."

Frank Brown was one of more than a million and a half men and women who sailed to the Pacific from San Francisco, the premier military command center and port of embarkation. The influx of people and wartime industry transformed the region and the state, changes that would last long after the war ended. Southern California became the center of Navy and Marine operations and aerospace manufacturing.

Northern California attracted thousands to its burgeoning shipbuilding industry. At the height of the war, fourteen shipyards in the Bay Area operated twenty-four hours a day, in three shifts, a pace that created opportunities for two groups that had been shut out of such work: blacks and women. Wielding tools and starring in patriotic videos, the women became known as Rosie the Riveters.

Federal dollars suddenly poured into California. In 1940, total federal spending was $728 million, mainly on social services. In 1945 alone, the federal government spent $8.5 billion in the Golden State, almost half the total personal income, which was triple what Californians had earned in 1939. The presence of the military and aerospace industries would drive growth and prosperity for the next two decades. The war years became a dividing line, an era that permanently altered California's economy, social structure, and urban development.

For Pat and Bernice and their children, the war years meant frequent air raid sirens and drills, blackout curtains that darkened windows at night, and a victory garden to help with fresh food. Bernice managed the coupon books that rationed food staples as well as gasoline and tires. Barbara wrote her uncles letters on tissue paper and helped collect tinfoil and grease. "I feel that we should live each day to the fullest and try to give it all that we have," Pat wrote to an old friend, predicting difficult times ahead. "I do not feel that we should have any time to waste on hating anybody and this includes the Japs and everyone else. We have to 'lick' them and kill them but we must do it like talking sharply to our children."

The lack of prejudice instilled in Pat by his mother made him an exception to the prevalent and long-standing racism against the large Japanese community that had settled in California. In the early part of the century, Japanese workers had replaced Chinese in many of the agricultural valleys, and many moved quickly from field hands to growers and businessmen. Like the Chinese, the Japanese became targets of racist, exclusionary policies. The Alien Land Initiative, passed in 1913 and strengthened in 1920, banned Japanese from owning property in California and made leasing land all but impossible. Nonetheless, Japanese came to California in record numbers. Most worked in agriculture. By 1940, more than five thousand Japanese-operated farms produced 42 percent of the state's crops.

They were people like Yoneo Bepp, born in California to Japanese immigrants, the same year as Pat Brown. Bepp had graduated in 1927 from Cal, where he majored in social science and math, played on the 130-pound basketball team, and led the Japanese Students Club. He managed a successful agricultural supply company in San Jose, and Pat was his lawyer. When the Japanese attacked Pearl Harbor, the Northern California Fertilizer Company had just incorporated and was preparing to issue stock.

On February 19, 1942, President Franklin Roosevelt signed Executive Order 9066, mandating the internment of all Japanese Americans in a broad swath of the West Coast defined as a military zone. More than a hundred thousand people of Japanese ancestry, most of them in California, most of them American citizens, were rounded up and imprisoned.

Bepp, his wife, Yoshi, their one-year-old daughter, Miyo, and his elderly parents, Kiroku and Sumi, were sent to Los Angeles and temporarily detained in the Santa Anita race track, one of a dozen hastily set up holding facilities, where families lived in converted horse stalls. From there they were sent to Heart Mountain, a Wyoming prison camp that already housed more than ten thousand people. The Bepps were late arrivals, squeezed into a small barracks room. Bepp sounded stoic when he wrote to Pat from block 2-11-E in the fall of 1942. The weather had not yet turned cold, and the dry air was healthful.

Pat's response reflected his perennial optimism, coupled with the tenor of the times:

> Whether the reason for the movement is for reasons of National Defense or protection of the Japanese people, it will, in the long run, turn out to be better for everybody. As a matter of fact I am quite a fatalist and believe that things always turn out for the best. When the war is over, and I hope it will be soon, your health and that of the family will probably be much better than that of us who remain in the Cities. With food rationing and tire and gasoline rationing, we will be pretty near as restricted in movement as you are. When I think of you up in the Country and the beautiful mountains of Wyoming, I am frankly somewhat envious. I hope that you will have time to do some of the things that you

probably wanted to do all your life and this enforced restriction
of movement will give you that opportunity.

Bepp dashed Pat's romantic notions. "This place is virtually a 'concentration' camp," he wrote, describing the surreal experience of living in a
village surrounded by barbed wire and manned watchtowers. "We have
no civil rights here and are subject to many restrictions, and our individual status is nothing more than that of a common laborer, all of which
contributes to make this existence very miserable." His family was healthy
so far, but medical care was scarce and a measles epidemic had spread.
They lived in one of 467 tarpaper barracks, each subdivided into small
rooms with a bed, light fixture, and stove for heating. Each block had a
communal mess hall and partitioned toilet and shower facilities. "Life as
we have lived it and enjoyed in the past was beautiful compared to the
circumstances and unnatural surroundings in which we now find
ourselves. We try to be philosophic about the whole thing, for after all,
this is war, and this is the sacrifice we have been called upon to make."

In January 1943, the temperature at Heart Mountain hit 28 below zero.
An official with the War Relocation Authority visited the camp and interviewed people who might be placed in jobs; Bepp asked Pat for a letter of
recommendation. "I can say without the slightest bit of hesitation that
Mr. Bepp is as much of an American as I am," Pat wrote. "He is not only
honest but competent and able and to me it is a tragedy that men of his
caliber should be immobilized during the war." By the end of the year,
the Navy hired Bepp to teach Japanese to intelligence officers at a school
in Colorado. He wrote Pat that he was happy not only to get out of the
camp, but to "be able to make my contribution to the war effort."

Bepp left the camp before he could help with a favor that Pat had
requested. He was planning to run for district attorney, Pat told his client,
and "if there are any people from San Francisco in Heart Mountain,
Wyoming, I would appreciate your marking their ballots for them."

Pat's 1943 campaign was his second run for district attorney. In 1939,
he had challenged sixteen-year incumbent Matthew Brady. A revived
Cincinnatus group helped Pat campaign, and though he lost by a substantial margin, he won a respectable 40 percent of the vote. He became
better known and positioned himself for a rematch. During the next few
years, Brady grew older and weaker, and the Democrats gained many

thousands of new registrants as voters changed parties, just as Pat had done.

Nonetheless, Pat knew he needed support from at least one of the city's four newspapers, all Republican-controlled and influential. The line between the editorial position of the papers and their news gathering was virtually nonexistent, so support translated into positive coverage. Opposition meant the paper would mention a candidate not at all, or only in negative terms. The Hearst family published the *San Francisco Examiner* in the morning and the *Call-Bulletin* in the afternoon; the de Young family owned the second morning paper, the *Chronicle*; and Scripps published the *Daily News* in the afternoon.

The incumbent district attorney leaked stories to the Hearst papers, so Pat judged he had the best shot with their competition. He visited the editor of the *Daily News* and said he would run only if he knew the *News* would support him. After he got the paper's blessing, he went to the *Chronicle* with the same pitch and won their endorsement. "He has the energy and the will to keep up with the tide of events," the *Chronicle* wrote. Their coverage helped transform Pat Brown from an ambitious young man to a serious contender.

His campaign cards showed Pat in an unusually serious pose, a young man with square-jawed determination, hair combed back, and wire-rimmed glasses already giving him the look that would lead to his "owl-like" epithet. "Born and reared in San Francisco, Edmund G. Brown has had an opportunity to absorb and study the human side of San Francisco—he knows its people as well as its politics—its shortcomings as well as its greatness," read his campaign literature. He promised to "get things done" to stem rising crime and juvenile delinquency rates in San Francisco. He viewed the office as not only punitive, but redemptive. He was particularly interested in preventive, educational programs for young people. "The District Attorney's office has more to do with the unhappiness of people than any other office. I am confident that it is a position that should be handled by a person who is really interested in the welfare of others," Pat wrote to a friend during the campaign. "The opportunity to bring the prestige of the District Attorney's office into the lives of people who might otherwise do wrong is one that I do not intend to pass up although I recognize the fact that it is one that may pass me up."

The campaign turned into the newspaper battle that Pat had foreseen. Brady, the incumbent, leaked stories to the Hearst papers; the *Daily News* and *Chronicle* favored Pat. Pat raised $20,000 for his campaign, all but $5,000 from his savings and the contributions of two friends. Joe Murphy, an Irish labor newspaper publisher and old-time San Francisco politician, taught Pat how to campaign in stores, barbershops, and restaurants, and how to work a room. Pat was a natural. He loved talking to people.

The candidate voted early on November 1, 1943, in time to get his picture in the afternoon paper. The vote count continued into the early morning hours. Art Belcher, captain of a quartermaster crew in Oakland, stayed glued to the radio all night for news of his childhood friend. "It felt as if the whole world depended on the outcome of the fight and when the race got nip and tuck I wanted to go out and find out what was wrong with the people," he wrote Pat the next day. "Didn't they know a good man when they saw him? Why didn't they vote for Pat? Then you would get a slight margin and I would grip my chair." Finally, Pat eked out a slim victory. Belcher thought back to their days together at Fremont Grammar School: "Remember how grand it was—win or lose—to know the gang was backing you and helping all they could to push one of them to the top of the heap. Well Pat, this is the big victory so far—one to be proud of winning."

Pat had overcome a last-minute smear that tied him to the Padre Club, an illegal gambling joint in the Tenderloin that he had incorporated as a social club a decade earlier as a favor for his father. Ida Brown was relieved the mudslinging campaign was over. When her son turned to her on election night, elated, and said the district attorney's office was just a stepping-stone, she was dismayed.

Most everyone else Pat knew was thrilled.

To Matilda Levy, he was still Edmund, and she voted with pleasure for the boy she had taught in grade school. "When I listened to the election returns and heard your sweeping success," she wrote, "it gave me a deep personal elation."

His Lowell fraternity brothers had been campaign boosters. "Norton Simon's dice games at the cigar stand may have put you thru college, but I'm certain your present post is the result of honest endeavor, intelligence and hard work," wrote Paul Klein, stationed with the 884th Ordnance Company.

Pat and Bernice went to Palm Springs for a week of rest. Congratulations trickled in as the news reached those stationed overseas. "Belated congratulations to an ex-Pythagorean and Grove Street slugger!" wrote Louis Laye when the newspaper story his brother had mailed arrived at the 733rd TSS in Fort Logan, Colorado. "Keep clicking on Success Boulevard, and we'll be calling on you, come 'V' time."

Many compared Pat with Earl Warren, a Republican who had served as district attorney in Alameda County, across the bay, before becoming California attorney general and then governor. Pat made an appointment to meet with Governor Warren, a popular moderate, to solicit ideas on how to revamp the office. They had what would be the first of many lunches in Sacramento just before Christmas.

One of the last letters of congratulation to arrive was from Pat's youngest brother, Frank. He wrote from "the other side of the world," a location he could not divulge, and he timed the letter to arrive as close as possible to when his brother took office. He still called his brother Ed, and wrote the whole family—Ed, Bern, Barbara, Cynthia, and Jerry.

"I wanted to tell you that I am very proud of you and know that you will do a swell job . . . only thing I would say is, do not lose sight of the fact that the people of San Francisco have placed you in a position of trust and responsibility and want results. You now belong to them and not to any of those who supported you in that hectic campaign." He told them he would be away longer than he had expected. "You cannot imagine how much more important an aspect your home and family take on when you are separated this way. It isn't only your family, it reaches to the common ordinary things like a ride thru Golden Gate Park, a hot dog at the beach, the name of a street." He begged them to write back.

Pat's father had not lived long enough to see his oldest son elected to the top law enforcement job in San Francisco, a prospect that might have filled him with both pride and trepidation. As the only daughter, Connie had assumed much of the burden of caring for her father after he had suffered a stroke. He wanted to move back to Grove Street, but Ida refused. Though he recovered and lived several more years, he was never fully himself. The Depression years were not good ones for any business, even gambling, and Harold and Pat took care of their father financially. He died on July 8, 1942. The mass was held in St. Agnes Church.

On January 8, 1944, Pat drove to City Hall for his swearing-in. His son rode with him in the car. Jerry, not yet six years old, had already distinguished himself with his penchant for asking questions. He wanted to know if Matthew Brady, the incumbent who had lost, would be at the ceremony, too. If his father was being sworn in, Jerry reasoned, it meant that the loser would have to be sworn out.

A new mayor also was taking office, and a large crowd gathered in the rotunda of City Hall. "The prosecutor must not become the persecutor, seeking vindictive punishment and exulting in its infliction," Pat said in his brief address. "It is most emphatically not a part of San Francisco's tradition, it will have no place in the district attorney's office in this city."

Referring to the mayor and other city officials, he concluded, "All of us, I am sure, love this great and fascinating city and, guided by that deep affection, all of us move forward in a firm determination to make it a city unique within the nation—unique perhaps in the entire world—a city whose golden gate is America's great portal to the awakening Far East."

5

Forest Hill

When the kids on Magellan Avenue played outside, as they did pretty much all the time, each family had a different signal to call their son home for dinner. Mitch Johnson's dad blew a bugle. Pete Roddy's mom rang a bell. Pat Brown yelled, *"Jer-ry!"*

Magellan Avenue was the kind of San Francisco neighborhood where the yard lines for touch football were painted indelibly on the curb, and if a parked car was in the way when the boys wanted to play, they knocked on doors till they found someone to move the car.

Bernice, the leader on practical decisions and finances, had chosen the house on the elm-lined street, a block full of young families in an upwardly mobile, heavily Irish neighborhood. They moved in shortly after her father died. Designed in 1912, three decades earlier, Forest Hill was a planned community advertised in unsubtle terms as an escape from urban riffraff, "a country home within the city." The Forest Hill Home-owners Association collected dues, maintained the private streets, and enforced covenants—single-family homes only, no Japanese, Chinese, or "Negros." The broad, curved streets followed the contours of the hills to embrace nature rather than impose an arbitrary grid. The height gave every street a scenic vista. The elegant Clubhouse, where the Boy Scouts and the garden club met, was designed by Bernard Maybeck, the renowned architect whose work included the city's Palace of Fine Arts, built for the World's Fair of 1915.

In February 1943, Jerry entered West Portal Elementary, two blocks from the Browns' modest two-story wood frame house. Pete Roddy introduced his neighbor to the kindergarten teacher: "This is Jerry Brown.

He's a character." When the local parish opened a grammar school in the fall of 1947, Pat Brown enrolled his son, who skipped ahead half a year and started fifth grade at St. Brendan. Jerry's teachers were Sister Mary Roseen and Sister Alice Joseph, the school principal; both marveled at Jerry's ability to question almost anything, and both would stay in touch with him the rest of their lives. Though Jerry chafed at the strict rules and old-fashioned teaching of the Dominican nuns, he internalized the Catholic ethos of right and wrong.

Jerry looked forward to summer, vacation, recess—any time outside of school. The Magellan Avenue boys careened down the steep hills on Flexies, sleds with wheels, and spent their allowance on ice cream cones at Shaw's. (Jerry's allowance was dependent on doing chores; he generally opted for no allowance and no chores.) Mark McGuinness's home became a gathering spot, with a basketball hoop, a light for night games, and plenty of food in the refrigerator. Jerry often ate his first dinner there, then hit Pete Roddy's house for dessert before going home for his second meal. Pat frequently worked late, and Bernice insisted they wait for him so the family could eat together.

Two competing trolley lines, the Muni and the privately owned Market Street Railroad, made San Francisco easy to navigate, even at a young age. Downtown was a short trolley ride from Forest Hill. With more than six hundred thousand people by 1940, San Francisco still felt like a small town. "The city" was San Francisco, "the lake" was Tahoe, and "the river" was the Russian. The city had Irish, Italian, Chinese, and Japanese enclaves, but regardless of ethnicity or religion, most people identified by their parish. When strangers met, the first question would invariably be "What parish do you live in?"

When Jerry was ten, he went to summer camp at St. Mary's College while his father attended the 1948 Democratic convention in Philadelphia and then spent a few days in New York. Pat wrote to his son about talking with President Truman and attending a Yankees game, a treat for a fan from a state with no major league baseball team, even if Joe DiMaggio struck out that night. Pat described the wonder of flying home on a Constellation, famous for its sleek, dolphinlike shape and triple-pronged tail. Lockheed built the planes at its Burbank plant, in Los Angeles County. Because the launch of the four-engine propeller-driven Constellations had coincided with the war, the planes had been initially converted to military transports. Now they had become popular for commercial flights, boasting some of the first pressurized cabins. Pat left New York City at nine A.M. on a TWA flight that arrived in San Francisco almost twelve hours later. Bernice was "amazed to see the huge plane land so smoothly."

"There are many, many interesting things that occurred and I will tell you about them on the way up to Yosemite on Monday," Pat wrote to his son. "I am sure that you brush your teeth, wash your hands and face, and say your prayers at least three times a day. Give my regards to the gang. I hope you have not gotten into any fights, but, if you have, I hope you haven't lost them."

Yosemite had not lost its importance for Pat, and summer visits to the park became a tradition that allowed him to pass on his love of the outdoors. He made time to join the family for a week or two most every summer, either at Yosemite or the Russian River. Jerry's earliest memory would be an unpleasant bath in the sink as a toddler at a cabin above the river, but his lasting affection for the place easily outweighed the disagreeable experience. He learned to swim as a five-year-old at Twain Harte, a private lake in the Sierra, and hiked the Ledge Trail at Yosemite the same year.

Friends who stayed in Yosemite at the Wawona urged Pat to give the more upscale hotel a try so he could play golf and mingle with business and political types. But the Browns were comfortable at Camp Curry. The small village of rustic log-frame cabins, stores, and recreational facilities dated back to 1899, when schoolteachers David and Jennie Curry created a tent camp that became a model for national park concessions. "I have two teen-age daughters who desire both male companionship and dancing and I must accommodate my gals," Pat wrote to friends. "Different boys every night, good dances, fine beach parties, excellent conversation, and bridge on the porch immediately after dinner."

Camp Curry also positioned them to watch the nightly event that drew crowds from throughout the park: the Firefall. Cars packed the roads and people jostled for position, waiting for the moment at nine o'clock when park officials would drop burning embers from the top of Glacier Point to the valley floor three thousand feet below. The crowd sang "Indian Love Call" as they watched the fire cascade, mimicking the park's famous waterfall. The nightly occurrence was beloved, its harm to the park's ecology overlooked.

Pat did not hesitate to use connections when he had problems obtaining the reservations he needed. In 1945, the Yosemite superintendent intervened to make arrangements for Pat at the request of the undersecretary of the interior, who had been contacted by the California Democratic Party chair. The Browns needed a comfortable cabin with two rooms and a bath for the month of July; Bernice was seven months pregnant. Their youngest daughter, Kathleen, was born at the end of September.

At work, Pat had moved quickly to make major changes. The new district attorney inherited sketchy records in ink-splattered ledgers. Bail money had been kept in a file drawer. Prisoners were brought into court in cages. Police decided on criminal charges with no input from the two dozen part-time attorneys in the DA's office, who spent most of their time on their private clients. Modeling changes on those Earl Warren had instituted across the bay, Pat made all his deputies work full time and reaffirmed the district attorney's right to decide on criminal complaints. The changes cost the police power as well as money, because defense attorneys could no longer bribe police to pursue lesser charges.

Pat focused his criminal prosecutions on gambling, prostitution, and abortion parlors, social issues that had become pressing during the wartime years as thousands of young men passed through the gateway to the Pacific. In addition to citizen complaints, the Army and Navy demanded action to protect the health of their recruits in the face of high rates of venereal disease. Rather than try widespread crackdowns, Pat waited for an event that might make his action more popular. A botched abortion on a teenager became a justification to pursue the infamous abortion clinic of Inez Burns, patronized by many notable women. With trap doors, secret cash compartments, and bribes to police, Burns had repeatedly evaded prosecution. Pat failed in his first two attempts, but finally obtained a conviction in the high-profile case.

As a son of San Francisco and a son of Ed Brown, Pat was familiar with many of the people running enterprises he investigated, particularly gambling. One of the men reputed to be at the center of various schemes had gone to grammar school with Pat's father and lent him money. When Pat ran into the gambler at his usual Friday lunch spot, the Exposition Fish Grotto, he did not mince words: Your father would turn over in his grave if he knew what you were doing, he told Pat.

"I have my greatest difficulty with the gambling situation," Pat wrote to a friend. He charged bookmakers with felonies instead of misdemeanors, but it made little difference. "As you know, San Francisco is a city that has gambled before I was born and will probably gamble long after I die. It is inbred in people of high moral principle and to eradicate it is like trying to cure a cancer."

Pat did make a difference, real and symbolic, with his appointments. He hired the first black assistant district attorney in the state and the first Chinese. Three of his twenty-six deputies were women. Several were Republicans.

His commitment to diversity came as the social and economic upheavals of the war years exacerbated racial tensions, amid early stirrings that would grow into the civil rights movement. The armed forces remained segregated until 1948. But the need for workers in the wartime industries had spurred President Roosevelt to issue an executive order in 1941 that required all defense department contractors to follow equal employment standards. That opened jobs for blacks, who had previously been denied membership in key craft unions that were now forced, grudgingly and sometimes under court order, to integrate. The wartime years drew about 150,000 blacks to California, most to the well-paying jobs in shipyards in the East Bay. The end of the war and returning veterans brought clashes over housing and jobs.

The civil rights movement in California, from its earliest years, was shaped by the state's large Mexican American population, particularly in Southern California. The influx of servicemen from around the country exacerbated discrimination against ethnic Mexicans, most prominently in a series of attacks in 1943 known as the Zoot Suit riots, named after the baggy suits popular among young Mexicans. For several days, mobs of servicemen roamed Los Angeles and attacked Mexicans in clashes inflamed by sensational media coverage. Two years later, Mexican American families in Orange County challenged their school districts' policies of segregating their children in inferior "Mexican" schools. The successful class action suit became a precedent cited nine years later by Thurgood Marshall when he argued the landmark *Brown v. Board of Education* case; Marshall had written the NAACP's supporting brief in the California case.

Pat viewed easing social tensions and promoting equality as part of his mandate. He formed a committee on race relations that investigated substandard housing. He set up a special court where women arrested for prostitution received medical examinations and treatment if needed; young women who had turned to prostitution after being stranded in the wartime city were given a bus ticket home. Pat focused in particular on young people, handing out a pamphlet titled "Youth, Don't Be a Chump," which promised to "aid the youth of San Francisco in playing The Game of Life." Demand was so high that 275,000 copies were printed in eight editions. The booklet detailed curfews, child labor laws, alcohol restrictions, truancy, and other laws pertaining to young people. Pat addressed the book "to every boy and girl in San Francisco of every race, creed and color: My office is, and always will be, open to you. Just walk in, tell the girl at the switchboard that you are a San Francisco boy or girl, that you want to talk to the district attorney, 'Pat' Brown."

The emphasis on prevention suited his staff, which had minimal capacity to conduct serious probes. His three investigators were friends, and only one did much investigating. One drove him around and arranged meetings. The third tried to generate stories that would help position Pat for his next campaign: California attorney general.

In 1946, less than three years into his term as district attorney, Pat made his first statewide run. Earl Warren headed the Republican ticket and, thanks to cross-filing, the Democratic ticket as well. Facing long odds, Pat viewed the race as a way to begin to develop a reputation outside San Francisco. "I want to be Attorney General of this state more than anything else in the world other than retaining my own self-respect," Pat wrote a supporter in June 1946. "I do not intend to compromise one iota in order to be elected. I intend to stand upon the things I think are right even though I may be wrong."

Pat had hired his friend Tom Lynch as his chief deputy, which facilitated cordial relations with Warren. Warren and Lynch had become friends when their offices shared the same lunchtime hangout, an Irish bar called the Waldorf. Lynch campaigned as a surrogate for Pat at meetings of dozens of small organizations that all expected a visit from the candidate: Ethnic groups like the Steuben Society, French Club, United Irish, and Sons of Little Italy. Neighborhood improvement clubs. Craft unions like the tile setters, bricklayers, carpenters, and sheet metal workers. The Oddfellows Hall, Native Sons, Eastern Star, and Daughters of Pocahontas.

Pat lost, as he had expected. He began to campaign almost immediately for a rematch. He coasted to an easy reelection as district attorney in 1947, cementing his stature as a leading California Democrat, albeit in a party that was all but moribund. He spent as much time as he could traveling around California to meet people, prop up the Democratic Party, and create his own political network.

His trips left Bernice to cope with two teenaged girls, a young boy, and a toddler. She strove to instill in them the frugality that had been part of her upbringing. She vetoed the puppy that a friend offered as the perfect hiking companion for Jerry. ("She says she has enough trouble with Jerry trying to keep the house clean," Pat wrote in declining the offer. "It really started a small-size riot in the family but the 'boss' generally wins.") She turned down Barbara's request to attend an all-night high school graduation party—only to have Pat come home, guilty about his long absences, and acquiesce.

Pat visited hot, dusty farm towns in the Central Valley and beautiful cities on the Central Coast, but he spent the most time in Los Angeles. That's where the votes were. As California's population grew from 6.9 to 10.6 million during the 1940s, most of the new arrivals had settled in Southern California. Even for Democrats whose base of support had been the more liberal, cosmopolitan north, the balance of political power began to shift south. The economy and lifestyle of Southern California had been transformed by World War II, first through military installations and then the postwar influx of veterans. The epic changes came with the speed that had been the hallmark of the Golden State since its earliest days.

The concentration of military personnel had begun right after the attack on Pearl Harbor, when General Patton started to train troops in the desert near Palm Springs. Soon, Southern California became home to the largest collection of military bases in the country. The Marines arrived in 1942 and turned a desolate area between Los Angeles and San Diego into Camp Pendleton. The Navy expanded its bases in San Diego and added facilities in Ventura, Long Beach, and Wilmington. The Army Air Force opened a training center in Santa Ana, in Orange County.

The combination of sunshine and open land spawned an aircraft industry that grew exponentially to meet the military's voracious appetite. To attract the women workers needed to accelerate wartime production, aviation plants became virtual villages, with onsite daycare, health clinics, counseling, and banking kiosks. Companies offered picnics, softball games, dances, and shows. In 1944, Lockheed employed ninety thousand workers and operated a cafeteria that covered an entire block and served sixty thousand meals a day, six days a week. To transport workers to and from Burbank, Lockheed gave out six thousand bicycles and operated 117 buses, one of the largest commuter bus systems in the country. In Santa Monica, the Douglas aircraft plant employed 162 police officers, the sixth-largest force in California. Workers got free Eskimo Pies at breaks, to bolster morale and to improve nutrition during wartime rationing.

When the war ended, many of the men who had first glimpsed California as military trainees chose to settle in the Golden State. About 850,000 veterans ended up in California, most of whom had lived somewhere else before the war. In the fall of 1947, veterans made up half the students at the University of Southern California and more than 40 percent at UCLA. The San Fernando Valley, north of downtown Los Angeles and still largely undeveloped, began to fill with subdivisions.

In 1949, as Pat Brown began to campaign in earnest, Los Angeles was the third-largest metropolitan region in the United States. Almost one third of the population had arrived since 1940. Though still overwhelmingly white, Los Angeles had more ethnic Mexicans than any city outside Mexico, a growing black population, and a sizable Japanese community.

"If you ever want to get to Sacramento, you will have to come by way of Los Angeles," wrote Pat's former law partner, Frank Mackin, who had moved to Los Angeles. He suggested Pat model himself, again, on Earl Warren. "What you should do, I think, is to Warren-ize yourself, become a Democrat who can get as much support, financial and otherwise, from the Republicans as from the Democrats."

Pat calculated that by the 1950 election, 42 percent of the voters in the state would live in Los Angeles County. He decided to spend several weeks in Los Angeles each summer, to cultivate financial and political support. He needed to find a Southern California finance chair who could raise at least $100,000 for billboards, radio time, and other publicity. Like all statewide campaigns in California, his would require separate committees in the north and south. The newspapers in Southern California were even more problematic than those in San Francisco, and just as important. The *Los Angeles Times*, owned by the Chandler family, was solidly conservative Republican. Although registered Democrats outnumbered Republicans in California, Pat believed that the biases of the major papers, and their attacks on Democrats, discouraged strong candidates and left the party with generally second-rate nominees.

In early 1950, Pat made his pitch to the political editor of the *Los Angeles Daily News*. He expected to raise $150,000 before the primary. He was president of the District Attorneys Association, supported by the Peace Officers Association, and hopeful of endorsements from two San Francisco papers. At the same time, Pat wrote a thirteen-page confidential letter to Frank Clarvoe, the editor of the *San Francisco News*, whose early support had been crucial in the district attorney race. Pat described the office he had inherited in 1944, the changes he had made, and the results. Before he arrived, one third of those charged with crimes had pleaded guilty. Today, 92 percent of those arrested pleaded guilty or were found guilty after trial. In six years the office had lost only six major cases. He was typically blunt in assessing his shortcomings: "We have failed to bring integrity into the San Francisco Police Department," where gambling protection continued to be a lucrative source of corruption. And the forty-five-year-old critiqued his own style. "I have been guilty of being too unguarded in my remarks. It has given me an impression of immaturity."

Pat emerged as the Democrats' best hope of winning a statewide race. In the U.S. Senate contest, Richard Nixon was waging a strong, vicious campaign against Helen Gahagan Douglas, whom he dubbed the Pink Lady for her alleged Communist ties. Governor Warren was so far ahead of his Democratic challenger, Jimmy Roosevelt, that the Republican declined to debate. As a result, the attorney general candidates engaged in the first televised debate for statewide office in California. Television was becoming a major factor in campaigns for the first time; almost half of all Americans owned TVs. Pat went low-tech, too, handing out notepads that said JOT IT DOWN . . . VOTE FOR BROWN.

Interest groups and Democratic clubs put together what they called slate cards, which listed all the endorsed candidates, and mailed them to all their members. The most important slate card was distributed by the Civic League of Improvement Clubs, San Francisco businessmen who charged money for the listing on the glossy two-page mailer sent to every registered voter. The mailer included a mock ballot card, which many people marked up and took into the voting booth. Voters would toss them on their way out, and in some precincts campaign workers

*Pat Brown's affinity for old-fashioned campaigning propelled him to victory in
1950, the only Democrat to win statewide office.*

pulled them out of the garbage to see how the vote was going during the
day. The results were known as the Garbage Poll.

For the first time in races for statewide office, there was a more traditional California poll, too. Mervin Field had become interested in survey
research as a teenager in New Jersey, where he worked part time for the
polling pioneer George Gallup in the early 1940s. After a wartime stint
in the Merchant Marine, Field settled in San Francisco. In 1947, he
launched the Field Poll, which became a California institution, one of the
most respected nonpartisan surveys in the country. Less than a month
before the 1950 election, the Field Poll showed the race for attorney general
was a dead heat. Pat reached out for help to a Republican—his high school
friend and fraternity brother Norton Simon, who had founded Hunt's
Foods and become a wealthy business entrepreneur. Simon's last-minute
contribution of $10,000 funded a billboard and newspaper ad campaign
that was credited with turning the race. In the ads called "Our Choice,"

Pat's photo appeared next to the governor's, with the slogan "Elect Warren and Brown." Pat had made sure in advance that Warren, who was not fond of Brown's opponent, would not object.

Pat won by a relatively slim margin of 225,000 votes, the only Democrat elected to statewide office. He piled up large pluralities in his hometown and did well in areas covered by the McClatchy-owned *Bee* newspapers, which supported him, compensating for weaker results in Southern California.

Ida Brown was there to see her son sworn in on January 8, 1951, just three days before her seventy-third birthday. She had sold the Grove Street house a few years earlier for $11,550 and moved to a studio apartment off Golden Gate Park. The studio had a closet big enough for her bed, and a little table and chair by the window where she could see the park. On her mantel she kept a picture of Jack Johnson, the prominent African American boxer. She took her shopping cart to buy groceries down the block at Park 'n Shop and took the bus to the beach to watch the ocean, which she loved. She organized a speakers program at the Howard Presbyterian Church, one of the oldest congregations in the city, a few blocks from her old Grove Street house. She knew all her neighbors, and they watched out for one another. She followed current events closely and spent time with her children and grandchildren, but spurned any suggestion that she give up her apartment and move in with family.

She didn't talk much about her early life in Colusa, though she went back from time to time to visit her brothers and sister. She played the role of family matriarch for the children, grandchildren, and cousins. Younger family members confided in Ida because she was accepting and nonjudgmental. She collected information, still the nosy girl who had steamed open letters, now the family linchpin who kept track of who was doing what and disseminated the news.

On Magellan Avenue, Pat's new job meant he was home even less, and Bernice juggled the demands of children who ranged in age from five to nineteen. Twelve-year-old Jerry lived in a makeshift bedroom off the kitchen; his parents and sisters slept upstairs. "Atty. General Pat Brown's children run the gamut; he has a girl in kindergarten, a boy in grammar school, a girl in high school and a girl at Cal—which makes life pretty complicated for Mrs. Brown," noted an item in the *San Francisco Examiner* gossip column. "She belongs to parent-teachers' groups in all four categories."

Barbara, a strong student like her mother, attended the University of California and lived at the Tri Delt house near the Berkeley campus. One of her sorority sisters was Joan Didion, who would later describe the university as "California's highest, most articulate idea of itself, the most coherent—perhaps the only coherent—expression of the California possibility." Barbara majored in English and journalism. She worked on the *Daily Cal* covering off-campus politics and tried as hard as she could to keep her family connections secret. She was eager to establish her own identity and resented the publicity.

Cynthia was a junior at Star of the Sea Catholic high school, with a boyfriend who would turn out to be far more than a teenage romance. Joe Kelly had attended St. Ignatius High School, putting himself through school during the war working a swing shift as a bellhop at the Franciscan Hotel. Teenagers were in demand for jobs because so many men had gone into the service. Most of the hotel's clients were military shipping out or on leave, and they tipped well. For a while, Joe earned as much as his father. By 1950, he was a student at the University of San Francisco, working part time for the phone company and coaching boys' basketball at Star of the Sea. On a ride home after practice one day so many people piled into the car that Cynthia Brown ended up on his lap. A few days later, she approached Joe through the chain link fence that separated the girls' high school from the coed grammar school and asked the nineteen-year-old to take her to the junior prom.

The Brown family, which would come to warmly embrace Joe Kelly, was at first a little wary, particularly the naturally reserved Bernice. For the first few years she would greet him at the door in a businesslike manner and show him to the living room to wait. That gave Jerry an opportunity to pepper the visitor with questions.

Jerry was finishing eighth grade at St. Brendan, where the class prophecy at graduation was that he would grow up to be New York State attorney general. Jerry wanted to attend the new Catholic high school, Riordan, where his friends were headed. Pat wanted his son to go to Lowell, his parents' alma mater. Pat objected that a new school lacked traditions. He may also have wanted to steer his son toward a less religious environment.

"I have heard that your son is interested in being a priest," Pat's cousin Burt Chandler, who was in a seminary, wrote in the summer of 1951. "I know that it does seem a little fantastic for a boy so young to be thinking along those lines, but very often God works just that way. He gives His vocations as He wants, some to the young and some to the older. Be sure and encourage him if he thinks that he wants the priestly life but by no means pressure him to it."

Pat and Jerry compromised. He would go to St. Ignatius, an elite high school with plenty of tradition. St. Ignatius traced its roots to a one-room school for boys the Jesuits had opened in 1855 on Market Street. The high school's goal, explained the catalog, was to train young minds to analyze, "to mold manhood, to develop the entire man, mind and heart, body and soul; to form as well as to inform."

Classes began at 8:40 A.M. and ended at 2:35 P.M. Attendance at the 8:00 A.M. daily mass in the chapel was mandatory on the first Friday of the month, encouraged on other days. Students studied Latin all four years, five hours a week, no exceptions. Honors students took Greek, the only other language offered.

Jerry distinguished himself on the debate team, a premier sport at St. Ignatius, which had a long-standing reputation as one of the strongest California teams in the National Forensic League. He won the Freshman Elocution Medal and was chosen as one of three to compete in the annual Silver Medal Debate between the freshman and sophomore classes. His team argued against the proposition that "all Americans should be subject to conscription for essential service in time of war." They lost to the older classmen.

The next year, Jerry won the Sophomore Oratorical Award and watched the juniors and seniors face off in the Gold Medal Debate. One of the judges was Attorney General Pat Brown. As a junior, Jerry argued in the Gold Medal Debate ("Resolved: The McCarran Act should be repealed," a debate on the 1950 immigration law approved over the veto of President Truman, who condemned as "un-American" the sweeping powers to investigate and deport immigrants deemed Communists or subversives). Again, Jerry's team was bested by the older classmen.

The debate team traveled by bus to tournaments around Northern California (once picking up Jerry at Magellan Avenue when he over-slept). Though he was not one of the team stars, Jerry found the competition intellectually stimulating. The readings on issues like NATO and free trade deepened his knowledge and interest in current events and political affairs.

The debate team regimen would prove relevant and useful in his future career. "It trains the student to read between the lines of newspaper and magazine articles, and to determine the causes and the solutions of difficulties presented to our democratic government," noted the *Ignatian*, the school yearbook. "Debating to the student, therefore, is a furthering of one's self in the poise and presentation of a subject; and the preparation for speaking with logic in future life."

Jerry mastered those skills at a young age, quick on his feet and self-assured in presentations that often ended with a quote he had garnered at the breakfast table: "As Attorney General Pat Brown says . . ." The very top debaters, like Jerry's friend John Coleman, put in more time on research. Coleman was one year ahead, a state champion, and a member of the teams that beat Jerry in the intramural battles. The son of a carpet layer, Coleman was as serious about his competition as Jerry was blasé. The rivalry did not diminish their bond in the small, intense world of high school debaters, who formed lifelong friendships.

Outside of the forensic league, Jerry was the quiet one in a close-knit circle of friends, almost all extroverts. To the extent he led it was by intelligence, though he was not a diligent student. In classes that he deemed a waste of time, he let his grades slip to barely passing. In classes he found intellectually stimulating, he engaged. The Jesuits' Socratic method fitted Jerry's penchant for asking questions, to the occasional annoyance of his teachers. Nor had he grown any fonder of rules. He was threatened with expulsion after tossing an Animal Crackers wrapper in the gutter; the vice principal, who had issued an antilittering edict, happened to observe the miscreant from his window. When the attorney general was informed, he "was about ready to explode," but he calmed down and ordered Jerry to return and apologize, which he did.

Every so often Jerry did something out of character, demonstrating an innate sense of the value of surprise and timing. He volunteered for the Senior Fight Night boxing match against his old friend Pete Roddy, who didn't bother training because Jerry was not much of an athlete, though the two frequently played golf together. But Jerry, determined to beat his friend, practiced at the Olympic Club, a San Francisco institution that proclaimed itself the oldest athletic club in the United States. Jerry knocked Roddy down and won on points, a victory he would lord over him for decades. Jerry also signed up as a cheerleader his sophomore and junior years, an uncharacteristic move for a nonjoiner who studiously disdained the rah-rah spirit that had marked his father's high school years.

St. Ignatius drew students from all over the city, its reputation based on achievement rather than the social stature of parents. Working-class kids mingled with children of the elite, embodying the California idea of education as the great equalizer and avenue to upward mobility. Jerry's crew included his Magellan Avenue neighbor Mark McGuinness and his cousin Baxter Rice, whose father was a liquor salesman; Peter Finnegan, one grade behind, whose uncle was vice principal; and Bart Lally, the son of a policeman. Their core group studied together, worked together, played together, and dated together. When they were young, Jerry and Bart went to the Boy Scouts' Camp Royaneh on the Russian River, and when they were old enough to drive they went up to the river on weekends and stayed with friends who had second homes or summer rentals. Sometimes Bart and Jerry went up to Sacramento with Pat, a ninety-mile trip that would take all day because Pat stopped to talk with people at every restaurant or bar along the way. He simply loved talking to people, and they responded to his warm, gregarious nature, his conversation punctuated by superlatives, and his memorable belly laugh. Bart lived nearby and spent a lot of time in the Magellan Avenue house. He viewed Pat as a surrogate father—supportive, respectful of Bernice, and paying special attention to Jerry, eager to expose his only son to his world.

Most of their teachers at St. Ignatius were Jesuit seminarians, fulfilling the three-year scholastic commitment that was part of the long path to becoming an ordained priest. The teachers were smart, dynamic, and not much older than their students. Their communal lifestyle was attractive for its social as well as religious aspects, and in their dedication they epitomized the Jesuit ideal of marshaling intellectual and moral force to change the world. The Jesuit education imparted a sense of destiny; the students as well as the teachers were chosen to lead and take on worldly challenges. The seminarians represented one path toward that goal, a life that seemed spiritually and intellectually exciting.

Jerry's seventeenth birthday fell on Holy Thursday in the spring of his senior year. He was late for his party because he stopped to worship at St. Brendan's Church. He liked the ceremony: the candlelit, incense-laden procession to place the blessed sacrament in the tabernacle, and the mysteries commemorated in the mass. When he finally arrived at the party, Pete Roddy had a black cassock waiting as a present for his friend.

Jerry informed his father that he wanted to enter the Jesuit seminary. Pat refused to give consent, which would be necessary until Jerry turned eighteen. In another compromise, he enrolled for the fall at Santa Clara University, the Jesuit school that had been the first college in California.

On June 10, 1955, Edmund G. Brown Jr. graduated from St. Ignatius High School with a classical diploma. He lacked the requisite years of Greek to receive the honorary classical diploma that Bart Lally and several others in their group achieved. Lally was also headed to Santa Clara in the fall. First, the two friends set out in Jerry's 1946 DeSoto for a summer in Idaho. Pat had gotten them jobs with the Ohio Match Company, owned by his friend Norton Simon. The teenagers cleared roads, part of the process of logging trees that would be cut down for matches.

Pat Brown had started his second term as attorney general after an easy election in 1954, when he won both the Democratic and Republican primaries. He was even supported by the *Los Angeles Times*, a rare break in the paper's practice of endorsing only Republicans. The token opposition didn't stop Pat from traveling the state to campaign. "I hope I do not seem too much of a glad-handing politician because I genuinely like people and like to talk with them," he wrote his cousin Burt Chandler after a campaign cocktail party. Pat left a week before the November election on a lengthy trip to South America, part vacation and part business. He was up in the Andes in Cuzco when the polls closed and didn't hear the results for several days.

Jerry Brown and (left to right) Mark McGuinness and Bart Lally at their junior prom. The Class of '55 friends would remain close the rest of their lives. (Courtesy of Bart Lally)

During Pat's second term, power shifts began within the California Republican Party that would soon affect both the state and the nation. Pat enjoyed strong professional and warm personal relationships with both Earl Warren and his successor in the governor's office, Goodwin Knight, another moderate Republican. They shared the sense of a common good and a belief that personal relationships trumped political affiliation among members of the "Party of California." Pat had visited Warren in Sacramento several times a year until he resigned in 1953 to become chief justice of the U.S. Supreme Court. Pat admired the older man's moral integrity and his dignified, gracious style, so different from his own. Over long lunches at the Del Paso Country Club, the longest-tenured governor in California history dispensed advice. Don't ever let them see your cards, Warren counseled the forthright and voluble attorney general.

Whereas Pat was almost always ready to forgive, Warren had a long memory. One of the people Warren never forgave was Richard Nixon, who had betrayed Warren in his long-shot bid for president in 1952. Nixon, then a U.S. senator, had publicly supported his fellow Californian, who hoped to emerge as a compromise candidate at a brokered convention. Privately, Nixon lobbied delegates to support Eisenhower and wangled the vice presidential nomination for himself. Eager to run for president in 1960, Vice President Nixon played an increasingly high-profile role in California Republican politics. Unlike Warren and Knight, Nixon continued and encouraged the red-baiting that had helped him initially win election to Congress. Although Pat was not yet a target (he worried a little that it was because they didn't think he was intellectual enough to be a Communist), he became enmeshed in the consequences.

The nation's Cold War battles played out most dramatically in California in Hollywood and at the University of California. The blacklisting of actors, writers, directors, and musicians began with the House Un-American Affairs Committee hearings in 1947 and the subsequent prosecution of the Hollywood Ten, who refused to answer questions before the committee and were sentenced to prison for contempt. California had its own Fact-Finding Committee on Un-American Affairs, which proposed in 1949 that the legislature assume the power to determine the loyalty of all university employees. To preempt such action, the University of California president suggested faculty sign a loyalty oath. The Regents adopted the requirement; students and faculty immediately denounced the oath as an impingement on academic freedom.

Governor Warren, who sat as president of the Regents, led opposition to the oath. Supporters of the oath tried to oust a Warren appointee who was a sitting judge arguing he could not hold both positions. At Warren's request, Attorney General Brown issued an opinion that allowed the Regent to stay. After months of negotiation and litigation, the Regents eventually rescinded the original oath requirement.

Pat was warned about Nixon by Democrats and Republicans alike. Liberal Carey McWilliams followed California politics closely, though he had moved east to edit the *Nation* magazine. Concerned about Nixon's rise, McWilliams sent Pat a story that detailed the vice president's strategy-planning dinner with Republican leaders, hosted by the *Los Angeles Times* political editor. In the capital, Pat heard more about Nixon's potential menace. "In a conversation with Governor Knight at 2:30 P.M. on April 19, 1955, at Sacramento, Mr. Brown was told that Governor Knight considered Vice President Richard Nixon one of the most dangerous men in the world," Pat wrote in a confidential memo for his files. "Knight told Mr. Brown that he had been double-crossed by Nixon on two occasions; that [U.S. Senator Thomas] Kuchel, [U.S. Senator William] Knowland and Warren had been treated the same way by Nixon; and that Nixon would in the opinion of Knight be the worst man imaginable for the Presidency of the United States." In a few years, Pat would spend a great deal of time worrying about Richard Nixon.

Two days after the conversation with Knight, Pat Brown turned fifty. His brother Harold threw a black tie birthday bash at the Nob Hill Room of the Fairmont Hotel. Friends chipped in to buy him a club chair and ottoman. In some ways, he was still the kid who joined every club. He was a dues-paying member of the Jonathan Club, the Native Sons of the Golden West, the Ancient Order of Hibernians, the Lawyers Club of San Francisco, the Moose Lodge, the Lowell Centennial Committee, the California State Auto Association, the State Bar, the Northern California Golf Association, and the Order of Elks. He subscribed to the *Catholic Lawyer*, *National Geographic*, *Atlantic Monthly*, *Democrat Free Press*, *Frontier Magazine*, the *New Republic*, and *America* magazine.

During his reelection campaign, Pat had made a speech in Los Angeles to a group of young professionals called the Diogenes Club. Two members were law school classmates and coeditors of the first *Stanford Law Review*, and both would become important advisers to the attorney general. Warren Christopher had clerked for U.S. Supreme Court Justice William

Douglas and returned to his hometown to join O'Melveny & Myers, Los Angeles's oldest law firm. Fred Dutton, a young lawyer interested in Democratic politics, was working for the gas company. He began to send Pat memos with suggestions. Pat arranged for Dutton to work on Adlai Stevenson's 1956 presidential campaign in California and then join the attorney general's staff. Dutton thought strategically about ideas and politics in ways different from the longtime friends and San Francisco Irish politicians who formed Pat's inner circle. Pat, always reading, recognized the need to broaden his sphere.

He and Dutton were thinking ahead to 1958, when the offices of governor and U.S. senator would both be on the ballot. Dutton articulated several precepts that Pat had learned about the realities of California politics. The first problem was the ineffectual Democratic Party, out of power for so many years, weakened by the lack of patronage jobs, the great mobility of the electorate, and the cross-filing system. Pat could not rely on the party structure; he needed to build a loyal team, committed to him. The geography of the state dictated a corollary hurdle: The Tehachapi Mountains divided Northern and Southern California into separate worlds, with different histories, economies, social structures, and leaders. Any future campaign would need two separate teams and strategies. Third, the era of campaigning largely in print was over. Radio and television were going to become the key media. Pat and Dutton began to talk regularly to formulate plans.

"California is a tremendous state," Pat wrote his cousin Burt Chandler. "As you go from one end of the state to another, you realize that California is destined to be the largest state in the Union. To think that I will have some part, good or bad, in shaping its destiny is sobering. I hope that I am not conceited because I know my limitations, but I do know also that with firm principles a person does not have to fear in the slightest degree. I know what is right and realize when I err."

6

The Governor and
the Seminarian

On the afternoon of August 14, 1956, as Jerry Brown and Frank Damrell approached a small town nestled in the Santa Clara Valley, they fished coins out of their pockets and tossed them out the car window onto State Road 17. They would not need money where they were going.

Damrell had met Jerry in high school when they competed in debates. His father was a judge in Modesto, in the heart of the state's Central Valley, and the two sons of Democratic politicians had gravitated to one another. They had both entered Santa Clara University and roomed together in Kenna Hall. Damrell, elected freshman class president, seemed most likely to follow in his father's footsteps.

Jerry was known for his night-owl hours, which included frequent visits to the senior who lived down the hall, Marc Poché, a scholarship student who earned extra money as a resident adviser. Jerry sought out Poché with atypical questions. He wanted to probe the difference between Kant and Greek philosophers, or the failure of democracies, or the reasons people didn't vote. The colloquies often ended with Poché sending Jerry to bed. Jerry continued to debate in public, too, and was chosen as one of three to compete against rival St. Mary's in the fifteenth annual Foch Medal Debate. The Santa Clara Broncos argued successfully that the multiparty system in the French parliament was detrimental to government stability.

Pat wrote his son regularly. He scolded Jerry for not paying his bill for the *San Francisco Chronicle* and emphasized the importance of a good credit rating. He lamented Adlai Stevenson's disappointing showing in the New Hampshire presidential primary. He urged Jerry to come back to Magellan Avenue on weekends. "Everybody at home is very well, but we miss you every single day you are away," Pat wrote.

His parents held out hope Jerry would stay at Santa Clara, but he had not wavered in his determination to become a Jesuit priest. Damrell made the same decision. So in June, Pat wrote friends on the East Coast and asked them to help entertain teenagers who wanted one last fling before embarking upon a monastic life. The friends spent a week in Boston, a week in D.C., and a week in New York, where they saw four plays. "A tremendous opportunity," Jerry wrote to his uncle Harold, "living like millionaires with an apartment on Park Avenue."

Eighteen years old, imbued with the confidence that he could play a significant role in the world, Jerry embraced the Jesuit seminary as a path to public service—and an alternative to the commercial politics of his father's world. "The prospect of a life devoted to religion and service of God struck me as far better than making a name in business or law or acquiring material goods," he explained fifteen years later. "The material world didn't interest me as much as a life of quiet contemplation. I didn't have any ambition to have a rich or powerful family, and I didn't want to lead an ordinary life in the suburbs. I thought it would be much more exciting saving the world for Christ."

Jerry and Damrell entered Sacred Heart seminary in Los Gatos on August 15, the anniversary of the date in 1534 when followers of Ignatius of Loyola took their vows and formed the Society of Jesus. On the eve of their formal entry into the Society, Jerry and Damrell met at a friend's house in San Francisco. Bart Lally, Jerry's childhood friend, picked up his classmates for the hour's drive south. Although they would be nearby, visiting would be strictly limited. Damrell's parents came from Modesto to say goodbye.

Pat missed the send-off. As the highest-ranking California Democrat, the attorney general led the state's delegation at the party's national convention in Chicago.

"The party for you—not just the few" was the slogan at the 1956 convention where Democrats expected to nominate Adlai Stevenson, who would again face President Dwight Eisenhower. The gathering marked only the second time national conventions were broadcast live on television, and the program offered a page of "You're on TV" tips: Stay in your seat until the broadcast ends. Ignore the cameras. And remember, "We're playing to the world's greatest audience."

An estimated 70 million viewers watched an unexpected floor fight unfold on live television. Stevenson was nominated for president and then announced he would throw open the vice presidential nomination for a vote the next day. Half a dozen candidates lobbied delegates throughout the night. Around three A.M., leaders of the California delegation met with Senator John F. Kennedy, the thirty-nine-year-old Massachusetts Democrat.

The California delegation was, as always, large, eclectic, undisciplined, and independent. They prided themselves on not taking orders from anyone. About two thirds favored Kennedy's principal opponent, Tennessee senator Estes Kefauver. Minnesota senator Humbert Humphrey also had support. Pat preferred Kennedy but did not attempt to pressure others. He also had trepidation about the promising young politician running on a ticket that would likely lose to Eisenhower and Nixon.

Hours later, the new anchor team of David Brinkley and Chet Huntley covered the action on NBC, boasting new "ultra-portable cameras" that enabled delegate interviews on the floor. On the first ballot California cast 33 votes for Kefauver, 23½ for Humphrey, and 10½ for Kennedy. In the bedlam, Pat could have voted the delegation almost any way he wanted, but he resisted the temptation to shift votes to Kennedy. The second ballot became a two-man race, and Kennedy pulled ahead. When he edged close to a majority, one by one, states shifted votes to Kefauver. When the result became inevitable, California asked to be recognized. Pat was so hoarse he could barely croak out the numbers: 50 votes for Kefauver, 18 for Kennedy. A few minutes later, Kennedy moved to nominate his rival by acclamation.

"I must confess that I was in doubt and confused as to what should be done," Pat wrote a few days later to Dick Nolan, political reporter for the *San Francisco Examiner*, who had described chaos among "the free, undirected, un-bossed" California delegation. "Confusion is understandable when you consider that California is low on the roll call, must vote almost immediately after the results are announced, and it is a tough job to reach 136 delegates, some of whom are in the mezzanine. What would you have done to have made history rather than have it pass you by?"

Jerry knew nothing of the history being made in Chicago; his new life required a virtual news blackout. Bart Lally had dropped off his friends, their trunks filled with heavy-duty shoes, tan denims, black jeans, and black trousers to wear under cassocks. He snapped a photo as the two stood in front of the large wooden door to their new home, Sacred Heart Novitiate, an imposing building on a vine-covered hillside. Waiting for the new entrants were their "angels," second-year novices paired with the new arrivals to help them adjust. Their names were entered in the daily ledger in Latin, the primary language they would use and the only subject they would study.

The first two years in the seminary were designed to immerse novices in the medieval, monastic way of life, to instill in them an understanding of the Jesuit motto "Contemplation in action." That was the mindset they would carry back to the world. They were to obey the dictum *Age quod agis*—Do what you are doing. Focus on the present. Look to the future, but don't let it dictate present actions. Be in the world, but not of it. The novitiate inculcated cerebral supremacy and emotional discipline that bordered on detachment. The ideal Jesuit was described as the teacher who, informed in the midst of a class that his mother has died, calmly continues with the lesson.

Opened in 1888, the H-shaped seminary in the rolling hills south of San Jose housed between 170 and 200 men. The chapel, dining hall, and administration offices were in the central part of the building. Novices lived in the west wing; juniors, who had taken their vows, lived in the east wing. Three or four novices shared a cubicle, with partition dividers about three quarters of the way to the ceiling and curtains for doors. Each had a bed, washbasin, closet, desk, and kneeler. They were instructed to keep the cubicle in perfect order—bed made, curtain drawn halfway except while dressing, only a crucifix on the desk.

On his first full day at Sacred Heart, 422 years after Ignatius took his vows, Edmundus G. Brown followed a schedule that had changed little since the eighteenth century. The details were recorded in the logbook: they rose at 5:50 A.M. that first day, though their normal wake-up time would be 5 A.M. Meditation began at 6:08 and continued until the 6:25 call to mass. At 8:45, make beds; at 9:08 the angels guided the novices in their first Reflection. At 9:20, Ordinary; at 9:50 they gathered at the wall outside; at 10:20 they stood in formation in front of the novice gate with new juniors. At 11:00 they had ten minutes of free time, followed by a half hour of *tempus scribendi* (writing time). At 11:40, call to Litanies, the common prayers, which began five minutes later and lasted until supper at noon. The afternoon was similar: 1:30, free, *licet siesta* (naps permitted); 2:15, spiritual reading; 2:30, Roman stations; 3:30, Rosary; 3:55, *licet* swim; 4:15, Pool *tempus*; 4:35, bell for benediction. Because juniors traditionally took their vows on August 15, after two years in the novitiate, the day concluded with a feast and special program. The next morning, the newcomers were warned about poison oak and fitted for their cassocks, to be worn at all times except during work or play. A simple ceremony a week later presenting the cassocks marked the start of formal training for the novices.

Their daily routine would vary little for the next two years, adding in Latin class, study periods, memory recitation, and chores. Manual labor assignments rotated; the class beadle, who kept logs and helped with administration, moved pegs with the novices' names to match slots on a wooden board that listed jobs—sweeping, cleaning, scullery, barbershop. All were done in silence, except outside jobs such as cleaning the chicken house and swimming pool. On Sundays they had *tempus scribendi*, time to write journal entries or letters to parents. Writing to other relatives was discouraged, with the exception of an occasional letter to a grandparent.

The novices received detailed instructions for their daily routines. Morning meditation on the life of Christ was done at the desk, kneeling, then standing, then sitting, then kneeling again during the colloquy, which ended when the priest began the mass. The afternoon meditation was on the Rules—kneeling, standing or sitting, then kneeling. Confession was once a week. The "Ordinary" reading period each day was a half hour set aside to study the Spanish Jesuit Alphonsus Rodriguez's classical work on asceticism, *The Practice of Perfection and Christian Virtues*, and *The Imitation of Christ*, by Thomas à Kempis. The "Extraordinary" reading period was another half hour devoted to learning the history of the Society and the lives of the saints. All books had to be sanctioned by the Father Master.

Corporal penance required explicit permission; "interior mortification and abnegation" were encouraged. Each novice was expected to say a *culpa* once a month, a public acknowledgment of a fault or breach of discipline. During supper, the novice knelt, made the sign of the cross, kissed the floor, folded his hands, said graces with the community, and then said his *culpa*. Other penances included saying graces with arms outstretched in the form of a cross, kissing the feet of members of the community, and kneeling while eating dinner. Novices were also subject to *Exercitium Caritatis*, in which their defects were pointed out by brothers who offered frank assessments that always began with, "It seems to me . . ." Silence was mandatory except during recreation, work or play outside, or with special permission.

"As in any 'boot-camp,' moments of deepest soul-searching and events of spontaneous hilarity weave together in the pattern of a novice's life to make these years the happiest and most rewarding a young man can know," explained the "Points for Parents" brochure the seminary sent home to help families adjust to their son's new vocation.

They sent personal letters as well. "You are probably beginning to feel the loss (apparent) of Jerry," Father Jim Straukamp wrote Pat and Bernice at the end of August 1956. "That is only natural and is part of the sacrifice of giving your boy to God. But just as you have been generous with Him, so will He return your generosity . . . a Jesuit remains closer to the family than one who gets married. It is God's way of making up for his departure. Jerry is a truly wonderful son . . . he'll make a perfect Jesuit. And for this reason we are expecting great things of him."

Jerry embraced the dramatically different life, though the night owl took some weeks to adjust to the early rising. "The change in routine was immediate and noticeable—especially having to get up when a few weeks before I was used to going to bed," he wrote to his uncle Harold. "Five o'clock in the morning around here is a beautiful time of the day—birds are chirping, the sun is coming up over Mount Hamilton casting a glow over the whole valley that joins with the dew to sparkle forth a freshness that you see at no other time." Time passed quickly, despite the unchanging daily routine. The goal of the novitiate, he explained, is "to furnish a man with an extended opportunity of looking into the meaning of life and then trying to come up with some basic answers . . . It opened up for me unthought possibilities. Becoming acquainted with Christianity in a serious way and the spiritual life that it implies was a tremendously expanding experience. It laid out a new world for me."

His father was finding more opportunities to exert his own core values as he rose in political prominence. When Pat was asked to introduce Adlai Stevenson a few weeks before the election, he chose a setting that spoke to the diversity of California. "We are here today to welcome our honored guest with a truly American throng composed of the descendants of people who have come to this city from all corners of the world," Pat said at a massive rally in San Francisco. He tied the virtues of the state to the candidate who had helped establish the United Nations in San Francisco a decade earlier. They stood in North Beach, home of Joe DiMaggio and scores of Italian American power brokers, Pat told the crowd of eighteen thousand people. A few blocks away was the largest Chinese community outside China. Nearby were communities of immigrants from Europe, South America, and Mexico. That mingling of cultures should be an example for the rest of the world, Pat said, at a time when technology had the power to draw people closer. Italy could be reached from California in less time than it had taken pioneers like August Schuckman to travel from Reno, Nevada, to San Francisco. "It is obvious we are all neighbors and should never be enemies," Pat said, stressing "the dignity of all men of all colors, races and creeds."

Three days later, Israel invaded Egypt in an attempt to gain control of the Suez Canal, and despite his natural optimism, Pat doubted that Stevenson could prevail. Pat found Eisenhower particularly impressive on television, which played a growing role in the campaign. "There are some people in public life who have a magnetic personality and Eisenhower is certainly one of them," he wrote to Jerry. "I never believe in underestimating the enemy." On Election Day, Eisenhower trounced Stevenson; he won all but seven states, including California, where his margin was more than ten points.

Pat tried to make it to Los Gatos for the monthly visits on Sunday from two to four in the afternoon. He and his son walked around the seminary's spacious grounds, unless the weather was bad or the outside area too crowded, and then they sat in the car. Jerry seemed content but hungry for news of the outside world. When his sister Cynthia visited with her fiancé, Joe Kelly, the novice was reluctant to end the conversation, and the car windows steamed up.

The novices had been at Sacred Heart more than six months before they were exposed to anything akin to the cultural life they had left behind. On May 8, 1957, they watched a performance of *Macbeth* staged by the juniors. John Coleman, who had been a year ahead of Jerry at St. Ignatius and bested him in the intraclass debates, played Macduff. "It was an excellent performance," Jerry wrote his parents. "This was my first real taste of anything along the intellectual line in the last few months and I enjoyed it very much. However I'm in no hurry to resume my studies again."

Aware that that would reinforce his parents' doubts, he tried to explain the importance of the early years in the lengthy path to become a Jesuit priest, ticking off the different stages. "Sometimes I get the impression that you think of the novitiate as some kind of necessary evil—something left over from another age and now outdated. Actually it is the most important part of our training. The time when the foundation is laid, the principles learned, and the defects eliminated. In the Juniorate we tackle the classics, in Philosophy we meet the great minds of history and consider the fundamental questions of life, in Regency the students, in Theology the truths of our religion, but in the Novitiate we face and with God's grace conquer the toughest opponent of all—ourselves. Many conquer others but only the great conquer themselves."

Pat responded quickly: "As usual, you have real discernment. I guess we do feel that the Novitiate is some kind of necessary evil because it is so difficult for us to understand a retreat from the stimulus of continued intellectual activity." He was impressed by Jerry's enthusiasm but eager for him to resume traditional classes, reading the works Pat had never had the opportunity to study. Pat read Jesuit publications and admired the rigorous thinking. But he wondered if the centuries-old traditions might not need to be updated. And then Pat Brown identified a trait that would be a lasting legacy of the Jesuit education and a well-known hallmark of his son: "I believe further that the Society will teach you to look at everything with skepticism and demand proof."

Father and son continued theological debates in person and by letter, along with lighter moments. (Pat urged Jerry to eat well: "It is my observation that fat friars are always happier.") Bernice refused to engage or apply her formidable intellect to understand the Jesuit theology or its appeal. She sometimes cried on the ride home after visits. Pat left books around the house and tried to persuade her to read Thomas à Kempis's *The Imitation of Christ*, to no avail. He urged Jerry to write about more mundane matters. "One of these days I expect her to reach for some of these books, merely to try to understand you and your determination. When she does, she will go after them with the same zeal with which she approaches everything else. At the present time, Mother enjoys hearing from you, but, very frankly, she cannot understand your objectives. This comes, of course, from a complete disinterest in religion."

Pat had more success in drawing Bernice into the public world of politics. The two flew to the opening of the Truman Library in Independence, Missouri, on the private plane of Ed Pauley, a Truman confidant, Democratic powerbroker, and oil baron. They mingled with Herbert Hoover, Dean Acheson, Sam Rayburn, and Earl Warren. "It was a most enjoyable trip and I think it was the very first time Mother really enjoyed politics," Pat wrote to his son. "She admitted it, which, I think, was quite an admission for her."

By the spring of 1957, Pat faced an important decision. He began to consult pretty much everyone, including his cloistered son. In 1958, all the statewide offices would be on the ballot, as well as a contest for U.S. senator. Pat could expect to easily win reelection as attorney general. Democrats were urging him to instead challenge either the incumbent Republican governor or senator. He was torn. "I love being Attorney General and cannot even think of anybody else sitting in this chair," he wrote to Jerry. "The United States Senate would open a completely new vista and permit me to have a box office seat on world affairs. The Governorship, of course, would be like your first two years at the Novitiate—tough but very enjoyable! I am being criticized by some of my Democratic friends for not making a decision, but I can't help it. I just don't know what I am going to do."

In fact, Pat had made a confidential pact with Clair Engle, a senior member of California's congressional delegation: If Engle challenged Senator William Knowland, scion of a powerful Bay Area family that owned the *Oakland Tribune*, Pat would run against Warren's successor, the amiable Goodwin Knight. But their political calculus was upended when the archconservative Knowland decided to challenge Knight for governor in the Republican primary. Suddenly the Senate seat had no incumbent, and Pat's angst increased.

Nineteen-year-old Jerry, ostensibly cut off from news, had plenty of advice. "Dear Dad, I thought I could write and give you a few of my ideas [about] your impending decision," he wrote in July 1957. He believed his father had decided to run for governor but vacillated out of fear he would lose, and Jerry fed those fears: Knowland would run a rough, well-financed race, because he saw the governorship as a stepping-stone to the presidency, and a loss would be career-ending. "Before running against him I think you should weigh your chances very carefully." He acknowledged that the deal with Engle complicated matters. But the skilled debater took the position that his father had a better chance of winning the open Senate seat, which would provide an equally good springboard to national prominence:

> The basic question seems to me to boil down to this: Where will you have the best opportunity of doing the most for God and country—which two ends are necessarily the same. As Senator you would have six uninterrupted years, untroubled by election entanglements to devote to your work. You would be the only senator of the majority party from the biggest state in the Union (if the population continues to grow at the present rate).
>
> If you are really interested in national health insurance and flood (calamity) insurance, capital punishment, and other sundry plans that you have talked to me about in the past, you can do far more to further these ambitions as one of our national leaders—to wit, a Senator. In my opinion, if you are ever to emerge from local politics (by that I mean California politics) you will have to do it pretty soon.
>
> The question you must answer is: Where can I do the most in solving these problems. Will I be able to do more as a Senator or as Governor? . . . when you come right down to it I can't say much about your political future except that you have a duty to God and your religion, upon which your decisions ought to be much in accordance with. Please excuse inaccuracies in this brief analysis as I have little experience and am far away from the political scene. With love, Jerry.
>
> PS My advice: make a retreat and ask God's help. You can't do it all alone.

His son's grasp of the political terrain surprised Pat. He acknowledged concern about the odds of a gubernatorial victory and worried whether he could win support from newspapers and raise sufficient money. But he also contended that issues facing California—providing water, energy, schools, and universities for the booming state—were as important as national concerns, and a governor could accomplish more than a junior senator. He planned to decide by October. "After I cross the Rubicon there will be no returning."

Fred Dutton, the politically savvy lawyer Pat had hired to expand his circle of advisers, thought the real choice was between a risky run for governor and secure reelection to a job Pat loved. Bernice might be warming to politics, but she understood a gubernatorial race would mean a quantum leap into the political fishbowl. Dutton impressed upon Pat the need to curb his habit of thinking out loud: "You have come into a position where what you say and do has a significant effect far beyond just you personally. I assume that is an uncomfortable status for you— and objectionable to your family. But it would still seem to be one of the inescapable realities."

Dutton's comments were sparked by a July 23, 1957, story in the *San Francisco Chronicle* in which Pat sent signals in all directions: He said he had received an attractive offer from the private sector, a gubernatorial race would cost half a million dollars, national Democrats wanted him to run for Senate, he preferred to run for reelection, and oil magnate Ed Pauley would not help him run for governor. He left a damaging image of "vacillation, confusion, superficiality," Dutton said. "You have to decide what you really want—in a personal and public sense. Then we need to go after it. . . . Only you and your wife can make that decision."

Eighteen years younger than Pat, Dutton was short, with a receding hairline, big glasses, a quick wit, and a ready laugh. He had grown up in San Francisco, interrupted his college education to join the Army, and returned home with a Bronze Star and Purple Heart after being wounded in the Battle of the Bulge and held prisoner of war. After finishing Cal and then Stanford Law School, he had been looking for a way into public service when he met Pat Brown. Dutton pushed Pat to run for governor. He knew Pauley supported Knight for reelection and wanted to maneuver Pat into a Senate race. So Dutton was concerned when Pat accepted an invitation for the family to spend ten days at Coconut Island, Pauley's private Hawaiian compound. "They have slides in the bedrooms going down into the water, so when you wake up in the morning the first thing you do is to get onto the slide and slide right down into the ocean," Pat wrote to eleven-year-old Kathy, who was away at camp, describing their upcoming adventure.

Worried that Pauley would use the vacation to pressure Pat to run for Senate, Dutton had sent a survey to dozens of key California Democrats asking what Pat should do. "Run for governor" was the overwhelming response. Every day Dutton airmailed piles of letters to Pat in Hawaii.

"I believe you should give serious thought to an early announcement of whatever your decision is," Dutton wrote. Knowland would make his official announcement in a few weeks. Knight was clearly rattled. "We no longer have a conventional political situation."

Coconut Island would be Pat's last break. "After that, it's back to the salt mines and probably the most important year that I will ever face," he wrote to Jerry. "I have almost determined to run for Governor even though all the odds seem to be against me . . . I intend to make no public announcement until after I have made a retreat because only in silence, meditation and prayer can I really work this one out."

Jerry spent his summer vacation at a different sort of compound. Once a week, the novices took a one-hour hike, three abreast in assigned trios, across State Road 17 and up a fire road that led to the Villa Joseph, owned by the Jesuits. In summer they camped out at the Villa for several weeks in June and August. They slept in tents among the redwoods, hiked, swam, played softball, and barbecued on the outdoor grill.

The end of the summer brought another change of pace. Two thirds of the seminary's financial support came from the Novitiate Winery, adjacent to Sacred Heart, which produced a black Muscat that frequently won prizes at the California State Fair. The Jesuits' nearby vineyards had appreciated considerably as the area became a popular San Jose suburb and agricultural fields gave way to development. The Jesuits debated selling the Santa Clara vineyards and buying cheaper land farther away, but they postponed the decision in part because the grape harvest was integral to the novitiate experience. Each season, novices worked in the fields for about five weeks during harvest. Their work helped the winery's bottom line and reinforced the virtue of manual labor. Each morning, two dozen novices in jeans and denim "grape jackets" balanced in the back of a flatbed truck for the drive to the fields, where they picked grapes in silence for an hour. Then the whistle blew, and they were allowed to talk. Competition was encouraged and the names of the five fastest pickers were posted daily. Just as in high school, John Coleman, the champion debater, always wanted to make the list. Jerry was noted more for asking provocative philosophical questions during the time they were allowed to talk.

Before the grape harvest ended, Pat Brown had made his decision. On October 30, 1957, his twenty-seventh wedding anniversary, he announced his candidacy for governor. He promised leadership to meet the rapidly growing state's needs for classrooms, highways, and water. He articulated a vision of ambitious expansion: "I deeply believe we have a great state to build."

A week later, Governor Knight walked out of the office of Vice President Nixon, whom Knight had called one of the most dangerous men in the world, and announced he would run for Knowland's Senate seat. A bitter Knight had little choice. Nixon had mediated the deal to avoid a damaging intraparty fight. Delighted Democrats promptly dubbed the Republican maneuver "the Big Switch." Instead of a popular, moderate incumbent, the Republican candidate running against Pat would be a conservative Washington insider with presidential ambitions.

Dutton, the man Pat called his Svengali, began crafting the message for an election more than a year away. He recruited help from his friend Warren Christopher, who was becoming a prominent lawyer in Los Angeles. Christopher wrote position papers and speeches. Dutton commissioned papers from experts and writers, including author Wallace Stegner and journalist Carey McWilliams. Dutton and Christopher brainstormed about how to increase Pat's profile in Southern California, where he still was not well known. "You will have the 4 major papers against you here in Los Angeles as far as editorial support is concerned. BUT you will have the majority of the *working press* for you," journalist Adele Rogers St. John wrote Dutton. To offset the dominance of the conservative *Los Angeles Times*, the Brown team cultivated smaller Southern California papers whose editorial positions were particularly influential with the thousands of voters who had recently moved to California.

California was growing so fast it was projected to gain at least six congressional seats after the next census. The 1958 election would be crucial because the next legislature would control reapportionment, the redrawing of congressional boundaries. For California Democrats, the election also became a test of a multiyear effort to rebuild, not through the weak state party but around it. In 1952, Democrats had fared so poorly that their Senate nominee lost his own primary. The only bright spot had been the energy of young people drawn to Adlai Stevenson's candidacy, who formed local political clubs. The Stevenson Clubs became the nucleus of a grassroots organization called the California Democratic Council, known as the CDC, founded in early 1953. Within two years, the CDC had four hundred clubs, and their members helped Democrats win all the party's primaries for the first time since crossfiling had begun. In addition to actively supporting Democrats before the primaries—which the state party was barred from doing—the clubs supplied dozens of volunteers to type, label, and send out flyers, important for campaigns that still depended on mailings. Though the liberal, intellectual CDC leadership was somewhat suspicious of Pat Brown's roots in Irish San Francisco machine politics, he easily won their endorsement at the January 10, 1958, convention, where the Democrats' emblem was a small silver broom with the slogan "Sweep the State in '58."

Because the Democrats' dysfunctional party had been out of power so long, Dutton traveled cross-country to glean strategies from five Democrat-controlled states—New York, New Jersey, Massachusetts, Pennsylvania, and Michigan. He reported that top Democratic office-holders campaigned year-round. They spent "beyond anything conceived of in practical terms in California" and raised money year-round in a systematic manner. Unlike in California, successful Democrats didn't rely on a small group of wealthy donors, nor did they allow donors to decide how money should be spent. Campaign professionals made those determinations. One result was in-depth public opinion surveys conducted several times a year.

So Dutton consulted Lou Harris, a pioneer in the field who had recently launched his own polling business. "Survey research is rapidly being recognized as an indispensable arm of the modern election campaign," Harris wrote Dutton. "Ticket splitting and switch voting have reached unprecedented proportions . . . more and more voters are casting their ballots for (or against) the individual man rather than for any party or set of party principles." Given the weakness of party loyalty in California, this would be especially true. Dutton outlined for Harris areas they should poll: What was the popular image of Pat Brown? Stature? Honesty? Vacillation? Did Catholicism hurt a candidate? How did opinions vary between north, south, and central California?

Pat's personality—buoyant, optimistic, embracing—lent itself to the "nice guy" campaign Dutton designed. Pat avoided strong partisanship and appealed to independents and liberal Republicans, in the tradition of Earl Warren and the "Party of California." Pat had spent the last eight years visiting all fifty-eight counties; he understood both statewide and local concerns. The results showed in the June 3 primary: Pat won 22.5 percent of the Republican vote, almost twice as large a share as Knowland's 13.6 percent showing in the Democratic primary.

Pat Brown's logo in his 1958 campaign

"The guy is as natural as an old shoe," Republican voter Thomas Curry wrote George Brewer, a Shell Oil executive and childhood friend of Pat who had formed "New York Republicans for Brown." Curry ran into Pat on the golf course, where the candidate abandoned his game and rushed over to the seventeenth tee to exclaim about their mutual friend's support. "He was as elated as a sailor with a 6 day pass. In my book it is not beyond the realm of possibility that one day in the not too distant future he may very well land in the No. 1 spot in the White House. As an Irishman once said—may the wind be ever at his back."

Most of the larger donors to Pat's campaign were Republicans. His campaign chair and principal fundraiser was Benjamin Swig, a real estate mogul, major philanthropic and political force in San Francisco, and close friend of Earl Warren. The businessman met the then governor in 1944 aboard the *City of San Francisco* when Swig traveled by train from Chicago to buy a San Francisco landmark, the St. Francis Hotel. By then, Swig was on his way to becoming one of the largest individual real estate operators in the country. A few years later, he bought the Fairmont Hotel, in part because his wife wanted to live in the penthouse, an opulent suite that would become the site of many political fundraisers. One of the first things Swig did was lift the hotel's ban on black guests. Swig became a Democrat after sitting next to Helen Gahagan Douglas on a plane; he apologized for the dirty red-baiting campaign Nixon had run when he defeated her for Senate, and then got so angry about it that he changed his registration. He still voted for Republicans like Warren and Knight, but he had become a major booster of Pat Brown. One of Swig's storied techniques was to host a luncheon and tell people the doors would remain locked until they all wrote checks.

As often happened in California, an unrelated ballot proposition played a critical role in the electoral race. Union membership and clout had been steadily rising in the 1950s. In response, conservatives placed on the ballot a so-called right-to-work initiative that would amend the constitution and deny unions the ability to require membership as a condition of employment. Knowland campaigned for the change; Pat opposed the measure. He thus became the indirect beneficiary of a million-dollar campaign to defeat Proposition 18, waged by national labor organizations that viewed California as a bellwether. Organized labor also conducted a voter registration campaign that helped Democrats widen their enrollment edge, though many of the new residents were conservative Democrats from the Midwest or South who often voted Republican.

The fight over the proposition helped sharpen the ideological differences between the candidates. The *Oakland Tribune*, the Knowland family paper, did all it could for its favorite son, including a caricature of Pat with a dog collar that was captioned LABOR'S STOOGE. But the Republican campaign was so dismal that one of the three major Republican papers, the *San Francisco Chronicle*, rescinded its earlier endorsement of Knowland. By the end of the summer, Dutton predicted Pat would win by more than a million votes. They launched the general election campaign after Labor Day with half a dozen kickoff rallies in San Diego, Long Beach, and Los Angeles, ferrying reporters on a presidential-campaign-style press bus outfitted with a bar, mimeograph machine, typewriter, and work space. Aides arranged for Western Union to pick up reporters' copy at various times to meet their deadlines.

For the first time in decades, a Democrat appeared poised to lead California. A *Time* magazine reporter trailed Pat for several weeks, filing reams of dispatches that captured how the candidate's warmth put people at ease no matter where he went. Within minutes, strangers in restaurants and taxis called him Pat. The *Time* story portrayed Pat's victory as all but certain and nationally significant, through an East Coast lens that marveled at how a "second rate administrator with a notorious inability to make decisions" could be so popular. The story mentioned Pat's drooping socks and tendency to worry, but omitted many of the more thoughtful comments from friends and colleagues who portrayed him as more complex than the "Just Plain Pat" who graced the cover of *Time* on September 15, 1958.

In one of the correspondent's outtakes, Norton Simon praised Pat for surrounding himself with talent to compensate for areas in which he felt weak. "So few of us are willing to recognize our own inadequacies," Simon said. "But Pat recognizes where true character lies and what to lean on. I have that feeling very deeply and I recognized this in Pat in his youth. This man is very, very real."

Only once in a while did Pat feel his brilliant advisers took too much credit. As they sat around a Palo Alto swimming pool analyzing the primary results, Dutton and others focused on the impact of the recession and their weak opponent. Pat was hurt. "I know what you all are thinking, that I lucked into this one," he said. "Let me tell you something. I've been selling Pat Brown for forty years. I've been working this. I had something to do with this election. The people like me." Then he got up, in his trunks and Hawaiian shirt, and walked around the pool, stopping at the first table he reached. "My name is Pat Brown. I'm running for governor . . ."

At Sacred Heart, the novices finished harvesting grapes, and Jerry was deep into his new studies. On August 15, 1958, two years after he entered the seminary, he had taken his vows of poverty, chastity, and obedience and become a junior. Jerry plunged into a classical education and spent much of his time in the library. He marveled over Cicero's speeches ("the clearest you would ever want to read and they roll out like a symphony. He worked over every line so the whole thing would be a finished masterpiece of literature as well as persuasive oratory"), discovered that English translations of Virgil's *Aeneid* lost the music, rhythm, and imagery of the original, and found Socrates's *Apology* "not only a well thought out defense, but an inspiring picture of a man that was ready and eager to die for his ideals." He was less impressed by the survey courses in Shakespeare, Western civilization, public speaking, and English, which he felt rushed to cover too much ground. Jerry preferred to burrow deeply into one subject rather than skim the surface of many.

The juniors could talk, study, read, and discuss ideas. But rules and regimen remained strict. Latin was to be used whenever possible, and conversations were to be brief; long discussions required special permission. The reading list was tightly controlled. Magazines and newspapers

Jerry Brown stands in front of the Lourdes Shrine on the grounds of Sacred Heart Novitiate in October 1958, two years into his studies to become a Jesuit priest. The shrine was a replica of the French grotto. (Courtesy of the office of Governor Edmund G. Brown Jr.)

were off limits. No one told Pat that the subscriptions to the *Atlantic, Fortune, Foreign Affairs,* and *Harper's* that he sent as gifts to the Sacred Heart Novitiate library were banned reading. For a small group of juniors, including Jerry Brown, the admonishments to unquestioningly follow orders, the repressive rules, and the restricted reading seemed to clash with their new intellectual course of study.

In both Rome and Sacramento, changes with profound implications for sacred and secular institutions were on the horizon.

On November 4, 1958, almost 80 percent of California voters cast ballots, a record for a nonpresidential year. Jerry, five months shy of his twenty-first birthday, was not among the seminarians at Los Gatos who went to the polls. The one television at the Sacred Heart Novitiate was off limits, but that evening the authorities made an exception. "After early election returns indicated the strong Democratic trend," the minister recorded in his logbook, "Bro. Edmund G. Brown was allowed to view telecast made by his father Governor-elect Edmund G. Brown."

Pat Brown won 60 percent of the vote, and his million-vote margin led a Democratic sweep. For the first time since 1889, Democrats captured every statewide office except secretary of state. They gained seven state Senate seats and ten in the Assembly to take control of both houses. Clair Engle was elected to the U.S. Senate, and the congressional delegation flipped to a slim Democratic majority.

The following day was equally historic. At Los Gatos, all the novices and juniors were allowed the rare opportunity to watch television: a live broadcast of the coronation of Pope John XXIII. His reign would prove momentous. Even before the pope convened Vatican II, the church council that would redefine the relationship of the Church to the modern world, the sense of impending change and concomitant apprehension began to permeate a novitiate where customs and practices had changed little for centuries. The rector at Los Gatos worried that the new Spiritual Father who worked with the juniors was too outspoken in his comments about the need to reform outmoded practices, which "caused some uneasiness and considerable discussion among the Juniors about their Novitiate training." Old-timers bemoaned changes in how Latin was taught, a de-emphasis that presaged the Church's decision to switch from Latin to the vernacular in saying the mass. And the authorities worried about the lengthy conversations that Father William Burman, a well-liked Latin teacher, engaged in with some juniors, including Jerry.

Jerry was granted the unusual privilege of leaving the seminary in January to attend his father's inauguration. Pat snatched a few quiet moments in a car on the way to Sacramento to dictate a letter explaining how Inauguration Day would unfold. "When your calls average thirty to thirty-five a day and then, in addition, you have from forty to fifty people coming into your office, you have very little time for what would be called in your institution 'meditation,'" he wrote. The thought of governing a state of 15 million people, larger than most countries, weighed on him, especially the responsibility to do right by those most dependent on the state. He would summon his best salesmanship to overcome parochial interests and unite the vast and varied regions of the state, making "above all an appeal to legislators to recognize the greatness of California and all its potential."

Pat had prevailed upon Warren Christopher to take a short leave from his position as a partner in O'Melveny & Myers and help launch the new administration. Christopher believed he could help set a tone and sketch out what he called "the architecture" for the new administration, then leave the building to others. His first job was to draft the inaugural address. Explaining the governor's philosophy, Christopher coined the phrase that would become Pat Brown's mantra: "responsible liberalism."

Inauguration Day was a celebration tailored for the former yell leader from Lowell High. The ceremony ended with the state song, "I Love You, California," the sentimentality of its lyrics matched by the sincerity of Pat's devotion to his state:

> When the snow-crowned Golden Sierras
> Keep their watch o'er the valleys' bloom,
> It is there I would be in our land by the sea,
> Every breeze bearing rich perfume.
> It is here nature gives of her rarest. It is Home Sweet Home to me,
> And I know when I die I shall breathe my last sigh
> For my sunny California.

Afterward, the Browns headed to the Governor's Mansion at Sixteenth and H for a private dinner, although the family would not move in to the historic home for some time. "You see, this is the only time we will have an opportunity to be all together," Bernice told a reporter. "Jerry is at Sacred Heart Novitiate in Los Gatos studying for the priesthood and this will be his only chance to see our new home. It is really for him that I arranged this family party." They posed for photos around the dining room table, Ida Brown with a great-grandchild on her lap, Jerry standing in his cassock.

In the evening the first couple made a grand entrance at the inaugural ball, Bernice elegant in a satin gown designed for her by the Academy Award–winning costumer Charles LeMaire, who chose turquoise blue to set off the first lady's silver-streaked hair and blue eyes. To headline the ball, Pat had chosen Nat King Cole, known for his activism as well as his voice. Cole had used his celebrity to speak out against racism on a national stage and then closer to home, when his move into the all-white Hancock Park neighborhood of Los Angeles triggered protests. Legislation to bar discrimination in employment and housing were among Pat's top priorities.

Pat assembled a cabinet that included minorities and women along with lifelong friends. Fred Dutton, the chief of staff, fired off what he called "mee-mos"; Pat studied them intently. He underlined words Dutton used over and over: The governor must show "<u>decisiveness, strength and stature.</u>" Pat's warmth and humanity were enormous assets, Dutton wrote, but as governor he was an administrator and policymaker who must establish his image as a clear-thinking, knowledgeable, decisive political leader.

The state had doubled in size in the last ten years. The tax structure had remained largely unchanged, revenues falling far short of spending needed to accommodate the growing population. Pat faced a $100 million budget deficit. He presented a budget that asked for $202 million in new taxes, a combination of income and sales levies, including a three-cent-per-package tax on cigarettes. "I think they were rather shocked," Pat wrote the day he delivered the budget to the legislature. "It was a courageous, challenging budget. I have nothing but contempt for those who say that no taxes are necessary. I have difficulty concealing it from the press."

For the first time in his life, Pat Brown tried to keep a diary. He was not a writer, and the sporadic entries were mostly short, prosaic sentences, scrawled in bad handwriting, usually in the early morning hours when doubts kept him from sleep.

"Worried very much about Gridiron speech—don't like it but can't think of anything better. Could be worst flop in history. Worried about mother. Can't see her because of work. Haven't heard from Jerry who is out of this world. Kathleen is disruptive. Slept very badly."

The traditional, off-the-record keynote at the Gridiron Club dinner, an annual gathering of Washington politicians and journalists, had to be witty. Warren Christopher, a serious, soft-spoken lawyer who did not consider himself funny, was an unusual choice to draft the address. He enjoyed the assignment and enlisted help from various people, including the humorist Art Hoppe, a columnist at the *Chronicle*. The speech was a hit. "California seems to have come up with a new product suitable for export to other states for national use," reported Hearst news. "His name is Gov. Edmund G. 'Pat' Brown, a Democrat of California. Brown passed with highest marks a test that has knocked off the aspirations to national office of many a politician."

Pat marveled at it all. "It amazes me sometimes that I am writing letters on the stationery of the Governor of the State of California," he wrote to a friend. He tried to execute Dutton's mantra of decisive leadership by using his big victory to push an ambitious agenda quickly. "I can see some real thunderheads in the offing because we are really treading on some pretty sacred cows," he wrote to Jerry. "I am trying to be very, very fair, but I sometimes find out that politics is not a matter of fairness but really doing something for your friends (which is human nature, I suppose). We have a labor bill, a water bill, and a budget that will really cause consternation. If all the forces join together, I am afraid both Governor Brown and the State will be in trouble. There is one thing I am certain they won't say, however, and that is that I am indecisive or unable to make up my mind. People closest to me know that I really want to accomplish things and that I am not too much afraid of people I think are wrong."

He celebrated his fifty-fourth birthday in the Mansion on April 21. Ida came by bus from San Francisco. "Happy birthday Daddy love Kathy," his daughter wrote in Pat's diary. "The tough part is ahead however but I do not intend to retreat on what I think is best for all the people," Pat wrote beneath his daughter's birthday greeting. He was clear about his goal: to make "life a little more comfortable for the average human being."

When the legislative session ended in June, Pat faced decisions on whether to sign two thousand bills. "The mere reading of them is laborious let alone the responsibility of making right decisions," he wrote in his diary. "I want to give California the best administration it has ever had. I wish Jerry was with me. He is missing a stimulating life as the son of the governor."

Jerry was finishing up the June vacation week at the Villa Joseph. The seminarians played bridge, swam, entertained high school students from St. Ignatius, picnicked at Lower Lake, barbecued for visitors, and held song fests at night. The more relaxed pace at the Villa also presented opportunities for breaking the rules with private conversations. Several juniors, careful to avoid the rest of their peers, began to share doubts about their vocation. Jerry struggled with the idea of unquestioning acceptance of church dogma. The clandestine conversations with his childhood friend Peter Finnegan and his high school friend Frank Damrell went largely unnoticed by their peers, but not by their superiors. The juniors were admonished to discuss concerns with priests, not one another. Juniors had been allowed to walk on outings in pairs; they were made to walk in three-somes again, so that conversations could be better monitored.

Jerry turned for counsel to Bill Burman, a kind, quietly charismatic scholar twenty-five years his senior. During dozens of visits, Jerry talked, and Burman listened. A worldly, multilingual intellectual who had studied in half a dozen countries, Burman was going through his own vocational crisis. As the censor of books, he had his own library. He lent Jerry two proscribed books that influenced him profoundly. In *Man's Search for Himself*, existential theologian and psychologist Rollo May wrote about the path to understanding self. In *Spirit and Reality*, Nikolai Berdyaev, a Russian Orthodox Church theologian, criticized Jesuit ascet-icism as inconsistent with freedom of the spirit. He offered a religious alternative to Jesuit obedience.

Burman felt a responsibility to counsel the juniors, and he was unapologetic when his conversations were reported to the rector as subversive behavior. "I felt that the best service I could render would be to lend them a willing ear as they worked out their own solutions," he wrote in response to a complaint. "I wanted them to feel free to talk about anything that troubled them. It was my firm intention not to influence them in any way. It was certainly not my desire to criticize the training of the Society or the guidance that they had received from any individual."

The conflicted juniors continued their furtive conversations during the late August vacation at the Villa, with visits to one another's tents in between the Follies of the Saints variety show and the ball games between teams dubbed the Octopii and the Eucalyptii. The juniors' conversations were reported to the rector, who spoke to each at length, chiding them not to talk to one another during Villa days and not to discuss vocational doubts.

On the Sunday before Christmas, Pat visited Jerry alone. The two took a long walk. The rector watched from his window and felt certain he knew what they were discussing.

"I visited my son at the Sacred Heart Novitiate," Pat wrote in his diary that day, December 20, 1959. "He is a fine wonderful boy. He told me that he would probably leave his studies for the priesthood. He felt that it had been a wonderful 3½ years, that his Catholicism was stronger than ever but that what they had taught him had caused him to logically feel that the 'rules of Obedience' were not valid. That there were times when freedom of the conscience was more important. He stated that he would like to go to the University of California, take some premed courses and then study medicine. I didn't advise him one way or the other but told him that I would help whatever choice he made."

Ten days later, the rector received the visit he had been expecting. Brother Edmund G. Brown requested a dispensation from his vows. "His reason? No vocation," the rector wrote to the Father Provincial. "To do what he is obliged to do by rule, is not difficult, he says; but to do it because of the rule is not for him. 'Don't fence me in' seems to express his attitude toward rules, regulations, and, it seems to me, even vows." Ever since he took his vows, the rector noted, Jerry had demonstrated "his manifestations of nonconformance."

Jerry's dislike of rules would continue the rest of his life, as would his nonconformism. At the same time, his Jesuit training would shape his core beliefs. He would repeat the mantra *Age quod agis*—Do what you are doing—and confer the motto on one of the institutions that mattered to him most. He would retain the Jesuit idea of thinking about the future while acting in the present. But he would have agency over the decisions and paths he took.

The rector made little effort to counsel Jerry to stay. "I know that his father, and especially his mother and grandmother, opposed his entrance into the Society . . . Frankly, I see no hope of saving the young man. And I doubt seriously about the wisdom of trying further to save him. Considerable unrest has been caused among the Juniors by the attitudes of Brothers Brown [and] Finnegan."

Two days later, Finnegan made the same request. The rector agreed that he, too, should leave.

Jerry had told his parents he was in no hurry and might stay another month or more. He left on January 23, 1960. Frank Damrell stayed several more months. By spring, the rector reported happily to his superiors that the spirit among the juniors had improved considerably:

> The California Juniors who were given their papers during the past year seem to have developed the same attitudes toward religious life. And they expressed those attitudes in about the same words. They stated that their personalities and abilities could not develop in an atmosphere where rules and regulations and

common life are considered to be so important. All seemed convinced that they possessed abilities which would better develop in the freer atmosphere of the world. All openly stated or intimated that the Society's methods of training were anti-quated, effective in the days of St. Ignatius, but not so today.

Jerry's return to civilian life elicited joy in Sacramento. His mother understood the issue clearly: Her son could not abide quashing his inquiring mind and spirit in the name of obedience to dogma. Jerry's father was equally glad to have his only son home, though he did not dwell on the reasons. Pat no longer made annual retreats, but the Jesuits' lessons stayed with him.

During the day, the governor would effusively greet each person he encountered. When Pat walked out of his office for lunch and saw school-children in the halls, he went up to them and said, "Do you know who I am? I'm the governor!" He wanted the kids to know they'd met the governor. He took an almost childish delight in his position and wanted to share that joy with everyone he saw.

At night, when he said his prayers, Pat remembered what he had learned on his first Jesuit retreat. They had knelt and prayed for the most forgotten soul in purgatory, that their prayers might help that soul reach heaven. Every night when he prayed in the Governor's Mansion, Pat later recalled, "I'd pray for the most forgotten soul in the State of California. That somewhere, the works that I did would reach out, and reach that most forgotten soul in California."

7

Fiat Lux

In the summer of 1930, just before Bernice Layne Brown eloped, a revolutionary dormitory opened on the campus of her alma mater. International House welcomed Cal students to the first coeducational dorm west of the Mississippi, a cultural center that would be a rare mingling place for men and women, Americans and foreigners, whites and blacks.

The sprawling Spanish Colonial Revival building with its Moorish tiles and ceilings, sunken patios, and domed tower was known as I-House, the second such facility underwritten by John D. Rockefeller Jr. He had opened I-House New York near Columbia University six years earlier "as a laboratory for a new kind of experiment—the day-to-day practice of international fellowship among men and women." Its success led Rockefeller to donate $1.8 million to construct the dorm at Berkeley, a window to the Pacific, with a particular mission to draw Asian students out of substandard, ghettoized housing. Its founders deliberately located I-House on Piedmont Avenue, the same street as the Cal fraternities and sororities that excluded Jews, blacks, Latinos, and Asians. When the project was discussed at community meetings, hundreds turned out to protest the integrated dorm.

I-House opened with 338 men and 115 women, mostly graduate students, living in single rooms. I-House hosted Sunday suppers, concerts, and cultural festivals. In 1942, the director spoke out against the Japanese internment and helped delay the deportation of Japanese students. After the war, Holocaust survivors were in residence. I-House students led efforts to desegregate restaurants and housing in Berkeley and helped the city test compliance with antidiscrimination laws. Heated debates between radicals and conservatives from around the world were commonplace in the lounges and dining hall. THAT BROTHERHOOD MAY PREVAIL was the motto on the International House seal.

Jerry Brown moved into I-House in the spring term of 1960. He knew about the dorm from his sister Barbara, who had lived there when she took classes for her teaching credential and enjoyed the intellectual cama-raderie. Although he aspired to become a psychiatrist, Jerry enrolled as a classics major because his prior course work dovetailed with requirements, giving him standing as a second semester junior. He benefited from his status as the governor's son, though he hid rather than flaunted his connections and often seemed oblivious to the implications. Reunited with Marc Poché, the senior adviser on Jerry's floor at Santa Clara who was now a law student at Berkeley, Jerry expressed to Poché surprise that despite his late arrival at an appointment with the registrar, all his requests were pleasantly accommodated.

Jerry plunged from one extreme to another, from the cloistered world of the seminary with restricted reading lists and banned books into the cultural ferment of Berkeley. He read Camus. He ate chop suey and rice at Robbie's on Telegraph and thought, this is where Allen Ginsberg hung out when he wrote "Howl." Jerry studied Yeats, Conrad, Foster, and Joyce with the literary critic Mark Schorer, who had been a star witness for the defense a few years earlier when police confiscated copies of "Howl" and charged poet and City Lights bookstore owner Lawrence Ferlinghetti with selling obscenity. The lengthy trial and acquittal had brought national attention to the Beats.

Schorer was one of three professors who made a lasting impression on Jerry. Intellectual historian Carl Schorske was another. Schorske had turned down Cal a few years earlier because of lingering concerns about the loyalty oath controversy. After guest lecturing, he was so taken with the electric environment that he changed his mind. Unlike the elite East Coast schools, Cal drew students from a wide range of social, economic, and religious backgrounds. The diversity was visible in their dress, everything from ties to jeans. The community was intellec-tually and socially open and welcoming. Schorske thought Berkeley the nearest thing to a European university in America. California reminded him of Thuringia, a series of German towns including Weimar, a volatile mix of creativity and instability.

Schorske gained an appreciation of teaching as a vocation from the junior political science professor who became his close friend and Jerry's third influential teacher, Sheldon Wolin. Wolin's book *Politics and Vision* had recently catapulted him into the ranks of significant political theorists. He was credited with resuscitating the then declining field of political philosophy by showing the relevance of history in analyzing the present, and the limits and possibilities of popular democracy. Five decades later, Jerry would still ponder his answer to the blue book exam question in Wolin's Political Science 116B: Explain the Marxian theory of power.

"Fine boy but too intense," Pat wrote in his diary after spending a March Sunday morning on campus with his son. "I wish he were closer to home."

The turmoil that would make Berkeley a household name was still a few years away, but Jerry's three semesters there coincided with a quieter tumult that had equally profound consequences— a debate over the future of not only Cal, but all public colleges and universities in California. The political and educational deliberations set in motion far-reaching changes for the country's largest system of public higher education. Ultimately, the resolution augured a national embrace of universal access to college.

"I knew exactly what I wanted to do," Pat Brown wrote to a friend a decade later, describing his commitment to the agreement known as the Master Plan for higher education. "I realized that in the next 20 years people would continue to come to California and there was absolutely no way to stop it. I gave the highest priority to education, because I felt the greatness of California would depend upon an educated people."

California had been growing by about half a million people a year, almost two thirds of the increase newcomers lured by the weather and lifestyle, the strong economy and booming defense industry, and the start of a technology industry near Stanford University, encroaching on the lush agricultural fields of the Santa Clara Valley. The migration, coupled with the postwar baby boom, meant more students of all ages. During the 1950s, the state needed to open the equivalent of one high school a week. The patchwork system of public colleges and universities was overloaded and poorly aligned to meet demands that would only increase.

California's commitment to free higher education dated from the first constitutional convention in 1849, at which delegates expressed the desire to establish a public university. Not quite two decades later, on March 23, 1868, the governor signed a charter that established the University of California, run by a constitutionally autonomous Board of Regents. "In the most quiet and unobtrusive manner possible, an event took place yesterday destined, we trust, to exercise an incalculable influence upon the future of this State," reported the newspaper *Alta California* in September 1869. "The University of California commenced its functions." The first classes met in Oakland, and the campus moved to Berkeley in 1873. Tuition was free for all Californians.

From the start, the openness and commitment to access distinguished the University of California from the prestigious East Coast schools it would soon consider intellectual rivals. While Cal modeled itself in part on Yale, the university admitted its first seventeen women in 1870, almost a century before Yale became coeducational. Phoebe Apperson Hearst, whose husband, George, had made a fortune in mining, endowed scholarships to help women support themselves while in college. Hearst was the first woman Regent, serving from 1897 until her death twenty-two years later. She financed an international design competition for the Berkeley campus, raised money for cultural activities, and founded the museum of anthropology.

The university achieved a series of firsts in the early decades of the twentieth century. In 1923, the year before Bernice Layne arrived, enrollment topped fourteen thousand, making Cal the largest university in the world. In 1929, Ernest Lawrence became the school's first Nobel laureate for his invention of the cyclotron. In 1930, the university became the first with multiple campuses, adding an agricultural school in Davis and a "Southern Branch" in Los Angeles.

When the Regents decided the schools needed individual leaders, Clark Kerr was named chancellor of the Berkeley campus in 1952. Six years later, the balding, bespectacled Quaker took over as president of the whole university, a few months before Pat was elected governor. Kerr would craft a blueprint that gave Californians an unparalleled system of public higher education, which in turn became a model for modern research universities across the country. Pat Brown would embrace the plan and use his political weight to shepherd it through the legislature and Regents.

Kerr was a few years younger than Pat, born in 1911 on a Pennsylvania farm and educated in a one-room school. The town was so small that when someone died, the church bell tolled once for each year; by counting the rings, it was said, people knew whom to mourn. Kerr became part of the 5 percent of his generation who attended college. President of the student government at Swarthmore, he planned to attend Columbia Law

School until a summer Quaker program in California set him on a different path. He enrolled in graduate school at Stanford in labor economics, then transferred to Cal to work with Paul Taylor, an expert on farm labor and the husband of photographer Dorothea Lange. Taylor sent Kerr to the Central Valley cotton fields to interview workers during a violent 1933 strike. Kerr finished his studies, found a job at the University of Washington, and wistfully left the Berkeley hills where he and his wife would watch the morning fog rise through the eucalyptus trees. In 1945, Governor Warren, concerned about postwar labor strife, created an institute on industrial relations at Cal, his alma mater. Kerr became the first director. It was his dream job.

Kerr gained prominence on campus during the controversy over the Regents' demand that faculty sign a loyalty oath. He signed, but became the leader of faculty opposition. He was chosen as chancellor partly on the strength of his role in persuading the Regents to rescind the oath requirement. The Berkeley campus was still more commuter school than intellectual community when Kerr took over in 1952, in the midst of a transition from teaching institution to research university. Student life centered on fraternities. Kerr initiated a shift to the "English model," adding more dorms, a student union, cultural facilities, and walking paths. Fraternities and sororities receded in importance, ROTC became optional, study abroad programs began. By 1959, a liberal student group had wrested the leadership of the Associated Student Union Council away from fraternities and sororities for the first time. Students began to press the university to take positions on nuclear disarmament and the recognition of Cuba. The Regents adopted a nondiscrimination policy for student housing and activities. A prestigious faculty grew stronger as Kerr lured top humanities scholars to complement the esteemed science faculty. Instead of vying for top rank among public universities, Cal began to view its competition as the Ivy League.

As demand grew, the university held to its commitment to provide a free undergraduate education to any California resident who qualified for admission. For tens of thousands of Californians from working families, that meant a passport to upward mobility. A 1959 survey found that 45 percent of the undergraduates came from families with limited income. Almost one third of the students at Cal reported they were self-supporting. Californians didn't need statistics to know that the university helped determine social position and earning power. Cal was the place to go to make connections that lasted long past graduation. Loyalty to Cal became a way of life and a family tradition.

By the time Jerry enrolled at Cal in 1960, the University of California had about fifty thousand students spread out over seven campuses, including an agricultural college at Davis that had evolved from the University Farm, a small liberal arts school in Riverside that developed around the world-famous Citrus Experiment Station, and a teachers' college for women in Santa Barbara. Overcrowding at the two premier campuses had become so severe that Kerr proposed to cap enrollment at Cal. At UCLA, the chancellor warned that the school's growth without adequate dorms—from seventy-five hundred students two decades earlier to more than twenty thousand—triggered complaints from neighbors and parking nightmares: ten thousand cars vied each day for seventy-eight hundred parking spots. Yet UCLA chancellor Raymond Bernard Allen found the school remarkable. "Never have I been on a campus where more dreams were being dreamed, more plans under way, more projects in the works."

Tensions grew between the campuses. Berkeley was still and always would be Cal, from the days when it *was* the university. As the university had absorbed existing schools around the state, those campuses chafed at their lesser status and wanted independent identities. The problem was particularly acute in Los Angeles, where UCLA's position as stepchild to Cal clashed with the rising political power of Southern California and caused conflict on the Board of Regents. The majority of the Regents were appointed by the governor, and many of the positions went to wealthy supporters. By 1958, half the Regents came from Southern California.

On top of the intrauniversity rivalries came friction with the state colleges, a separate system that reported to the state Board of Education. They, too, had grown rapidly, far beyond their original mission as teacher training schools opened in the 1850s in San Francisco and San Jose. The colleges lobbied for status as research schools that could grant graduate degrees and operate with autonomy comparable to that of the universities.

The third tier of the system, the two-year community colleges, remained under the jurisdiction of local K-12 school districts, uncoordinated with the four-year institutions that their graduates increasingly wanted to attend. Together the three systems educated about 80 percent of the college students in California.

Kerr became principal architect of a study that evolved into the California Master Plan, which guided future development of public higher education for decades. A process that began as a desperate attempt to cope with a deluge of students and competing demands ended up as a grand vision. "The master plan was a product of stark necessity, of political calculations, and of pragmatic transactions," Kerr wrote in his autobiography. The crafters were not thinking of achieving the California dream, he wrote, but of avoiding a nightmare. Yet the Master Plan that Pat Brown signed into law on April 26, 1960, expressed a vision for the state as much as for the university, a commitment to increased economic and social mobility for young people, to a higher quality of academic research, and to broader access to higher education. The Master Plan effectively made California the first state to guarantee universal access to higher education, an idea beginning to gain popular acceptance.

"Californians are proud of their university network, and well they might be. It is huge, young, brilliant, aggressive, progressive," reported *Time* in an October 17, 1960, story that landed Clark Kerr on the cover of the national magazine.

For the University of California, the Master Plan was a commitment to multiple flagship campuses, each with its own identity and specialties. The university became more selective, admitting only those high school seniors in the top 12.5 percent of their class.

Research and doctorates remained the purview of the university, but state colleges would report to a new Board of Trustees. Four campuses were slated to join the existing fifteen, and the colleges would admit students in the top third of their graduating class.

Community colleges would expand from 63 to 85 campuses, maintain open admissions, and guarantee that their graduates could transfer to a four-year public college.

"What the railroads did for the second half of the last century and the automobile for the first half of this century may be done for the second half of this century by the knowledge industry," Kerr said in a 1963 talk at Harvard in which he traced the development of what he dubbed the multiversity. "Knowledge is now central to society. It is wanted, even demanded, by more people and institutions than ever before."

Pat's self-consciousness about his lack of higher education only deepened his boosterism for the university, particularly Cal, his wife's alma mater. He was committed to provide access to a commodity he had missed. He loved to hear reports of accomplishments at Regents meetings and beamed when other governors told him they envied what he called "my university."

From 1962 to 1966, California voters authorized nearly a billion dollars in bonds for construction of colleges and universities. Each new state college cost about $120 million, and the university campuses twice as much—about the prices, respectively, of a nuclear submarine and an aircraft carrier. Kerr oversaw the planning, design, and conceptual framework of three campuses, each with a different intellectual focus and a physical design to match its setting. San Diego's La Jolla campus added an undergraduate college to the existing graduate science programs built around the Scripps Institution of Oceanography. Santa Cruz featured twenty small residential colleges on a redwood-lined campus that overlooked a crescent of Monterey Bay. Irvine was designed as the center of a new city for two hundred thousand people in Orange County, built on ninety thousand acres of the Irvine Company ranch that had been citrus groves and grazing land for sheep and cattle.

"This is perhaps the most striking introduction to democracy in California: that the free state university takes for a new campus (and can afford to take) some of the best and most desirable land in the state," wrote sociologist Nathan Glazer. Dissenting from his Eastern intellectual colleagues' disdain for Southern California, Glazer marveled at the vitality of a place shaped by people who had chosen to make it their home.

Over the next decade, enrollment in the state's public schools would more than double, to more than 100,000 students at the universities, 210,000 at the colleges, and 665,000 at the two-year schools. No other state offered free tuition—only the City University of New York. "Only in California can a young man or woman who has ability go from kindergarten through graduate school without paying one cent in tuition," Pat wrote.

In the spring of 1961, Pat's son was completing his studies on the Berkeley campus, not entirely enamored by his experience. He found the university big, impersonal, and bureaucratic. He did not like the rules at Berkeley any better than he had at St. Brendan, St. Ignatius, or Sacred Heart.

After taking a chemistry lab, Jerry had ruled out psychiatry as a profession. (Bart Lally, a medical student in St. Louis, was bemused when his friend called and said he had left the seminary and wanted to become a doctor. Lally could not envision Jerry sitting through the years of grinding work in classes and laboratories.) When Jerry expressed interest in clinical psychology, his mother suggested Pat set up visits to state institutions. Jerry visited psychologists at San Quentin and Vacaville prisons and state facilities for youth. "I was very impressed with his modesty, sensitivity and keen social awareness, traits not often found in young men today," psychologist Robert G. Kaplan wrote Pat after meeting with Jerry. "I'm not too sure what kind of impression we made on your boy. I think he saw a different aspect of professional psychologists than he sees in the classroom of the university, perhaps the human side sans ivy towers."

What Jerry saw pushed him away from psychology and toward the law. Bernice, aware that her husband would love nothing better, admonished Pat not to push law school too hard for fear that his typical strong approach would backfire. Instead she soft-pedaled the idea to Jerry, pointing out that law had proved to be a good career for his father, uncles, and brothers-in-law and merited consideration.

Jerry turned for advice to his father's friend Mathew Tobriner, now a judge on the appellate court. "I know you will be pleased to hear that I've had some fine talks with Jerry," Tobriner wrote to Pat after taking Jerry to lunch with two California Supreme Court justices. "We were truly impressed with his modesty, charm and his probing, searching mind." Tobriner regretted his own choice of Harvard Law School and promoted Yale as smaller, more socially conscious, and oriented toward the relationship of law to social science and philosophy.

"Mr. Brown is not interested in the mechanics of law as such," Tobriner wrote in his recommendation to Yale. "He is one of those who wants to probe deeply into the meaning of the legal process." He described Jerry as mature, unspoiled by his father's status, and a B+ student. "My conversations with him disclose that he is thoroughly versed in political theory; that he has a philosophical and searching turn of mind."

Jerry was interested in Yale because it had no required courses after the first six months. Private law schools cost money, so Pat called upon his friend Louis Lurie, a San Francisco financier and real estate mogul with a fondness for the Browns. Lurie could be found most days at lunch at his table at Jack's, the French restaurant and San Francisco institution that had counted among its regulars Cary Grant, Clark Gable, Ingrid Bergman, and Ernest Hemingway. Lurie gave Pat movie and theater passes, which he often passed on to his mother, in an era when such gifts were commonplace. Lurie also had set up a fund to help pay tuition for children of politicians, on the grounds that they sacrificed more lucrative professions to serve the public good. Lurie had donated to Sacred Heart. When Jerry enrolled in Cal, he gave him ballet tickets and took him to lunch at Jack's. "Uncle Lou" said he would be delighted to help Jerry with tuition at Yale, but he teased Pat about his son's choice: "I thought you were a real Californian—what's the matter with Cal or Stanford?"

Jerry took for granted his father's connections and his own privileged position, but he also wanted to escape. He headed to New Haven, where no one would know his name—in contrast to his college graduation, at which Governor Edmund G. Brown had welcomed the graduates and their families and then personally bestowed a diploma on a slightly embarrassed Edmund G. Brown Jr.

Jerry had already left Berkeley when President John F. Kennedy came to speak the following spring at Charter Day, the annual celebration of the university's founding in 1868. Extra chairs were placed on the Memorial Stadium field to accommodate the record crowd of ninety-two thousand students, alumni, and guests. Kennedy spoke about the university's importance in the civic and scientific life of the country. He harkened back a hundred years, to the foresight of President Lincoln, in the midst of the Civil War, in signing legislation that created the nation's land grant colleges. Among the first graduating class at Cal, often referred to as the Twelve Apostles, were a future California governor, congressman, judge, assemblyman, clergyman, doctor, and lawyer. "This college therefore from its earliest beginnings has recognized and its graduates have recognized that the purpose of education is not merely to advance the economic self-interest of its graduates," Kennedy said, running down a long list of more recent prominent graduates who had gone into public service.

A year earlier, Kennedy had famously promised to put a man on the moon. Berkeley researchers played critical roles in the space race, and the president paid tribute to the university's contributions to science, through its faculty as well as the Los Alamos and Livermore labs that it operated. Clark Kerr had built a multiversity that boasted more Nobel laureates than any other faculty in the world. "It is a disturbing fact to me, and it may be to some of you, that the new frontier owes as much to Berkeley as it does to Harvard University," said the man from Massachusetts, and the governor of California applauded loudly.

Kennedy ended with a story about the French marshal Hubert Lyautey, who asked his gardener to plant a tree. The gardener objected that the tree grew slowly and would not reach maturity for a hundred years. In that case, the marshal said, we have no time to lose. Plant it this afternoon. "Today a world of knowledge, a world of cooperation, a just and lasting peace, may be years away," Kennedy said. "But we have no time to lose. Let us plant our trees this afternoon."

During the eight years Pat Brown was governor, the University of California doubled in size, to eight campuses, with eighty-eight thousand students and seven thousand faculty. Its presence spread from the nineteenth-century Lick Observatory on Mount Hamilton to the Riverside smog station, from the agricultural station in the Salinas fields to the Scripps marine research facility in San Diego. In anticipation of the university's centennial, Kerr commissioned a project to document the size, scope, reach, and potential of the university. He asked renowned photographer Ansel Adams to capture in images the history of the university and project its future. "It is a bold and challenging idea, and we are naturally deeply moved by the thought that you want to consider us for it," Adams wrote to Kerr.

Adams spent four years visiting every campus, research station, and outpost. He produced a body of work second in size only to his images of Yosemite. He became convinced, as he updated university officials, that "the University and the State of California are inseparable." He sought to document "the intimate and effective relationship of the University and the people of California," the symbiotic relationship that touched every aspect of life. Adams photographed the nuclear weapons lab at Livermore, the medical school opened by a doctor who had come to San Francisco during the Gold Rush, the Irvine campus rising phoenixlike in the midst of citrus groves. He illustrated cutting-edge projects—videotaped lectures that could reach thousands, bicycle-only lanes on the Davis campus. He published a book of selected images he titled *Fiat Lux*, the motto of the university: "Let there be light."

"To look at the University of California is to look at California itself—its land, its people, and their problems—into the civilization rushing toward us from the future," Adams wrote in the introduction. "What happens—or does not happen—to California in its attempts to solve the problems of population and industrialization will affect the world. The challenge to the University of California today is nothing less than to help bring forth the civilization of the future."

8

Down but Not Out

Only a bit of smog marred the view as Democrats from around the country arrived at Los Angeles International Airport to mariachi serenades, fresh California orange juice, and a winking donkey logo for their luggage. A thirty-five-piece brass band greeted each governor with his state song. A car and driver whisked them downtown where they found a fifth of liquor waiting in their hotel rooms as a welcome present from their host, Governor Pat Brown.

"Your Party, and mine, has chosen to recognize the growing strength and influence of the West by holding its great quadrennial nominating convention in Los Angeles," Pat wrote in his welcome message to the Democratic Party delegates who gathered July 11, 1960, for the first Democratic National Convention in the City of Angels. Home to six million people, more than one third of the state's population, Los Angeles County had grown by almost half over the previous decade. "Here, where growth of population and expansion of the economy are regarded not with timid concern, but with enthusiastic vigor, let us begin to meet the challenges of the modern world with courage and confidence."

Two hundred fifty "Golden Girls" offered tours of the area's attractions—Grauman's Chinese Theatre, Capitol Records, the Griffith Park observatory, the Santa Monica beach. Disneyland, which had opened five years earlier, had just added the 147-foot-high Matterhorn, the first tubular steel track roller coaster in the world and the tallest structure in Orange County. Delegates were invited to the Miss National Convention Beauty Contest at the Ambassador Hotel swimming pool and a premiere of *Inherit the Wind* at the Screen Directors' Guild Theater. "Modern Los

Angeles is a city bulging with muscle; vibrating with confidence and enthusiasm; always looking ahead to things that can be accomplished in the future," the program explained. "Here, in the fastest growing area in the United States, extraordinary statistics have become commonplace."

Pat loved to show off California, and the national convention had promised an opportunity for both the man and the state to shine. Instead, the four-day party left him politically weakened at home and tarnished in the eyes of the Kennedy clan who would soon be ensconced in Washington, D.C.

His first year as governor had seen success after success: bipartisan support for new taxes, agreement on a major water project, a fair employment commission. By the end of 1959, the *New York Times Magazine* profiled Pat Brown as an influential figure in the upcoming national campaign, a dark horse candidate for vice president, or even a compromise presidential choice.

Then came the case of death row inmate Caryl Chessman. The political missteps that sent Pat's popularity plummeting were rooted in a case that would be a relatively minor historical footnote, yet would dog Pat the rest of his life.

Chessman was an infamous career criminal, nicknamed the Red Light Bandit because he shined a light into the cars of couples parked in secluded spots in Los Angeles, robbed them at gunpoint, and in two cases raped the young women. Convicted in 1948, he was sentenced under a statute passed after the kidnapping of Charles Lindbergh's baby, which made assault while kidnapping a capital crime. While in prison, Chessman wrote several bestselling books, including *Cell 2455, Death Row*, which became a major motion picture. His case became a rallying point for death penalty opponents, partly because his crimes did not involve murder, partly because of his flamboyant personality. His books were translated into a dozen languages, his case became an international sensation, and religious leaders and celebrities rallied to his cause. He proclaimed his innocence, said he had been coerced into a confession, and insisted on representing himself at trial. He found ways to delay his execution for a record eleven years, during an era when death row inmates were executed relatively swiftly.

An execution date for Chessman approached a few months after Pat Brown took office. His executive clemency secretary, Cecil Poole, buried himself in files that dated back to the Earl Warren years. Advocates of the death penalty were as vocal as the Chessman defenders, deluging the office with calls and mail. By the time it was over, the governor's office had installed extra telephone lines to handle the volume and Poole calculated his office had received 2.5 million communications from around the world.

Poole was born in Birmingham, Alabama, in 1914 and grew up in Pittsburgh. An African American lawyer with degrees from the University of Michigan and Harvard, he worked for the National Labor Relations Board until he was drafted. In officer training school in Alabama, Poole refused an order to do his swim training in the blacks-only pool. He had friends in Oakland and decided to move there after the war, part of the second great migration of blacks to California. Three years later, he became the first black deputy in the San Francisco district attorney's office. In his job interview, Pat told Poole there would be some cases he wouldn't want him to handle, such as a black man arrested for assaulting a white woman. Poole got up to leave, and Pat's friend and deputy Tom Lynch intervened. With his trademark candor, Pat apologized and said he was wrong. Poole took the job. When Pat became governor, he brought Poole to Sacramento, where his job included reviewing death penalty cases.

"Chessman hearing. Toughest decision I will make," Pat wrote in his diary on October 15, 1959. "11 years on death row and they are still crying for blood. It seems barbaric to me but I must like everyone else obey the law. Chessman is a tough guy but to me it is the state that suffers not Mr. Chessman—open minded but leaning towards clemency." After consulting Poole, Pat concluded that because of Chessman's prior felonies, the governor could not commute the sentence without permission from the California Supreme Court. In private conversations, the chief justice told Pat he did not have the votes to make that happen. "Wrote statement at 3:30 am denying clemency to Chessman," Pat wrote on October 17. "My conscience tells me to commute his sentence but my reason tells me that if I do I will be unable to commute anyone else on the row or if I do everything else will be measured against this emotional issue."

Pat Brown the lawyer had correctly concluded he had no legal recourse. Pat Brown the Catholic humanitarian longed to find a way to avoid a state-sponsored killing that he felt was morally wrong. He believed Chessman was guilty but should not face the death penalty. After appeals and delays that dragged on for months, Chessman's attorneys exhausted all options. The execution was scheduled for February 19, 1960.

The Winter Olympics would begin the same day in Squaw Valley, a remote California ski resort in the Sierra Nevada. Pat was to have taken part in the opening ceremonies the night before. Because he needed to stay by the phone during the execution, he dispatched Bernice and Kathleen to represent the family. On February 18, three of his aides took Pat out to dinner—Poole, press secretary Hale Champion, and travel secretary Dick Tuck. They knew Pat's big heart and impulsive nature, and they loved him for it. They wanted to take no chance that he would change his mind at the last minute. After dinner, Pat went home while Poole and Champion returned to the office. Protesters ringed the capitol, and thousands of telegrams arrived every hour, urging the governor to spare Chessman's life. When Poole's phone rang, he knew from the special white light that it was the governor. Pat said he was thinking about a sixty- to ninety-day stay, in hopes that he could persuade the legislature to overturn the death penalty. Poole ran down the hall to get Champion; they grabbed a state car and raced the dozen blocks to the Mansion.

"And there was Pat. He had been talking to Jerry," Poole recalled, years later. "When we walked in there I said, 'Pat, I don't know how you can do this. You can't get the court; you won't get the legislature.' And he said, 'Well, talk to my son.' And I did talk to him. Then he [Pat], Champion, and I sat there in the Governor's living room and went back and forth over this thing, back and forth, back and forth. The Governor was determined to do it. We tried to point out to him all the consequences, conceding the depth of his feeling about it."

Pat had also talked to Sacramento bishop Joseph McGucken and California Episcopal bishop James Pike, who had been crusading on Chessman's behalf. But it was the argument of Jerry, just a month out of the seminary, that gave Pat the excuse he wanted: Even if the chance were a thousand to one that he might save Chessman's life, shouldn't he take the chance? The legislature would never overturn the death penalty, Poole reminded Pat. The chief justice had repeated a day earlier that he could not get a majority on the court. The phone rang. They had a rule that only Poole or Champion would take calls. When the guard said it was a reporter, Pat grabbed the phone and blurted out the news. He was going to give Chessman a reprieve and ask the legislature to repeal the death penalty. "Champion and I looked at each other," Poole said, vividly recalling the scene seventeen years later. "Because . . . when it gets down to it, he's the governor. And he had made a decision."

One hundred miles to the northeast, Squaw Valley had been transformed from a wilderness outpost to the first Olympic village. Bernice and Kathleen watched an opening pageant orchestrated by Walt Disney, featuring a cast of five thousand people, two thousand doves, and thirty thousand balloons. Disney's role as chair of the Pageantry Committee, coupled with the first sale of live television rights, turned the formerly low-key athletic event into a spectacle that set the pattern for all future Olympics. Bernice had been concerned about leaving Pat alone and tried to call home before dinner, but the swarm of international press tied up the phone lines for hours. By the time she got through, it was too late. "I often wonder how the course of history would have changed if I had gotten him," she said years later. "I don't know whether I would have been able to prevail . . . But he was sitting there alone in that Mansion. It's a big house, and he was sitting there alone and pondering this thing. Then Jerry called, and Jerry can be persuasive."

The governor's old friend Mathew Tobriner applauded and sent Pat an article about the racial inequities of the death penalty. "I have no doubt but that your handling of the Chessman matter will add to your stature. Whatever the initial reaction, the longtime evaluation will prove you to have been not only 'courageous' but merciful and humane." Tobriner was a distinct minority. Death penalty supporters were angry, opponents unappeased. Pat was pilloried in the news. His staff was sullen. He brought his mother, Jerry, Cynthia, and Kathleen to the opening game at Candlestick Park, the San Francisco Giants' new stadium, only to be booed. Pat and Bernice escaped for a few days on a fishing trip in Mexico, where he read a biography of Roosevelt. "Greatest attribute of Roosevelt—able to sell his product. My greatest fault inability to do the same," he wrote in his diary.

"Since the Chessman reprieve it has been very tough—no sleep—boos—attacks by your own members of the Democratic party," Pat wrote in the early morning hours of March 10, the day the legislature would debate his proposal to abolish the death penalty. The arguments went on past one o'clock, but the outcome was a forgone conclusion. To spare Pat as much embarrassment as possible, the committee rejected the measure by one vote.

The stay ran out. On May 1, the eve of the execution, picketers marched and chanted around the Mansion all night. Pat went out to talk with them in the morning, then headed to the capitol and sat at his desk, a few feet from where Cecil Poole camped out in a secretary's office on the phone with an open line to the warden at San Quentin. Preparations had begun. "It is now 9:50 AM. Chessman will be executed in 10 minutes," Pat wrote. "I feel that it is better to get it over. Up until now I have had a terrific sympathy for Chessman but now that it's almost over I feel quite calm." Poole came in the office with an update. "Just heard the Warden stated that Chessman said he was ready to go. You have to be governor to know the context but there is nothing I can do—I am happy that I have not the responsibility."

Pat's handling of the Chessman case, morally courageous and politically suicidal, earned him the epithet Tower of Jell-O. Even those most angry about Pat's actions, like Fred Dutton, thought the characterization unfair. Pat often sought advice endlessly, responded to people he should ignore, and debated his decisions out loud. That engaging style earned him ridicule, but the image belied a more complex intellect that sought information to grow. Pat was always in motion, physically and mentally. You don't need brains to succeed in politics, he used to say, you need good glands. Dutton was frustrated that Pat had sacrificed credibility and effectiveness for a futile gesture. His handling of the Chessman case would reinforce an image of indecisiveness that Dutton felt was debilitating, if undeserved. He believed Pat when he said Jerry just gave his father a reason to do what he wanted. Dutton also agreed with Pat's assessment of the long-term damage. He would never fully recover politically.

The consequences quickly became clear. A month after Chessman's execution came the California Democratic presidential primary. Pat was on the ballot as a favorite son, not because he had a realistic path to the nomination, though he briefly harbored long-shot hopes, but as a strategy to hold together the always fractious California Democrats and leverage their role at the convention. California was one of only sixteen states that held primaries in 1960; most delegates were chosen at closed-door caucuses, and the decisive votes took place at the convention. In March, Pat had met with John F. Kennedy at the senator's Georgetown home and urged him not to enter the California contest, which he would likely win but at the cost of splintering the state party. As a favorite son, Pat would hold the large block of delegates together, uncommitted until the final moment, then deliver them to Kennedy at the convention. In return for staying out of the California primary, Kennedy asked that Pat promise not to accept a vice presidential nomination from another candidate. Such a move would of political necessity pit the two Catholics against each other. Pat agreed. He came away from the meeting impressed with Kennedy. "He has around him the best brains in the country," he wrote in his diary that night.

The Kennedys were everything Pat Brown was not: polished, glamorous, wealthy, Harvard-educated, and ruthless. The Lowell yell leader was always out of place in Camelot, no matter how hard he tried. He would always be slightly awed and uncomfortable in their presence. At the same time, his success confounded the Kennedys, who never understood how such an effective, accomplished governor could prove such a weak political leader. The Kennedys shared the view of California common among the East Coast political establishment: a byzantine world of geographic divisions, weak party discipline, and a lamentable lack of party bosses. Tom Lynch told a story about Pat's bewilderment when Abraham Ribicoff, a Kennedy cabinet secretary and former governor of Connecticut, asked Pat who had decided he should run for governor. *I did*, Pat responded, baffled at the idea that party bosses would make such decisions.

Pat was justifiably apprehensive on June 7, as he played his traditional Election Day golf game with Bernice. His opponent in the presidential primary was little known, but he had attacked Pat for the Chessman reprieve. The governor won, but with far less of the vote than he should have had. He was shaken, and the loss of prestige eroded his position heading into a convention that should have been a triumphant celebration of the coming of age of his beloved state.

In the days leading up to the convention, the Kennedys pressed hard for Pat to release the California delegates and publicly endorse the Massachusetts senator. Pat refused, arguing the move would backfire because of strong support for rival Adlai Stevenson. The governor expected the California delegation would fall in line once the depth of support for Kennedy was clear. He misjudged. In a rancorous session on the eve of the convention, a majority rejected Pat's plea to support Kennedy. Liberal Democrats stuck by Stevenson, who also became a stalking horse for Lyndon Johnson, who hoped to deny Kennedy a first ballot victory. "Stop

Kennedy" leaflets called him "the candidate of an overly ambitious father with unlimited wealth." Pat struggled to muster a majority for Kennedy. "I pleaded, urged and cajoled," he wrote. "It did no good. I told them it would humiliate me. It did no good."

The delegation's vote on the convention floor gave Kennedy 33½ votes, two more than Stevenson. The Kennedys had known they didn't need the California votes to win on the first ballot, but Pat's determination to hold the delegation neutral till the last minute only reinforced his image as a weak leader. "I tried to let the people know that this was an Independent Delegation not controlled by me. This was my first and fatal mistake," he wrote in his diary. "A Governor Can Not Abdicate Leadership. It is better to lose."

His friend and adviser Hale Champion put it this way, writing a friend: "Pat is just not a whipcracker at heart and people know it and like him for it. This time, however, this reputation for being a nice guy hurt instead of helped."

Dutton stressed familiar points: Pat needed to focus, deliberate in private, and act decisively in public. Dutton's keen political instincts had impressed Kennedy and would soon lead to a job in the new administration. In his last days in Sacramento, Dutton again demonstrated his foresight. Pat needed to transition to become a leader for the new decades, Dutton warned: "Less reliance on approaches fashioned for the 1950s in California and more scrutiny of the realities of the present and immediate future."

Those realities emerged sharply from the 1960 election: Political power in California had begun to shift from north to south. Future campaigns would be run on television, not in print. And cracks had appeared in the infatuation with growth, presaging the time when bigger would no longer be better.

From the time the first limited access highway in the country opened in 1940, connecting downtown Los Angeles and Pasadena, the state could not build roads fast enough to keep up with traffic. Consequences of the unbridled growth became more apparent. The spike in traffic accidents led to so many personal injury lawsuits that the legislature authorized fifty new judgeships. Pat proposed mandatory blood tests for suspected drunk drivers, who were responsible for increasing numbers of fatalities. Despite millions of dollars allocated for new highways, traffic at key intersections did not improve. With five million passengers a year arriving at LAX, access roads to the airport were jammed; a key interchange designed to handle two hundred thousand cars a day was already carrying three hundred fifty thousand.

Congestion emerged as more than an inconvenience. Recent research had conclusively linked traffic to smog, upending earlier assumptions. The low-lying Los Angeles basin had long suffered from polluted air that remained trapped between the mountains and the sea, sometimes limiting visibility to a few blocks. For many years, stationary sources had been blamed for the yellow-gray air that hid the nearby mountains and irritated eyes and lungs. In 1947, Los Angeles had formed the first air pollution control district in the country, empowered to regulate emissions from power plants and oil refineries. But the noxious smog only worsened.

In his Pasadena lab, Caltech biochemist Dr. Arie J. Haagen-Smit, who had made his name as a scientific detective by identifying the compounds that gave pineapple its flavor, started to investigate what was causing discolored leaves and stunted flowers in his garden. His experiments pinpointed the culprit as ozone, a substance created when sunlight interacted with molecules in car emissions. Though the automobile industry disputed the finding, by the time Pat became governor there was a widespread consensus that cars were the primary source of smog. Local officials lobbied for the state to take action. "The industry which causes air pollution should be required to solve it," Los Angeles County supervisor Kenneth Hahn wrote Pat, urging the governor to call a special session of the legislature. A landmark law passed a few months later required new cars to be equipped with the first types of pollution control devices.

Warren Christopher tackled the air pollution problem on another front during his brief tenure with the Brown administration. Before state officials could regulate air quality, they would have to create agreed-upon standards. Christopher traveled the state visiting local officials who had initiated antismog efforts and scientists who studied air pollution. His findings led to the creation of the Motor Vehicle Pollution Control Board, which made California the first state empowered to promulgate and enforce air quality standards.

In his zeal to master issues like air pollution and be well read, Pat always carried around at least two briefcases, so overstuffed with books and documents that they never closed. Sometimes his executive secretary went through the contents to create a priority reading list, an exercise that revealed an eclectic assortment of journals far removed from state business. Pat dragged the briefcases with him on planes and in the car and took them home on evenings and weekends.

A favorite reading spot at home became the pool, added to the Mansion during 1959. When they first moved in, Pat often threw a bathrobe over his swimsuit and walked across the street to use the pool at the Mansion Inn. Bernice, with her strict sense of decorum, was mortified to discover that the governor changed in a hotel bathroom. Friends raised money for the kidney-shaped backyard pool, which became a place where Pat could mix work and family. On weekends he caught up with reading while children and grandchildren played. His daughter Cynthia and her husband, Joe Kelly, had moved into the Magellan Avenue house and had two small children. Barbara and her husband, Pat Casey, had two sons. Pat took particular delight in his oldest grandson, Charlie, who laughed at his grandfather's jokes.

Many mornings, Bernice would get halfway down the back stairs in her bathrobe only to hear Pat already at work, deep in conversation in the breakfast room. Often the guest was Bernice's younger sister, May Layne Bonnell, who had known Pat since she was six and now worked as his appointments secretary. Bonnell had followed her sister to Cal and majored in political science, then learned typing and shorthand in order to get a job. Her lack of political experience or connections made her an ideal appointments secretary, loyal only to Pat. She found the best time to get his attention was in the breakfast room around seven thirty A.M. Even then they would be interrupted by calls.

Bernice slowly embraced her new public role. She looked the part. Whereas Pat struggled with his weight and wore rumpled socks, Bernice was svelte and strikingly elegant. After years of wearing black, she added colors to her wardrobe. With her usual intensity, she focused on the art of entertaining, with meticulous attention to style and detail. Finding only mismatched sets of silver at the Mansion, she ordered a special pattern with a design drawn from the state's Bear Flag. She requested round tops to be put over card tables, to facilitate conversation. When she noticed legislators all talked shop while their wives sat silent (there were only two women lawmakers), she had guests pick numbers to ensure they sat at different tables from their spouses. She ordered tulip-shaped champagne glasses she had liked at a White House reception, selected by Jackie Kennedy.

Fred Dutton admired Bernice, whom he viewed as an analytical thinker who could have been an intellectual had she not opted for the more traditional female role. Her combination of dignity, candor, and reserve was often mistaken for coldness, but close friends found her warm and witty. Dutton knew Pat relied on Bern in private, and he thought she could be an asset in public as well. He encouraged her to develop greater comfort with public appearances through visits to state social services institutions, comparable to Eleanor Roosevelt's activities as first lady of New York.

By their second summer in Sacramento, Bernice appeared regularly before women's groups, where she spoke about life at the Mansion, catering to unexpected guests, and babysitting grandchildren. In her forthright manner, she made clear that she had political opinions, which she chose not to share. A wife, she said, should be a good listener and a sounding board and contribute a suggestion from time to time. She continued to say she would never have chosen life in the political world, "but of course I've become deeply interested."

She had witnessed huge changes in politics since going door to door on San Francisco streets for her twenty-three-year-old boyfriend more than three decades earlier. Now she had a front row seat for the first presidential election of the modern era, when television had become the dominant force. By 1960, almost nine out of ten American households owned a television set—a tenfold increase in a decade. TV coverage ushered in a radically different age of campaigning, in which style and sound bites could matter more than deep knowledge or well-thought-out positions. Television would soon lead to profound changes in the role of money in campaigns as well, as candidates needed to raise larger and larger sums to buy TV airtime.

Senator Kennedy, the young, relatively inexperienced underdog, lagged in polls against Vice President Nixon, a well-established politician and California native. When the two met in the first high-level political debate since Lincoln-Douglas, the televised images propelled Kennedy into the lead for the first time. Radio listeners judged Nixon the winner, but his gaunt, sallow looks, shifting eyes, and five-o'clock shadow cost him with the estimated 70 million viewers who tuned in on September 26, 1960. The charismatic senator from Massachusetts looked straight at the camera, his telegenic looks and vigor giving him the clear edge over the dour Nixon.

Pat's mother, Ida, who steadfastly shied away from political events, made an exception for a campaign tea at the Fairmont Hotel hosted by Rose Kennedy, the candidate's mother. Ida was given a place of honor on the dais and introduced to the crowd of a thousand women. "When I saw this report of the crowd at the tea, I was a little uneasy but your mother tells me the affair was 'very, very nice,' was handled very well," an aide wrote to Pat. "I think she was pleased although she said she would have preferred just to have remained in the crowd."

Ida resumed her low profile. She refused to let her son send a car and took the bus to visit Sacramento. "Why should I trouble anybody?" she said in a rare interview. When Pat wanted her to come to a senior citizens event, she told him her hair was a mess. Bernice suggested a chartered bus to bring Ida's friends to the Mansion for a birthday party. Ida said they'd need a fleet of ambulances. She downplayed her role in Pat's career, or in any of her children's successes. "They were go-getters from the start. It's their drive, not mine." "Go-getter," her children said, was a word they had learned at home.

As always, Pat and Bernice's wedding anniversary fell a week before the election. Pat rose early, took a swim, and played golf with Bern. They celebrated their thirtieth anniversary with a family dinner at the Mansion, joined by Ida, Pat's brother Frank, Barbara, Cynthia, Jerry, Kathleen, and four grandchildren. "They may say I vacillate (I don't) but from the moment I saw Bernice Layne I knew I loved her," Pat wrote in his diary. "Never in 37 years have I regretted my choice. I should tell her more often—I should have told all the family at dinner . . . Wonderful day."

Pat predicted Kennedy would carry California by a million votes. The legislature had abolished cross-filing, which meant that no candidate could win both parties' primaries. As a result, all state and local races were contested on the November ballot. Democrats had conducted voter registration drives, which gave them a majority for the first time in all eight southern California counties. Orange and Santa Barbara were last to flip. The most prominent registration drive was financed by the national labor movement and targeted California's growing Mexican American community, a campaign overseen by a young community organizer named Cesar Chavez. Mexican Americans were drawn to the charismatic young candidate vying to be the first Catholic president, and Viva Kennedy clubs sprang up in the barrios. All told, 1.6 million new voters registered, an increase of more than 28 percent.

On Election Day, more than 70 percent of the registered voters in California cast ballots. The result was so close that the count took several days. Nixon eked out a 36,000-vote victory amid a record turnout of 6.6 million. Nationwide, Nixon lost the popular vote by a tiny percentage—113,000 votes out of 68 million—but lost the Electoral College decisively. At his press conference the day after the election, Nixon raised the possibility of running for governor of his home state in 1962. "He would be tough opposition but I would have united democratic support," Pat wrote in his diary.

By the time Nixon announced his candidacy for governor on September 27, 1961, Pat Brown's approval rating was at an all-time low. Only 38 percent thought he was doing a good job. Nixon led in polls by as much as 16 points. He had never lost a race in California. He had the backing of most major newspapers, wealthy supporters, and ruthless professional advisers. Pat had confidence in his ability and pride in his accomplishments, but doubts about his skill at conveying those achievements. He was self-conscious about his lack of education and occasional mispronunciations, worried about his image as a bumbler, and aware he was not viewed as what he called "a great brain."

Nixon's interest in the governorship was widely seen as a precursor to another presidential run. Although the Kennedys viewed Pat as politically inept, they had a strong interest in denying Nixon a platform from which to run another national campaign. So the president made several trips to California, where his approval rating was roughly twice as high as that of the governor.

"Pat Brown said that I would carry this state by a million votes," Kennedy opened his talk at a November 18, 1961, fundraiser at the Hollywood Palladium, good-naturedly ribbing Pat. "Cruel!" said Pat, laughing heartily along with the crowd. "And I prophesy he's going to win, which is the important thing," Kennedy continued. "This state above all others in the union must continue to move forward." The president singled out Pat's commitment to doubling the size of the higher education system in California as a national model. "He recognizes that this country will be as strong and as free in direct proportion to how well educated and motivated our children are."

Kennedy's greatest contribution to the campaign was to bolster Pat Brown's self-confidence. Early in 1962, Pat delivered one of his best speeches to a packed room at the National Press Club in Washington,

D.C. With command of facts and figures, he talked confidently about the state he knew so well and all that had been accomplished during his three years as governor. He contrasted his own experience to that of Nixon, with a national pedigree and foreign policy expertise but little knowledge of his home state. This would be Pat's most important campaign theme: Nixon was interested in Sacramento only as a stepping-stone to the White House. Pat's performance at the Press Club was so strong and his ode to California so persuasive that when he asked for questions, there was a long pause, until someone stood up and said, "Governor, what's the price of a one-way ticket?"

Afterward, Pat went to the White House, where the president, briefed on Pat's speech, greeted him warmly. Kennedy sat with Pat in front of a fire and reminded him what happened when national politicians tried to go home: It didn't work. The presidential support coupled with the successful speech helped change the narrative. Don't count Pat Brown out yet, the national press wrote, a refrain soon echoed in California papers.

Pat took lessons in Los Angeles to improve his appearance on television and better manage his feet and hands. He worked on his diction. And then his diet. For a month, he and Bernice went out at six every morning and played golf without a caddie or cart, walking as fast as they could and playing the course in half the normal time. He lost thirty pounds by cutting out carbohydrates and alcohol, dropping to a comfortable weight of 180 on his five-foot ten-and-a-half-inch frame. In February he made a three-day retreat at El Retiro, the Jesuit center. He gained self-assurance and improved his performance on the campaign trail. By spring, Pat had inched ahead of Nixon in polls for the first time.

Pat's friendship with Earl Warren had deepened during the latter's years on the Supreme Court. Though Warren's deep dislike of Nixon was well known, as chief justice he could not play a role in the campaign. But his son, Earl Warren Jr., became a prominent Brown supporter. And Warren found ways to help. On an official appearance in California, the chief justice went out of his way to laud the state's economic health, stable taxes, and lower unemployment. The chief and the governor were often photographed on their annual duck hunts at a Colusa ranch owned by a friend of Warren's. Warren was fond of traditions; the weekends always began with a cracked crab dinner on Friday night, followed by a poker game. Warren often brought his sons, and during the Christmas break in 1960 and 1961, Pat brought Jerry.

On one trip to Colusa, Pat took Jerry for the first, and potentially the last, time to see the old Mountain House. Frank Schuckman had died in the spring of 1959. With his frugal habits and money lending, he had amassed an estate worth more than $1 million, which he divided among his nieces and nephews. Pat's brother Harold was executor of the estate, and in the probate process, the Mountain House was put up for sale. "Let's buy this place. We can probably borrow substantially on it and I think we ought to keep it in the family," Pat wrote Harold. But the brothers lacked sufficient money, and their siblings had no interest.

In the summer of 1962, uncertain whether he would still have a job in a few months, Pat took action. At the last minute, with a sale of the property all but closed, Pat and Harold recruited several wealthier friends and purchased the Mountain House with a corporation they called Rancho Venada. (They were so distant from the place that they misspelled Venado.) "I guess I'm an old sentimentalist," Gertrude Schuckman Rosenback wrote to her cousin Pat, in appreciation of his action. She was "all Schuckman," Gertrude added, and loved conversations with her Aunt Ida. "When she talks to me it is as if I heard my father." Pat replied that he, too, was a sentimentalist. "When I think of our grandfather and grandmother coming across the plains and building the things they did, it gives me greater determination as Governor of this State to get more things accomplished," he wrote back. "I bought that old Mountain House just because I didn't want it to go completely out of the Schuckman family."

By the end of the summer, Pat was even in the polls, though the majority of voters viewed him unfavorably. He had strong support among Catholics, Jews, and blacks, but had made no headway with Protestants, who favored Nixon by a large margin. Overwhelmingly, voters believed Nixon's real interest was the presidency, while they viewed Pat as sincere and acting on behalf of Californians, particularly minorities and the elderly. Strategists urged Pat to do as much as possible in person, where his warmth and friendliness shone in a way that did not translate on television, even at his best. "The battle between the two titans of California politics is on for keeps," reported a confidential Harris poll done for the Democrat. "And it will drive straight to the wire."

Pat hammered Nixon as a shady political opportunist. Billboards advertised the governor as "The Man Californians Can Trust." Nixon relied on the strategy that had worked in earlier campaigns, attacking his opponent as soft on Communism. His own pollsters cautioned Nixon that the tactic fell flat. Pat Brown was well known as a Catholic, and not an exceedingly liberal Democrat.

Events conspired to help the Democrats. First, the campaign was relegated to the back pages in early October by one of the biggest sports stories to hit a state that had only recently acquired major league teams: The Los Angeles Dodgers and San Francisco Giants finished the season with identical records and played a tie-breaking series to determine the National League pennant. The first game coincided with the only joint appearance by the two candidates for governor, much to Pat's glee.

Warren Christopher, Pat's negotiator, had worked to minimize debates without appearing to shirk them. Pat was nervous at the prospect of going up against a college debater. The compromise was one joint appearance before the UPI Editors Meeting at the Fairmont Hotel, broadcast live on radio and television. Pat opened by saying California would soon pass New York as the largest state, an event he had thought about and planned for since he took office. Contrasting his upbeat views with his opponent's gloomy demeanor, he concluded, "I tell you that we are on the way to the stars, and I want to be the navigator for the next four years."

Nixon spoke in generalities about the need for new leadership, lower taxes, and removing "chiselers" from welfare. "I have never lost California," he said. "I am not taking the easy road to win it." Just as in the Nixon-Kennedy debates, he came across worse on television than in person or on radio. Though Pat lacked Kennedy's polish, his sincerity and nice-guy image contrasted well with Nixon's pugnacious manner.

For the next two weeks, political news took a backseat as the Giants battled the Yankees in the World Series, a competition not decided until the seventh inning of the seventh game in San Francisco's Candlestick Park. Three days after the Giants' loss, the California poll showed the Nixon-Brown race a virtual dead heat, with 8 percent undecided and Nixon gaining. Three days later came the Cuban missile crisis.

Pat flew to Washington for briefings at the Pentagon, one of six governors who met with the president and secretary of defense. He returned home and announced he would suspend campaigning during the crisis. For once, Bernice got to spend a quiet wedding anniversary at home. A frustrated Nixon compounded the damage by buying a half hour on television to speak "not as a candidate but as a private citizen." The effort to demonstrate his foreign policy expertise backfired. "Nixon climaxed a shoddy campaign with an attempt to turn the Cuban crisis into personal political gain," said former lieutenant governor Harold Powers, one of several prominent Republicans who defected. "Nixon has failed to come up with a single, solitary program beneficial to California."

When the votes were counted, Pat defeated Nixon comfortably, with 52 percent of the vote. He joined Earl Warren and Hiram Johnson as only the third California governor elected to two consecutive terms in the past century, and the first Democrat. The significance of the victory transcended Pat Brown: The results marked the return of the two-party system to California. The Democratic sweep of 1958 that broke the Republican stranglehold had not been a fluke. Democrats had significantly increased their registration edge—4.29 million to 3 million Republicans. They exploited control of the reapportionment process to carve out favorable districts for Democrats at a time when the phenomenal growth had given California eight more congressional seats. Democrats emerged from the election with twenty-four of the thirty-eight House seats.

The openly partisan California press, long controlled by the Hearsts, Chandlers, and Knowlands, had achieved a new maturity that played a role in the election, too. The most significant change was at the *Los Angeles Times*, whose new publisher, Otis Chandler, had hired professional political reporters from other papers. Unlike earlier years when the paper's political editor hosted gatherings of Republican leaders, the new team covered the news straight. Nixon, accustomed to favorable treatment from the paper, was surprised and angry. He blamed the reporters, whom he singled out in his famous, bitter concession speech: "As I leave you, I want you to know, just think how much you're going to be missing. You won't have Nixon to kick around anymore because, gentlemen, this is my last press conference."

When Kennedy called the Mansion to congratulate Pat, the two agreed that Nixon was finished. "I will tell you this. You reduced him to the nut house. God, that last farewell speech of his," Kennedy said. "I don't see how he can ever recover," Pat said. "I really think that he is psychotic. He's an able man, but he's nuts." Before he hung up, Pat asked the president for a favor. "Would you just do one thing for me? Just say hello to my son, Jerry, who came back from Yale Law School and really put me over in San Francisco?" The president greeted Jerry, who assured Kennedy he would carry California by "ten times as much as you did before."

A few weeks later, the governor was in Washington, D.C., with Hale Champion, who had become state finance director. Pat was scheduled to have dinner with Earl Warren, and he invited Champion along. The celebratory meal included many toasts. "They were two happy old buddies who'd just scored one of the great victories of their lives," Champion recalled some years later. "And every once in a while they would lift the glass and say, 'To what's-his-name, wherever he is tonight.' And would laugh and pour it down." Champion left them in the restaurant, talking and laughing and toasting the great victory late into the night.

9

"Water for People. For Living"

In a way, the problem of water in California was simple. Most of the water was in the north, most of the people were in the south, and in the center lay a rich alluvial plain the size of Denmark that could grow more food than any other valley in the world.

From its earliest days of statehood, California wrestled with whether and how to move water from where it fell, flowed, and flooded to the semi-arid climes where the people and the crops always wanted more. The fights pitted north against south, fields against cities, land barons against family farms, developers against environmentalists.

Pat Brown knew when he became governor in 1959 that no other issue he tackled would have a more profound impact on the future of California. With his innate exuberance and optimism, he turned the decades-old water wars on their head. The charged political battles had revolved around how to allocate a scarce resource. Pat started from the assumption there was plenty of water for everyone. The question was how much to move and how to move it. He reframed the debate as an engineering challenge, and that helped him to negotiate where others had failed.

"I want you to know that I consider the water problem the most vital in California and I think that its satisfactory solution is a key to my entire administration," Pat wrote to a Northern California newspaper publisher his second week as governor. Pat did not see himself as the adjudicator of regional disputes; his role was to unify his state behind an audacious water project that benefited everyone, including him.

Pat traced his interest in water to his pioneer ancestors who had settled in the northern California county of Colusa. When he visited the Mountain House as a boy, he saw life on a ranch without well water, where the household and the farm depended on rainfall. His mother told him that when she was a child, her father gathered the family after he planted and everyone knelt and prayed for rain. Sometimes the prayers were answered, sometimes not. Drought wasn't the only worry. The pioneers also contended with floods, when the rivers swelled from heavy winter rains and spring snowmelts in the High Sierra peaks. August Schuckman had noted in his diary that he sought land on high ground, far enough from the Sacramento River to avoid the annual floods that washed away livestock, crops, and people.

In the late nineteenth century, floods were exacerbated by the large-scale hydraulic mining operations that replaced the solo prospectors of the early Gold Rush years. The mining companies diverted the Sacramento River and its tributaries, redirecting massive volumes of water under high pressure to blast away gravel and soft stone. The mining debris was dumped into waterways, where the silt and gravel choked rivers used for navigation, increased erosion, and poisoned water that farmers used to irrigate their fields. Hydraulic mining was eventually outlawed. But the miners had shown that ditches and canals could be used to move great quantities of water from one place to another.

As early as 1878, the year Ida Schuckman Brown was born, California appointed its first state engineer and allocated $100,000 for a comprehensive inventory of water resources. Over several years, William Hammond Hall surveyed the Sacramento, Feather, American, and San Joaquin rivers and assessed irrigation needs in the Central Valley. He proposed a long-range plan to redistribute water that would include storage reservoirs in the north and aqueducts to carry the water south. A half century later, his plan would form the basis of a federal water project.

In the meantime, groups of landowners and local governments tackled the problem on their own. In 1887, the state legislature embraced the idea that providing water was a public service and established a new legal entity, the irrigation district. Dozens formed. They created small canals and dams, as well as a tradition of turf battles between powerful independent districts. Epic legal fights over water rights ensued. When Hiram Johnson was elected governor in 1910, the Progressives moved to assert more state control. A 1914 referendum established municipal water use as a priority over agriculture and set up a state water commission to resolve claims, though the commission had little power over court cases.

The two largest metropolitan areas, meanwhile, had temporarily solved their own water needs. Southern California, still relatively sparsely populated, infamously grabbed water from the Owens Valley on the northeastern edge of the state and built a 233-mile aqueduct that ended in the hills north of the Los Angeles city line. Water began to flow in 1913. "There it is, take it!" the engineer William Mulholland said, as crowds in suits and long skirts clambered over the hills to watch the first water pour through the sluice. The aqueduct facilitated development of the San Fernando Valley, enriched a small group of prominent landowners, and eventually doubled the size of Los Angeles, making it the largest city in the United States.

San Francisco had obtained permission from the federal government in 1909 to dam the Tuolumne River and flood the spectacular valley of Hetch Hetchy, on the northwest edge of Yosemite National Park. John Muir led a lengthy battle to derail the project, which would irrevocably damage the park he had fought so hard to protect. The dam would submerge a valley comparable in beauty to Yosemite itself, Muir pleaded with President Theodore Roosevelt, who had camped in the park with Muir just a few years earlier. Roosevelt and his two successors declined to intervene. Before the valley disappeared underwater, the Sierra Club led a final mournful outing to Hetch Hetchy in 1914, months before Muir died on Christmas Eve.

Pat followed the developments during his regular summer pilgrimages to Yosemite. He entered night law school just as the dam was completed in 1923. Though the course was not relevant to anything he anticipated needing in his practice, Pat enrolled in a summer class taught by Simon Weil, the preeminent Western water lawyer of the day. Water rights had become a complicated legal specialty. And the most critical water issues revolved around the 425-mile-long Central Valley, the heart of the state's largest industry.

Two principal rivers flow through the Central Valley, dividing the giant plain into the smaller Sacramento Valley in the north and the San Joaquin Valley, roughly twice the size. The Sacramento River starts high up in the Klamath Mountains near the Oregon border, wends its way south to within a mile of the state capitol, and then enters the vast Sacramento–San Joaquin Delta, a sprawling estuary and ecosystem that leads to San Francisco Bay. The San Joaquin River forms a lopsided U, starting in the High Sierra and heading southwest into the San Joaquin Valley past Fresno, then turning northwest past Modesto, Merced, and Stockton to feed into the Delta. From there, the rivers squeeze through the narrow Carquinez Straits and rush out to sea through San Francisco Bay.

The annual rainfall in the south end of the San Joaquin Valley was less than five inches. Even in the wetter north, rivers and streams dried up in summer, just when the water was needed most. Crops required reliable sources of water at certain times of year. Landowners with limited or no access to river water relied on wells, forced to dig deeper and deeper every year, extracting so much water that the ground began to sink. The deeper the wells, the costlier the power to raise the water up to ground level. Growers kept paying, until the Depression hit in 1929.

The Depression fueled both a greater demand for government intervention and greater bipartisan support for major public works projects, to provide badly needed jobs. The idea proposed decades earlier by the first state engineer gained new currency: Build dams on the northern ends of the Sacramento and San Joaquin rivers to create reservoirs that stored water, and aqueducts to function as man-made rivers transporting the water south. In 1933, the California legislature passed a $171 million plan that was approved by voters on December 19. But in the midst of the Depression, the state had no way to float bonds to raise the money. So officials turned to the federal government.

On December 2, 1935, the U.S. Bureau of Reclamation took over the Central Valley Project, with a price tag of $228 million. Over the next sixteen years, a workforce of more than five thousand built the Shasta Dam on the Sacramento River, twelve miles north of Redding, and then the Friant Dam on the San Joaquin River, twenty miles north of Fresno. Pumping stations propelled the water high enough that gravity did the rest, pulling water through 350 miles of canals. Hydroelectric plants turned the rushing water into energy, and the sale of excess power offset the costs of operations, helping the bureau sell water at far below market rates.

The cheap water came with a catch. The Bureau of Reclamation fell under the Newlands Act of 1902. Designed to encourage family farmers to settle the West, the act restricted subsidies to farms no larger than 160 acres. Many small landowners remained in the Central Valley, but the vast majority of acreage was in large tracts owned by a handful of corporate giants, including the Southern Pacific Railroad and Standard Oil. The federal government agreed to sell the large landowners water if they signed contracts promising to sell excess acres within a certain number of years. They signed—and then promptly began lobbying to void the restriction. The Central Valley grew roughly half the country's fresh fruit, one third of the dried fruit, one third of truck crops, and one third of canned fruits and vegetables; by 1959, the value of California's two hundred agricultural products topped $3 billion. As California's prime industry and a supplier of food to the nation, agriculture was a powerful force. The economic wisdom of breaking up large farms became a debate that pitted the Jeffersonian ideal against the reality of mass-produced crops.

Secretary of the Interior Harold Ickes, who oversaw the Bureau of Reclamation, was not receptive to the industry's complaints. In part, he was influenced by the publication of two seminal books: John Steinbeck's novel *The Grapes of Wrath* and Carey McWilliams's treatise *Factories in the Field*. Published in 1939, both detailed the exploitation of farmworkers in California, where thousands of Dust Bowl refugees lived in shantytowns and struggled to survive. Earlier generations of farmworkers had been primarily immigrants, first Chinese, then Japanese, Filipino, and Mexican. Now many of the workers were Okies like Steinbeck's Joad family, and their plight evoked widespread outrage. *The Grapes of Wrath* became a bestseller and then a blockbuster movie. Ickes was unsympathetic to growers who underpaid and mistreated workers and now wanted cheap water on their own terms. The Bureau of Reclamation commissioned an anthropologist at the University of California to study and compare two valley towns, Dinuba, which had primarily small farms, and Arvin, which had large ones. The study concluded that the average quality of life and income were significantly better in Dinuba. In 1943, Ickes and Roosevelt reaffirmed their commitment to the 160-acre limitation.

Pat Brown was first exposed to the fierce divisions and passions involving water when he traversed the Central Valley as a candidate for attorney general. By the time he ran in 1950, the deadline for divesting land loomed. Big agriculture was agitating for a state takeover of the water project to get out from under the impending federal restrictions.

Failing that, they wanted California to build its own project. The newly created State Water Resources Board had prepared a statewide plan that estimated even with the existing reservoirs, 40 percent of the river water ended up as ocean runoff—or, in the terminology used by advocates of more dams, "wasted." The myriad environmental consequences of reengineering the powerful rivers were not yet part of the public debate.

Water rights were so complex that the *California Law Review* devoted its October 1950 issue to water. Academics, engineers, and lawyers analyzed whether the Central Valley Project should be owned and operated by the state, the ramifications of the 160-acre limit, and a dispute over whether public or private utilities should have the first right to buy the project's excess power. Pat read and reread the law journal several times. He pledged support for a state project, but was noncommittal on details.

One of the first decisions he confronted as attorney general in 1951 was the state's position on a landmark legal challenge to the 160-acre limitation. The case, known as *Ivanhoe*, was brought by irrigation districts, which argued that any limit imposed by the federal government violated the California constitution's guarantee that water be equally distributed. Pat's predecessor had supported the districts. Pat reversed course and argued the federal government had a right to limit the subsidies and the state had a right to enter into agreements that imposed those restrictions.

The key legal scholar behind the state's reasoning in the *Ivanhoe* case was Deputy Attorney General Abbott Goldberg, who became one of Pat's most trusted and influential advisers. Goldberg had grown up in Massachusetts and graduated from Harvard Law School shortly before the United States entered World War II. A stint in the Army ended in illness and recuperation at a military hospital in San Francisco. He fell in love with the city and decided to stay, choosing a job in the attorney general's office because the work seemed interesting and the state offered good medical benefits, uncommon in the private sector. Goldberg knew nothing about water law when Pat assigned him to research the *Ivanhoe* case. But he had a fine legal mind and was an expert on relationships between state and federal governments. He argued that the government had the right to impose restrictions and that simply owning more land did not constitute a legal right to a greater subsidy. Although the position angered the large farm interests, Pat gave Goldberg full support. The state lost at every level until the case reached the U.S. Supreme Court, which ruled unanimously in California's favor. The implications of the case for state-federal cooperation went beyond water and established the right of either party to attach conditions on joint projects. It would prove key to Pat's future water plans.

The second water decision the attorney general tackled that would rebound to his later benefit was the so-called County of Origin opinion, based on a plan adopted by the legislature in 1931. Pat signed an opinion that gave the northern counties the right to stop sending water south if they demonstrated a future need. Pat considered the opinion sufficiently vague as to be meaningless, but necessary to reassure the northerners that they would not find themselves in a situation comparable to the Owens Valley, where the lake and economy had dried up when the water went to Los Angeles. Pat told the north that the decision gave them protection, while he assured the south that the opinion meant nothing because "origin" was not defined.

Perhaps most important for the future, the state reformed the crazy-quilt bureaucracy that governed water. In 1956, an Assembly committee chaired by Republican Caspar Weinberger found more than fifty-two state agencies handled different aspects of water regulations. California had passed seventy laws that were used to create 165 irrigation districts, 69 county water districts, 55 reclamation districts, 39 water districts, 35 county waterworks districts, and 19 municipal water districts. Weinberger proposed a single department with centralized power that could efficiently plan and manage water. He asked for backing from Pat Brown, the only statewide-elected Democrat and one who was deeply involved in water litigation. Pat's endorsement gave the Weinberger plan a bipartisan cast. On July 5, 1956, the Department of Water Resources was created, effectively giving the governor broad control over water policy. Within a year, the department proposed the construction of new dams and aqueducts.

The genesis of the State Water Project had been pressure from the large landowners who wanted to evade the 160-acre limitation. But the explosive growth in California made water a key concern everywhere. California was adding roughly half a million people a year, the new state agency pointed out in a brochure, "Water for a Growing State." The state had more than doubled from its prewar population of 7 million and projections were for a population as high as 56 million by 2020. Half the people would live south of the Tehachapi Mountains, the dividing line between Northern and Southern California. While 70 percent of the water originated in the northern third of the state, 77 percent of the need was in the southern two thirds. In the northwest corner of the state, average rainfall was 110 inches per year. In the desert, it was two.

During his 1958 campaign, Pat supported the idea of a state project, "as essential to the future of the northern part of the State as it is to the south." The state plan called for a dam high up on the Feather River, the major tributary of the Sacramento and the one large river still untamed. Both northerners and southerners wanted the plan approved through a constitutional amendment, in order to guarantee that whatever deal they reached could not be changed by future lawmakers. For the past two years, the legislature had been deadlocked, far short of the two-thirds majority needed to place a constitutional amendment on the ballot.

When Pat became governor in 1959, the Department of Water Resources's second annual report was ready to be distributed, with an introduction from the director that urged approval of a constitutional amendment. The Brown administration intercepted the booklets at the printing plant and ordered the introduction ripped out of all six thousand copies. Abbott Goldberg had convinced Pat there was an alternative to the constitutional route. If the legislature authorized debt, subject to popular approval, the law could prescribe specific uses of the money, immutable for the life of the bonds. A simple majority vote could provide ironclad guarantees that would satisfy all sides.

A project born from the demands of Central Valley land barons morphed into a mission to address future needs of the whole state, a shift that reflected California's transition from agricultural empire to sophisticated technological pioneer. Though he had always lived in San Francisco, Pat considered the project particularly crucial for the development of Southern California. He weighed cautionary arguments that less water would force slower growth in a semiarid area not destined by nature to support the thousands who arrived every month. He was convinced that people would come anyway. And they would need water. Pat adopted a line coined by one of his advisers: Better to have problems with water than problems without water. His missionary zeal was matched by Goldberg and other advisers who viewed themselves as following in the tradition of pioneers, conquering the Western wilderness by "doing the Lord's work" to bring communities the element most needed to prosper.

Pat had recognized he would be strongest in the early months, coming into office with his million-vote margin. He asked Warren Christopher to craft a special message on water, which Pat delivered to an unusual joint session of the legislature on January 22, 1959. He framed the issue as one whose solution would strengthen the whole state, rather than tear it apart:

> It has become the fashion in recent years to dwell on our water problems as being awesome and impossibly complicated. We have brooded over the expense and become lost in a forest of fear . . . this stalemate must come to an end.
>
> I would emphasize that our problem lies, not so much in the control and use of our rivers, as in ourselves. Let us resolve to prove that we are one state, one people, and that we can produce one good water program. Let us grow with the strength of unity, as we begin to fulfill our destiny of greatness.

Pat's timing was auspicious. Nineteen fifty-nine was a very dry year. Crops withered in parts of the San Joaquin Valley. Groundwater tables had dropped by thirty feet and seawater intrusion was ruining wells. Santa Cruz and parts of San Diego faced potential water rationing by summer. In Southern California, the giant Metropolitan Water District, which supplied Los Angeles and San Diego communities, was a defendant in a suit that threatened to reduce its share of water from the Colorado River. In Palo Alto and other rapidly growing cities south of San Francisco, residents were angry at paying higher rates for Hetch Hetchy water in order to subsidize the city.

The plan Pat sent the legislature in May was designed to meet the state's needs through 1985 with a bond issue of $1.75 billion, a sum almost as large as the entire state budget. That still would fall short of financing the whole project, but with money from oil tax funds and potential collaboration with the federal government, the bond issue would come close.

Pat was honest about his selfish determination to leave behind a lasting physical legacy. But he was also farsighted in his vision for the state and unusual in his commitment to projects that would be completed long after he left office. At best, water would not flow through the state aqueduct to

Southern California for another decade. In a letter to a Central Valley lawyer, he tied the need for water to the state Master Plan—three new universities, ten state colleges, and a medical school all in the works. "In planning a water program I have to think of all of the things, not only for now but in planning for the next twenty-five years," Pat wrote. "Very frankly, in my opinion there has not been sufficient planning at the state level in the past."

State officials estimated that 27 million acre-feet of water from Northern California ran off into the ocean. The most optimistic projections were that in a hundred years they could use only half that amount. Because all the rivers met and mingled in the Delta, the state plan envisioned the Delta as a pool with a giant spigot that could be opened as needed to funnel water south. Each river contributed only its excess water, so no one area could go dry, as had happened in the Owens Valley. Still, Northern Californians worried they would never get water back if they had need for it. Southern Californians worried they would pay the brunt of the construction costs and then not get enough water. The valley people worried about pressure to take water away from crops if it was needed for people. Pat pointed to the County of Origin opinion, but opposition remained strong, especially in the north.

The state Senate posed the most significant political hurdle. While the balance of power in the state was tilting south, the Senate was immune: Districts were drawn around county lines regardless of population. The lone senator from Los Angeles, representing six million constituents, carried the same weight as the senator from Inyo, Mono, and Alpine counties with a combined population of fifteen thousand. Pat turned for help to Senate President Pro Tem Hugh Burns, a conservative Democrat from Fresno, the largest producer of agricultural products of any county in the country. Burns wanted the industry-friendly state insurance commissioner reappointed. The Republican commissioner kept his job; Burns carried the water bill. His support reassured the agricultural interests in the valley, his most influential constituents.

The major opposition came from the "River Rats"—senators with districts along the Sacramento River and the Delta, who would lose water. The governor called in every favor he had. He promised appointments and cut deals. Senator Pauline Davis demanded small lakes in her district on tributaries of the Feather River; "Pauline's Puddles" went in the bill and she signed on. The bill was so technical and complicated that in an unusual move, which would later be banned, top aides to the governor sat on the floor of the legislature during the debate to answer questions. Even then, many did not understand what they voted for. "I believe that the bill got through the Legislature as much on the basis of unequivocal loyalty to Pat, faith in Harvey and you, and anxiety on the part of most of us to 'do something' in solution of the water problem as it did on its merits," Assemblyman Thomas McBride wrote to one of the two aides.

The bill passed 50–30 in the Assembly and 25–12 in the Senate, with votes split on geographic rather than partisan lines.

"Water bill passed. Hurrah," Pat wrote in his diary on June 17, 1959. "The end of five months of the toughest kind of work." He noted more personal triumphs the same day, too. His son-in-law Joe Kelly was admitted to the bar. Cynthia went to the reception for her husband four days after giving birth to their second child, fortitude Pat credited to her pioneer ancestors. The only discordant note came from a quarrel with his youngest daughter. "Kathleen wanted to go to a show with a boy. She is only 13 and I said no. She is very unhappy and so am I."

Pat signed the water bill a few weeks later, calling it the crowning achievement of the legislative session. "This will remove the last great obstacle to California's full growth and prosperity," he said. By 1985, he estimated the project would serve 21 million of 35 million Californians, more than twice the state's population at the time the bill passed. Though his projections proved high—population growth slowed with legalized abortion and birth control—he correctly foresaw the enormous impact on Southern California.

"Your place in history will be assured as the Governor who made it possible for Southern Californians to die of smog, strangulated freeways, and claustrophobia, instead of thirst. Their gratitude should be enduring," one of the deputies who handled water litigation in the attorney general's office wrote to Pat. "My place in history will be assured after the water bill is passed and the structure built and after I have completely dissipated smog in Los Angeles," Pat retorted.

The water bond still needed to be approved by California voters. Although the election was more than a year away, Fred Dutton worried they were late in organizing and cautioned that the complicated issue needed to be reduced to its simplest message, "not left as a technical water problem." The $1.75 billion number scared people; they needed to break it down into smaller, year-by-year expenditures and compare the amount to dollars spent on schools and roads. "The quickest way to beat the bonds is to let the campaign be run by specialists and experts who will make it too complex for the public mind," Dutton wrote Pat. "You will either settle it on the basis of the need for more water, or not at all."

Construction and planning began with seed money, and Pat presided at a groundbreaking on the Feather River for what would be the first new dam. All the streams in the area had dried up in April, three months earlier than usual. The new reservoir would not only stabilize supplies but create a recreation area. He stressed the urgency of pushing ahead, even in the face of uncertainty about the gigantic bond issue. He was his typical honest self, never overly confident but always ebullient. "I must confess that deep down in my heart I had qualms" about whether his water program would pass, Pat said. But he had faith that he could overcome the mistrust that had stymied earlier efforts. "We had been overlooking the one fear that we should have—that the necessary works would not be constructed in time . . . We must *build* no matter how the other questions are resolved. For the first time, the State is assuming a responsibility to see that water is available and is taking action to meet that responsibility." No matter the myriad details that remained, he stressed the campaign motto: "Water for people. For living. For income. For pleasure."

Environmental concerns that would later become key to water wars were not yet paramount. The project was not subject to any environmental review. The importance of the wild rivers as spawning grounds and the protection of fish stock got scant attention. To win support from the small cadre of conservationists, a proposed peripheral canal was added to the project to channel water around the Delta to protect fish.

The campaign for the bond issue stressed the economic ties between the state's regions, which depended on one another to buy and sell goods and services. Backing up the idea of a "public good" with more pragmatic benefits, supporters estimated the construction phase would be worth more than half a billion dollars to the economy of each major region— north, south, and central. "Water or no water—that is the question," Los Angeles mayor Norris Poulson repeated in speech after speech. The Republican mayor became key to the campaign. With six million people in his county, he said, "this will be won or lost in Los Angeles County."

An uneasy alliance prevailed between the bond act's two biggest beneficiaries, Southern California, served primarily by the giant Metropolitan

Water District, and the agricultural interests of the Central Valley. Each suspected the other would try to shirk their share of costs, and each tried to lock in as much water as possible. Mayor Poulson threatened to replace his appointees on the Met board if they did not support the project. Days before the election, the board signed a contract to pay upfront for water not expected to flow until 1972. Those payments would be essential to pay back bonds that financed the construction. "Water delivery to Southern California is the cash register," Pat said.

The building trade unions supported the bond issue because it would mean jobs, an estimated 12 percent of all money spent on construction in the next decade. But the California Federation of Labor was opposed, painting the project as a bonanza for agribusiness at a time the labor movement was trying to organize farmworkers. The *San Francisco Chronicle* was the most vocal opponent. Stories proclaimed desalination would be commonplace and affordable long before the mammoth water works were complete. Proponents dismissed that as fantasy. Pat chided all sides, reminding them of the need for water to fulfill the state's destiny. "We must put an end to endless argument in which each speaks only his own self-interest," he told a business group. "There is a need to recognize the larger interest that benefits and brings together all of our state."

On November 8, 1960, the water bond passed by only 173,944 votes out of more than 5.8 million. Pat was relieved, but he wrote friends that he still was baffled that so many people voted no. Earl Warren was one of the first to send congratulations on "a great step forward. As time passes and our State continues to grow at an unprecedented rate, I become more firmly convinced than ever that it can outgrow most of its growing pains without permanent injury if it first solves its basic water problems."

"It was a tough, hard and frustrating fight," Pat responded. "You won some tough ones when you were Governor, and can realize how much I enjoyed this one."

The Central Valley Project had been a mammoth endeavor; the 600-foot-tall Shasta Dam had a spillway three times the height of Niagara Falls. The State Water Project would dwarf its federal counterpart in complexity. To oversee the project and its myriad hurdles once the water bond passed, Pat turned to William Warne, whom he called the best administrator he knew in state government.

Warne had no formal training in engineering, but his life had been shaped since childhood by the water woes of California. His family had moved to California from rural Indiana when Bill was eight because his father accepted a job on the irrigation project that brought Colorado River water to the Imperial Valley. Warne grew up on a 160-acre dairy farm, attended a two-room school, and did homework by coal lamp because electricity didn't come to the valley until he was in college. He followed his three older brothers to Cal, where he majored in English even though he was expected to return to the family farm. Warne went into journalism instead. He developed expertise in writing about water. In Washington as a regional correspondent in 1933, he wrote mainly about water projects. He asked so many questions at Interior Department Secretary Harold Ickes's weekly press conferences that Ickes offered him a job. Warne worked for the Bureau of Reclamation and became an expert on irrigation.

Warne met Pat when he came through Washington for meetings as attorney general, and they stayed in touch. When Pat was elected governor, he appointed Warne to head the Department of Fish and Game and consulted him frequently about water matters. Warne organized a pack trip the first summer to take reporters to see the golden trout program near Mount Whitney, the highest peak in California, where the state captured and transplanted stock to safe areas. Pat went along. They rode horseback over trails into the wilderness and got lost, but there was a pitcher of martinis waiting when they finally reached the camp. They caught golden trout with barbless hooks and put them in ten-gallon milk cans to transport them to new waters. The pack trips became an annual tradition, and Pat went on every one except the year he had a broken ankle. He loved the trips and talked about them for months. At night they played poker, and before breakfast Pat plunged into the icy waters of the nearest lake.

Warne was one of the few to call attention to the impact of the water projects on the fish he was charged with protecting. He had sounded an alarm when the flow of water from the federal Friant Dam was reduced, threatening to devastate the salmon fisheries and a catch worth more than $1 million a year. As soon as the bond issue passed, he wrote memos about the need to protect wildlife during construction and find ways to compensate for the loss of spawning grounds.

When he became head of the Department of Water Resources in 1961, Warne took on a project that, like so much in California, was characterized by superlatives: The largest dam in the world. The biggest water and power development in the country. "The greatest mass movement of water ever conceived by man is charted to become a reality in California's State Water Project," Warne said in advertisements circulated around the world to entice civil, mechanical, and electrical engineers. The project included 16 dams, 444 miles of aqueduct, and multiple power plants and pumping plants. By 1965, the construction costs were $1 million a day. "California must always in the future be willing, as no one else is willing, to sustain growth and development," Warne said in a speech he called "California Comes of Age."

One of the greatest engineering challenges was how to pump water up 3,415 feet over the Tehachapi Mountains, which formed the northern border of Los Angeles County. There was no model or precedent. Admiral Hyman Rickover, in charge of developing nuclear propulsion for the Navy, proposed a demonstration nuclear power plant that the federal government would help finance. California signed a contract with the Atomic Energy Commission to construct and operate a breeder reactor, but at the last minute the deal fell through. Federal officials said the cladding on the fuel rods was not strong enough to prevent radiation from polluting the cooling waters. Warne and his team went back to more conventional solutions, ultimately putting in place a system that lifted 4,100 cubic feet of water a second the last two thousand feet over the Tehachapis.

The second significant collaboration with the federal government went more smoothly. One of the final pieces of the federal water project was to be the San Luis Reservoir, created by a massive dam on the San Joaquin River. In order to save costs and avoid duplication, the State Water Plan assumed the state and federal governments would jointly build and use the dam. The Interior Department set a deadline of December 30, 1961, to reach an agreement, or the Bureau of Reclamation would proceed alone and not include capacity needed for the state project. At the very last minute, they made a deal. The state would have the right to use its share of the water without restrictions imposed by the 160-acre federal limit—an agreement made possible because Pat Brown and Abbott Goldberg had successfully argued the *Ivanhoe* case up to the U.S. Supreme Court.

Four pipes emanate from one of the five pumping plants that lift water more than 2,000 feet over the Tehachapi mountains that separate northern and southern California. (Courtesy of California Department of Water Resources)

The groundbreaking for the San Luis Dam took place on August 18, 1962. President John F. Kennedy's helicopter landed in a cloud of dust near a platform erected in the middle of a grassy slope facing the saddle that would become the dam. Kennedy arrived from Yosemite, where he had been the first president to visit the park since Theodore Roosevelt. He talked about the importance of people from the East Coast, who have water everywhere, seeing firsthand what water means in the West. He described what he saw out the window on his flight from Yosemite, "the greenest and most richest earth producing the greatest and richest crops in the country, and that a mile away see the same earth and see it brown and dusty and useless, all because there is water in one place and there isn't in another."

The joint project, he said, was a model of how Americans could work together:

There is no other project in the history of the United States where a state has put in such a large contribution to the development of its own resources, and where the national government has joined with the state . . . the benefits that will come from it are unique and special. All those years when people in this state said it was impossible, and those who had water wanted to hug it and not make it available to all those who lived in dry areas. Many state administrations in California, including some of the most distinguished, wrestled with this problem, but I believe that all Californians will remember the leadership which your distinguished governor has given to this great cause of making water available to the people of this state.

Engineers had planted multicolored smoke bombs across the center of the dam-to-be, marking the diameter of the large span. Bill Warne would look back a decade later and remember the next moments as the most memorable of his career, when the president turned to the governor and said, "It is a pleasure for me to come out here and help blow up this valley, in the cause of progress. We are able to do anything on this occasion."

Amid laughter and applause, on the count of three, the men simultaneously lowered the handles of two plungers, and colored fireworks raced across the valley.

10

The Turbulent Term

In the spring of 1961, Pat Brown cut short his Easter vacation and left Acapulco on a two A.M. flight to return home for the Sierra Club's seventh biennial wilderness conference. He arrived in San Francisco in time to board an Army helicopter to tour the Point Reyes seashore with the newly appointed interior secretary, Stewart Udall, who was working to preserve the area as a national park. From the air, Pat pointed out Muir Woods, Rattlesnake Camp, Big Lagoon—places he had hiked in his youth. He proudly said he had slept on the beach, only to be told the state had since outlawed the practice.

"In California, as elsewhere, the face of the wilderness is less and less apparent, and the struggle to retain it grows more difficult," Pat said that evening in an address to conservationists. He reminisced about spending summers as a student hiking in Yosemite. "The effect that it had upon me lives with me every day."

Udall followed Pat to the podium at the Palace Hotel and read a letter he had recently been handed by the writer Wallace Stegner. "It was so powerful and so eloquent and so poetic a statement concerning wilderness that I thought, when I attempted later to write a text of my own, that it would be foolish not to read it," Udall said. Stegner, who lived in Los Altos, a few miles from the Jesuit center where Pat had gone on retreats, had penned a plea to preserve wilderness areas not only for recreation but as spiritual sanctuaries, essential ties to the frontier history of the West. Stegner would later marvel that a letter written in half a day spread around the world faster than novels he had worked on for years. The final four words that Udall read were the ones that resonated so strongly:

Stegner called the prairies, deserts, mountains, and forests an essential part of "the geography of hope."

Stegner and Pat crossed paths only a few times; in 1958, the Stanford professor helped draft a campaign speech, and four years later, Stegner would sign on to a Professors for Brown committee. Their disparate worlds overlapped in a shared reverence for the Western landscape and the fear that it might disappear. "The most beautiful place in the entire world is a little High Sierra camp near Glen Aulin," Pat wrote when asked to name his favorite spot in California. "It lies at the base of a waterfall on the Tuolumne River. In early summer when the water is rushing down, it is one of the most remarkable works of nature that I have ever seen. It is quiet, except for the roar of the river and the beautiful aspens, ferns and pines." Always an optimist, Pat Brown instinctively embraced the geography of hope.

Ansel Adams, whose images of Yosemite had etched the valley in the national imagination, spoke to the Sierra Club conference about the historic arc of wilderness in California. For August Schuckman's generation, wilderness had been an environment to overcome, tame, and exploit. Once conquered, wilderness had become over time a source of recreation and inspiration. "We painfully realize there is not much wilderness in this category left to us and to the future," Adams said. "The next few years are to tell a tragic or a wonderful story."

Adams's warning presaged the tensions that would frame Pat's second term. For months, he had anticipated the moment California would pass New York to become the most populous state. An electronic counter installed on a billboard near the Bay Bridge tracked the numbers: one more Californian every 54 seconds. By the end of 1962, the counter hit the magic number: 17,341,416. Pat proclaimed New Year's Eve the start of a four-day "California First Days" celebration.

Stegner watched the governor chortle with delight at reaching the long-awaited milestone. Long before Pat recognized that bigger might not always be better, Stegner foresaw how the magnificent present would beget a complicated future:

> More spectacularly endowed than any other of the 50 states, culmination of the American movement westward, neighbor to Asia, raw, young, powerful, yet with oases of extraordinary sophistication and a smattering of every cultivated grace,

California is a place where you can find whatever you came looking for, and right next to it that which you most hoped to avoid.

In the mid-1960s, California became the world's fifth-largest economy, a state of more than 18 million. Every day for a decade, planners calculated, a thousand people had moved to California, and another thousand babies had been born. The new arrivals gravitated to the cities, and each year, two hundred square miles of rural land turned into housing, shops, and urban landscape. California built the equivalent of a city a week, erected a thousand traffic lights a month. Smog worsened, and even the Bay Area suffered days when the air burned the eyes. Public transit in Los Angeles was all but nonexistent, isolating people too poor to own cars. At Yosemite, the old Camp Curry apple orchard had been turned into an asphalt parking lot, as many as five thousand visitors crowded into one square mile on summer days, and the bumper-to-bumper traffic prompted calls to end the famous Firefall. "It stood to lose what it most loved and treasured—its magnificent landscape and brilliant climate, its easy, spacious, lavish way of living, its cosmopolitan cities—the whole proud young California civilization," Ansel Adams wrote.

The growth strained municipal budgets. Officials estimated every new arrival cost California $13,000 the first year in capital outlays—and paid no taxes until the following year. The legislature rebuffed Pat's proposals to institute tax withholding to help balance the state budget. Roy Bell, assistant director of finance, had started in the Warren administration, when his main job in the postwar years was finding "little pockets" in which to squirrel away surplus money. By the early 1960s, all the pockets were empty. The legislature approved only temporary one-year taxes, while the gap between revenues and expenditures grew. The state compensated in part by its resourcefulness at obtaining federal funds. California became a popular testing ground for programs such as migrant education and Kennedy's "New Frontier" poverty initiatives. Often out front and always outsized, California in turn influenced how regulations were written and programs administered.

"California plans big because it has no choice," Stegner wrote. "And just as certain California acts such as the compulsory smog-control device on automobiles have set examples taken up by the whole nation, so some of the state's preparations for further growth offer models of how far a single commonwealth can go to solve its problems."

That tradition of independent self-reliance had built unprecedented waterworks, colleges, and freeways, a record that had propelled Pat Brown to his come-from-behind victory over Richard Nixon. He celebrated the start of his second term with a lavish inaugural celebration, undeterred by the looming financial problems. The *Sacramento Bee* described the 1963 inaugural festivities as "more glitter and glamour than Sacramento has seen in many a day . . . one of the most outstanding social events ever held in the city." Dean Martin sang "I Left My Heart in San Francisco." Gene Kelly danced a soft shoe routine. Frank Sinatra's medley included a special request from seventeen-year-old Kathy Brown, "All the Way." Steve Allen joked, with more prescience than anyone realized, "If Dick Nixon had won, you'd be sitting here listening to Roy Rogers and Ronald Reagan." Ida Brown partied until three A.M. "I didn't dance," she told a reporter a few days later. "After all—I am 85—but I so enjoyed meeting the people there."

Pat spent some time with Earl Warren, hosting a dinner at the Mansion before the inauguration and joining Warren at the Rose Bowl game in Pasadena and the East-West Shrine Game in San Francisco, traditions the chief justice observed faithfully. Pat often sought Warren's advice and envied his calm, relaxed demeanor, a contrast to his own peripatetic nature. "I have a deep sense of urgency in a state that is growing as fast as California," Pat wrote to Warren, enclosing his inaugural message that outlined plans for the second term. "There are some of these that I am sure we will win and others that I am sure we will not, but I thought this was a great opportunity to speak out on all of the things I believe in."

It soon became clear he would lose more than he would win. Pat did not have a million-vote majority to strengthen his hand this time, nor did he have support from Democratic Assembly Speaker Jesse Unruh, who had his own gubernatorial ambitions and little interest in helping the incumbent. He had barely started his second term when aides urged Pat to fight hard on losing battles—to set the stage for a future campaign. "Everything you say should be aimed at the people, over the heads of the senators," press secretary Jack Burby wrote. He urged Pat to open up press conferences to television. "It is an inevitable move and you may as well be known as the governor who took the step and get the credit and the gratitude of the television industry." (Print journalists, on the other hand, were so annoyed when TV cameras were allowed at the press conferences

August Schuckman at the Mountain House, the Colusa County ranch that the Prussian immigrant acquired in 1878. The land has been in the family ever since. COURTESY OF KARIN SURBER

August Schuckman, third from left, outside the Mountain House inn and tavern, a popular stage-coach stop. His son Frank is at far left; his son Charles and his wife, Mary, and their daughter at right.
COURTESY OF KARIN SURBER

Ida Schuckman, August's youngest child, was nineteen when she married Edmund Joseph Brown, a twenty-six-year-old native of San Francisco. COURTESY OF KARIN SURBER

Ed Brown in 1902 behind the counter of his cigar store in San Francisco's Tenderloin district. He ran a lucrative gambling operation in the back. COURTESY OF KARIN SURBER

The Brown family: Ed and Ida with their three oldest children, Edmund, Connie, and Harold. COURTESY OF KARIN SURBER

The Browns—Ed and Ida with Connie, Frank, Edmund, and Harold—in front of the Wawona Tunnel Tree, a giant sequoia in the Mariposa Grove in Yosemite National Park. The tree was part of an effort by the National Park Service to promote the park as automobiles became more common. Seven feet wide and nine feet high, the tunnel was a popular tourist attraction from 1881 until the tree was felled by heavy snow in 1969. COURTESY OF KARIN SURBER

TOP: Pat Brown and his daughters Barbara, five, and Cynthia, three, were among the two hundred thousand people who walked across the Golden Gate Bridge on opening day, May 27, 1937.
EDMUND G. BROWN PAPERS, BANC PIC 1968.011-PIC, COURTESY OF THE BANCROFT LIBRARY, UNIVERSITY OF CALIFORNIA, BERKELEY

BOTTOM: Pat Brown took photographs with his family each time he ran for election. In 1943, as he launched his campaign for San Francisco district attorney, he and Bernice posed with Barbara, Cynthia, and Jerry, who was five years old.
SAN FRANCISCO HISTORY CENTER, SAN FRANCISCO PUBLIC LIBRARY

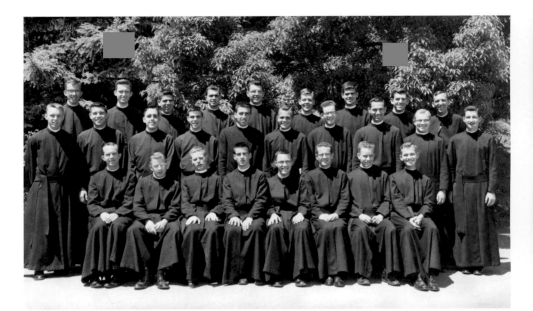

In August 1958, Jerry Brown (front row, fourth from left) took his vows after two years at the Jesuit seminary in Los Gatos. His college roommate and lifelong friend Frank Damrell (back row, fourth from right) also became a junior at the Sacred Heart Novitiate. CALIFORNIA JESUIT ARCHIVES

Pat Brown gives his mother, Ida, a kiss as he declares victory on election night 1958, winning the governor's race by more than a million votes. Bernice and their daughters Kathy and Cynthia look on. SAN FRANCISCO HISTORY CENTER, SAN FRANCISCO PUBLIC LIBRARY

TOP: After winning the 1958 election, Pat and Bernice headed for vacation in Palm Springs. Pat, an avid reader, brought along the just-published Cold War political novel *The Ugly American*. While Pat's golf game never seemed to improve, Bernice had perfected her form at a driving range so that she was proficient from the first time she set foot on a course.
COURTESY OF THE BROWN FAMILY

BOTTOM: When he was sworn in as governor, Pat Brown introduced his family: Bernice; Jerry, who was allowed to leave the seminary to attend the ceremony; his mother, Ida; and daughters Barbara (behind Ida), Kathleen, and Cynthia. COURTESY OF THE OFFICE OF GOVERNOR EDMUND G. BROWN JR.

Pat Brown had spent summers in Yosemite as a youth and loved to hike, swim, and camp in the High Sierra. As governor, he went on annual Fish and Game Department trips. In August 1959, he fished for golden trout on a pack trip that traveled to an area near Mt. Whitney.

that they used obscenities in questions to render the video footage unusable.) Burby echoed advice Fred Dutton had passed on four years earlier when Pat's first chief of staff visited other states: "I no longer believe it is possible to quit campaigning altogether. You can never stop being a candidate and be only the Governor any more than you could stop being Governor and be only a candidate during the recent campaign."

Politics and government blurred seamlessly in an era with few ethical qualms or rules. State staff worked on campaigns. Neither officials nor lobbyists reported dinners, Christmas presents, or gift memberships. Movie theaters sent free passes, which Pat often passed on to his mother. When Frank Sinatra saw Pat's shabby golf clubs, the entertainer surprised the governor with a new set. Pat was among the select few who received a Disneyland Gold Pass each year, signed by Walt Disney, good for free admission and VIP treatment for six guests.

He received similar treatment when he traveled abroad. In the summer of 1963, the Browns embarked on a leisurely European trip, combining a minimal amount of work with six weeks of sightseeing in seven countries. They were welcomed with roses and champagne, fruit baskets and designer scarves. A San Francisco television reporter who tagged along captured memorable moments, both serious and lighthearted: At the Berlin Wall, the Browns climbed onto the platform where Kennedy had delivered his famous address and peered into East Germany. In London, Pat's desire to visit Parliament lost out to Bernice's wish to visit Shakespeare's home in Stratford-on-Avon. In Paris, Bernice visited Givenchy and Yves Saint Laurent, where designers compared her figure to that of Jackie Kennedy.

In Paris, the Browns also reunited with Jerry, who was working as a summer intern at NATO headquarters, a job arranged through Fred Dutton. Jerry traveled with the family to Rome, where they had an audience with Pope Paul VI. The third-year law student told a reporter that he intended to become a trial attorney in San Francisco and that his role model was Vincent Hallinan, a Jesuit-educated Irishman who had run for president for the Progressive Party. He would succeed, Jerry said, "without help from Dad. I'm going to make it alone."

His sister Kathy brought along on the trip her best friend and former neighbor from Magellan Avenue, Barbara DiGiorgio, whose father was one of the largest grape and vegetable growers in the San Joaquin Valley and a staunch Republican. In Paris, Kathy drew notice when she went off to see the Eiffel Tower in a miniskirt. "A pretty good politician in her own right, Kathy says also that Paris is great—but her favorite city remains unaltered—it's San Francisco," reported KGO-TV.

Kathleen returned from Europe to enroll as a freshman at Stanford, a campus roiled by twin forces reshaping the political landscape—the civil rights movement and student protests.

In June, NAACP leader Medgar Evers had been assassinated in Mississippi. As the Browns toured Venice, hundreds of thousands of people converged on the nation's capital for the March on Washington. Millions more watched on television as Martin Luther King Jr. proclaimed on August 28, 1963, "I have a dream . . ." While the Browns gazed at the Berlin Wall, court-ordered school integration in Birmingham was foiled by explosions. The Sunday before freshman orientation at Stanford, Ku Klux Klan members planted a bomb at the 16th Street Baptist Church in Birmingham, Alabama, killing four young girls.

Thousands of miles removed, the palm-lined drives and red-roofed limestone quads of the Stanford campus had a direct link to the civil rights struggles in the South. The charismatic young political activist Allard Lowenstein had taught at Stanford until two years earlier and maintained close ties with the university. In late October 1963, he was coordinating voter registration campaigns in Mississippi and called friends at Stanford with an urgent plea: Send student volunteers to help organize a mock election with "Freedom Ballots," an effort to demonstrate the extent of black disenfranchisement. Four Stanford students left the next day, their departure bannered on the front page of the Stanford *Daily*, overshadowing news about the football team's upset victory over Notre Dame. Two more carloads left the day after.

The Stanford undergraduates became the first orchestrated contingent of students to work under civil rights leaders in the South, a prelude to the Freedom Summer that followed. On campus, students collected $5,000 to help cover bail expenses in Mississippi. When Lowenstein announced the funds at a rally, "the place went wild," he told the *Daily*. "This is what can stop the intimidation, the force of someone from the outside." The presence of the overwhelmingly white students drew media attention and more visible federal law enforcement. Braving violence and threats, more than eighty thousand black voters cast ballots at polling places set up by the civil rights activists—four times the number of blacks allowed to vote in the state-run election for governor.

Students returned to Stanford shaken and energized, eager to share stories about fear, police brutality, and heroic struggle. Stanford became the western hub where national civil rights leaders coordinated student recruitment for what became the 1964 Mississippi Summer Project. Students from dozens of western colleges gathered in Palo Alto in April for a three-day conference with a keynote address by Reverend King. "Human progress never merely rolls in on the wheels of inevitability. There is always a right time to do right . . . and that time is now," King told the overflow crowd. "Come south this summer to help create a movement so large it cannot be ignored, pressure so great the federal government will be forced to act."

Kathleen, crammed into the back of Memorial Auditorium on April 23, 1964, found the message so powerful she signed up; Pat promptly vetoed the idea as too dangerous. Kathleen helped raise money instead. Even her decision to attend Stanford had required a minor act of rebellion. She had spent the last two years of high school at Santa Catalina, a small Catholic girls' boarding school in Monterey. After a mediocre Sacramento public school, Kathleen found the intense intellectual environment life-changing. She applied to Stanford because it was hard to get in (she was one of 1,282 freshmen and just 434 women) and because almost everyone else in the family had gone to Cal. She sidestepped an argument with her parents by signing their names on the application, then enlisted the diminutive but steely school principal, Sister Mary Kieran, to overcome her father's steadfast conviction that his daughter belonged at Cal.

The Stanford freshman class had students from almost every state and sixteen countries. Kathleen mixed easily in different groups, from the preppy crowd to the existentialist intellectuals in black turtlenecks. She got her ears pierced and decided to major in social sciences. Like her brother, she received tuition assistance from Louis Lurie, the San Francisco financier and family friend, and wrote him letters in exchange. "My Brown brain has been taxed considerably and the reward has been neither in a monetary nor in a grade sense, but rather as an achievement sense, self earned and self satisfying," she wrote. "I love it. I have discovered the excitement of spontaneous seminars that last until the wee hours of the morning and which encompass such a range of subjects, from politics to love. These gab groups are composed of my motley contemporaries who are perched upon that same precarious brink of discovery that I find myself upon. It is all new and excitingly different.

I guess that I have inherited that extemporaneous gift for gab that my illustrious 'pop' has."

The summer after her freshman year she raised money for the Mississippi project, worked at the Saks Fifth Avenue store in San Francisco, then went to Washington to help on the Democratic platform committee under the direction of Fred Dutton. "Being in that international political hotbed made my head spin and what's more convinced me that I must go back there after graduation and work for the government," she wrote Uncle Lou. "Once again the 'father' in me crept out of its hiding place."

Her brother wrote letters to Uncle Lou, too. Jerry was a not particularly diligent student with eclectic interests. At Yale, he took classes in Roman law, psychiatry and the law (taught by Anna Freud), and secured financing, which he found absorbing. "This is a new field for me and quite fascinating," he wrote to Uncle Lou in an annual appeal for tuition assistance. "Don't tell my father, but I'm finding these financing problems as interesting as politics. Who knows, I might even become a banker."

Jerry followed California politics closely from New Haven, requesting from his parents clips about political events and subscriptions to the *San Francisco Chronicle* and *Examiner*. He did not advertise his connections—his close friend Tony Kline, who lived in the same entryway, did not realize for several months that Pat was Jerry's father—but did not hesitate to use them, either. When Yale students were recruited to help in Mississippi in 1963, Jerry went but stayed only a few days. The level of fear he witnessed was so strong he thought it prudent to check in for protection with Governor Ross Barnett, a Democrat but a committed segregationist. Jerry wrote his father repeatedly on behalf of a South African doctor and antiapartheid activist who faced extradition and needed a waiver of a Justice Department rule. "Would you please be sure to do something as soon as possible," he wrote, urging Pat to contact Attorney General Robert Kennedy. "I know this is a minor detail in comparison to the hundred and one problems that are facing you now, but I think it is worth your doing whatever you can."

In the summer of 1964, Pat faced his own civil rights battle. With his ingrained sense of equality, Pat had pushed during his first term to establish a Fair Employment Practices Commission to police discrimination in the workplace. In 1963, he proudly signed the Rumford Fair Housing Act, named after its sponsor, William Byron Rumford, a Berkeley pharmacist who had been the first black elected official from Northern

Pat Brown passed on to his family his love of the outdoors. He and Jerry hiked in Desolation Wilderness, which straddles the Sierra Nevada. (Courtesy of the office of Governor Edmund G. Brown Jr.)

California. The act outlawed discrimination by landlords on the basis of race or ethnicity, though it had been watered down to exempt single-family homes not financed with government-backed loans, and apartment dwellings of fewer than five units. The real estate industry immediately launched an effort to nullify the law through an initiative, framed as a crusade to protect property rights. Proposition 14 easily qualified for the November 1964 ballot. The campaign was a thinly veiled appeal to prejudice, wrapped up in Californians' fierce attachment to property. Homeowners, Prop 14 supporters declared, should be able to sell or rent to anyone they chose. Their slogan was "A Man's Home Is His Castle."

"In any California vote where human rights conflict with what people choose to call 'property rights'—in this case the right to discriminate—property will win," observed Wallace Stegner. "It will win because from the multi-million-dollar development corporations to the littlest tract dweller with a GI loan, the state is property-crazy."

Proponents of the Rumford Act portrayed the Prop 14 supporters as right-wing, out of touch, and opposed to basic civil rights. Dozens of officials of both parties and mainstream organizations urged a no vote. The Unitarian Church campaigned to save the Rumford Act, only the second time the church had adopted a political stance since the Civil War. The moral issue seemed so clear-cut to Pat that he did not hesitate to call Proposition 14 supporters bigots. Some advisers grimaced, aware that the term would antagonize middle-class whites who saw themselves as belea-guered homeowners, not racists. Pat campaigned the way he always did, sure that if he could just reach people, one by one, he could win them over. By Election Day, he was realistic about the prospects. But he was shaken by the two-to-one margin of defeat. The results revealed deep fissures that would only harden in coming months. "You could draw but one conclusion from the vote on 14 and that is that the white is just afraid of the Negro," Pat wrote to Kathleen a week after the election. "The Negroes have a long way to go before there is any acceptance by the white majority in our state. There is absolutely no reason to feel this way about it, but it is something that all of the eloquence in the world cannot change."

The 1964 elections brought other harbingers that California was on the leading edge of a political transformation. In California's GOP presiden-tial primary, conservative candidate Barry Goldwater defeated New York governor Nelson Rockefeller, a moderate Republican in the tradition of Earl Warren. The high point of the Goldwater campaign came in a nation-ally televised speech delivered October 27, 1964, by his surrogate Ronald Reagan, a Hollywood actor who had switched party allegiance a scant two years earlier. Reagan's thirty-minute address, "A Time to Choose," articulated basic conservative principles: Government was bloated and meddlesome, taxes were too high, Communism was a serious threat. The speech was an immediate hit. *Washington Post* columnist David Broder called it "the most successful national political debut since William Jennings Bryan electrified the 1896 Democratic convention with the 'Cross of Gold' speech." By the time Reagan spoke to the elec-tion night crowd at the Ambassador Hotel in Los Angeles, he was the conservatives' rising star and presumptive candidate for governor two years hence.

In Northern California, events were unfolding that would provide Reagan with his most potent rallying cry in that gubernatorial campaign. The hub of campus protest had shifted from Stanford fifty miles north to Berkeley, the school and city whose name would become synonymous with student rebellion.

Like their Stanford counterparts, Cal students had increasingly been caught up in the civil rights movement. In the early 1960s, campus branches of the Student Nonviolent Coordinating Committee (SNCC) and Congress of Racial Equality (CORE) organized protests that focused on bias in hiring. With pickets and sit-ins, students drew attention to the increased discrimination that had followed a shift in the Bay Area economy as San Francisco transitioned from an industrial center to a financial and tourist mecca. Blacks who had been able to find work in manufacturing and industry were denied the more visible jobs in banks, hotels, stores, and restaurants. Picket lines by Cal students that targeted well-known businesses like Mel's Drive-In, Lucky grocery stores, and the Palace Hotel raised political consciousness on campus in ways that would help fuel the coming struggles.

Students had some reason to believe their protests would be supported by Pat Brown and University of California president Clark Kerr, outspoken civil rights advocates. "I say: Thank God for the spectacle of students picketing—even when they are picketing me at Sacramento and I think they are wrong," Pat said in a 1961 commencement speech at Santa Clara University. "The colleges have become boot camps for citizenship." When hundreds of students were arrested for blocking the entrance to the Palace Hotel in San Francisco, the governor and Kerr defended the students' rights to practice civil disobedience.

Kerr and the Regents had liberalized several rules, including an earlier ban on controversial speakers that had blocked such mainstream leaders as presidential candidate Adlai Stevenson from speaking on campus. In 1963, the Regents revoked a ban on Communist speakers and allowed student groups to invite speakers without permission from the administration. Carl Schorske, Jerry's professor, moderated a conversation with the first American Communist invited to speak on campus. But the university continued to make a distinction between free speech and political advocacy. The infamous Rule 17 banned students on school property from collecting money for political causes or soliciting participation in demonstrations—activities that had become central to the increasingly politicized students.

The battle that birthed the Free Speech Movement began, on its surface, with a bureaucratic tussle. Student groups had traditionally used an area just outside a campus gate to solicit for political causes. When the university took that land for a new building, Kerr proposed that students shift to a small area at the intersection of Bancroft and Telegraph on land the university would donate to the city. As students returned to school in September 1964, they were informed the land had never been transferred and political advocacy was banned. Student leaders, fresh from the Mississippi summer, imbued with passion for fighting injustice and sophistication about the mechanics of orchestrating protests, reacted with outrage.

On September 30, 1964, student political groups set up tables in Sproul Plaza, the entryway to campus. Five student leaders were told to report to the Dean's Office for disciplinary action. More than three hundred showed up. The following day the chancellor announced eight students would be suspended indefinitely. As students assembled to protest, a campus police officer arrested Jack Weinberg, a recent Cal graduate manning the CORE table, and placed him in a police car. Hundreds of students swarmed the car, lying down in front and behind. A charismatic student leader named Mario Savio removed his shoes, jumped on top of the car, and enumerated their demands: The university must drop all disciplinary actions and agree to meet with students to revise the freedom of speech regulations. "I am right now publicly serving a notice of warning, and I should say, threat, to this administration they will be subject to continuous direct action by us, and it's going to be damn embarrassing for them. We're going to get foreign press, we're going to get domestic press, we're going to get all sorts of organizations against them until they accede to these legitimate demands."

Savio, a junior and a philosophy major, led dozens of students into Sproul Hall, where they blocked egress and trapped the deans inside. A group of faculty members attempted to mediate between students and administration, periodically updating the crowd. By late afternoon, demonstrators voted by acclamation to withdraw from Sproul Hall but continue to surround the police car until charges against the original eight students were dropped.

The governor's reaction was not sympathetic. "This is not a matter of freedom of speech on the campuses," Pat said that afternoon after a speech in San Francisco. "This will not be tolerated. We must have—and will continue to have—law and order on our campuses."

By evening, the crowd in Sproul Plaza had swelled to more than twenty-five hundred, alternately shouting, singing, and swearing. The roof of the police car sagged as speaker after speaker used it as a platform to address the crowd. Savio urged calm as fraternity brothers threw eggs and burning cigarettes at the demonstrators. The sun rose on a plaza strewn with sleeping bags, books, blankets, and debris, the lone police car still stranded in the middle. Thousands more joined the crowd as negotiations continued and police began to mass around the perimeter of the campus.

Around seven thirty P.M., Savio mounted the police car one more time to read the agreement that had been reached: Students would refrain from illegal activity; a committee of students, faculty, and administrators would make recommendations on political activity on campus; the university would not press charges against Weinberg; and the proposed suspension of the other students would be submitted to a committee of the Academic Senate for review. The next day, the new student organization was formally announced as the Free Speech Movement.

For a month, an uneasy truce prevailed, punctuated by occasional sit-ins and rallies. Students set up tables and violated regulations with only sporadic, minimal enforcement. The Regents modified rules to permit fundraising and recruitment, but they refused to clear the records of those sanctioned in recent months. Unexpectedly, over the Thanksgiving break, the chancellor informed four students, including Savio, that they would be disciplined for their actions back in October.

On December 2, hundreds of students gathered in the plaza and Savio addressed them from the steps of Sproul Hall: "There is a time when the operation of the machine becomes so odious, makes you so sick at heart, that you can't take part, you can't even tacitly take part, and you've got to put your bodies upon the gears and upon the wheels, upon the levers, upon all the apparatus, and you've got to make it stop. And you've got to indicate to the people who run it, to the people who own it, that unless you're free, the machine will be prevented from working at all."

As Joan Baez sang "We Shall Overcome" and a song recently written by Bob Dylan, "The Times They Are a-Changin'," almost eight hundred students rushed into Sproul Hall. With blankets, books, and food, they settled in for a well-organized, orderly occupation of the administration building. The fourth floor was designated for quiet study, the second floor for classes and showing movies.

Kerr, a Quaker and a labor mediator, favored police intervention only as a last resort. While he did not condone the students' actions, he understood why they felt betrayed. He spoke twice with the governor, who was in Los Angeles at a gala hospital fundraiser headlined by Frank Sinatra and Bob Hope. Pat agreed to wait until the morning and then accompany Kerr into Sproul Hall to try to negotiate a peaceful end. Hours later, an inspector from the California Highway Patrol and Assistant Alameda County District Attorney Ed Meese reached out and told Pat the situation was out of control. They urged him to send in state police. Pat agreed, without consulting Kerr. He was, as he said often, a former law enforcement official who believed laws must be obeyed.

Police stormed Sproul Hall around three in the morning and over the next twelve hours carried out more than six hundred students, dragging their limp bodies one by one down flights of stairs as cameras rolled and the crowd sang "We Shall Not Be Moved" and "Ain't Gonna Let Governor Brown Turn Me 'Round." Of the 735 people arrested, all but 47 were students, 80 percent of them undergraduates.

"It isn't often that a great university suddenly goes smash, yet this is what happened to the Berkeley campus during the first week of December, 1964," Sheldon Wolin, one of the faculty leaders who supported the students, wrote a few weeks later. "Campus authority vanished, academic routines were reduced to a shambles, and the prophecy of Mario Savio was fulfilled: the 'machine' came to a 'grinding halt.'"

Wolin, who helped craft the resolutions that brought the machine back to life, argued that the Free Speech Movement "rediscovered" the democratic political process. The students were idealistic and nonviolent. In pictures of the October sit-in, the policeman was smiling. The Faculty Senate's support of the students was instrumental in persuading the administration to back down. An angry, divided Board of Regents finally accepted Kerr's recommendation to endorse the faculty resolutions, which included amnesty and broadening free speech to include political activity. After a week of strikes and strife, some semblance of normality resumed.

Pat Brown was hurt, outraged, bewildered. He could not comprehend why students who should be grateful had flouted the law. He lacked advisers who might have helped him understand the students' alienation and rage, which would soon intensify and turn against the war in Vietnam and the university's role in scientific research for military purposes. "What had been peaceful demonstrations, which I have always protected, had turned into violations of state law and the actual threat of anarchy," Pat wrote to the many constituents who questioned his actions. "I took a strong stand to preserve law and order; but I have been working just as hard to guarantee that the students on campus are not denied their civil liberties."

Student grievances broadened into an attack on what they dubbed the "knowledge factory," a research-oriented institution where undergraduates could easily spend four years without speaking directly to a professor. "These students broke the rules and the law in an agonizing effort to compel an Administration which, by its unwillingness to listen to their just claims and to treat them as participating members of a community of the intellect, inevitably brought about its own moral downfall and forfeited its claim to willing obedience," Wolin wrote.

One of Wolin's former students, Jerry Brown, had a ringside seat to the unfolding student protests. Through a mutual friend, he had arranged a phone call between his father and Savio early in the confrontation. The conversation resolved little. Though Jerry empathized with the portrayal of Berkeley as a mechanistic knowledge factory, he, like his father, had little tolerance for unlawful protests. Jerry had graduated from Yale and started work in the fall of 1964 as a clerk to Mathew Tobriner, whom Pat had elevated to the California Supreme Court. An esteemed judge who had his pick of clerks in a highly competitive process, Tobriner accepted Jerry at once when his friend's son requested one of the coveted positions.

"He has a thoughtful mind and an original point of view; he has a fine and contagious enthusiasm and a sensitive feeling of obligation to his community. He is a liberal in the best sense," Tobriner wrote to Pat. "I will consider it a privilege to have him with me, and I think we will have lots of fun together."

For part of his clerkship, Jerry shared the ground floor of a Victorian house in Berkeley with his law school friend Tony Kline, also a Supreme Court clerk. Most of their Yale classmates were from the East Coast, and historically the path from Yale law had led to a New York firm or a clerkship. National firms did not yet have offices in California, but Los Angeles firms like O'Melveny & Myers began to show up on the East Coast radar. Jerry's class of 1964 broke tradition when a significant number of graduates took jobs in California, in part because of interest in the largest state at the forefront of the 1960s revolutions, and in part because the

California Supreme Court had established a reputation as arguably the best in the country.

Tobriner, key to that reputation, found his new clerk more like Bernice than Pat, a quick-witted loner. His work showed a willingness to improvise and a reluctance to be bound by precedent. He earned another distinction, as the only one of Tobriner's clerks to fail the bar exam. Jerry had not bothered to study much. His father arranged for tutoring and settled his son in a third-floor bedroom of the Governor's Mansion. He took the exam again in March, and passed.

On June 14, 1965, Pat and Bernice sat in the front row of Veterans Memorial Auditorium in San Francisco to watch their son sworn in to the California bar. "It's a big day in his life," Pat said, "and it is a big day in mine." Asked about his future plans, Jerry said: "I have some political ambitions, when the time is right."

He did not explain until many decades later the moment in the Mansion that had triggered those ambitions. While studying for the bar, a task he found tedious, Jerry would wander out onto the stair landing to eavesdrop on conversations downstairs. One day, he overheard his father engaged in a heated dispute with Assembly Speaker Jesse Unruh, a Democrat who had become an adversary rather than an ally. Unruh argued that it was his turn to run for governor in 1966. Pat denied he had ever agreed to step down after two terms. The conversation was about power. Jerry found it riveting.

Pat, determined to run for a third term in part to block Unruh, knew he would face a difficult campaign. In August 1965, he and Bernice set off on a month-long European summer vacation that would be his last long respite. So it happened that when another California city became a symbol of protest and mayhem, the governor was in Greece.

Among the many things that had increased along with the explosive growth in Southern California were income inequality and de facto segregation. By 1965, the poor were concentrated in a heavily black swath of south Los Angeles, while the white middle class moved farther and farther from the center, to self-contained suburban enclaves. In four communities in the center of the city, seventy-five thousand whites moved out between 1950 and 1960, and more than a hundred thousand blacks moved in.

Between 1940 and 1965, the population of Los Angeles County tripled, while the black population increased almost tenfold. Many came from the South seeking the promise of the Golden State and found instead restrictive housing covenants, racist police, and jobs that were claimed by returning veterans. By 1965, the map of heavily black neighborhoods and the map of poverty had largely the same contours. Two thirds of the approximately 650,000 blacks in Los Angeles lived in and around the community of Watts, which had become almost 90 percent black. As families crammed into dilapidated housing projects, density increased, unemployment among men climbed to 35 percent, and the median income declined. Two thirds of the students did not graduate from high school. The population was young, poor, and disillusioned. The passage of Prop 14 had reinforced whites' commitment to segregation, one more effort to roll back the gains that had been made during the war.

The sprawling, carcentric geography and culture of Los Angeles added problems not found in other urban ghettos. Los Angeles had the worst public transportation system of any major city, leaving the carless with extremely limited options for shopping, entertainment, or basic services. Neighborhood stores sold outdated food at inflated prices. A pediatrician in Watts saw patients in groups to accommodate his caseload of ten thousand. Because most people in Los Angeles drove, and there was little reason for nonresidents to drive through Watts, poor people in the center of the city became largely invisible. Their physical and social isolation made their rising anger and desperation easy to ignore.

That indifference was shattered by a sequence of events that began with a police stop in Watts on Thursday, August 12, 1965. A fight broke out after a black motorist was arrested for drunk driving. A crowd gathered, accusations of police brutality spread, and violence escalated. Residents, who had long complained about police harassment, pelted officers with rocks and concrete chunks. Skirmishes continued through the night. A meeting the next morning failed to calm the crowds. Los Angeles police chief William Parker asked for a thousand National Guard troops. Hale Champion, Pat's finance director, reached the governor in Athens and told him to come home as quickly as possible.

For several days, Watts was torched and looted, mobs roamed the streets, and shots rang out as National Guard troops struggled to gain control. Fires were visible miles away. Scenes that resembled foreign war zones filled television screens. Traditional sources of leadership in the black community, such as churches and the NAACP, were based outside Watts in more affluent areas and largely rejected by the community. Martin Luther King Jr. came to Watts during the riots, and he was booed.

Pat reached Los Angeles late Saturday night after a twenty-four-hour journey, during which he used layovers in Rome, New York, and Omaha to talk with state and federal officials. He toured Watts on Sunday and held a news conference. "Most of us, whatever our race, now stand hesitantly between fear and hope," he noted, "not only in Los Angeles, but in New York, in Philadelphia, in Chicago, in Detroit—all across the land . . . it is here in Los Angeles, however, that fear seems closest and hope the most distant at this hour—here that the greatest toll of riot, arson and bloodshed in our nation's recent history haunts our minds and hearts, clouds our vision and briefly blights our faith in ourselves and in our neighbors." He added a heartfelt caution: "While poverty is no excuse for violence, let us remember, too, that violence is no excuse for indifference to poverty."

By Monday, there were thirteen thousand National Guard troops in the curfew area, and the worst of the rioting was over. On Tuesday, the National Guard began to withdraw. By the end of the week, there had been four thousand arrests. Five hundred buildings were burned and looted, with damages estimated at $40 million. More than a thousand people were wounded. Thirty-four died.

William Warne, the director of the California Department of Water Resources, saw images on television that reminded him of scenes he had witnessed when he worked in Iran and Korea, mobs that had "slipped all restraints . . . young men and women smashing windows and setting fires; children laughing as they and their mothers carried home loot." Warne felt so strongly about the need for a government project to address the underlying causes of the disturbance that he proposed taking on that task and handing off the water project. "People said plainly, if inarticulately, that they saw the privileges around them but had no contact with the people who enjoyed them, and they resented that of which they were not a part," Warne wrote to the governor. "Why is it that the American genius is able to diagnose the ills of others and to prescribe and apply remedies, but has not recognized, let alone treated, the illness at home?"

Pat did not take him up on the offer. He appointed a high-level commission and dispatched his top aide for human rights, Bill Becker, to the riot area. Becker had grown up in New Jersey and taken a job organizing farmworkers in the San Joaquin Valley in 1948 when his child's health required a hot, dry climate. He went on to work for the Jewish Labor Committee in San Francisco and formed a coalition that lobbied for civil rights legislation, including the Rumford Act. After its passage, Pat hired Becker. In Watts, Becker spent weeks in conversations and meetings before filing a report. "Although they express many different grievances and have a variety of attitudes toward the riot, these people reflected an almost universal *bitterness* toward the 'establishment,' both white and Negro," Becker wrote to the governor. "They do not feel beaten or humbled, but rather more self-confident and even more united."

Becker concluded that their anger focused on the police in part because that was the only government agency most people encountered. They complained about Los Angeles mayor Sam Yorty and Police Chief Parker, about being overcharged by discourteous shopkeepers for inferior produce, about slum landlords and streets that were cleaned only before elections. The teenagers talked about rats eating popcorn around their feet and running across the screen during movies. They described libraries with so few books they were useless for school assignments. Becker summed up their feelings: "We want the kind of life the white man has."

The commission chaired by former CIA director John McCone held hearings, took testimony, and issued a report that pleased no one. The report was criticized as too lenient by conservatives who favored harsher law enforcement and denounced by liberals who argued it glossed over underlying causes of the riot and downplayed racism. The U.S. Commission on Civil Rights said the recommendations were for "aspirin where surgery is required."

Pat understood the political consequences as he headed into an election year. "The white backlash is understandably very severe and a governor must in every utterance he makes maintain the rule of law," Pat wrote to the columnist Drew Pearson. "On the other hand, I have a deep and, I hope, understanding sympathy for the Negro and would rather not be reelected Governor than to let them think some of the white people do not appreciate the terrible problems of poverty and prejudice."

By Thanksgiving, it was clear that Pat would face a campaign in which "Berkeley" and "Watts" were shorthand for a state out of control. Pat put that aside as four generations of Browns gathered at the Mansion for the traditional turkey dinner. "We have an awful lot to be thankful for," Pat said, surrounded by his eighty-seven-year-old mother, his three daughters, and their families, including eight grandchildren. "The turkey's bigger than you are," Pat said to the youngest, newborn Hilary Rice.

Hilary was the daughter of Kathleen. In 1964, the fall of Kathleen's sophomore year at Stanford, she had reconnected with a junior she had known in high school in Sacramento, George A. Rice III, known as Jeep. Kathleen had volunteered to canvass for President Lyndon Johnson in the largely Mexican American neighborhood of East San Jose, and she invited Jeep to come along. He was just back from a year studying in France that had turned him from a nominal Republican into a liberal Democrat, and the heady atmosphere of Stanford was pulling him further left. He came from a family of educators who had attended and taught at Cal. Like Kathleen, he had defied tradition by choosing Stanford. He, too, had liked the challenge, one of only three in his high school class admitted. He was prelaw. They quickly became a couple. Like her parents, Kathleen decided to elope. Just as Pat and Bernice had done, Kathleen and Jeep were married in Nevada. Like her parents' elopement, Kathleen's marriage was front page news, with a photo of the couple on skis at an impromptu reception at the Lake Tahoe chalet where the family was staying. As the Laynes had done, the Browns welcomed their new son-in-law despite the surprise announcement. When Hilary was born, the photogenic baby quickly became the youngest member of the family to live in the public spotlight, showing up with her grandfather in photos during budget deliberations and campaign literature. When Kathleen turned twenty-one and registered to vote, Hilary shared the photo in the *Sacramento Bee*.

Kathleen would cast her first vote in what shaped up to be her father's toughest race. On January 4, 1966, Ronald Reagan formally opened his campaign for governor with a scathing critique of moral decay and disorder in California, couched in optimistic tones. "Our problems are many," he said, "but our capacity for solving them is limitless." Reagan faced a primary challenge from an established politician and moderate Republican, San Francisco mayor George Christopher. In the first of many political miscalculations, the Brown team covertly sabotaged Christopher, believing the inexperienced actor would be an easier opponent. Reagan, an amiable, conservative outsider unencumbered by political ties, a fresh face with a strong television presence, was the ideal foil to Pat Brown.

Two-term governors have accumulated baggage. They have said no to too many people, or, in Pat's case, he had said yes to too many people and then failed to deliver. He so hated to disappoint people that they often left his office believing they had his support, only to discover later that an opposing party believed the same thing. Pat's feud with Assembly Speaker Unruh meant the governor's agenda had been largely stymied. The defense industry was battered by cuts, housing starts were down, unemployment was up, and the governor was blamed. Pat was pilloried by the right for Berkeley and Watts and derided as a supporter of minorities at the expense of the white majority. He was abandoned by the left for his handling of student protests and his support for President Johnson and the increasingly unpopular war in Vietnam. Pat Brown was a creature of the 1950s fighting to stay alive in a radically different decade.

"The Watts problem is likely to have more effect on the November election than all your TV spots and local campaign appearances combined," Fred Dutton wrote Pat in May 1966. "For many people the situation will unconsciously but inevitably be a prime test of how effective a governor you now really are." The second time Pat called and asked for his help, Dutton put his private Washington law practice on hold and flew out to California, though he suspected it was too late. He found a governor who had grown more comfortable, less creative, and less hungry, no longer the scrappy Irish kid from South of Market and now the established politician chauffeured in black limousines. Pat was still lovable, gregarious, and prone to very human gaffes. He had always been an easy target to caricature and proudly displayed the framed cartoons on his wall. Now his verbal missteps were used against him, objects of ridicule, derided by Reagan as "Brownisms."

Pat faced a primary challenge from Sam Yorty, a conservative known for red-baiting, race-baiting, and opposing progressive causes such as recycling. Nominally a Democrat, the Los Angeles mayor had openly supported Nixon over Kennedy in 1960. In the primary, Yorty won a substantial 37 percent of the Democratic vote, further weakening Pat. Demoralized, the governor took a few days off to go fishing.

Dutton saw the primary results as a warning, not just for California. He wrote to Bill Moyers, a senior White House official, to impress upon the Johnson administration the national implications of the California contest. Contrary to the East Coast view, Dutton pointed out, California "has followed national voting trends throughout this century with startling closeness." The state's voters were a mix from all regions, and included the highest proportion of young voters, who would be key in the 1968 presidential election. Though Lyndon Johnson and Pat Brown differed significantly in personality, both came from an older generation. Neither was wearing well as the country underwent "a major political cultural water-shed," Dutton wrote. He warned that for liberal Democrats, Vietnam had become the overriding issue. "They feel more intensely about this issue than anything since the mid-1930s and cannot be taken for granted or disregarded without lasting consequence."

Pat's failure to understand the importance of symbolism had undercut his support with another small but important constituency, Mexican Americans. By 1966, the civil rights struggle in California had become most visible in an unlikely venue, the impoverished farmworker towns and labor camps that dotted the length of the Central Valley. The Mexican American civil rights movement gained prominence first in the fields, and the face of *la causa* was Cesar Chavez, the improbable charismatic leader.

Chavez began in the fields because that was the world he knew best; he had come to California as a twelve-year-old in a migrant family that had lost its Arizona ranch at the end of the Depression. Farmworkers were excluded from virtually all labor, health, and safety laws, underpaid, fired at will, treated like just another farm implement. It was the loss of dignity and the lack of respect as much as the physical and economic hardship that drove Chavez's anger, and when he grasped the potential of community organizing, he leaped at the opportunity to force change.

He had a ten-year apprenticeship working for and then directing the first grassroots organization for Mexican Americans, the Community Service Organization, founded in Los Angeles in 1947. His first experience with farmworkers and labor came in 1959 in Oxnard, just north of Los Angeles, when he fought to win jobs for local workers who were being illegally passed over in favor of Mexican guest workers. His ally was the newly elected governor, who dispatched labor officials to help. Two years later, Pat Brown proudly signed a law that had been the CSO's top priority for several years, making noncitizens eligible for state-funded old age pensions. He would later cite the bill as one of the things he felt best about—the state rectified a historic injustice and provided a little money for people who had earned it, an action that would change their lives.

The victories in organizing field workers in Oxnard propelled Chavez to leave the CSO and set out on his own in 1962 with the quixotic goal of forming a union for farmworkers. By 1965, he was leading what would be a five-year strike in the vineyards of the San Joaquin Valley, challenging the most powerful industry in the state. He took lessons and gained volunteers from the civil rights movement, and he understood, just as Allard Lowenstein had understood in Mississippi, that it was the eyes and voice and power of outsiders that would be needed to win. He didn't just invite outsiders to the union's headquarters in Delano, in the heart of the San Joaquin Valley; he brought the struggle to them. In the spring of 1966, Chavez led farmworkers on a three-hundred-mile pilgrimage from Delano to Sacramento, walking along Highway 99 up the spine of the valley, with a rally every night in a different town. The images told the story. Chavez, limping. The banner of Our Lady of Guadalupe, patron saint of Mexicans, leading the march. Farmworkers doing what they could never have imagined, walking along the highway proudly waving a union flag. The march swelled at each stop until thousands massed in the park outside the state capitol on Easter Sunday. They demanded to see the governor.

Pat had made plans to spend Easter with his family at the Palm Springs home of Frank Sinatra. Jerry argued that his father should go to Sacramento. Pat refused to change his plans; Easter vacation in the desert oasis had become a family tradition. He offered to meet on Saturday or Monday. Chavez declined. He would meet on his terms or not at all. Chavez thrived on having a good enemy, and the governor's absence only made the rally stronger.

A few months later, Pat interceded in a matter of far greater consequence to Chavez. The farmworkers had targeted the DiGiorgio Company, the largest grower in the San Joaquin Valley, urging consumers to boycott DiGiorgio produce until the company recognized the union and negotiated a contract. Pat prevailed on his former neighbor Robert DiGiorgio, whose daughter had accompanied the Browns to Europe and been a guest at the inaugural ball, to allow the state to conduct an election to see if workers wanted union representation. Pat appointed a special mediator, who proposed ground rules that gave Chavez's union a fighting chance. The victory in the first secret-ballot election for farmworkers was an enormous boost for Chavez and the union's credibility.

As governor, Pat appointed Mexican Americans as judges, commissioners, and staff, in all about sixty-five appointments, compared with only three during the four terms of his Republican predecessors. The Viva Pat Brown campaign literature in 1966 included endorsements from key Mexican American leaders, including Chavez: "In its first statewide political endorsement, our union has unanimously voted to support the reelection of Governor Brown . . . Governor Brown made history in bringing about the first free and open representation elections for farm workers in the history of agriculture in America." But the lasting image was of a governor relaxing in Palm Springs while the pilgrims rallied outside his office in the capitol.

"I've had a rough campaign out here and I've got my work cut out for me," Pat told President Johnson in a phone call after the June primary. He described Reagan as "part of the kook crowd in the United States. He's to the right of Goldwater." Johnson tried to be reassuring. "I know all your weaknesses and all your disadvantages but I don't want you to point them out because you're selling everyone on the fact that you can't win. I think we got to get our tail up, get bushy tailed and chin up, and let's go."

The Democrats' attempt to paint Reagan as a know-nothing actor and a kook backfired, at odds with the genial, reasonable-seeming candidate the public saw. Reagan's political consultants turned his lack of experience into a positive. They billed him as a citizen politician whose ignorance of state issues was a refreshing counterpoint to the career politician. Working-class Democrats defected, embracing the outsider image that would soon gain national appeal. In 1958, Pat had been supported by 78 percent of white union members and their families. Against Reagan, his support dropped by 20 points.

In Democrats' polls, the word "Berkeley" consistently elicited the strongest negative response. Berkeley meant drugs, hippies, lack of order, sit-ins, and antiwar protests. "Clean up the mess at Berkeley" became a Reagan slogan and applause line. He received fresh ammunition in May 1966 when the state Senate Subcommittee on Un-American Activities issued a report that blamed Clark Kerr and liberals for turning Berkeley into what Reagan called "a rallying point for Communists and a center of sexual misconduct."

The same month, the California Supreme Court struck down Proposition 14, which had gutted the fair housing law. Ruling in a suit brought by the NAACP, the court declared that Prop 14 violated the Equal Protection Clause of the Fourteenth Amendment of the U.S. Constitution. When the decision was appealed to the U.S. Supreme Court, both Pat and his friend Tom Lynch, the attorney general, refused to defend Proposition 14. Reagan pledged to find a way to overturn the Rumford Fair Housing Act, a bad law, he said, that "invaded one of our most basic and cherished rights—a right held by all our citizens—the right to dispose of property to whom we see fit and as we see fit."

Liberal voters who should have applauded Pat's commitment to fair housing instead deserted him over his refusal to denounce the escalating Vietnam War. The draft ratcheted up, and so did protests on campuses, where student deferments were no longer automatic. Only students who scored high enough on a test designed by the Selective Service, or had grades that translated into a sufficiently high college rank, would be exempt. At Stanford, David Harris led a three-day occupation of the president's office to protest the testing policy. Pat tried to duck the issue by saying Vietnam was a national problem. But when pressed, he supported the president. He was booed at the convention of the California Democratic Council. *Ramparts* magazine ran a cover with Reagan and Brown labeled Tweedledum and Tweedledee.

Friends and family tried to help. Longtime supporters hosted star-studded fundraisers. Jerry, who had recently moved to Los Angeles, spent some time in the campaign office. Tony Kline stayed with his law school friend for a few months while he headed Young Democrats for Brown. Bernice campaigned and discussed substantive issues for the first time. She had become an early conservationist, warning people to "guard your environment" and protect the state's natural beauty. She cited predictions that the state's population would double to 38 million by 2000. "That means double everything—homes, schools, libraries, freeways. It's almost frightening. We have to prepare for this tremendous increase in population." She was optimistic that Californians were starting to think beyond their narrow self-interest: "I think people have really developed an environmental conscience."

By the final week of the campaign, Pat looked unusually grim as he took his seat on the dais at the candidate forum sponsored by Pacific Gas & Electric, the state's largest utility. Chairman Robert Gerdes remarked that they had started together as young lawyers but Pat beat him to the bar by one year. "He has kept well ahead of me since that time in all respects except one: I have an easier time getting reelected than he does." Pat burst into his trademark infectious guffaws, mouth wide open, head tilted back.

Then he stood up with his big binder and read a speech that was, like most of the campaign, defensive. "I have to base my campaign against him on three things," he said, then caught himself, too late: "Not against him—my own campaign." Reagan would end free tuition at the university. He would cut down trees. How could the people trust someone who had no experience at all, a motion picture actor?

When it was Reagan's turn, he was introduced as "the boy next door" who "made good on everything he took on in life." Relaxed, occasionally consulting note cards, he spoke of a new spirit and ridiculed Pat as a career politician: "I've never held public office—and he's never held any other kind of job." Reagan said his aides had asked if they should go around and tape Pat's speeches, the way Pat had aides follow Reagan around with a recorder. "I agreed on one condition: that I don't have to listen." He received a standing ovation.

On Election Day, Pat asked his son-in-law Joe Kelly to set up lunch with a group of his old San Francisco friends at the Merced Golf Club. Afterward, Kelly drove Pat to the airport so he could fly down to Los Angeles to await results. When Pat said he needed to stop en route to visit his mother, Kelly knew that Pat had given up hope.

Pat entered the Ambassador Hotel in Los Angeles just after ten o'clock that evening to prolonged cheers, though some in the crowd were already weeping. "The people of California have been very, very good to me. I can only say that I have tried to reciprocate," he said in his concession speech. "We have a fight to keep going. Our principles are right. We lose a battle but we'll win the war." The developer Ben Swig found his friend almost in a daze. Later, Pat would remember Swig's kindness, and his immediate assurance that he would put Pat on retainer as a legal counsel at $10,000 a year for five years, whatever firm he chose to join.

The next morning, a small crowd waiting on the tarmac in Sacramento broke into "For He's a Jolly Good Fellow" as Pat and Bernice stepped off the state plane. Bernice said she was relieved to have the campaign over; Pat was philosophical. In the final count, he lost by almost a million votes, out of 6.5 million ballots cast. The only statewide Democrat who prevailed was his childhood friend Tom Lynch, whom Pat had appointed attorney general when a vacancy occurred in 1964.

People had trouble staying mad at Pat. George Christopher, who had lost the Republican primary in part because of smears by the Brown campaign, wrote to set up a lunch date. "Now that our political careers have ended perhaps we will have a little spare time to see each other and to reminisce about the old days when we were just fledgling aspirants in the political world."

Before he left office, Pat signed a contract with the state's three major utilities to pump the man-made river of water over the Tehachapi Mountains. Bill Warne hurried to finish up as much of the water project as he could; thirty water districts had signed contracts, providing funds to repay the original bonds, although water would not reach the southern San Joaquin Valley until 1968 and Los Angeles a few years later. The governor made a raft of last-minute appointments, filling many judgeships. He promoted his brother Harold to the appellate court; criticism about nepotism no longer mattered.

Of all the letters and telegrams that poured in after the election, one that mattered perhaps the most to Pat came from a Republican, a throwback to the generation that grew up in the Party of California, without partisan elections. "Nina and I voted for you two weeks ago and since then have been praying that there would be enough thinking voters in California to insure your reelection," Earl Warren wrote. The Chief Justice sought to reassure Pat that he was the victim of forces beyond his control:

> You have given our state good, progressive government for eight years and that is all any man could have done . . . Some day the people of California will comprehend just how silly and shallow was the campaign to unseat you, but until that time arrives, I hope you will content yourself with a sense of duty well performed, which in the last analysis is the greatest satisfaction that can come to any public servant.

Pat was always prone to superlatives, which reflected genuine feeling at the moment of the utterance. Every dinner with friends was "the best one yet." His response to Warren reflected a more lasting sentiment: "I think you know that I respect and admire you more than any man I have ever met. To have earned your respect and admiration too, the greatest Governor in California's history, is something that makes all of the effort and all of the troubles (and even the defeat) worthwhile. You were Governor of California longer than any man in its history. I wanted to equal or even better your record, but it just couldn't be done."

11

The Browns of Los Angeles

Though their past life and friendships had been closely tied to Northern California, Pat and Bernice Brown decided to build their future in Los Angeles, a place that seemed to hold the most promise for new beginnings. Pat accepted a position as a rainmaker with Ball, Hunt & Hart, a well-known and politically connected law firm. Bernice found a house she liked atop Benedict Canyon in Beverly Hills, with a pool where Pat could swim and a view of the Santa Monica Mountains that reminded him of Yosemite.

Los Angeles was not like their San Francisco, where everyone knew your parish and your parents and politics was personal. Los Angeles was a city in transition, with an aging Protestant elite and never-ending streams of newcomers, a spreading metropolis where a history of rigid racism was giving way to large emerging ethnic communities and predominantly white suburbs. The vast sprawl, condemned by sociologists and planners, masked the city's kaleidoscope appeal, the sense of movement and openness, the tabula rasa personality that matched the landscape. By the end of the 1960s, Los Angeles had a Mexican American congressman, a viable black candidate for mayor, and Jewish law partners. The geography of dramatic extremes, from the Santa Monica Mountains to the Mojave Desert to the Malibu beaches, attracted settlers and industry: Hollywood, aerospace, science and technology, and a booming port. All had been enticed and nurtured by the sunny, dependable climate. Los Angeles, Carey McWilliams wrote, was "a paradox: a desert that faces an ocean."

People in the Bay Area might regard Southern California with disdain as a cultural wasteland, but people in Los Angeles didn't much care. The city was developing cultural institutions of its own. In 1964, the Dorothy Chandler Pavilion had opened in downtown Los Angeles, anchoring the Music Center that would be home to the Los Angeles Philharmonic and the Los Angeles Opera, familiar to millions from televised Oscar presentations. A year later, the Los Angeles County Museum of Art opened, and two years later the Mark Taper Forum, which premiered groundbreaking theater. The mingling of classes began to break down long-standing cultural barriers. The Music Center was the first institution to integrate Jews into the philanthropic world of greater Los Angeles. The openness to experimentation produced creative collaborations. Frank Zappa and the Mothers of Invention teamed up with Zubin Mehta and the Los Angeles Philharmonic to perform a concert at UCLA.

The Browns' move to Los Angeles marked a symbolic end to the era when the locus of political power was firmly in the Bay Area. The clout of Southern California had been further strengthened when the legislature finally complied with federal court orders and reapportioned the state Senate on the basis of population. In 1966, Los Angeles went from one senator to fourteen. The eight Southern California counties controlled more legislative seats than the other fifty counties combined. More than half of California voters lived in the Los Angeles television market. Among Pat Brown's miscalculations had been underestimating the degree to which political power had shifted south.

His son was not going to repeat that mistake.

Jerry Brown accepted a job at Tuttle & Taylor, a boutique law firm in Los Angeles with a reputation for hiring former U.S. Supreme Court clerks and the highest-achieving law students. The partner who had hand-picked most of the firm's dozen lawyers was Bill Norris, a gregarious optimist who loved the law, politics, and public service. Norris was the fourth lawyer when he joined the firm in 1956, the same year Warren Christopher brought Norris to Adlai Stevenson's headquarters and introduced him to Fred Dutton. Norris became active in the California Democratic Council and was appointed by Pat Brown to the Board of Education and then the Board of Trustees for the California State University system. He viewed Pat as a mentor, and when he heard his son was looking for a job in Los Angeles, Norris reached out to Jerry.

Tuttle & Taylor had about a dozen lawyers when Jerry arrived in March 1966. Eli Chernow, who joined at the same time, was a more typical hire. He had grown up in the San Fernando Valley after his parents moved from Pittsburgh, drawn like so many by the promised health benefits of the warm, dry climate. They ran an upholstery business and settled in North Hollywood, delighted to find a house with a big yard and five fruit trees. Chernow joined the Young Democrats at Hollywood High School and then formed a chapter when he attended Caltech. Bill Norris met Chernow when he was active in the 1960 campaign, tracked him through Harvard Law School, and offered him a job. Chernow admired Norris's commitment to a life that combined law with public service, a value Tuttle & Taylor embraced. The firm's average of sixteen hundred billable hours per lawyer per year, far below the demands of larger corporate firms, left plenty of time for outside interests.

Tuttle & Taylor's thirteenth-floor office was at the top of a 1925 terra-cotta and enameled brick building at the corner of Sixth and Grand, a Spanish Romanesque structure designed by the architectural firm of Walker & Eisen, whose work dominated the 1920s Art Deco building boom that shaped downtown Los Angeles. Around the corner was the Yorkshire Grill, the office hangout and lunch spot. Jerry was notorious for never having any money. His colleagues found him smart, unconventional, and inquisitive. He had reverted to night-owl hours and was as likely to be found in the office at three A.M. as at three P.M. He arrived for meetings at the last minute, rushing down the hallway, tie flying behind him as he struggled into his jacket. He often filed papers right on deadline, racing to the courthouse in the old white Chevy Malibu that his father had given him as a consolation present when he failed the bar exam. Gloria Lujan, one of the secretaries, had to slide over and out the driver's side to run up the courthouse steps because the passenger side door was tied on with rope. Lujan was about the same age as Jerry, and she appreciated his curiosity, candor, and lack of pretense. Her parents were Mexican American, and Jerry often asked about their views.

Los Angeles did not become a magnet for young people nor a symbol of the counterculture in the same way as San Francisco, where the Summer of Love in 1967 ushered in cultural and social change that lasted long after LSD became illegal, the Grateful Dead left Haight-Ashbury, and psychedelic rock went mainstream. But the spirit of protest, liberation, and experimentation permeated Southern California as well. Lujan and the other women in the office joined the National Organization for Women soon after it was founded in October 1966. Their workplace protests were small and well received. One day all the women wore pant-suits. They ended the ritual of fetching coffee for their bosses when they arrived each morning. They attended rallies and demonstrations, for the farmworkers and against the war.

As the American bombing campaigns and casualties escalated, the Vietnam War dominated conversations and divided the country, insti-tutions, and families, including the Browns. Pat staunchly supported the president. Jerry opposed the war. Vietnam became the cause that drew him into his first political foray.

By 1967, the civil rights and antiwar movements increasingly over-lapped. Leaders from Martin Luther King Jr. to Allard Lowenstein argued that not only was the war immoral, but the billions of dollars spent on the conflict deprived communities like Watts of the funds needed to combat the pernicious effects of decades of racism. "If we spend thirty-five billion dollars a year to fight an ill-conceived war in Vietnam and twenty billion dollars to put a man on the moon, we can spend billions of dollars to put God's children on their own two feet, right now," King said at Stanford on April 14, 1967, in a speech he called "The Other America." Millions walked the streets looking for jobs that did not exist, he said, "perishing on a lonely island of poverty in the midst of a vast ocean of material prosperity." The struggle for economic equality in an increasingly divided country was harder than the civil rights battles of a decade earlier, King said. "It's much easier to integrate a lunch counter than it is to guarantee a livable income and a good solid job." Then he flew to New York to appear the next day at the Spring Mobilization to End the War in Vietnam, while his wife, Coretta Scott King, addressed the West Coast peace rally in San Francisco.

The California Democratic Council, the grassroots group formed back in 1953, voted at its annual convention to field a Peace Slate in the 1968 presidential primary, with delegates pledged to a cause rather than a candidate. Easterners thought they needed a candidate before building an organization; the California approach was to create the grassroots movement, which would attract a candidate. The strategy, CDC presi-dent Gerald Hill argued, was to demonstrate that President Johnson was so unpopular he could not win reelection.

By fall, the California idea had gained momentum around the country. National Democrats awaited the outcome as twenty-five hundred CDC delegates and observers gathered on September 30, 1967, at the Long Beach Arena. After four hours of debate, delegates approved a resolution that called for a slate pledged to a candidate who promised an immediate end to the bombing of North Vietnam and negotiations to withdraw all American forces. A walkout by blacks was averted with a compromise that included more minority representation on the steering committee and a clause tying the end of war to the struggles of oppressed minorities.

"We are still in control of our destiny. There is still a difference between the right course and the wrong," said economist John Kenneth Galbraith, the national chair of Americans for Democratic Action, in his keynote address to the convention. "As liberal Democrats, we need not accept either the apologies of conservatives or the reproaches of the left." He told them public sentiment had turned against the war as people began to understand the conflict better.

Among the seventy-five delegates elected to the CDC steering committee to oversee the Peace Slate for the June 4, 1968, California primary was a familiar name, Edmund G. Brown Jr., who also volunteered as finance committee chair for Southern California. Eli Chernow joined his colleague on the committee, along with two young politicians launching their careers after leading the Young Democrats, Henry Waxman and Howard Berman.

By mid-November, the steering committee for the Peace Slate urged Minnesota senator Eugene McCarthy to enter the race, but stopped short of an endorsement to appease a faction that hoped New York senator Robert F. Kennedy would jump in. When McCarthy announced his candidacy on November 30, the CDC voted a formal endorsement. McCarthy met with the steering committee in Fresno on January 12, 1968, at the Hacienda Motel (the Peace Slate got a special rate, $9 per room). Jerry was named to the committee that would sponsor the McCarthy slate for the primary, joining major liberal Democratic donors like Max Palevsky and Stanley Sheinbaum.

For thirty-year-old Jerry, who had been around politicians all his life, Gene McCarthy offered a strikingly different and appealing model—a former seminarian, an intellectual, a poet with an ironic wit. His campaign stressed ideas rather than personality, and the importance of institutions rather than the individual. He disdained the traditional trappings of politics that Pat Brown embraced. Speaking on the candidate's behalf at a Democratic women's meeting in the Los Angeles suburb of Sherman Oaks on February 8, 1968. Jerry pointedly dismissed the politics of "hoopla and streamers." The McCarthy campaign was serious. "It's time for a voice of reason and McCarthy is that voice," Jerry said. "The past two weeks of horror and destruction in Vietnam has made it a thousand times more necessary."

One week later, Cesar Chavez began a fast to protest violence closer to home. The grape strike was in its third year, some of the union's supporters had grown frustrated, and incidents of violence threatened to mar the image of the United Farm Workers and undercut its support. Like the march to Sacramento two years earlier, Chavez's fast became a powerful symbol. His sacrifice drew hundreds to the union's headquarters in Delano for the nightly mass and drew the world's attention to the farm-workers' struggle. On the twenty-fifth day, too weak to walk, Chavez broke his fast sitting next to Robert Kennedy. Five days later, Kennedy announced his candidacy for president.

The same day, March 16, 1968, Martin Luther King Jr. addressed the California Democratic Council convention and praised the decision to endorse McCarthy, "one of the truly outstanding, capable, brilliant, dedicated Americans." King spoke again about the two Americas: one that flourished, with food, culture, and education for all, the other with millions of unemployed, substandard housing, pitiful overcrowded schools, "a daily ugliness about it that transforms the buoyancy of hope into the fatigue of despair." Again, he tied the problems to the war in Vietnam: "It has made the great society a myth and replaced it with a troubled and confused society."

Less than three weeks later, King was assassinated on the balcony of the Lorraine Motel in Memphis.

By then, President Johnson had stunned even his close advisers by with-drawing from the race, facing, as Gerald Hill had predicted a year earlier, the strong likelihood that his own party might reject him. Vice President Hubert Humphrey scrambled to win over the Johnson delegates. Fred Dutton became Kennedy's campaign manager in California. Pat Brown split with his former Svengali and supported Humphrey.

"I have been trying for weeks to get my father to support McCarthy," Jerry said. "Of course Humphrey is a good man but he represents the old guard of the party. We need new blood in the Democratic Party and we need a presidential candidate free enough from past mistakes that he will be able to chart a new course for the country. As far as I can see, Gene McCarthy is the only candidate who can do this."

Cesar Chavez was a Kennedy delegate, loyal to the man who had lent his charismatic support to the farmworkers' cause. In the final weeks of the campaign the veteran organizer brought a hundred farmworkers and volunteers to Los Angeles, where they methodically canvassed Mexican American neighborhoods in East Los Angeles. They set up a headquarters in one house on each block and visited every voter at least twice. On Election Day, turnout in some precincts was 100 percent. The votes were key to Kennedy's narrow margin of victory, 46 to 42 percent over McCarthy.

Fred Dutton was part of the scrum guiding Kennedy toward the press room after his victory speech at the Ambassador as he walked through the hotel kitchen, shook the busboy's hand, and was shot three times. Dutton rode in the ambulance to the hospital, where Kennedy died the next day. "The lights went out for me," Dutton said later, explaining why he never worked on another campaign.

Jerry was not the only member of the Brown family to oppose the war. His aunt Connie and her husband, raising two children in San Francisco, participated in antiwar demonstrations. Like her mother, Connie was involved with the Unitarian Church. She joined a study group on Islam. When her children were in high school, she went back to finish college and became a teacher. Ida lived nearby and shared her daughter's liberal politics and opposition to the war. Ida had voted for the progressive Henry Wallace when he challenged Harry Truman in 1948 (which she proudly announced to Truman's campaign manager at a cocktail party hosted by Pat, much to his chagrin). Ida told her daughter that President Johnson should be chloroformed.

Ida continued to rebuff suggestions she move in with one of her children. She loved to walk in the fog in nearby Golden Gate Park. She drank scotch on the rocks, several times a week. Her children organized a birthday party each January, though Ida preferred to avoid the spotlight. "I like it quiet," she said at one of the parties. "My son Pat says I'm anti-social." She was content to read and listen to the radio in her studio apartment decorated with photographs of the family, handmade birthday cards from her great-grandchildren, a map of the United States, two Italian miniatures from Harold's wife, a watercolor painted by one of Kathleen's friends, and a print of "The End of the Trail," the famous image of an American Indian, slumped over on his horse, despondent. "The foregoing might not say much for interior decorating, but it says an awful lot to me," Connie wrote to Pat. "Pride, love, involvement, acceptance—so very much."

Pat was still adjusting to life as a private citizen in a new city. "The first two years out of public service have been interesting and stimulating, but I would be less than frank if I didn't tell you that I miss the challenge of public office," he wrote in a holiday letter to friends. He was more open with his brother Harold: "I am trying awfully hard to get re-established here in Southern California."

Pat and Bernice traveled extensively, first for pleasure, then for business. At the coronation of the king of Tonga, where he was sent as a representative of President Johnson, Pat stayed in the presidential palace and played golf with General Suharto, who had recently seized power and become president of Indonesia. That connection would lead to Pat's most lucrative business enterprise. He became an adviser to Pertamina, the Indonesian military dictatorship's oil company, and the authorized agent for importing oil into the United States. "It seems to me that, for 23 years, I have fought hard for things that I think are right. I would like to assure myself of some degree of material security in whatever years I have ahead of me," Pat wrote to a friend.

In the fall of 1969, he attended an event on the University of California, Santa Barbara, campus in honor of the *Santa Barbara News Press* publisher and editor, Thomas Storke, whose crusading editorials about the John Birch Society had won a Pulitzer Prize. The building dedication was bittersweet. One of Governor Reagan's first acts had been to fire Clark Kerr. "When I looked at that Santa Barbara campus I couldn't help but think men do effect change and men do things and it is important who publishes a paper and who governs a state," Pat wrote to Storke. "In my opinion Reagan has done more to wreck the greatest university in the land and hinder the whole educational system than I ever thought possible." Then, ever the optimist, he looked ahead. "I have a son, Edmund G. Brown, Jr., who made a speech at Santa Barbara a few weeks ago and everybody tells me it was very good. He is stronger than the old man because he is just like his mother."

Unlike his mother, however, Jerry Brown was very interested in politics. Under the Master Plan, junior colleges continued to be run by individual school districts. By 1965, the Los Angeles Unified School District operated with a half-billion-dollar budget that financed 7 two-year colleges, 28 adult schools, 126 secondary schools, and 438 elementary schools. Pressure grew, especially from faculty, to split off the colleges so they would receive more attention and be differentiated from the high schools. A state law created the Los Angeles Community College District, which would be governed by seven elected trustees.

When elections for the new board were announced, Jerry went to see Joe Cerrell, only a few years older but already an experienced political operative. Cerrell had started the Trojan Democratic Club as an undergraduate at the University of Southern California, worked on Pat Brown's campaign in 1958, and become director of the state Democratic Party the following year. Cerrell was from Queens, and he understood the difference between politics on the East Coast and in California. If he had stayed in New York, he would have started as an assistant precinct captain; in California, he became state party director at twenty-four. By 1968 he had forged a new path as a political consultant, a specialty that had been the provenance of Republicans. Jerry asked Cerrell what he needed to do to win a seat on the new college board. The answer was, put his name on the ballot. BROWN'S SON IN FIRST BID FOR POLITICAL POST, read the headline in the *Los Angeles Times* on January 1, 1969.

Though he had been known his whole life as Jerry, Pat Brown's son launched his political career as Edmund G. Brown Jr.

Unburdened by the need to campaign seriously, Jerry began to build the network of relationships that would be central to his future career. He enlisted help from a friend he had met several years earlier during a trip to South America. Richard Maullin, a doctoral student at UCLA working for the Rand Corporation, had met Jerry in Bogotá, Colombia, at a dinner hosted by a Yale Law School classmate. Maullin reconnected with Jerry during the 1966 gubernatorial campaign. He did not know Pat Brown, but Maullin volunteered out of gratitude for the Master Plan, which had enabled a kid from Boyle Heights who put himself through UCLA cleaning swimming pools to attend a first-rate school, tuition free. Maullin never considered Ivy League colleges, though he had the grades, because of the cost and the quotas for Jews. During the 1966 campaign, he went out every weekend and registered voters in his old neighborhood, now largely Mexican. Jerry went along sometimes, interested in the process, asking questions about the mechanics. Maullin had limited political experience but a sharp mind for data and a wide-ranging intellect. When Jerry announced for the community college board, Maullin agreed to help with the campaign.

At a Democratic candidates forum, Jerry met Tom Quinn, a young journalist running for the school board. He, too, was following in the family business; his father, Joseph, had worked for Mayor Sam Yorty, been the Los Angeles bureau chief for United Press International, and then founded City News Service, a wire service that covered Southern California. Tom had majored in journalism, worked at a Sacramento television station, spent a year at City News, and then started an audio version called Radio News West, which sent feeds to forty-five stations.

One of the popular ways to campaign in California was on "slate mailers," a postcard or brochure sent to voters that endorsed a list of candidates. The principal criterion for the endorsement was the candidate's willingness to pay to join the slate. Quinn, always enterprising, decided that rather than pay to join someone else's slate, he would form his own. Edmund G. Brown Jr. seemed like a good name to have on a slate, so he approached the community college board candidate with the proposition of an education-oriented slate. The two hit it off and continued the conversation at a Chinese restaurant, then closed a bar at two in the morning. Their respective offices were nearby, and Jerry began dropping in to Radio News West to talk strategy with Quinn.

Jerry also sought advice from his old mentor at Los Gatos, Bill Burman. Burman had left the seminary in 1962 and taught for a couple of years at Santa Clara University. He fell in love with one of the students in his summer class on Horace. He was released from the Jesuit order in 1964, married, and moved to Los Angeles to start a family. Jerry had stayed in touch throughout the years. The Burmans attended parties at the Mansion and at Pat and Bernice's summer home in Los Angeles. In 1969, shortly before the college board election, Burman was promoted to associate professor of philosophy at Valley College, one of the Los Angeles junior colleges to be run by the new board.

Voters could choose seven board trustees in the April 1, 1969, primary. Out of 133 candidates, Edmund G. Brown Jr. finished first. He received 186,000 votes, 50,000 more than his nearest rival.

Though the novelty of the college board election garnered some attention, the contest that dominated the news was the race for mayor of Los Angeles. City councilman Tom Bradley, an African American, had forged a coalition of black and Jewish support that enabled him to mount a strong challenge to the incumbent, Sam Yorty. Bradley, a retired Los Angeles Police Department lieutenant, won the endorsement of the *Los Angeles Times* and bested Yorty in the primary, nearly clearing the 50 percent threshold necessary to avoid a runoff. Yorty rebounded with a race-baiting campaign that portrayed Bradley as a tool of Communists and the Black Panthers. The scare tactics were so effective that more people voted in the May 27 runoff than in any Los Angeles mayoral race before or since. Yorty won with 53 percent of the vote.

Jerry finished first again among fourteen candidates in the runoff for the school board post. Taking office on July 1, he found himself on the losing end of most votes on a board with a conservative majority. None of the trustees had held other office or had any experience on a school board; several viewed it as a springboard to higher office. Six weeks after they were sworn in, the board voted 5–2 to dismiss two Valley College teachers for reading in class an allegedly pornographic poem that one of them had written. Jerry called the dismissals rash, paternalistic decisions likely to be overturned in court. "Students can assess what they hear. The central fact of the case is that students are not infantile and can make up their own minds about what they can or cannot read."

The conservative majority meddled in affairs of the eight colleges to such a degree that they endangered the schools' accreditation, engaging in what Jerry termed paranoia and "partisanship that binds them so closely it's like a religious cult." In one of the more publicized episodes, the board rejected, by its customary 4–3 vote, a request by students to honor Martin Luther King's birthday. Trustee Michael Antonovich called King a lawbreaker and compared him with Sirhan Sirhan, the assassin of Robert Kennedy.

From the start, Jerry evinced a frugality that he attributed to his mother. His lack of interest in material goods also made for good politics. He opposed the board's decision to spend $700 per trustee on new office furniture, arguing that the metal desks and plain chairs were sufficient. He condemned an extra $23,000 for public relations as "press agents to toot our own horns." He chastised the board for its focus on trivial issues like the placement of vending machines. "The people who never come to community colleges or who drop out in a few weeks are the problems we should try to solve," he said. "We have an $85 million budget but we do not know how to make major decisions about it."

By August 1969, less than two months after Jerry took office, his father told friends his son might run for California secretary of state the following year. Frank Jordan, who had held the office for more than a quarter century, had suffered a stroke and was incapacitated. The race would be wide open. In December, Pat hosted the first fundraising lunch for Jerry at the Century Plaza Hotel.

Jerry asked Tom Quinn to manage the campaign. Quinn was twenty-five, had never run a campaign, and did not hesitate to accept. He would redirect into politics the combination of charm, chutzpah, and connections that had served him well as a journalist. (When Robert Kennedy visited Los Angeles amid rumors he was about to declare for president, Quinn figured out he might be staying with Pierre Salinger, whom he knew, talked his way into the house during a rainstorm, waited while the senator napped, and got his interview.) Both the candidate and the campaign manager had supreme confidence in their ability to craft a strategy superior to that cf any Democratic establishment politicians. Jerry sent Quinn to Pat, who set him up in the law library of his Beverly Hills firm with a stack of "mee-mos" from Fred Dutton. Dutton had also been a political novice in 1958 when he masterminded Pat's campaign. The memos were Tom Quinn's education in running a statewide campaign.

Jerry had a clear sense of what he did not want to do. He would not wear silly hats, a literal position that came to stand metaphorically for a rejection of the traditional political trappings. He did not hug people or kiss babies. He rarely smiled. Bernice had coined a term for her husband's old-style campaigning: low comedy. Jerry avoided it at all costs.

He also did not want to take money from people who expected favors. His desire to take office not beholden to supporters dovetailed with what emerged as his central theme: the need for transparency in campaign finance reports, which were regulated by the secretary of state. Looking for issues to run on, Jerry had researched the law and concluded the office had far greater power than had been exercised. Most candidates listed their source of donations as "various friends" or "cocktail party" or "other." Money had become increasingly important as campaigns moved into television, which made Jerry's demand for accurate reporting a potent issue.

On March 2, 1970, Jerry made his formal announcement, first in Los Angeles and then in San Francisco. He said he would insist on detailed reports of all campaign contributions and refuse to certify any election whose funding was not clearly itemized. He called the dependence on money from lobbyists and special interests "inherently corrupting."

Quinn wanted a Northern California setting that would emphasize Jerry's roots in San Francisco, so they staged a press conference at the Magellan Avenue house where he had grown up, now home to Jerry's sister Cynthia and her husband, Joe Kelly. Jerry met the press in the living room, surrounded by three nieces and a nephew who were allowed to play hooky to attend the event. "I wanted my grandmother to be here," Jerry told reporters. "But she's ninety-two years old, and you guys scare her."

Asked what sort of advice his father dispensed, Jerry parried the question: "Actually, he doesn't give me political advice as much as personal advice. For instance, he tells me when to get a haircut." In another interview, he addressed the impact of his name in a typically straightforward manner: "Pretty simple: some people will vote for me because they liked my father; some will vote against me because they didn't like him."

Pat's excitement over his son's interest in politics was tempered by his own dashed, fleeting hopes of a comeback. Lacking a strong candidate, some Democrats had approached him about running against Reagan again. The same day as Jerry's announcement, Pat's secretary requested the necessary state filing forms. But Bernice said there could not be two Edmund G. Browns on the ballot, and it was Jerry's turn. "I do think I was a good governor and sometimes almost great, but I don't think I was ever able to articulate my inner philosophy of life," Pat wrote to Tom McBride, a friend and former assemblyman, now a federal judge, who scolded him for even considering another run.

Pat had many friends, and he turned to them all for help. He even appealed for votes for his son in Colusa, one of the most Republican counties in the state. Pat and Harold had hired a local rancher in Williams, Floyd "Bud" Marsh, to oversee the Mountain House. Marsh reported "a good crop of barley this year, but we need rain in the next few weeks to keep it from maturing too rapidly." Illegal hunters had cut fences and killed one of Marsh's cows. In reply, Pat wrote, "Anything you can do to help Edmund Jr. would be very much appreciated by me. Colusa County is not very big, but every vote counts."

Pat's former campaign finance chair Ben Swig hosted events in his Fairmont Hotel penthouse suite. Jerry reported in May that he had raised $38,404, plus a $10,000 loan, half from his father and half from the son of one of his father's friends, department store magnate Cyril Magnin.

Several of Pat's friends donated $1,000 each, including actor Burt Lancaster and oil magnate Ed Pauley.

Jerry's younger sister, Kathleen, helped out on the campaign, too, in between raising a family and finishing up her Stanford degree long distance. She had left college a year early when her husband, Jeep, began Harvard Law School. For the daughter of California's greatest booster, who had imbued his family with the notion that California had it all, Cambridge had been a revelation. She loved the seasons and the community. She returned from visits to California with a suitcase filled with artichokes and tortillas and cooked the exotic food for friends who had never heard of tacos. When Jeep graduated in 1969, they chose to live in Los Angeles, for much the same reasons as other members of the family. They both liked its openness and entrepreneurial culture. Los Angeles had mountains, beaches, the entertainment industry, ethnic communities, and opportunity. Jeep joined forty-one other lawyers at Latham & Watkins and advanced quickly, working on complex cases that would have required years of seniority at an older San Francisco firm. Jeep, who had grown up with a typical Northern California sense of superiority, found that in Los Angeles, merit, wits, and hard work were more relevant to advancement than connections.

Tom Quinn sent Kathleen to campaign as a surrogate for her brother in small media markets, where her arrival was guaranteed to be big news. She was a good speaker and enjoyed the campaign. Her father always told all his children they should run for office; now friends and strangers began to tell Kathleen the same thing.

Early in the campaign, Jerry did an interview at Channel 9 in Los Angeles, on the Paramount Studios lot on Melrose Avenue. Quinn was with him; they finished around noon and decided to try the Mexican restaurant across the street. El Adobe was owned by Lucy Casado and her husband, Frank, one of the founders of the Mexican American Political Association. When Casado overheard a conversation about politics, he joined the table. By the end of lunch, he asked for Quinn's card. Quinn didn't have cards, so he gave Casado the number of the campaign office. Quinn had taken Pat's advice not to waste money on rent and found free space in the basement of a building at 3540 Wilshire Boulevard, a few blocks from the Ambassador Hotel. Casado called and asked Quinn to hire his daughter to work on the campaign; her father would pay her salary so she could get experience. Patty Casado had recently graduated from high school. Quinn needed a gofer. She was not only a good worker, she brought food from the restaurant for lunch. The staff began hanging out at El Adobe for the free dinners, and then for the friendship. The Casados had built a business where they served in loco parentis for a generation of young musicians and journalists. Jerry became as comfortable in Lucy Casado's kitchen as he had been in Mark McGuinness's home on Magellan Avenue.

Mexican Americans were emerging as a political force in Los Angeles, as Frank Casado's generation gave way to more militant activists who turned the word Chicano from a term of derision to a source of ethnic pride. Inspired in part by the farmworker movement and the success of Cesar Chavez, Chicanos had been demanding improvements in their second-class schools and city services. School walkouts in East Los Angeles in 1968 increased political awareness. Young leaders protested police brutality, racism, and a Selective Service System that disproportionately drafted Mexican Americans, who were less likely to have college deferments. The Chicano Moratorium on August 29, 1970, drew more than twenty thousand antiwar marchers to the streets of Los Angeles and into Laguna Park, where the marchers were gassed and clubbed by sheriffs. Three people died, including *Los Angeles Times* journalist Ruben Salazar, hit in the head with a projectile a deputy sheriff fired through the window of a restaurant where the reporter was having a drink.

Across the country, there had been more than three hundred major protests on college campuses since the Berkeley Free Speech Movement in 1964. The tenor of the clashes changed markedly, especially after the violence and arrests at the 1968 Democratic convention in Chicago. Berkeley again was in the vanguard. In the spring of 1969, a coalition of students, radicals, and neighbors had taken over an abandoned university-owned lot a few blocks south of campus. Families and students, counter-culture hippies and political activists joined together to lay sod, plant flowers, and create what they christened People's Park. On May 15, 1969, acting on orders from Governor Reagan, police surrounded and seized the park, ripped out the improvements, and fenced it off. Led by Mario Savio and other veterans of the movement, students rallied on campus and marched toward People's Park. Police fired tear gas and then shotguns. One bystander was killed, another blinded. The next day, Reagan sent two thousand National Guardsmen with rifles, bayonets, and tear gas. Violent clashes continued for two weeks. National Guard helicopters sprayed tear gas over much of the campus. Almost five hundred students were arrested and dozens injured. Writing in the *New York Review of Books*, Sheldon Wolin called People's Park "the first application of systematic terror directed at an American campus by its own authorities," shocking violence that soon became commonplace. Within a year, four unarmed students were gunned down by the Ohio National Guard during an anti–Vietnam War demonstration at Kent State University.

Despite his long-standing opposition to the war, Jerry took a conservative position on student protests. Students who broke rules should be suspended or expelled. At a fundraising event organized by Ben Swig, Jerry said he favored a statewide campus police force operating under the governor. He argued that the unrest and violence at public schools would only hasten support for imposing tuition. "We are going to have a lily-white system of public college education in California open only to the children of the rich and the middle class," he told students at Valley Community College. "The poor, the black, the people who are out of the mainstream who really need education won't get it. This violence is a real indulgence that the radical students don't think a lot about."

The campaign for secretary of state, a low-profile job with little-known responsibilities, garnered unusual publicity because of Jerry's name and obvious ambition. He did little to dampen speculation. "I don't intend to remain secretary of state as long as Frank Jordan," Jerry said, referring to the most recent office holder. "I'm interested in the office itself. But after that, who knows?"

In the primary, Jerry easily defeated Hugh Burns, the conservative Fresno Democrat who had led the Senate and helped push through Pat's water plan. On Election Day, Jerry defeated Republican James Flournoy by almost 5 percentage points, carrying most of the large counties. He lost Colusa by only two votes. He lost the solidly Republican coastal counties of Ventura, Santa Barbara, San Luis Obispo, Monterey, and Santa Cruz but carried most of the Central Valley, which boasted a Democratic enrollment edge. With a margin of victory of just over 300,000 votes, he became the only Democrat in a statewide constitutional office. Ronald Reagan easily won reelection, defeating Jesse Unruh.

After a scant year and a half on the local school board, Jerry was sworn in to statewide office on January 4, 1971, in a dark blue pinstripe suit and polka dot tie. Recently retired Chief Justice Earl Warren administered the oath of office, another portent the new secretary of state would have far from the usual low profile. "I want to thank my mother for having the good sense to name me after my father," Jerry said. "I never really liked that name, but I came to appreciate it as the campaign wore on." He thanked his father for giving him the inspiration to run.

"Times change," Pat said after the ceremony. "The young must take over. Little did I think four years ago that I'd be up here for my son's inauguration." Jerry was thirty-two. He had barely been sworn in when the chatter began about his possible gubernatorial candidacy in 1974. "You can never tell," Pat said. "Funnier things have happened."

Dozens of old friends, from the Magellan Avenue gang through his Yale classmates, sent congratulatory notes. Rose Bird, a friend from International House who had become a lawyer, thanked Jerry for the invitation to the inauguration and welcomed him as "a breath of fresh air in that oppressive police state atmosphere which Governor Reagan has created. There are many of us in the hinterlands who look forward to your administration and hope that it is only the first step in a long and successful political career."

For all but two of the past sixty years, the secretary of state had been a Jordan: Frank C., from 1910 until 1940, and his son Frank M. since 1943. The elder Jordan was an ally of the Southern Pacific Railroad, so Governor Hiram Johnson had stripped the office of much of its power. Many of the duties involved routine registrations, licenses, and election oversight. Nonetheless, Jerry found plenty of laws that had gone unenforced.

He threatened to prosecute 134 candidates for failing to properly report campaign contributions. He sued nine who refused to correct the mistakes and said he would bar them from running again unless they complied. Five were Democrats. Campaign finance laws, which dated back to the nineteenth century, had been generally followed until the 1940s, when the increased costs of campaigns prompted candidates to fudge the sources of donations. "When Mr. Shanahan, known incidentally as the Tall Sycamore of Shasta County, introduced the bill in 1893, he clearly intended that these be intelligible statements that people could understand and that the amounts and the names and the nature of the items referred to be specified on the report," Jerry said. He was quickly getting a reputation for rhetoric that invariably included Latin phrases or historical references.

Jerry sued the campaign committee that had defeated a proposition to divert gas taxes from highway construction to smog control and mass transit, forcing the committee to reveal that they had received $65,000 in contributions from Gulf and Standard Oil. He personally argued the case before the California Supreme Court and won a unanimous decision that established the need for full disclosure by corporations and organizations that contributed to ballot measures.

In his first three months, Jerry issued more press releases than Jordan had in four years. By the second year, he churned out an average of three a week. He lobbied for lower postal rates for political mail and equal time requirements for candidates on radio and television. He foresaw that candidates would increasingly need to be independently wealthy: "Public office rapidly is becoming a rich man's preserve." He explored voting by mail, which would not become widespread for more than a decade. His office distributed the first voters' guide materials in Spanish.

Secretary of State Jerry Brown and his younger sister Kathleen work on a voter registration campaign in 1972. (Courtesy of George A. Rice)

The escalation of the Vietnam War had intensified demands that those old enough to be drafted should have the right to vote. A few months after Jerry took office, the national voting age was lowered to eighteen, which set off a legal battle over whether students could vote from their school address. The Republican attorney general had ruled that California students must register at their home. When Jerry was named as a defendant in a lawsuit challenging that decision, he turned around and sided with the plaintiffs, filing an amicus brief on their behalf. They prevailed. Richard Maullin, who had become a deputy secretary of state, estimated the lower voting age could add 1.2 million first-time voters in California. Jerry wasted no time reaching out to his future constituents. "The collective voice of students will be heard," he told students at Berkeley High School. He explained the Greek derivation of democracy and exhorted them to civic participation. "Self-government should occupy as much time as baseball or TV."

Speculation about his political future increased, fueled by media interest in the story of the two Browns, the younger one so little known that writers still referred to him as Gerry, Ed, or Edmund Jr. A father-son appearance on *The Merv Griffin Show* reached a national audience and drew letters from old friends. "What impressed me the most was how much you are the same" as the Yale student she remembered, wrote Peggy Byrnes, whose brother had been a law school classmate. "I remember your being so quietly proud of California and all that was being done for education and prison reform. You were so confident that the Democrats were the better party, saying they were twenty years ahead of the Republicans."

Early polls on the 1974 gubernatorial race showed Jerry as the leading Democrat in a crowded field of seasoned politicians. The most common reason cited for a favorable view of Jerry was his father. The most common reason cited by those who viewed him unfavorably was his father.

Memories fade fast. Jerry was well aware that to exploit his father's name, he needed to move quickly. As he had done in the past, he capitalized on his father's reputation and connections even as he sought to distance himself from Pat Brown's style.

"I don't quite enjoy the crowds and the handshaking like my father did," Jerry said soon after he took office. "I don't take to it like a duck to water. I'm not yet ready to sentence myself to a life in politics." He did not disguise his doubts about the power of government to solve problems nor his dislike of the political trappings. "I think you get stale staying around politics too long . . . public life is spiritually debilitating—the falseness, the applause, the phoniness. To get mesmerized by all this folderol is a mistake. I view with some skepticism the ability of government to make people happy."

His youth and intensity, his unconventional path and habits, and his disarming frankness generated attention wherever he went. So did his piercing eyes, bushy eyebrows, and graying sideburns. He accepted speaking engagements around the state and answered all his mail. He wrote notes and outlines for speeches on whatever was handy. A list of assignments on a cardboard shirt insert from the cleaners. Notes for a speech to the Native Sons of the Golden West Grand Banquet on the program menu: "Asked what sec do? Asked aren't you rather young to be sec" scrawled over Shrimp Louie Salad and Cross Rib of Beef. He edited himself heavily, crossing out sentences and moving paragraphs around. He reviewed routine responses to correspondence and frequently red-penciled staff drafts, impatient with loquacious answers. "This is bureaucratic mush!" he wrote, a red line through the four-paragraph answer to a query about a school bingo game that didn't fall within his jurisdiction. "Mush!" on another. "Too impersonal!" "Wordy!"

There had not been a California governor younger than forty in more than a century. In interviews, he dismissed talk about a run for higher office. "But you have to have a goal, don't you, or at least a reason to live, something to keep you moving?" he said, as if in a colloquy with himself. "That's what I like about the stars, I guess—in politics and the movies. They have a certain quality, an élan vital, a sense of being alive and vibrant. So many people these days act like they're dead, just going through the motions."

He rented a house in Malibu that belonged to the dancers Marge and Gower Champion. "It's quiet on the beach," he told an interviewer. "I can be alone. In politics, you're always being thrown in with other people, all day long. You don't get much time by yourself, for privacy and reflection." Neither he nor his deputies, Quinn and Maullin, wanted to live in Sacramento, although the office was based in the capitol. Jerry spent a day or two a week there. He toyed with the idea of renting an office in Santa Monica ("if that wouldn't be too outrageous," he wrote to a friend). They ended up with an office in West Los Angeles.

On April 7, 1971, Jerry turned thirty-three. He was in Sacramento that day and his father sent a telegram to the state capitol. "Dear Jerry, congratulations, and happy birthday. I was 33 when you were born. You can't match that. But you've gone further in politics than I at your age. You have a great future, and we're both very proud of you. See you Saturday. Best wishes. Love Mother and Dad."

Another birthday card came from an old girlfriend. Jerry wrote back and described his new calling:

> I have been almost totally absorbed in my work. I'm beginning to get a sense of just what I can do in politics. It is very important. The world is so shaky and what we do in this country could make quite a difference. And there are so many jerks running things. I'm learning what can be done and that I can do it. It is a crazy job I have. It seems to fit just what I can do and what I like doing. Now that the furniture is out of the way I'm re-organizing these 140 strange souls entrusted to my care. Within a year or two I'll have this place doing as much as it will ever do for the state. After that and after the next president is elected, then the real fun begins.

12

The Candidate

In its prime, the Alexandria had been the fanciest hotel in Los Angeles, the first to boast centralized steam heat and private baths in every room. The Beaux Arts building with opulent ballrooms and a Tiffany skylight opened in 1906 and hosted Presidents Roosevelt, Taft, and Wilson. Charlie Chaplin danced in the lobby. Over time, the hotel at Fifth and Spring fell into decline along with the rest of downtown. The city's financial center shifted west, leaving behind the elegant Art Deco buildings and theaters in the once bustling commercial corridor along Broadway and Spring. The Alexandria Hotel sheltered transients instead of movie stars.

Decades later, the landmark building was restored by S. Jon Kreedman, a carpenter from Detroit who had become a major developer in Southern California. Kreedman had learned construction as a teenager and settled in Los Angeles after serving in World War II. He started building tract homes during the postwar expansion and made his name with big, innovative projects on the west side of Los Angeles. He built the first high-rise apartments in Beverly Hills. He converted the I. M. Pei–designed Century City Towers into some of the earliest condominiums. In 1971, he refurbished the Alexandria as part of a largely unsuccessful effort to revive downtown Los Angeles.

Two years later, room 343 of the Alexandria Hotel was the staging grounds for far more sweeping change, and the vanguard of the revolution was an ex-nun who taught political science at a small Catholic liberal arts college.

The role of radical was nothing new for Mary Jean Pew. She had grown up in Los Angeles and, like Jerry Brown, postponed her entry into the novitiate by a year because her parents insisted she try college first. She persisted and spent nineteen years as an Immaculate Heart sister. She left in 1968, shortly before the Los Angeles nuns' proposals for modest reforms led to a standoff with conservative Cardinal James Francis McIntyre. Their battle foreshadowed the coming feminist struggles within the Catholic Church and led to an internationally publicized schism with the Vatican. The entire community of more than two hundred nuns renounced their vows. Pew had a PhD in government and had taught at Immaculate Heart College in Hollywood since 1961. As chair of the History and Government Department, she hired Tom Hayden to teach a class on Vietnam and the antiwar movement using the Pentagon Papers as a text; Hayden, one of the founders of Students for a Democratic Society, was free on appeal from his conviction as one of the Chicago Seven, charged with inciting a riot at the 1968 Democratic convention.

Pew had heard Jerry Brown speak at Immaculate Heart College on behalf of Eugene McCarthy during the 1968 presidential campaign. She was a Kennedy supporter, but she found Jerry impressive. Two years later, when he called the school seeking student volunteers for his secretary of state campaign, Pew decided to sign up herself. She thought she should get some practical experience after years of teaching political science and social justice. Pew was smart, witty, passionate, and organized. She fit in on the unorthodox, ragtag Brown campaign team. She also drew the attention of a Tom Quinn protégé, Doug Faigin, who had taken over running Radio News West when Quinn went to work full time for Jerry. On their first date, Faigin took Pew to the Santa Claus Lane Parade, a traditional Hollywood extravaganza the Sunday after Thanksgiving.

By 1973, Pew and Faigin had married, Faigin was Jerry's press secretary, and Pew had been recruited by Quinn as campaign coordinator to lay the groundwork for a gubernatorial race. She set up shop in room 343 of the Alexandria Hotel because Kreedman offered free space. At age forty-four, Pew was often the oldest person at any strategy session. "It's largely an ad hoc job," she said. "None of us has ever run or been involved to any great degree in a gubernatorial race before; we're all kind of learning. It's creative, in its best moments."

She spent the fall of 1973 working to find a state headquarters, recruit volunteers, and develop contacts in the black and Chicano communities. Still carrying a full-time teaching load, she worked on the campaign at least forty hours a week, every afternoon into late evening and weekends.

When Pew and Faigin went to see *The Sting* at Christmas, they both fell asleep in the movie theater.

Pat's initial response to Jerry's earliest musings about a gubernatorial campaign had been alarm. Pat took Quinn to breakfast at the Polo Lounge to try to persuade him that Jerry was too young and inexperienced. A run for governor in the crowded Democratic primary field in 1974 would ruin his career. Quinn was unfazed. Jerry was undeterred. Like his father before him, he was in a hurry. Once the decision was clear, Pat embraced the campaign. In the dozens of letters he dictated each week, barely a missive went out that did not include a reference to Jerry. When early polls showed Jerry would beat Ronald Reagan, Pat sent copies to dozens of opinion makers, including every U.S. senator and California representative and newscasters Walter Cronkite and John Chancellor. Pat enclosed a short note: "I thought you might be interested in knowing that I have a son to carry on."

Reagan, however, declined to run for a third term, creating the first gubernatorial contest with no incumbent since 1958, the year Pat Brown was elected. The wide-open race drew several prominent, experienced contenders, including Assembly Speaker Bob Moretti, San Francisco mayor Joseph Alioto, and Congressman Jerome Waldie.

Reagan had chosen not to run for reelection so that he might focus on a presidential bid, a decision predicated on the assumption that Nixon would complete his second term and the 1976 race would be wide open. Events intervened; the Watergate break-in and subsequent investigations would culminate in Nixon's resignation and enable Gerald Ford to run for reelection as an incumbent. As inconvenient as Watergate proved for Reagan, the drama that played out in 1973 could not have come at a better time for Jerry Brown.

Watergate resonated with a theme Jerry had hammered since his campaign for secretary of state: the corrupting influence of money and the importance of campaign finance reform. On a subtler level, the unfolding scandal generated interest in fresh faces. In a gubernatorial primary against established old-school politicians, Jerry's relative lack of experience became an advantage, just as it had been for Reagan in 1966.

The week the Senate Watergate Committee began the riveting, nationally televised hearings that helped bring down a president, Jerry spoke at a Town Hall Forum in Los Angeles. He decried the secrecy and lies that caused people to lose confidence in government. Ten years ago, he said,

75 percent of the people trusted their government; by 1972, the figure had dropped to 45 percent. "Without secret money, the Watergate scandal would have been impossible," he said in the May 1973 speech. "Secrecy is dangerous, but something far worse often follows it—government deception. Nothing is more destructive of public confidence than outright lying by those in high places. Yet, in the last ten years, deceit by public officials has become commonplace." Jerry called for Nixon's impeachment.

His father wrote to the president expressing sympathy. Pat always wanted to think the best of people. He still thought Lyndon Johnson must have been right on Vietnam. ("He wanted to be a great president so much, and he wanted to do so many things for people, and I just can't believe that a man that would do the things for the poor and the blacks, that he would be such a great man in that field and such a villain in the other.") Watching Nixon's troubles deepen, Pat recalled a small gesture of kindness in 1960 from the then vice president. "You and I were at the opening of the new baseball stadium at Candlestick Park in San Francisco," Pat wrote to Nixon. "This was soon after I had given Chessman a 60-day reprieve. I was booed unmercifully. I will never forget your quietly saying to me, 'That is nothing, you should have heard some of the booing I have taken.'" Pat offered to help Nixon in any way.

A week later, as the U.S. attorney general designate reviewed candidates to appoint as a special Watergate prosecutor, Nixon made a suggestion, more calculated than it sounded. "I threw in a name," he said to his chief of staff, Alexander Haig. "Pat Brown . . . Former district attorney, attorney general, governor, Democrat. Ran against the president. He's a decent man. Everybody would believe him." The idea went nowhere.

Jerry had another Watergate card to play. More than a year of delicate negotiations with two citizens' groups had produced agreement on the Political Reform Act, a far-reaching initiative better known as Proposition 9. The measure would limit spending on statewide offices and ballot measure campaigns; require complete disclosure of contributions by candidates for state office; bar lobbyists from contributing to campaigns, limit their gifts to elected officials and staff to $10 a month, and require monthly disclosure; establish conflict of interest rules; and create the Fair Political Practices Commission to administer the new law. In the wake of Watergate, what might have been a backburner initiative became front page news. Prop 9 easily qualified for the June 1974 ballot—when Jerry would compete in the gubernatorial primary. "This commission will absolutely prevent Watergate scandals in California," Jerry said when he filed the initiative. "It is by far the most powerful body of its type ever conceived in the United States."

He calculated that lobbyists in Sacramento spent an average of $6,875 a day to entertain state officials. Adding in their salaries, Jerry estimated they spent $10.4 million a year to influence state policy. "Two hamburgers and a coke" became the campaign's shorthand for the proposal to limit lobbyists to $10 per month per public official. That alone was an affront to the social and political culture of a capital accustomed to doing business over expense account meals, drinks, and cigars. It was only a sign of things to come from the brash young candidate.

The primary drafter and negotiator of the initiative was Dan Lowenstein, one of two aggressive lawyers Jerry had hired to invigorate the ossified Office of the Secretary of State. Lowenstein had grown up in New York City, attended Yale and then Harvard Law School, graduating at the time that the first legal services organizations started. He took a job with California Rural Legal Assistance (CRLA), a federally funded group that helped farmworkers, and moved to Modesto, in the heart of the Central Valley. He met his wife there, a Japanese American who had been born in an internment camp. One of the founders of CRLA who had been at law school with Jerry heard that the secretary of state needed an attorney and recommended Lowenstein. Lowenstein shaved off his beard and registered as a Democrat for the first time, not because he thought Jerry would care, but because his politics had changed. He could no longer be a Republican after watching Reagan attack government and cut services for those most in need.

Lowenstein, five years younger than Jerry, admired his boss's intelligence. He grew comfortable with his management style and adept at reading his sometimes enigmatic cues. Not everyone did. The characteristics shared by the small staff foreshadowed the qualities Jerry would look for when he recruited dozens of high-level appointees. Lowenstein never worried about what he said to Jerry. He could be blunt and even insulting. He could argue any position, on two conditions: that he gave Jerry all relevant facts, including ones that might not support his own view, and that he accepted and supported the boss's final decision. People who worked for Jerry didn't need or expect his approval; they were a self-confident bunch. "I want ideas from them," Jerry said when he took office. "I don't want a bunch of sycophants around me. I want bright guys who aren't afraid to tell me what they think."

Lowenstein respected Jerry's ability to immerse himself in details and focus so intently on a problem that he found solutions that others had overlooked. While Jerry Brown the public official dived into issues in minute detail, Jerry Brown the candidate worked hard to do the opposite. The campaign strategy he devised with Quinn and Maullin was to stay as vague as possible. Jerry outlined four key areas of focus: education, environment, economic growth, and political reform. He took a handful of general positions. He was for decriminalization of marijuana, equal rights for women and minorities, progressive taxation, and collective bargaining for public employees. "I'm against the death penalty. I'm for Cesar Chavez." He condemned junkets and called for an end to "back-room politics." His campaign slogan was geared to the times: "Edmund G. Brown Jr., Democrat for Governor. He could make you believe in government again."

Jerry took lessons from his father's defeat eight years earlier. Reagan had effectively packaged the idea that government was the problem, Sacramento was out of control, and a fresh face was necessary to clean up the mess. Jerry saw those themes as critical to electability, and he adapted and adopted them as his own. "A new spirit" became his campaign mantra. "California has its problems," Jerry said in his formal announcement on January 28, 1974, an echo of Reagan's announcement eight years earlier. "But I love this state . . . and I intend to do all I possibly can to see California develop in a healthy and worthwhile manner."

A March campaign piece sent to Democrats opened with dramatic white block lettering on a black page: THE NEXT ELEVEN WEEKS. Inside was a long letter to the voter, in a conversational style. "A lot of people are running for governor. I know because I'm one of them. And though I don't look forward to the fatigue, the confusion, the loss of privacy, my job is going to be easier than yours. You have to listen to all of us. You have to judge, interpret, separate and distill a clutter of promises and positions. Maybe I can help you with my part in that process."

Jerry dealt with the issue of his father head-on: "Anyone who says I'm lucky to have my father's name is absolutely right. I'm also lucky to have his counsel and support. But he's not running for anything this year, and I am. I ask you to judge me, my record, and my ideas."

Behind the scenes, Pat played an active, indispensable role. He set up a campaign office in exile at his law firm, hired his own travel secretary, and arranged meetings with old friends and supporters around the state. He made introductions, hosted events, and collected checks. Wealthy individuals could contribute unlimited amounts, and the bulk of the campaign's funds came from a handful of people. Others sent Pat money for Jerry in gratitude for favors long ago. A Central Valley farmer sent $500 because Pat had helped Kern County get water—and written a law school recommendation for his son.

Big donors wanted to meet the candidate. Jerry was uncomfortable at the small gatherings with his father's friends. Sometimes he escaped to the kitchen, more relaxed talking with the workers. "Jerry is much more like his mother than he is like me," Pat wrote to a friend who found the candidate diffident, cocky, and brash, criticisms Pat heard frequently. "His aloofness is not arrogance but rather bashfulness. I know he doesn't come through this way, but that is the way he has been all of his life."

On occasion Jerry found common ground with one of Pat's friends, like Joseph Houghteling, a Yale graduate, antiwar activist, and environmental planner who owned a string of small papers in the Santa Clara Valley. Houghteling had started as a kid on the *Sunnyvale Standard* doing a little of everything, shooting photos of high school football games and selling ads in the planned community of five thousand with the slogan "Watch us grow!" He wasn't yet twenty-five when he bought his first paper in 1949, the *Gilroy Dispatch*, circulation thirteen hundred. The biggest event in town was the annual rodeo, upstaged a few years later by the Gilroy Garlic Festival. Houghteling volunteered on the 1952 Stevenson campaign and made friends among the Jewish business community in San Francisco that supported Democrats. One night Houghteling ended up with Jerry at the bar at Rickey's, a Palo Alto institution. Jerry asked why the newspaper publisher would support him. Three reasons, Houghteling said. You've done a pretty good job as secretary of state. I admire your parents and respect your father's record as governor. And third, you're going to win. Jerry made Houghteling treasurer for Northern California.

Even more than his father had done in 1958, Jerry campaigned outside the Democratic Party structure, relying on his own instincts and an ad hoc team led by Quinn and Maullin. Lucy Casado became a director of Californians for Brown, and her El Adobe restaurant displayed campaign literature. Jeep Rice took a six-month leave from his law firm and worked full time as a travel secretary for his brother-in-law. Joe Kelly worked on the campaign committee in San Francisco. Ray Fisher, a top litigator at Tuttle & Taylor, drove Jerry around in his Alfa Romeo. Pop star Helen Reddy emceed the opening ceremonies at the campaign headquarters at the corner of Sunset and Vine, a couple of blocks from her star on the Hollywood Walk of Fame. Brown headquarters was above the legendary Wallichs Music City, named after Capitol Records founder Glenn Wallichs. The music store had been the first to seal record covers so they could be displayed and browsed in racks. The glass listening booths where customers sampled records drew a young trendy crowd into the early morning hours, about the time the campaign staff straggled out and headed home.

In the L-shaped office, volunteers sat along the windows that overlooked Sunset. The executive staff had offices along Vine. Mary Jean Pew, on leave from her teaching job, recruited a handful of her recent students. In an era of changing mores, Pew served as a role model for young women as she worked to dispel stereotypes that lingered even among her colleagues. "There's still the notion that a woman is best suited to typing and doing the secretarial work," she said. "It's a struggle for some of them to accept a woman as a thinking being. But most of them, I must say, in four years I've noticed a real change. They've become more conscious of how they have looked on women in the past."

The Brown campaign did compete for the support of two traditional Democratic groups that could turn out votes in a primary— organized labor and the California Democratic Council.

The Bay Area had long been the heart of organized labor in California, a union stronghold since a bloody 1934 longshoremen's strike led by Harry Bridges turned into a general strike that shut down the city. Now, forty years later, San Francisco mayor Joe Alioto counted on an endorsement from the state labor federation, which could be decisive in a close contest. He did not know he would have to reckon with Stephen Reinhardt and Blackie Leavitt. Reinhardt, a politically active liberal Democrat and labor lawyer in Los Angeles, had been an informal adviser to Jerry since 1970. One of his clients was Leavitt, head of the Los Angeles board of the Culinary Workers Union and a vice president of the Hotel and Restaurant Employees and Bartenders International. Leavitt wanted an entrée into politics. The Culinary Workers were powerful enough to block Alioto from winning the state labor federation endorsement. Instead, the organization voiced support for all four leading candidates.

experimented with planned communities that would minimize driving. After zoning restrictions foiled a housing cooperative in the San Fernando Valley, many of the prospective residents ended up in Laurel Canyon. Eckbo helped design Wonderland Park, sixty-five homes built on a graded, filled-in shelf on the west side of the canyon. In 1950, he built his own home on a half-acre lot, at an elevation of 1,600 feet.

Six years later, the Aluminum Company of America (ALCOA) asked Eckbo if he would be interested in creating an experimental garden with aluminum. The material had been widely used during the war years as a component in airplane manufacture, and ALCOA wanted to promote peacetime uses for the lightweight metal. Eckbo had developed a respect for basic materials when he worked for several years designing migrant labor camps in the Central Valley for the federal Farm Housing Agency. He accepted the ALCOA challenge and designed a garden for his own house using large quantities of aluminum in screens, trellises, sunbreaks, and most spectacularly in a centerpiece fountain shaped like an abstract flower.

When Jerry arrived in the early 1970s, Laurel Canyon had a flourishing music scene, less well chronicled than that of Greenwich Village and Haight-Ashbury but just as influential. Musicians had clustered in the relatively affordable, secluded houses that Joni Mitchell sang about in "Ladies of the Canyon." She lived with Graham Nash in the home memorialized in Nash's hit "Our House." For the cover photo of the first Crosby, Stills and Nash album, the band posed on the porch of a canyon house. Mama Cass Elliot, Jim Morrison, Jackson Browne, Don Henley, and Glenn Frey were drawn to the community of singer-songwriters and the easy proximity to clubs like the Troubadour and Whisky a Go Go, just down the hill. They worked in relative anonymity in a setting only Los Angeles could offer—bucolic beauty within minutes of an urban scene.

Jerry bought Garrett Eckbo's house, most of the ALCOA "Forest Garden" still intact. The wood-and-glass house had echoes of Japan, where Eckbo had spent a lot of time. "It's rather isolated, with lots of trees around it, the way Jerry likes," said Bernice, who had approved of the purchase. Jerry valued his privacy, especially now. "It takes a very strong sense of yourself to be yourself," he said four days before the election. "The inevitable tendency is to become what everyone wants you to be."

On election night, a handful of friends awaited results with him at the Laurel Canyon house, including Tony Kline, his law school classmate. Pat and Bernice hosted a dinner for fifty family and friends at one of their favorite spots, Perrino's, a legendary restaurant from the golden age of Hollywood. Pat was nervous.

The margins were narrow, but Jerry was ahead all night. He headed downtown to the ballroom where his supporters waited. Always conscious of symbolism, he had rejected the Democrats' traditional Beverly Hills Hotel in favor of the utilitarian downtown convention center. The music was mariachis, jazz, and a Sufi choir. The food was Mexican, Italian, and Chinese. Two big banners hung on the ballroom wall: "We are not satisfied, and we will not be satisfied until justice rolls down like waters and righteousness like a mighty stream—Martin Luther King Jr.," and the Jesuit motto, "Age Quod Agis." Do what you are doing.

On his way into the hall, Jerry was philosophical about the slim margin, neither visibly distressed nor dismissive. "What's the name of that book by Maxwell Taylor? *The Uncertain Trumpet*? Or something like that? That's what this mandate is, an uncertain trumpet." He won by 2.9 points, or 180,000 votes. It was the closest election for governor in California since 1920. Turnout was 64 percent, the lowest since 1946. Of the eligible voters, only 46 percent cast ballots. Nixon's resignation and Ford's pardon of his predecessor, just a few months before the election, helped Democrats do well across the country.

Pat and Bernice mounted the bandstand in the cavernous convention center alongside their son. "Some say I got here because of my father, but it's actually my mother," Jerry said. Bernice smiled. Unlike primary night, Pat took the microphone, albeit briefly: "I just want to say that I had something to do with it." His son agreed. "I'm just glad he didn't run against me—he's the only one who could have beaten me," Jerry said.

"People have always come to California to find a place in the sun. We have the resources, but we lack the will. We can be a model for the whole country," he said. The biggest problem was not the recession sparked by the 1973 oil embargo and energy crisis, he said: "The main crisis is the *human* energy crisis."

In the following days, the congratulations poured in, everyone from Marlon Brando to Sister Alice Joseph, the former principal of St. Brendan school, who kept on her office wall a framed copy of the *Time* magazine cover with Jerry's picture.

The father of an old girlfriend recalled a conversation in Jerry's office when the secretary of state looked out the window. "You pointed to the

Mansion and said, 'it really is not far from here to there,'" he wrote. "More power to you, Jerry."

Father William J. Finnegan, the former vice principal at St. Ignatius and uncle of Jerry's childhood friend and fellow seminarian Peter, wrote to Pat and Bernice, thrilled at the victory. "Who, twenty years ago, would have thought things would turn out this way?"

"If Jerry does a good job, his mother and father will take the credit—if anything happens we are going to blame it on the Jesuit Community," Pat wrote back. "I seriously believe the 3½ years he spent at Los Gatos, the year at Santa Clara, and the 4 years at St. Ignatius left an indelible effect upon his mind and actions. I don't believe you fathers ever realize the impact you have upon human beings and particularly those of us who go into politics."

On this, father and son agreed. In an interview for an *Esquire* magazine profile that ran just before the election, Jerry offered one of his clearest articulations of the relationship of his Jesuit training to his political career:

> The Jesuit ideal is that you should prefer neither a long life nor a short life, neither riches nor poverty, neither health nor illness; it's all a matter of indifference. All you care about is the greater glory of God. You try to reach that state of mind. When you do, then you are ready for God to use you as his instrument. But you must take direct action. You can't just wait. The Jesuits say, "You act as though everything depended on you, although you realize that everything depends on God." I don't think I have achieved this mental outlook, and I don't know that I ever will. But I haven't forgotten it. It's in the sense that your self has to diminish, that you try to transcend your own ego. That's the concept. Obviously in my structure of the world, when I deal with uncertainty, the unknown, I have certain habits of mind that I fall back on and rely upon . . . I want to understand the world, fit into it, and make whatever splash and contribution I can.

Ida Brown did not live to see her favorite grandson elected governor, though she did witness his victory in the Democratic primary. Until the last year of her life, she had continued in good health and spirits. At her ninety-fourth birthday party at Jack's restaurant, she downed a scotch on the rocks and talked about her daily walks around her neighborhood. Many of her seventeen grandchildren and eleven great-grandchildren were there to celebrate, and she regarded the secretary of state with particular affection: "A fine boy."

Hardly ever sick her whole life, she was diagnosed with cancer the next year. After several operations, she was forced to give up the independence and apartment she had cherished. She moved in with her youngest son, Frank, who had always been a favorite. Smart, gifted, and accomplished at an early age, Frank's struggles with alcoholism had made him alternately the troubled child and the prodigal son.

Ida's last birthday party was at the Browns' old Magellan Avenue home on January 11, 1974. At ninety-six, she said she was content. "I'm not a social person," she said. "I love to read." Jerry presented his grandmother with *Portraits from North American Indian Life*, by Edward S. Curtis, which reminded Ida of reading early California histories by Hubert Bancroft. "I'm so glad my eyes are good so I can still read," she said. "It seems to me that many old people waste their time. They don't seem to know about reading."

She was still strong enough to attend fundraisers for Jerry during his gubernatorial campaign. Pat sent her copies of Jerry's speeches. He called his mother every day unless he was overseas and couldn't get a line. When they talked on July 5, 1974, Ida told Pat that Frank had taken her out to the loveliest lunch at the Palace Hotel. She recited what she had ordered, including a scotch and soda. She died the next afternoon.

"You may have gotten lots of your warmth and charm from the Irish side. But I always sensed in your mother an individual of tremendous human poise and strength and intuitive understanding about all that was going on, as well as having about as sharp an intellect and knowledge as anyone could," Fred Dutton wrote to Pat. "It was the convergence of all those various facets in you, that I came to conclude, provided the initial foundation for all that you've come to achieve."

Joseph Houghteling wrote how much he had enjoyed seeing Ida at events, first for Pat and then for Jerry: "She was so deservedly proud of her family and her presence not only showed this pride but also gave the rest of us the understanding of the heritage she passed on to her children and, in time, the successive generations of that fine Brown family."

In her old age, Ida had called herself a "mountain woman," embracing the past she had long ago escaped. She was buried in Colusa, not far from where she was born. On her gravestone, at the suggestion of Frank's daughter Faye, was the quote Ida had so often recited to her grandchildren: WHAT DOTH THE LORD REQUIRE OF THEE BUT TO DO JUSTLY AND TO LOVE MERCY AND TO WALK HUMBLY WITH THY GOD? Pat and Harold waited until November to have the stone engraved and placed in the Williams cemetery. There were the names and professions of her four children: Edmund, governor, Harold, judge, Constance, teacher, and Frank, attorney. And at the very bottom: GRANDMOTHER OF EDMUND G. BROWN JR., 34TH GOVERNOR OF CALIFORNIA.

13

The New Spirit

The invitation to the Brown transition team Christmas potluck opened with a quote from a letter written in 1915 by the German poet Rainer Maria Rilke: "I often have to turn, asking what force is perhaps now passing there behind me to its work, each to its work, and the way of so many, leads through the center of our heart."

Those who expected Edmund G. Brown Jr. to govern in the tradition of his namesake—and there were many—were soon disabused of such notions. From its outset, Jerry Brown's administration was an attack on the status quo.

To his father's dismay, Jerry canceled the inaugural ball and reception. "I really believe the problems that face us are not just material problems," Jerry said at the traditional prayer breakfast on inauguration morning, January 6, 1975. "I think the crisis is not just that of energy or the environment, I think it's a crisis of the spirit. We don't lack for anything in this country. What we really lack is leadership."

The crowd moved from the convention center to the capitol, gathering in the Assembly chamber. In the balcony, surrounded by their three daughters and ten grandchildren, Pat and Bernice watched their son sworn in as governor. His seven-minute inaugural address set a record for brevity. Speeches turned off young people, Jerry said; besides, he had not started writing until the night before. He had stayed up reading all the inaugural addresses back to Hiram Johnson and found them full of repetitive promises. The thirty-six-year-old governor issued instead a rebuke to the standing-room-only audience of more than seven hundred, most of them veteran politicians:

What have we learned? More than half the people who could have
voted refused, apparently believing that what we do has so little
impact on their lives that they need not pass judgment on it. In
other words, the biggest vote of all in November was a vote of no
confidence. So our first order of business is to regain the trust and
confidence of the people we serve. And we can begin by following
not only the letter but the spirit of the political reform initiative,
the biggest vote getter of all in the primary election.

He left for San Francisco, where he was greeted at City Hall by his
vanquished rival, Mayor Alioto, then flew south to speak at Los Angeles
City Hall, now presided over by Mayor Tom Bradley, who had succeeded
in his second attempt and become one of the first black mayors in an overwhelmingly white city. The inaugural party had dinner at Man Fook
Low, across from the wholesale produce market in the city's old Chinatown, a decades-old Cantonese restaurant with a following that included
Mae West.

Jerry Brown took office after the failure of the Vietnam War, the
scandal of Watergate, and the crippling impact of the 1973 oil embargo
and ensuing recession. Voters who had endorsed Ronald Reagan and his
outsider's critique of bloated government did not want a return to expan-
sive state spending or Pat Brown's "responsible liberalism." Jerry's ascet-
icism and belief in limits suited the reduced expectations of the 1970s. In
a political world where television was the medium, Californians embraced
this unconventional politician who was neither warm nor fuzzy but
promised honest, incorruptible leadership. His candor was refreshing and
his unusual style appealing, even if his agenda remained murky.

California was continuing to grow, but the school-age population stag-
nated as the baby boom generation grew up. Efforts to integrate schools
through busing tore districts apart and spurred white flight. Traffic and
pollution worsened. Inflation eroded incomes. The recession of the early
1970s had left behind an altered economy. Aerospace and the defense
industries, long the economic engines of the state, were in decline. Technology companies were transitioning to a peacetime economy in an area
of Santa Clara County near the Los Gatos seminary.

Jerry demonstrated an ability to intuit what mattered to people and
home in on their concerns in direct, frank language. He welcomed crises
as a way to spur action. He did not avoid delivering bad news. "You have

to be optimistic and visionary," he said. "But there's a darker side, a tragic side, that cannot be overturned . . . I think this country has to come to terms with its limits and to make its choices."

Jerry Brown took office as the youngest California governor in memory, tested in campaigns but a novice in the world of governing. He had made almost no campaign promises and owed no political debts. He had antagonized much of the political establishment with his crusade for reform and its inherent implication that legislators were easily bought and sold. He surrounded himself with people he valued for their intelligence, creativity, and willingness to challenge authority. They were either idealistic and inspiring or arrogant and brash, depending on your point of view, or maybe all of the above. Pat Brown had worked hard to accomplish things within the system. Jerry came to blow the system up.

Those who spent time with the two Governor Browns in private described their relationship as that of a typical father-son, neither warm and easy nor full of friction, despite all the speculation to that effect. Jerry's lack of interest in his father's counsel, particularly his suggestions for appointees, reflected a desire to establish a separate identity but also grew out of his starkly different worldview. They shared core values; they differed fundamentally in philosophy, politics, and personality.

Pat's warmth was so genuine, his belly laugh so contagious, he immediately put people at ease and seemed like an old friend after a five-minute conversation. "Let me use my good offices to help you" was his standard response to the myriad people who called asking for favors. "Perhaps my best quality is that I like people," Pat said, comparing himself with the son whose diffidence Pat defended as shyness rather than arrogance. "I never can believe that I can't make people like me." Pat hugged strangers; Jerry shook hands with his father.

Jerry disdained small talk, often appeared aloof, and was most comfortable with those who did not want anything from him. He tried to preserve his privacy and relaxed with visits to the Tassajara Zen Center and a Trappist monastery in Northern California. "You know, Thomas à Kempis cites Seneca to the effect that 'every time I leave my cell and go out among men, I come back less a man,'" Jerry said on the eve of his election. "Sometimes I feel that way."

Pat plunged into group activities, as he had since childhood. He founded a policy group he called the Wild Ones and eagerly took part in the One-Shot Antelope Hunt in Wyoming. "I may not be a great lawyer or a successful politician, but I am a damn good joiner," Pat wrote a friend, urging him to come to the male-only Bohemian Club's annual retreat on the Russian River.

Jerry described himself as an observer, whether in Mississippi during the civil rights movement or outside San Quentin prison protesting an execution. Even while immersed in politics, he viewed his own actions from a certain distance. His idea of fun was reading Oliver Wendell Holmes or matching wits on television with William F. Buckley on *Firing Line*.

Pat had married his high school sweetheart; Jerry dated movie stars Liv Ullmann and Natalie Wood. He said marriage was incompatible with his job. "For two people to be together constantly takes a lot of consideration and attention. I don't have the time right now." Nor did he want to subject a family to the role of political prop. "Too often people display their families," Jerry said. Each time Pat Brown had filed paperwork to run for office, he had commissioned a family portrait that became a campaign handout. "My father liked to share his family with the body politic. We were always paraded out front," Kathleen told *Time* magazine.

"I was attracted and repelled by what I saw of politics in my father's house," Jerry told an interviewer. "The adventure, the opportunity. The grasping, the artificiality, the obvious manipulation and role-playing, the repetition of emotion without feeling, particularly that the repetition of emotion." Pat had run for district attorney the year after his son was born; there was never a time Jerry was not exposed to his father's brand of politics. "I've always felt I could see its limitations because I was brought up in it," Jerry said. He also readily acknowledged that he would not be governor and perhaps not a politician at all if not for his father's career. He described his conflicted feelings as typical of any father-son relationship. "Some would say that carrying on the family business is a high form of admiration," he said shortly after taking office.

Jerry dismissed the idea of image ("I have always felt uncomfortable with the notion that I had an image, something separate and apart from what I really am") even as he quickly acquired one. He shunned the state's Cadillac limousine and opted for a blue Plymouth. (Actually, two; one in Sacramento, and one in Los Angeles.) He denounced the large suburban home the Reagans had chosen as the governor's residence and lived in an apartment furnished with little more than a box spring and mattress on the floor. He flew commercial. He discontinued the purchase of new briefcases for state officials (forty thousand were already in use)

Father and son shared core values, but approached the job of governor in radically different ways, a function of their personalities and the times in which they governed. (Courtesy of the office of Governor Edmund G. Brown Jr.)

to slow "the blizzard of state paperwork" and jettisoned three paper shredders in his office. He got rid of the automatic signature pen; nothing would go out under his name that he had not read. He banned the acceptance of any gifts. These were the things people around the country would remember about Jerry Brown long after they forgot his accomplishments or failures.

His choices required little sacrifice, given his penchant for a spartan lifestyle, and they proved politically popular and symbolically valuable. "To the extent that what I'm doing has some basic connection with where we're going in this country, it can symbolize the restraint and the limits that all people are up against," Jerry said. He returned hundreds of gifts in the first few months, including an encyclopedia, a painting assessed at $2,000, seventy-five books, season tickets to UCLA football, a membership in the St. Francis Yacht Club, a gold Frisbee, an edition of *Peter Rabbit* in Latin, and the Gold Pass to Disneyland. A package of marigold seeds was sent back with a form letter explaining the new policy. A handmade paperweight was returned to the daughter of Marc Poché, Jerry's freshman dorm adviser. When a flag from the Veterans of Foreign Wars was rejected, an angry barrage of letters followed. "No, Governor Brown doesn't consider the flag just another gift," his press secretary wrote apologetically.

Jesuit priest and antiwar activist Daniel Berrigan sent a copy of one of his books with a note that acknowledged the no-gift policy and suggested the governor consider it a loan. "I appreciate the 'loan' of your book," Jerry responded, "but I think I'd like to keep it permanently, so enclosed is my check for the cost."

Secretary of State Brown had been happy to send autographed pictures; Governor Brown refused. "He feels that distributing such memorabilia contributes to a misplaced cult of personality which too often grows up around our political leaders," read the reply to hundreds of requests received each month. Mark Leonard, a Cub Scout in Boise, Idaho, who had collected forty-nine gubernatorial photos, wrote Jerry three times, enclosed a stamped envelope, and then appealed to Pat Brown. "I know you want your autographed pictures to be collector's items and I know that you are a very, very busy Governor, but I assure you that complying with a few requests would not be burdensome," Pat wrote Jerry. To the Cub Scout, he was philosophical: "I have written my son and told him that I thought he should send you an autographed picture. Sons don't always pay attention to their fathers, however."

Jerry drew from his Jesuit education a detachment about exercising power and a predilection to question everything. He viewed information with skepticism, challenged the source, and sought alternative views. He tested arguments for depth, cut people off and circled back later to test for consistency, probed for courage of convictions. He told a story about the time he had accompanied his father, when Pat was governor, to a multistate conference to discuss the construction of bomb shelters. Jerry wanted to know why they were needed, a question dismissed as unworthy of consideration. "Conventional wisdom and group thinking almost conspire to prevent serious challenge to widely shared assumptions," Jerry said. "I take it as a very important thing in government that assumptions in the inner circles be challenged again and again."

To that end, Jerry built an unconventional inner circle composed of friends from all parts of his life and interesting characters he met along the way. For the group that called themselves Brownies, it was a heady time. The governor preached an era of fiscal limits, but there were no bounds on the ambition or novelty of ideas. Like Steve Jobs and Steve Wozniak, who were building the prototype of the Apple 1 in Jobs's Los Altos garage, the Brownies needed minimal capital, just vision and determination.

Jerry filled key positions with people who were smart, curious, and eager to challenge preconceptions. If anything, experience was a black mark. "He is contentious, an intellectual provocateur," said Tony Kline, who left his job at the nonprofit public interest law firm he cofounded to become Jerry's legal affairs secretary, an amorphous title with a broad mandate. "He has contempt for the ability of people, particularly politicians, to question fundamental assumptions. Should government be involved in this? Can government do anything about the problem? Should anything be done? That can appear to be contempt for the process itself, or for people."

In response to Watergate, Jerry was adamantly opposed to gatekeepers. He would have no one in a role comparable to that of Bob Haldeman or John Ehrlichman in the Nixon administration. Tom Quinn and Richard Maullin were placed in key positions—but outside the governor's office. There would be no suggestion, as had surfaced during the campaign, that his advisers were calling the shots. Quinn and Maullin took over the Air Resources Board and the Energy Commission, respectively, two recently created commissions with sweeping regulatory powers. Neither had any background, and both spearheaded groundbreaking regulations that dismayed industry.

Many of Jerry's first calls went to old friends. Two days before the inauguration, around midnight, Jerry called Marc Poché, his friend since Santa Clara college days, and asked him to serve as finance director. Poché protested that he was totally unqualified. He also had a wife, three children, and three jobs. Jerry insisted Poché go to Sacramento the next day to meet people. Poché made the two-hour drive; Jerry was not there. Poché wandered around the capitol and drove home. Jerry called again. He had arranged leaves for Poché from his academic and congressional jobs. Poché became legislative secretary, with the often thankless job of introducing the governor to older lawmakers wary and resentful of Pat Brown's son.

Uncomfortable with displays of gratitude, Jerry avoided making formal, or even informal, job offers. After the Political Reform Act passed, he started talking to Dan Lowenstein about what would need to be done to set up and run the new Fair Political Practices Commission; Lowenstein, knowing his boss, understood that meant he was being offered the job. He became the first chair of the new commission.

Don Burns, an ex-seminarian and friend from Yale, was practicing law in Washington, D.C. Finding himself in San Francisco the week after the election, he called to congratulate Jerry, who invited Burns to Los Angeles. They stayed up until three A.M., just as they had done in law school. Jerry asked Burns to help in the transition and signal if there were a job that interested him. Burns shut down his law practice, worked on the transition team, and didn't talk to Jerry again for weeks. Only when they walked out of a big group dinner at Lucy's El Adobe did Burns find out he would be secretary for business and transportation.

Rose Bird, a friend from when she and Jerry both lived in International House, had been a public defender and taught criminal law at Stanford. When she declined Jerry's offer to head the environmental agency, he made her cabinet secretary of the Agriculture and Services Agency. Baxter Rice, a friend from St. Ignatius High School and the seminary, took over the Alcoholic Beverage Control Department. Eli Chernow, Jerry's former colleague at Tuttle & Taylor, went to work for the Air Resources Board. Ray Fisher took a leave from Tuttle & Taylor to work as a special adviser and help fulfill one of Jerry's only campaign promises, collective bargaining for state employees. Mary Jean Pew was appointed to the California State University Board of Trustees. Several of Pew's former students ended up on the governor's staff, part of a cadre of twentysomething Brownies thrust into a world they found transformative.

Michael Picker had grown up in a blue-collar family in Garden Grove, an Orange County suburb. After high school, he worked as a printer. Prodded by his former guidance counselor, Picker entered Immaculate Heart College, where Pew changed his view of education. Since Picker worked part time at a liquor store, Pew recruited him to tend bar at a Democratic fundraiser in 1974. After graduation, Pew put him to work in the Brown campaign, running errands and driving the candidate. Picker watched Jerry get into the car, pen in hand, mark up a press release, get out, mark it up some more, and wait while the staff retyped the handout. Picker studied the way Jerry crafted his message. At the end of the campaign, the twenty-two-year-old helped close down the Los Angeles office, returned campaign cars, and prepared daily news summaries, clipping articles from the Southern California papers and shipping them overnight on PSA Airlines to the capitol. Then he moved to Sacramento for a job in the mailroom. In his off hours, he volunteered with the farmworker support group and joined Tom Hayden's new organization, the Campaign for Economic Democracy. Suddenly Picker was thinking further ahead than the next semester.

Diana and Dan Dooley had grown up in the small Central Valley town of Hanford. First in her family to graduate from college, Diana was happy to land a civil service job and then thrilled to be chosen for a spot in the governor's office as an assistant to the labor relations adviser. Dan came from a farming family and had just graduated from law school. At a backyard barbecue, he met Rose Bird, who was seeking attorneys who understood agriculture. At twenty-six, he went to work crafting state policy on pesticide regulation.

The Brownies soaked up the intellectual ferment in an office that filled with a rotating cast of eclectic thinkers. Wendell Berry gave poetry readings. E. F. Schumacher, author of *Small Is Beautiful*, which Jerry often cited and made required reading, gave a talk for the staff. Gary Snyder, a Zen master and Pulitzer Prize–winning poet, became the first chair of the California Arts Council.

Jerry had met Snyder through the San Francisco Zen Center. Shortly after his victory in 1974, the governor-elect had arrived unannounced at the gates of Tassajara, an isolated Buddhist monastery run by the Zen Center, deep in a forest near Big Sur, at the end of a steep fifteen-mile dirt road. The head of the Zen Center was summoned, and eventually Jerry was admitted to Tassajara, the first Zen training monastery established outside Asia. Thus began Jerry's friendship with the Zen Center's abbot, Richard Baker, and Jerry's entrée to the salon of intellectuals and artists assembled by the charismatic Buddhist leader.

Jerry traced his interest in Buddhism back to a 1961 lecture by Aldous Huxley at a San Francisco symposium. Huxley had condemned modern education. When Jerry asked for an explanation, Huxley told the college senior to read *Zen Flesh, Zen Bones*. The book of short Zen stories and riddles intrigued Jerry. After his election as governor, Jerry became a frequent overnight guest at the Zen Center, a complex wedged between a freeway and a housing project in San Francisco's Hayes Valley neighborhood. Drawn to the combination of community and monastic life, the governor became a regular at dinner parties hosted by the abbot, known as Baker Roshi. Some of the guests became Jerry's friends. Some became employees.

Through Baker, Jerry met Stewart Brand, publisher of the counterculture classic the *Whole Earth Catalog*, a technologically and ecologically oriented journal that fused essays with reviews of products and tools, broadly defined. Jerry hired Brand as an adviser; his job was to bring interesting people to Sacramento. Brand ran a speaker series for the governor's staff that he called "What's ACTUALLY Happening," with guests like Ken Kesey, Buckminster Fuller, and Amory Lovins. Others were less well known names doing cutting-edge work: Ridgeway Banks, an engineer at Lawrence Livermore Labs who had built the first engine out of nitinol, an alloy with shape memory; Milton Kotler, an activist author who advocated a return to strong neighborhood government control; Jay Forrester, a pioneer in the field of computer modeling who was applying the approach to urban problems and population growth.

The liberal Democratic activist Allard Lowenstein moved his family across the country and into Jerry's Laurel Canyon house for a summer to work on special projects. "Al was like an energy source," Jerry said a few years later, describing his friend as someone in perpetual motion. "He was a source of inspiration, and my sense of government is this inert mass of conventional thinking, and it needs to be constantly agitated, pushed, confronted, challenged, inspired, energized. He had that quality of openness and playfulness, or excitement."

Committed to the idea that government must look more like the governed, Jerry appointed women and minorities to hundreds of high-level jobs and commission posts, many for the first time. Women assumed visible, nontraditional jobs, becoming the secretaries of agriculture, transportation, navigation and ocean development, and veterans' affairs. Ed Roberts, a paralyzed polio victim who crusaded for the rights of the disabled, became head the Department of Vocational Rehabilitation—an agency that had once deemed Roberts too disabled to hold a job. Jerry signed a law mandating that lay people be the majority on boards that regulated most industries, and then enraged doctors by appointing chiropractors to committees that reviewed physician discipline cases.

In his most prominent and lasting effort to subvert the established power structure, he reshaped the state's judiciary. California courts had three times as many judges as the entire federal system. Almost all were white men. The first year, half of Jerry's fifty-seven judicial appointees were black, Mexican American, Asian, or female. The judicial establishment, accustomed to having great input in appointments, found the traditional ways of doing business challenged and upended.

"I'm like a windshield wiper," Jerry said, "cleaning the windows so we can see where we are going."

Where he sought expertise, Jerry looked outside the traditional Democratic networks. Ron Robie had graduated from Cal one year ahead of Jerry and worked on water issues, first as a legislative aide during Pat Brown's administration and then as a member of the state water commission. Allied with environmentalists, Robie had been frustrated by the power of special interests like the utilities to block progressive measures. As the new head of the Department of Water Resources, Robie found himself part of an administration that didn't care who was important and flaunted its independence. Ideas and persuasive arguments were the currency that mattered. He was exhilarated by the spirit of exploding traditional ideas of power.

"Anyone who had energy and talent and was philosophically disposed to want to make government more interesting and responsive and creative, then they were welcome," Jerry reflected a few years later. "My general methodology—which I think is somewhat unique—I could be sitting in a restaurant and if someone would engage me in conversation I would start talking with them and they might be working for me two months down the road."

Marty Morgenstern, a union organizer who had consulted with the Brown campaign briefly, ended up as the governor's labor adviser after running into Jerry in a restaurant and debating the merits of binding arbitration for public employees. State labor leaders were unhappy that the governor's chief negotiator came from outside their ranks, another pointed reminder that Jerry bypassed traditional Democratic channels. Though Morgenstern came from an East Coast background and lacked the long-standing ties of some in the inner circle, he fit in well as an intellectual sparring partner. He had recently turned forty, which made him the old man in the crowd.

The pace and lifestyle was geared to the young, mainly single, staff. Their work days often started in late morning and ended at three o'clock the next morning. Jerry's habit of arriving around eleven A.M. and eating takeout hamburgers and fries drew concern from the state health department nutritionist, who worked with the capitol cafeteria to provide healthier alternatives. The governor was notoriously late, kept people waiting for hours, and refused to adhere to a schedule that would cramp his ability to pursue conversations as long as he wished. He thought nothing of making calls at any hour, or directing others to do so. Cabinet meetings began in the early evening and might run till midnight; Jerry rarely attended, and it was left to his chief of staff, Gray Davis, to try to impose order. The conversations continued into the early morning at David's Brass Rail, across the street from the capitol. At the legal closing time of two A.M., David locked the doors and served free liquor. City transplants stuck in a small, provincial town, the Brownies formed a close-knit community and lifelong friendships. In Los Angeles, the staff sometimes met at El Adobe, or at the Malibu home of Jerry's girlfriend, singer-songwriter Linda Ronstadt.

Jerry was still infamous for never having any money on him; his friends joked that the vow of poverty in the seminary was not one he had had trouble obeying. When a businessman's friends refused to believe his story about a chance encounter, he wrote Jerry: "Dear Governor Brown: I am still trying to convince my friends and associates that Jerry Brown borrowed 10¢ from me to make a telephone call. Can you be of any assistance in my plight?" (Jerry wrote back and sent him a dime.)

When Jerry's advance man Wally McGuire was in Sacramento, he sometimes stayed in the other apartment on Jerry's floor, kept empty for security reasons, and furnished with a futon bed. The two men often talked into the early morning hours. Later in the day, Jerry might walk past McGuire in the capitol and barely say hello. Those who were bothered by that level of detachment didn't stick around. "This is no place to be if you need positive feedback to keep going," said Rose Bird. "Jerry doesn't need approval and he doesn't think other people do."

Jerry immersed himself deeply in the details of issues that interested him, ignoring that which bored him or intruded on his focus at a given moment. When Assemblyman John Knox, a Bay Area Democrat, arrived to discuss a judicial appointment, the governor was on the speakerphone with a turtle expert in Florida. Jerry had to decide whether to sign a bill that would allow a Grand Cayman Islands farm to export green sea turtle meat to California. Jerry drew Knox into an hour-long conversation with the professor about the endangered species, ultimately convincing the legislator he had voted the wrong way on the bill.

"Green sea turtles make soup, pretty shells and cosmetic oil," Jerry wrote in his veto message. "Once there were tens of millions, now there are only thousands making their mysterious voyage through the seas from nesting beaches to distant feeding grounds. Some say farming green sea turtles in captivity will bring them back. Others see such commercial ventures as just expanding the appetite for this threatened creature. I incline to the latter and believe what turtles need is less people taking their eggs and depleting their species." The *Los Angeles Times* editorial board called it one of the best veto messages they had ever read.

Jerry used the budget, the most far-reaching tool for setting an agenda, to demonstrate both his command of details and his commitment to limits. In his first news conference, he invoked "a time of lowered expectations" and expressed pessimism about revenue projections, "probably based on my theological training more than my economic analysis." He trimmed the published book that outlined the budget by more than half, briefed reporters on the overview, and invited them to return and quiz him about the document once they had had time to read it through. "I went over it word by word, comma by comma," he said about his budget message. "I want you to understand my philosophy."

The budget laid out three core principles: Government should not spend more than it takes in, larger expenditures do not equate with better government, and there are no sacred cows. In many ways, the proposal resembled those of Ronald Reagan more than those of Pat Brown, with reduced spending for some state agencies and minimal increases for others. Jerry supported spending that achieved clear impact, such as an increase in grants to the aged, blind, and disabled. "This is money that goes to people," he said. "They get the checks and they can use them for their own judgment. It does not go through a pretzel palace, it does not hire planners, it doesn't expand the Xerox machine capacity of the state, it doesn't write comprehensive plans . . . one of the few things that government does well is to send out checks. When it gets more complicated than that, watch out."

He advocated and implemented a flat pay raise for state employees, from "judges to janitors," rather than a percentage increase. All state workers received an extra $70 a month in 1976, a boon for lower-wage workers like Mike Picker in the mailroom, whose monthly pay was $440. "We should reduce the great disparities that exist in public service," Jerry said. "I think often times those at the top have meaningful jobs and shouldn't really get paid additionally for them but ought to be happy for the opportunity to serve people in that particular capacity. It's kind of a variant on 'virtue is its own reward.' . . . I grant you that is not the orthodox perception but that's the way I think."

In response to those dismayed by his failure to restore cuts imposed during the Reagan years, Jerry pointed to the issue that had drawn him into politics: Vietnam. The billions of dollars the United States spent in Vietnam failed to win the war. "There is an overblown rhetoric and an overblown expectation that if there is a problem, there must be a program to solve it. I think that in many ways is the lesson of Vietnam . . . we lost because we lacked the political will to carry out a particular objective," he told William F. Buckley on *Firing Line*, filmed before a live audience in Sacramento in a conversation called "The Practical Limits of Liberalism." Students sat on the studio floor watching Jerry, gray sideburns, dark hair long enough to touch his jacket collar, dark gray pinstripe three-piece suit, purple tie tucked into his vest.

"Creative inaction" was an underrated option, Jerry argued. Additional laws, like additional funds, were often the wrong remedy. He refused to support a law that would abolish minimum milk prices, citing their effectiveness during the Depression when price controls were hailed as a great reform. "Before you dump something over, you better figure out what it is you are doing . . . precipitous action is rarely needed, and then only with adequate justification."

A strong leader knew when not to act, Jerry said. "In my view, a leader has only a few great decisions to make or, perhaps, a few colossal mistakes to avoid," he said. President Johnson's political victories in establishing social programs were overshadowed by his legacy in Vietnam, Jerry argued. "If President Johnson had had the detachment and the vision that a great man should possess, it's conceivable that he might have foreseen the Vietnam debacle and avoided it."

All the personae of the young governor—intellectual provocateur, skeptic, self-confident antiestablishmentarian, cheapskate, and public servant—coalesced in his prolonged struggle to change the culture of the University of California, a painful, frustrating experience for all concerned. To compensate for budget cuts under Reagan, the university had imposed an "educational fee" that amounted to tuition. By 1975, California undergraduates paid $630 in annual tuition and fees; affordable, but a symbolic break with the commitment to free tuition. Battered by Reagan-era cuts but still stewards of the best public system in the world, university leaders had expected Jerry to be their champion. Instead, the university found itself under attack. In public and in private, Jerry tried to jolt the academic community out of its traditional ways and sense of entitlement, to inculcate the idea of limits, and to refocus the school in accordance with his vision of a liberal arts education as a force for communal good.

In his first year, Jerry cut the budget request from $567 million to $542 million and vetoed additions that state lawmakers restored. He reminded the Regents they were competing for dollars with the old, the disabled, the unemployed, public schools, and every other state agency, and dismissed their complaints as "delusions of grandeur." He criticized university president David Saxon's $60,000 salary: "Low salaries draw better people into public service. Look at Gandhi; he didn't make any money and he was pretty successful. And Ho Chi Minh and Mao. What have they got going for them that we don't have?" One Sunday, Jerry showed up without warning at Saxon's house and stayed to talk for six hours. Saxon had a saying: Reagan hated public institutions; Jerry hated all institutions.

Jerry dismissed the university's five-year plan as an example of "the squid process—an abstract statement that tells me absolutely nothing . . . spurts of ink spread across many pages in patterns that look like words but mean nothing." He bemoaned the lack of transparency and difficulty obtaining answers to basic questions. "To identify anything requires a Sherlock Holmes approach on the part of not only the department of finance but myself. I find it extremely difficult to extract a clear sentence about what those people want to do—about anything." At Regents meetings, he outraged academics by questioning basic precepts: Why were smaller classes better? Why weren't admissions officers weighing essay questions more heavily than standardized tests? Why were no women or minorities considered for a chancellor's position? What did marginal students do after they graduated and how did they contribute to society? He suggested professors accept lower salaries because their work should provide "psychic income."

The questions reminded Richard McCurdy of the restless mind in his English class at St. Ignatius High two decades earlier. "If you made a statement, he could push you to the wall to back it up. You couldn't get away with anything," said McCurdy, the teacher Jerry credited with instilling in him an appreciation of literature. McCurdy had entered the seminary with Jerry, become a Jesuit priest, and returned to St. Ignatius as principal. "He learned the Socratic approach to learning," McCurdy said about the young governor. "Some of the things that have happened in Sacramento, like his responses to complaints from the University Regents, are traceable to this approach, which is also the Jesuit way."

Jerry appointed the first Asian American and the first Latino Regents. As an ally in challenging the educational status quo, he recruited Gregory Bateson, an English anthropologist and idiosyncratic intellectual who pioneered the science of cybernetics. Stewart Brand had decided Jerry should meet Bateson, who taught part time at the University of California at Santa Cruz. Brand and Bateson arrived at the capitol for a six P.M. appointment; the conversation began at eleven thirty P.M., the tape recorder running as they sat on Jerry's office floor. Bateson told Jerry that the elite students he taught knew very little.

"They don't know the multiplication tables. They don't know the Lord's Prayer." "In English or Latin?" Jerry interjected. "Certainly not in Latin, but they don't even know it in English. They don't know any Shakespeare or any Blake."

"And these are the best. So what are we getting for our millions?" Jerry asked. "God only knows," Bateson responded. Among his students, he said, "there are really ten percent who are worth teaching." Jerry appointed Bateson to the Board of Regents.

After a year as a Regent, Bateson wrote the chairman that he was "simply unable to decide or even to have an opinion on most of the matters . . . To correct my incompetence and ignorance, it would be necessary to do a very great deal of work." He was not motivated to do the work for matters he considered trivial. He wondered what Saint Augustine would say if he attended a Regents meeting. Jerry engaged Bateson in colloquies at meetings and defended his appointment: "He's added a new dimension and proven that even Regents can think and consider the important issues, and that the governance of a University is about ideas, as well as parking lots and capital improvement."

"The fact that the U.C. law schools are listed as being among the top 10 in the country is not a sign of glory, but of failure," Jerry wrote, arguing schools were measured by the wrong criteria. "Never before has education been so irrelevant for so many kids in this country . . . That is why I raise questions about the University. Not because I don't respect, not because I don't even love them, not because I don't think it is a great place, I believe it is. It is the greatest in the world. But I look at the law schools and I ask myself, how does that affect the least of the people who live in this society?"

No matter how provocative or persistent, he ultimately had little impact on a giant bureaucracy resistant to change. Unable or unwilling to negotiate with a power structure that viewed him as an alien threat, Jerry succeeded largely in making the university more defensive, while his budgets, on top of the Reagan cuts, weakened the schools.

His critiques, however, consistent with Jerry's other public comments, resonated with a larger audience. In national polls, Americans overwhelmingly agreed about the need to reduce consumption, a trend that dated back to the recession that followed the oil embargo. Before the end of his first year, 85 percent of Californians viewed Jerry Brown favorably. "He's a phenomenon of sorts, because as a result of his promising less, he's the most popular governor the state has ever known," said Morley Safer, in the introduction to an interview on *60 Minutes*.

"He has been elevated from Mr. Clean to Junior Enigma," wrote *Sacramento Bee* editorial page editor Peter Schrag. "He goes around town with a sandwich board that says 'Repent.' Is he running for Vice President or for the still-to-be-created position of Public Monk?"

East Coast journalists descended to dissect the phenomenon. They gravitated to the shibboleths about wacky California. The governor sleeps on a mattress on the floor, drives a Plymouth, works all night. "'What's your program?' That's all you Washington reporters want to know," Jerry said to David Broder, who was writing a piece for the *Atlantic*. "What the hell does that mean? The program is to confront the confusion and hypocrisy of government; that's the program."

"Jerry Brown is different," reported the *New York Times Magazine*. "He is the most interesting politician in the United States. And, at the moment, he is one of the most popular"—despite the fact that "he is not a particularly likeable young man" who asks "hostile and irreverent questions."

Poet and City Lights bookstore owner Lawrence Ferlinghetti asked if Jerry would agree to have his writings included as part of a series of small books that would consist of quotes from "original brains—we hope to make it a really catalytic series of seminal works—short books in pocket format, no more than 64 pages." The slim book of collected quotes from the governor, *Thoughts*, sold seven thousand copies in two weeks.

"In all the Western states I visited there is a great deal of interest in you, in what you are saying and in the popularity you have gained and maintained in California," wrote Henry Grunwald, managing editor of *Time* magazine, after interviewing Jerry over arroz con pollo at El Adobe. "Your notion of 'lower expectations' has become a ready reference point for most political discussions. I also find that many professionals are fascinated by your attitude of not trying to give ready answers to major problems, but rather trying to define the questions. Frankly, they are also wondering just how long you can keep that up."

His father, as baffled by his son as he was proud, wondered, too. "You haven't paid very much attention to me during your first six months and I think that is all to the good, because if you had you wouldn't have achieved what I believe to be a great first six months," he wrote. Pat frequently recommended job candidates, undeterred by the knowledge that his suggestions were, as he put it, thrown in the wastebasket. "I do have some feeling for the problems of a former governor who is a strong proponent for his son," Carlotta Mellon, the governor's appointments secretary, wrote to Pat. "I am only sorry that I have not been able to make your batting average better . . . Hang in there." Many of Jerry's staff viewed Governor Pat with great affection and were happy to take calls that always opened with a simple question: "How's Jerry doing?"

After the president of Santa Clara University impersonated the pope in order to get Jerry to take his call, the governor agreed to deliver the commencement address at the school he had attended two decades earlier. Ben Swig, the wealthy San Francisco real estate developer and financial backer of both Browns, was on the university board. He knew Pat would want to hear his son's address and sent a helicopter to the Bohemian Grove encampment on the Russian River, where Pat was spending the weekend, to fly him to San Jose.

Jerry was displeased to find his father seated on the dais. Conforming to his reputation for brevity, he drew a cheer in the eight-minute address when he explained why he avoided public speeches: "If there is any vice that I see more than any other in public affairs, it is the surplus of rhetoric, meaningless generalizations, and an abuse of the English language." He exhorted the students not to look for government help in solving their problems but "to depend on your own energy and your own creative potential." He declined to wear academic robes, and as soon as he finished speaking, he changed from his dark suit to frayed blue jeans and a denim shirt for a flight to Northern California, where he made an unannounced visit to a Maidu Indian ceremonial ground where tribes held their annual bear dance.

Pat and Jerry differed sharply in their views about the limit of government to help people, but they shared certain values. As Pat had proselytized the importance of personal responsibility in his booklet "Youth, Don't Be a Chump," Jerry infused his decision making with a sense of individual responsibility. He opposed a bill that would have required motorcycle riders to wear helmets, saying the state should not be in loco parentis. People should face the consequences of their actions. He agonized over whether to sign a bill that would shield parents from liability if underage drinkers left a house party and drove drunk; at the last minute, he signed it.

Asked to name his objectives after six months, he said, "Reduce the sum of human misery a bit, I guess. Help people expand their lives a little bit, give them an awareness of their own potential."

Not all that different from his father's goal—to think of the poorest soul and help them exit from purgatory.

"Jerry is more private, a more private person, but I think he's just as compassionate as Pat, and I think he has the same commitment," Bernice said. "I think this is what Jerry gets from him—commitment to public service, and I think that's why he got into politics." Though she had been bewildered and upset by Jerry's years in the seminary, she credited the Jesuits with making her son a scholar and instilling values that became his yardstick for life. Jerry had never been particularly sensitive, Bernice said, but he showed flashes of thoughtfulness. He gave gifts only when he found something meaningful, not to conform with a set holiday like Christmas. When he did give presents, they showed a great deal of care. When the old photo of his father and sisters walking the Golden Gate Bridge on opening day began to fade, Jerry commissioned an oil painting to preserve the image.

He exhibited similar traits in his correspondence. Jerry put little in writing but took pains with the few epistles he penned. He wrote thoughtful condolence notes. Occasionally, a letter caught his attention. In September 1976, Mrs. H. M. Cullers sent the governor a photo of the second Mountain House, rebuilt by Frank Schuckman in 1907.

The land was still owned by Pat, his brother Harold, and two partners they had recruited to buy the Colusa property in 1962. They leased the fields to local farmers who grew barley and alfalfa and used the land to graze cattle. The property netted about $6,000 a year in income. A few barns and outbuildings remained, but the Mountain House had burned down in 1971, after years of sitting empty and abandoned, a graffiti-ridden hideout for local children.

Mrs. Cullers remembered the old inn well. She had grown up in nearby Hough Springs at the turn of the century and often ridden the stagecoach that stopped at the Mountain House. In December 1912, she married a man who hauled Bartlett Spring water to Williams via the Mountain House. "Hope you build a house up in that country," she wrote to the governor.

"I want to thank you for your nice letter," Jerry wrote back. "No definite plans have been made, but I have thought about the idea of starting a family farm near Williams. Sixty-four years is a long time to be married. I hope you and your husband will have a very happy anniversary celebration in December. Warmest regards."

14

Jerry and Cesar

In a three-evening interview with *Playboy* magazine that ended around two A.M. in the governor's office, Jerry Brown was asked to name people who have power. His first response was Cesar Chavez.

"A person in a significant position of power can lead by the questions he raises and the example he sets," Jerry said during the conversation early in his second year as governor. "A lot of political energy comes from a certain vision, a faith that communicates itself to other people. People who stand for an idea that has energy connected with it, that's power."

Cesar Chavez had launched a crusade that led 17 million Americans to boycott grapes so that California farmworkers might earn decent wages. He leveraged the boycott to force the state's most powerful industry to sign labor contracts with its poorest workers. Along his bumpy, historic path to win dignity and respect for the predominantly Mexican American farmworkers, Chavez had even extracted a rare campaign promise from candidate Jerry Brown.

One man had grown up in migrant labor camps and dropped out of school after eighth grade to work in the fields, the other had an elite education and often spouted Latin. Yet the two had more in common than their interest in power. Both had carved paths outside establishments they treated with disdain. Both sought to subvert the status quo. Both were spiritual Catholics, uninterested in material goods, steeped in a tradition of asceticism. Both preached the need to reduce consumption and valued individual sacrifice for a common good. Neither had much interest or patience for the mundane. Each an oddly charismatic leader in a nontraditional mold, they were drawn to each other by mutual need that evolved into admiration and even trust. They forged a partnership that achieved goals that most others would not even have attempted.

The relationship began when Jerry was secretary of state. The boycott had forced more than a hundred table grape growers to sign contracts with the United Farm Workers union in July 1970. The growers responded with the tool that Hiram Johnson had unleashed as a weapon against the railroad: the initiative. Agricultural interests gathered enough signatures to place on the November 1972 ballot a proposition that would invalidate existing contracts, outlaw the boycott, and effectively destroy any future opportunity to unionize farmworkers. The UFW's survival depended on defeating Proposition 22.

LeRoy Chatfield, a former Christian Brother who shed his vows to join Chavez's movement, was in charge of the No on 22 campaign. In the attic of the county registrar's office, Chatfield's wife, Bonnie, reviewed petitions that had been submitted to qualify the proposition, hoping to find some useful lead. She discovered hundreds of forged signatures. Chatfield dispatched volunteers to contact the petition signers. They began to unravel a well-orchestrated fraud; even many who signed their own names had been misled into thinking the proposition supported farmworkers' rights.

As the only Democrat in a statewide office in Sacramento, Jerry Brown was considered a nominal friend of Chavez and the union he founded, though contact between them had been slight. Jerry traced his interest in farmworkers back to his student days at Cal, when the AFL-CIO briefly attempted to organize in the California fields. Jerry had joined a student support group that picked strawberries for a day, then spent a night in Stockton listening to union speeches, slept on a church floor, and picked tomatoes the next day. In 1962, Chavez moved to the Central Valley city of Delano and began organizing what became the United Farm Workers. Jerry met Chavez briefly four years later when he came to see Pat Brown during the campaign to organize workers at the DiGiorgio vineyards. Dressed in his customary plaid work shirt, the short, dark-skinned Mexican American stood out from the usual visitors to the governor's house. Three years later, Jerry joined a UFW march to the Mexican border to protest the use of Mexican workers as strikebreakers. He stayed in the background as Senator Edward Kennedy and other politicians spoke. "I marched with Cesar Chavez" figured prominently in Jerry's subsequent campaign literature.

As secretary of state, Jerry was in charge of certifying ballot measures. Chatfield made an appointment to talk about Prop 22. He brought with him the union's lawyer and boxes of declarations by petition signers who said they had been duped. Jerry's initial response was a wary protestation that he could do little to help. "I'm not God," he said, a line Chatfield later repeated often. Tom Quinn grasped the political potential and calmed everyone down when Chatfield blew up and began to leave. Once Jerry focused, they quickly devised a plan. The UFW would gather sworn statements; Jerry would denounce the fraud in press conferences around the state, demand investigations, and call upon friendly district attorneys to draw further attention to the problem.

The quasilegal practices that the UFW uncovered and Jerry publicized highlighted a trend with broad ramifications: Initiatives were becoming a powerful, lucrative industry in California. Since 1912, with a few exceptions, there had been only a handful of initiatives each year; in 1972 there were ten. The new emphasis on single-issue politics was driven and facilitated in part by consultants, led by Whitaker & Baxter, who offered expertise for hire that enabled any interest group to buy its way onto the ballot. No longer was a genuine grassroots effort necessary. The publicity over Proposition 22 exposed tactics that were becoming commonplace, like petition gatherers paid by the signature.

"The initiative was an instrument to give the people the power to make their own laws, but it is very rapidly becoming a tool of the special interests," Jerry said at a state hearing on Proposition 22, where minors testified about illegally collecting signatures and petition gatherers explained the financial incentive to use deceptive practices to fill their sheets. They even had a name for the small cards they used to cover up the real description of the ballot proposition—"dodger cards."

Republicans like State Attorney General Evelle Younger, who learned on the radio that he had been asked to investigate Prop 22, dismissed the complaint as another example of Jerry Brown's publicity machine. "In the future, if you request an investigation of this office, it would be appropriate and deeply appreciated by me if you would communicate with us prior to holding a press conference," Younger wrote to the secretary of state. But the Los Angeles district attorney cited evidence of massive fraud, prompting editorials in the *Los Angeles Times*. Jerry hired fifteen hundred temporary clerks to check a million signatures and used their findings to sue to remove Prop 22 from the ballot. The suit failed, but the publicity enhanced his statewide profile, helped defeat Prop 22, and cemented important political and personal relationships.

Within a year, Jerry was running for governor and LeRoy Chatfield was heading his Northern California campaign, the first of numerous UFW volunteers to cross over. The overlap was not surprising; Jerry and Chavez attracted similar disciples. People who demonstrated an ability to make things happen rose rapidly to positions of responsibility. Fanaticism and single-minded devotion to the cause were highly valued.

Chatfield had grown up in Colusa, not far from the Mountain House. Like Ida Schuckman, he left as fast as he could and never looked back. At fifteen, he entered a Catholic monastic religious teaching order, then became a high school teacher and debate coach in Bakersfield. At a conference on social justice in 1965, he heard about Cesar Chavez's movement, based just a half hour north of Bakersfield and still virtually unknown. He visited Chavez in Delano and soon decided to work for him full time.

Chatfield was asked to join the Brown campaign in a typically elliptical manner. Jerry invited Chatfield to the Laurel Canyon house. He arrived to find a party under way and talked for much of the evening not to Jerry, but to a somewhat mysterious Frenchman named Jacques Barzaghi. Chatfield later realized the conversation had been a job interview. Barzaghi, customarily dressed in black and sporting a beret, was a loyal confidant who shadowed Jerry, performed tasks such as buying clothes, and served as an antenna, helping evaluate outsiders.

As the gubernatorial campaign progressed, Jerry and Chavez had reason to talk. Jerry visited an executive board meeting of the UFW in March 1974 to ask for the union's support. He was struck by the vitality and sense of mission among the dozens of volunteers who worked and lived at the isolated compound in the Tehachapi Mountains where Chavez had built a communal home that served as the movement headquarters. Nuns typed in the outer office and volunteers shared a vegetarian meal in the dining hall, where Chavez offered Jerry herbal tea. Under pressure amid continued turmoil in the fields, Chavez had reluctantly endorsed the idea of state legislation that would establish a mechanism for farmworker elections, similar to the National Labor Relations Act, which governed union activity but excluded agricultural laborers. Chavez feared a bad law would take away the union's freedom to boycott and impose a structure that favored agricultural interests. He wanted a commitment that Jerry would veto any bill the union disliked. They made an appointment to talk for half an hour; the conversation lasted almost two hours. The candidate was knowledgeable, and noncommittal.

Jerry hoped to avoid any promises that might bind his future actions or cost him votes. When a troublesome bill surfaced in Sacramento and the union reached out to Jerry and Tom Quinn, neither returned calls. Early one morning Chatfield arrived for work at the Brown headquarters in San Francisco and found the second-floor mezzanine outside his office filled with farmworkers. The UFW veteran recognized the sit-in as a warning, turned around, and went down to the ground floor coffee shop to quickly evaluate his options. He invited the workers into his office to lessen the chance of publicity. Sandy Nathan, a union lawyer who had organized the protest, had clear instructions: The workers would stay until the candidate agreed to issue a statement immediately that backed the union's position on legislation. Several hours and phone calls later, the demand was met.

The commitment figured prominently in Jerry's very brief inaugural address, one of the only substantive issues he mentioned. He vowed to bring peace to the fields after a decade of chaos, intraunion disputes, economic uncertainty, and mass civil disobedience. "It is time that we treat all workers alike, whether they work in the city or toil in the fields," he said. "It is time to extend the rule of law to the agriculture sector and establish the right of secret ballot elections for farm workers. The law I support will impose rights and responsibilities on both farmworker and farmer alike."

The promise took a back seat in the early whirlwind days of the new administration. To exert pressure, the UFW ramped up its national boycott of Gallo wine, targeting the well-known Central Valley vintner who had spurned the union. Consumers had lots of alternatives, and Gallo sales in California dropped six percent in the first quarter of 1975 while sales of other brands increased. Like many growers, Ernest Gallo had wearied of the harassment from a union that Chavez proudly described as "the nonviolent Viet Cong." The winemaker took out full-page ads urging that farmworkers be placed under the National Labor Relations Act. When the UFW organized a march on Gallo headquarters, the company hung a banner in San Francisco's Union Square, where the marchers gathered: MARCHING WRONG WAY, CESAR? The union should aim its power at Sacramento instead.

Four days and 110 miles later, the march reached Gallo headquarters in Modesto. "As the song says, we're going to roll this union on," Chavez told the cheering crowd of about ten thousand. "No doubt in our minds and our hearts that we're going to win." Then he addressed the governor, who had not been in touch: "Brothers and sisters, we have a final message to another person. We want to tell him, 'Dear Governor, you know, we once went to Sacramento to visit your daddy.'" The crowd cheered *"Si se puede"* (Yes we can) at the reference to the 1966 pilgrimage from Delano to the capitol, when Pat Brown snubbed the workers and spent Easter in Palm Springs.

Unlike most politicians, Jerry welcomed crises. They focused attention, spurred people to embrace change, and offered an opportunity to exert leadership. Three days after Chavez's jibe, farmworkers were on the agenda at the governor's weekly Monday meeting with Senate and Assembly leaders. Chatfield, who had segued from the campaign to the governor's office, placed an urgent call to UFW counsel Jerry Cohen: The governor wanted a full, detailed briefing on farm labor legislation before the Friday cabinet meeting.

On Saturday morning, March 15, Chavez and Cohen joined Jerry, Barzaghi, and Chatfield at the Laurel Canyon house. Chavez's strategy was to say as little as possible. "Find out where Brown stood. Let him know that legislation wasn't what we were after. We wanted damn contracts more than anything else," he explained to his executive board. He hoped to persuade the governor to use the threat of legislation to pressure growers to sign contracts. He thought his demands for proposed legislation were so favorable to the union that they could never be met. Chavez underestimated Jerry's determination and negotiating skill.

Jerry subtly wooed Chavez. The governor underscored their philosophical compatibility with unrelated references, like a comment about his contention that University of California professors were overpaid and underworked. And in the middle of deliberations, Jerry asked Cesar to go for a walk. Cohen and Chatfield exchanged glances. They knew Chavez avoided being alone with politicians. But he agreed. He instinctively trusted Jerry.

"We walked out, and that's where we made some deals," Chavez told his board. Jerry said he was serious, and Chavez said he was, too, but the bill had to have teeth, allow workers to choose the union of their choice, and impose penalties on employers who failed to negotiate in good faith. Chavez said if the bill passed, they wanted Jerry to speak at their convention. Jerry asked if they could win elections. Chavez said of course. Chavez gave Jerry a dozen specific points they needed, and Jerry indicated most were doable. As Chavez would learn, Jerry's negotiating style was marked by unusual transparency.

The two men agreed on a strategy: The governor would introduce a bill, and the union would attack and support a more radical alternative. The governor's bill would then be amended to become acceptable to all sides. On April 7, 1975, Jerry celebrated his thirty-seventh birthday at the Tassajara Zen retreat. Two days later, the governor unveiled his proposal. "This is a bill that attempts to give farmworkers self-determination through secret ballot elections," Jerry said. "It is a unique effort, and I enlist everyone's support for that endeavor."

The weeks that followed were a round robin of private negotiations and public posturing, long days and late-night sessions fueled by beer and wine. Chavez tossed insults. When he said the governor wouldn't know anything about potatoes, Jerry was miffed; he protested that he had had a victory garden when he was three years old. Chatfield organized what the governor called the necessary "theatrics," bringing in groups of clergy and labor allies, cultivating favorable press, courting legislators, and building momentum. Jerry spent hours in meetings and phone calls with supermarket executives, black clergy, prominent growers. He listened intently to all sides to understand what mattered to whom and who had room to move where.

A front page story in the *Wall Street Journal* on April 29, 1975, noted that the young governor was so popular in California he was already touted as a national candidate. Yet his fiscally conservative agenda had disappointed liberal supporters and he lacked any major accomplishments to date. "Jerry's mistrust of government isn't enough," Stephen Reinhardt, the labor lawyer who had played a key role in Jerry's campaign, told the newspaper. "His questioning has to lead to conclusions. Whether he's a serious national contender depends entirely on the next few years. He's got to do something."

Reinhardt's phone rang the next evening; only Jerry Brown, oblivious to all professional sports, would call while the Golden State Warriors were playing the Chicago Bulls in game 2 of the Western Conference Finals. Jerry challenged Reinhardt to come to Sacramento and help out in the denouement of historic legislation. Reinhardt accepted. He helped draft language during the early morning hours of the first weekend of May as Jerry shuttled from room to room among parties that had been implacable enemies for years. The UFW was in one room, Teamsters in another, growers in a third. Jerry drew upon his training as a debater and trial lawyer. He immersed himself in the smallest details and then emerged to summarize issues in clear, persuasive language and rebut counterarguments. He had studied the issue from every point of view, understood each protagonist's bottom line, and functioned as an honest broker. In the final negotiations, with impressive mastery of complex nuances, Jerry sold the UFW's adversaries a measure that had everything Cesar Chavez demanded.

California became the only state to grant basic labor rights to farmworkers. The law protected union activity, imposed penalties on employers who bargained in bad faith or retaliated against union leaders, and established a state agency to oversee secret-ballot union elections. The Agricultural Labor Relations Act was hailed as the most pro-labor law in the country, preserving the right to boycott under certain circumstances and giving labor unions the sole right to determine members in good standing.

"A law of itself can't solve human problems, but it can provide the framework," Jerry said as he signed the bill. "It gives for the first time a group of people in our society who are at the lowest end of the economic scale the self-determination to assert their own dignity and their own rights and their own views on what they want and what they don't want. And that is a very significant step forward."

Jerry saw himself as a catalyst who seized the right moment; without the power that Chavez had amassed and demonstrated, the others would not have been willing to deal. "Many problems depend on an intangible like that," he said. "On dedication, on a principle, on an idea. And an idea is more powerful than anything else. If that idea is grounded within the structure of a people, there is no stopping it if it fits with the time."

Jerry also understood that the victory marked a fundamental turning point that would change the nature of Chavez's movement and send him searching for the next crusade. That had been part of Jerry's argument to the growers. "Cesar needed a movement. His movement was drained of its, of its, what's the right word, its charisma, or its enthusiasm, by virtue of the domestication of the law," Jerry said a few years later. When

Chavez had said he did not really want a law, the concern was more than a negotiating ploy.

"The thing about Brown, I think, that's probably amazing, is that more than any other party, he played it straight with us," Sandy Nathan said to Jerry Cohen two weeks after the bill passed, as the two UFW attorneys relived the tumultuous past month. Cohen credited Jerry's respect for Cesar, the values of the movement, and its power. He also cited the increasing buzz about Jerry as a presidential candidate. "If Brown doesn't have national ambitions," Cohen said, "our strength isn't as great as it was."

Though Jerry had been in office less than a year, his unprecedented popularity in California and the lack of a clear Democratic front-runner in the 1976 race had fueled speculation about a presidential bid. "The success of his farm-labor negotiations had as much impact in New York as it did in Los Angeles—perhaps more," wrote California political reporter Ed Salzman in the summer of 1975, as the new law went into effect. What mattered was not the disenchantment of California liberals unhappy with budget decisions but the embrace of those on the East Coast, where Cesar Chavez and *la causa* had strong support.

Just after Labor Day, thousands of Mexican American farmworkers lined up at polling places in the California fields, many casting the first vote of their lives. The rival Teamsters union appealed to workers on bread-and-butter terms and tried to overcome its history of top-down, sweetheart contracts. By far the more popular choice was the organization workers simply called *"la union de Cesar Chavez."*

Jerry had delivered on his promise to Chavez to appoint a sympathetic board to oversee the new agency. LeRoy Chatfield was a member. As chair, Jerry tapped Fresno bishop Roger Mahony, the most knowledgeable cleric on farm labor issues and a key participant in negotiating the early UFW contracts. The intricacies of the unprecedented elections overwhelmed the board and challenged the young UFW organizers to develop strategies to play by a new set of rules. "The fact is, there is no deus ex machina that can drop in and solve this in one month," Jerry said. "To think that merely by signing a piece of paper and creating a board . . . that you can resolve the disputes of decades is a premise that just doesn't face the reality that we have to deal with."

He remained unusually engaged, committed to make the law work, and the UFW maintained the pressure necessary to hold his attention.

When farmworkers were fired unjustly for union activity, a group staged a multiday vigil outside the governor's office, sleeping on sofas and the floor. Jerry returned to Sacramento at midnight and talked to them for three hours. One worker placed his jacket on the governor's chair and snapped a photo, still in disbelief the conversation had happened. When sheriffs raided labor camps on the eve of an election and picked up key union supporters for immigration violations, the governor's office figured out a way to issue temporary permits so the workers could stay through the election. The workers returned triumphantly with their *permisos*, the kind of victory the UFW used to show the power of the movement.

That power was the quality that intrigued Jerry and that he sought to adapt to the political arena. "To be a politician in America is not generally to be a movement leader, and yet the need that I perceive is that there has got to be a coherent platform or vision that will be able to organize effective political action in a period of increasingly ineffective political action," he said. "That's what I'm working on. It's not easy. I don't see anyone else doing it."

On Friday March 12, 1976, talking with a few reporters around six P.M., Jerry Brown mentioned, almost in passing, that he planned to enter the Maryland presidential primary. He deliberately avoided a formal announcement. The deadline was the following Monday. Ignoring those who had urged him to jump in earlier, he had skipped the first sixteen primaries and followed his own dictum: Postpone decisions as long as possible, since they foreclose options.

"I represent a generation that came of age in the civil rights movement and the anti–Vietnam War movement and can put behind us the malaise of the 1960s, Watergate, the CIA and FBI violations," Jerry said as he launched his campaign. "I am unencumbered by the baggage of the last ten years."

He left California for the first time since his election sixteen months earlier. On the flight to Maryland with him was Allard Lowenstein, the liberal Democratic activist and former congressman who had worked briefly for Jerry; among Lowenstein's projects had been supervising interns who researched election laws on presidential primaries in all fifty states. Lowenstein, a networker before the term was in vogue, carried his legendary phone book with several thousand home numbers of key Democratic players around the country. "His unconventionality is his strongest trait," Lowenstein said on the flight to Maryland, dismissing

Jerry's relatively slim list of achievements as irrelevant. Like Robert F. Kennedy, Lowenstein said, Jerry Brown had the ability to convey to people the sense that they could accomplish things.

Jerry's quixotic campaign was based on the power of an idea. "What can a president do? He gets up in the morning and he goes to bed at night. There isn't all that much he can do except set a tone and chart a vision," he said at a rally. "I don't think the president runs the country, nor do I think the governor runs the state," he told supporters at a fundraiser. "Government is a part of an overall, complex equation—social, economic, and environmental. Within that limited framework, a leader can set a tone, can express a philosophy, and can describe a future that is either consistent with what is possible or not."

For a brief time, anything seemed possible. In Maryland the young governor was treated like a rock star. At his first rally, people reached out to touch him. Someone ripped a button off his suit. In later years, Jerry Brown would refer to the Maryland campaign as a political high that was hard to match. Months later, he would return to the state, anonymous and unrecognized.

Just as Pat Brown had lined up old-time political support for his son, Jerry benefited in Maryland from more traditional Democratic support through the connections of a young San Francisco politician, Nancy Pelosi, whose father and brother had served as Baltimore mayors. Jerry's stance as the outsider and his tactic of challenging assumptions won support from liberals and conservatives. His penchant for avoiding specifics made him the object of ridicule in the comic strip *Doonesbury*, which invented a new campaign chant for Brown supporters: "Hey, ho! Go with the flow!"

On May 18, 1976, Jerry Brown defeated front-runner Jimmy Carter in Maryland, 49 to 37 percent. The band played "California, Here I Come" as the candidate entered the victory party in his customary three-piece suit. Eating linguine at two A.M. in Baltimore's Little Italy, he said, "I can really win." His oldest friends were not surprised. "If Jerry Brown decides to run for president," said his former roommate Frank Damrell, "it's because he thinks he *can* be president."

Pat Brown dismissed suggestions that his son was too young. "Jerry's contemplative. He's not like your regular politician," Pat said. He had measured his own career by what he called the "laundry list" of accomplishments. His son was different. "He believes a president should lead the people to a better quality of life, and not read a laundry list. He's in this campaign just for himself because he is convinced that he is a leader."

Even as he savored the success, Jerry wrestled with his Jesuit values. He talked about the conflict between politics, which fed the ego, and the Christian admonition to rid oneself of selfish desires. "You've got to have purpose," he said. "Save souls, or bring about the new order, protect the environment, save the whale, provide full employment. This is my job. This is my vocation. This is what I'm supposed to be doing."

As the campaign moved into other states where election rules posed logistic hurdles in a tight timeframe, the Brown team needed lots of bodies and creative strategy. The solution to both came from the farmworker movement.

Action had slowed in the California fields. Excitement over the new law and pent-up demand by farmworkers had resulted in 423 elections in the first five months. By February 1976, the state agency had exhausted its initial appropriation. The legislature declined to allocate more, and the board shut down for the rest of the year, suspending all elections.

Jerry Brown and Linda Ronstadt, who met in 1971, were both public figures who valued their privacy. The couple did not often appear together at public events. But when Jerry ran for president, Ronstadt headlined a fundraising concert at the Capital Center in Maryland on May 14, 1976, four days before Jerry Brown won an upset victory in the Maryland primary. (Associated Press/Karin Vismara)

The UFW had dozens of volunteers with nothing to do. Cesar Chavez dispatched them to help his favorite politician.

Marshall Ganz, son of a Bakersfield rabbi, had spent the summer of 1964 in Mississippi and dropped out of Harvard to stay and work in the civil rights movement. A year later, he joined a different crusade, close to home, and learned to organize from Chavez. Ganz's only experience with a political campaign was watching Chavez turn out the vote for Robert Kennedy in 1968. Sent to Canada to stop the sale of grapes, Ganz had organized one of the union's most successful boycotts. Then he figured out tactics to win union elections under the new law. Both operations required ingenuity with little resources. Like all successful leaders in the union, Ganz knew how to make things happen, fast.

He landed in Oregon with a team of UFW volunteers dispatched to run a write-in campaign. They recruited and trained dozens of people and assigned them to specific polling places, where they would explain on Election Day how to vote for Jerry Brown, even though he was not on the ballot. The novelty of the campaign and the youth of the candidate drew large crowds. Students at the University of Oregon in Eugene hung out of balconies in the quad and climbed trees for a better view of the candidate in his double-breasted suit, who arrived late because he had signed a bill that morning that gave tax credits for solar heating installations. Jerry told the students the most important thing was to "restore honesty to Washington" and "rebuild the cities of America." Without that, "no matter how many missiles we have in our silo we lack the collective strength and political will to defend anything."

In the May 25, 1976, Oregon primary, Jerry was just edged out by Carter, an impressive showing for a write-in candidate. The next day, Ganz and his group of boycott volunteers were in the airport headed for New Jersey when they were paged and diverted to Rhode Island to tackle a tougher campaign. Jerry was not on the ballot. Write-ins were illegal. The only way for Jerry to win required voters to follow a complicated set of instructions and pull multiple levers to elect an uncommitted slate. The Brown team had five days, including Memorial Day weekend.

Most businesses were closed for the holiday. UFW volunteers went through the phone book until they found a union printer willing to produce posters, billboards, and handouts the next day. One group of volunteers hit the streets. They created instant rallies by using "the Dragnet"—a team swarmed through any offices near a campaign event and dragged people out into the street with them. Another team worked the phones, with sleeping bags under their desks. They called voter lists until they couldn't stay awake, slept on the floor, then started all over. Ganz divided the state into seven areas and assigned a coordinator to each, tasked with recruiting and training poll watchers for every precinct. On Memorial Day, 550 poll watchers gathered in a Catholic high school auditorium cheered loudly when Jerry arrived to address the volunteers.

The next day, Ganz adapted a tactic he had used in farmworker elections. Poll watchers handed out sample ballots that showed step by step exactly how to vote for the Brown slate. In a major upset, the uncommitted delegates edged out Carter, 32 to 30 percent.

Jerry won two more states—Nevada and California—and beat Carter in New Jersey with an uncommitted slate of delegates. He had entered too late to mount a serious challenge, but the meteoric campaign made the California governor a player. Jerry was already out of contention when a celebrity crowd that included Andy Warhol, Harry Chapin, Betty Comden, Earl McGrath, Bayard Rustin, and Diane von Fürstenburg gathered for a fundraiser on June 1 at the Central Park West apartment of Allard Lowenstein's brother.

"Every eight years I come to you to introduce some leading Jesuit theologian who has suddenly decided to run," Lowenstein said, and the guests looked over at Eugene McCarthy and laughed. Lowenstein recalled working with Jerry on the Peace Slate that morphed into the McCarthy campaign in 1968. For people bruised by the aftermath of that loss, "there is a feeling that again that somehow it's worth being involved," he said. "If this campaign has done nothing more than to make clear that it is not impossible to generate electricity and excitement and a sense of hopefulness . . . it will go down as a very significant contribution."

Jerry's campaign was "typically unorthodox," Lowenstein said. "So we have tonight somebody who is twice as frugal as Ronald Reagan, twice as Jesuit as Eugene McCarthy, twice as ruthless as Robert Kennedy, twice as garrulous as Hubert Humphrey."

Jerry said he had entered the race because he didn't see any candidate generating the necessary enthusiasm. The national campaign had reinforced cultural and geographic divides. In the West, people wanted less government. In the East, they wanted help in crises like the New York City financial bailout. "I think the very issue that people have raised about my candidacy is its greatest virtue and that is that I would come to Washington as a new force out of the West, unencumbered with a lot of the alliances of the past, not untried in the political process—I've been around it all my life and I think I understand it—but with the ability to bring people together, to inspire some hope and try to get this country back on the up-beat."

A month later he was back in New York City for the Democratic convention at Madison Square Garden. Among the 204 California Brown delegates were family members (Pat and Bernice Brown, Kathleen and Jeep Rice, Cynthia and Joe Kelly), Warren Beatty, Lucy Casado, Cesar Chavez, Marshall Ganz, and half a dozen other UFW organizers.

Jerry stayed in the ancient, once grand Hotel McAlpin on Herald Square, where rooms cost $28 a night and mice ran across the floor. In the evenings, he watched the convention on the black-and-white television in his room. The UFW volunteers, accustomed to working for room and board and $5 a week, felt right at home. They were the last guests in the hotel before it was torn down.

The UFW contingent found themselves in the unusual situation of having nothing to do. The union lived largely off donations, and the boycotters were accustomed to fundraising wherever they went. So they organized an event on the spur of the moment, a $10-a-person cocktail party with Jerry and Cesar. A restaurant owner offered to donate enough Mexican food and sangria for a thousand people. Boycotters cleaned the decrepit ballroom in the McAlpin. A farmworker supporter from the Bronx arrived with floral decorations. Someone found a mariachi band.

A day and a half after they hatched the idea, delegates from around the country waited half an hour for the ancient elevators to take them to the twenty-fourth floor of the McAlpin, where the crowd was packed in so tightly that sweat dripped off their faces. When they arrived, Jerry and Cesar could barely get through to the front of the room. Jane Fonda auctioned off six copies of a book about the UFW, autographed by Chavez and Jerry. Chavez thanked everyone for coming. Then they crammed into the elevators again and headed to the convention hall for an event that felt almost anticlimactic.

Jerry had asked Chavez to place his name in nomination. Chavez was not a good public speaker, and the address was unremarkable. But the symbolism was hard to miss. Chavez had led a revolution, Jerry said later, "not just against some grower in Madera County, but against what I might call the oligarchy, the power establishment elite, the governing class. And as a politician, that's the class you have to please, because if you don't you are then stigmatized as an oddball, a radical, a weirdo, not playing by the rules."

"This convention is just a beginning," Jerry said the next day, casting California's votes for Carter. His sister Kathleen said she was sad. "In some ways it seemed like the end . . . but this was just the moment of truth. I think Jerry handled these last few days, which could have been a real problem for him, with grace, dignity and style." She laughed when told that Carter's advisers already worried about a rematch four years later. "The Carter people think Jerry will run in 1980? Then they know more than Jerry. Jerry doesn't even know what he's going to do next Wednesday."

15

To the Moon and Back

Jerry Brown was a Californian by birth, a Jesuit by training, a politician by vocation, and a farsighted thinker by nature. The unusual combination shaped a governor whose sustained passion and lasting influence was as an advocate for better stewardship of the earth.

Forces that had drawn Jerry to the seminary, a world of ideas, philosophy, and absolutes, now attracted him to the realms of environment, science, and technology. The debates were about precious, often finite, resources. The impacts were clear. The needs were urgent. The scientific breakthroughs were stunning. The potential to effect change, and the opportunity for California to lead, were enormous. Jerry would be dismissed and even mocked for espousing ideas ahead of their time, an often fatal flaw in the world of traditional politics. In many ways, his views in the mid-1970s foreshadowed the seminal encyclical on the environment and human ecology that would be issued almost four decades later by the first Jesuit pope.

"Environmental issues get me more interested than most things. It seems to relate to something more in the nature of an absolute," Jerry said in the midst of his tenure in Sacramento. Like the fundamental realities he studied in the seminary, the stakes transcended material concerns. "If you actually put PCB in the drinking supply, you might poison the food-producing capacity of a whole region. That to me seems more serious than whether or not you have the capacity to buy a second car."

He found the clear, visible connections between actions and reactions appealing. More cars spewing ozone worsened pollution already so bad that schools canceled outdoor gym classes on dozens of days each year.

Conversely, investments in more efficient technology yielded tangible improvements. The parsimonious governor skeptical of so much "squid-like" spending on schools was more willing to commit money to obvious public goods. He told Resources Secretary Claire Dedrick that she was fortunate to be lobbying for the conservation of pristine land—he could see exactly where the money was going. "The state government has not come to terms with the environmental crisis facing California," he wrote in his first budget message, which included additional money for air and water pollution initiatives.

He tapped into a historic bipartisan vein of support in California for the natural world as a foundation of much of the economy, a source of recreation, and even, as in the case of Yosemite, an emblem of identity.

"We think of our wealth as represented in the accounting books by the economists and described on Wall Street. But our true wealth is our natural systems. Our land, our soil, our forests, our fishing industry, our water, our weather, that is the fundamental basis," Jerry said in a State of the State address in which he proposed investing in reforestation, fish hatcheries, and solar power. He warned about the need to manage water and quoted from Fernand Braudel's book *The Mediterranean* to caution that California must act to avoid the fate of earlier civilizations in similar climes: "The desert lies in wait for arable land and never lets go." Pat Brown had engineered the State Water Project by assuring Northern, Southern, and Central California that there was more than enough water for everyone. "We have lived with abundant water," his son said a decade later, in the midst of a drought. "We haven't had to worry about it. But we now have to manage it."

In Pat Brown's era, there had been no organized environmental advocacy, nor environmental reviews for massive projects like the water works. The modern environmental movement traced its roots to a 1969 disaster in Southern California, a huge oil spill off the coast of Santa Barbara. Oil derricks, part of the seaside landscape since the turn of the century, had moved close to shore after new technology enabled drillers to locate oil reserves near land. In the late 1960s, the federal government issued dozens of leases. On January 28, 1969, a Union Oil well blew out less than six miles from shore, unleashing what was then the largest spill in U.S. waters. Over ten days, between 80,000 and 100,000 barrels of crude oil spilled into the channel, washed up on shore, blanketed beaches with a six-inch layer of black goo, and killed thousands of fish and birds.

The disaster spurred two lawmakers active in the anti–Vietnam War movement, Congressman Pete McCloskey, a liberal Republican from California, and Senator Gaylord Nelson, a Wisconsin Democrat, to borrow tactics and channel energy from that struggle to raise awareness of environmental threats. On April 22, 1970, millions of Americans took part in teach-ins across the country during the first Earth Day. The participants were mostly young, liberal, and white; much of the rhetoric was antiestablishment and antiwar. The warnings from scientists were dire. "Halfway measures and business as usual cannot possibly pull us back from the edge of the precipice," newscaster Walter Cronkite concluded at the end of a special report that evening, *Earth Day: A Question of Survival.* "To clean up the air and earth and water in the few years science says are left to us means personal involvement and may mean personal sacrifice the likes of which Americans have never been asked to make in times of peace."

Such calls meshed with Jerry's beliefs and agenda. Environmental issues offered a tangible means to emphasize the importance of limits, in a way that coincided rather than conflicted with the goals of a traditional Democratic constituency upset at his insistence on limits in other realms.

In California, the natural world was so key to the state's identity that alliances transcended ideology. The importance of a robust environment for many of the state's leading industries blunted organized business opposition to government intervention. As governor, Ronald Reagan had ushered in a new brand of conservativism, but despite his harsh rhetoric about bloated government, he used the force of the state to protect rivers, coasts, air quality, Indian burial grounds, and scenic wilderness. While he would later be remembered for antienvironmental actions as president, Governor Reagan put in place structures his successor would use to great effect.

Three regulatory bodies with far-reaching powers, the Water Resources Control Board, the Energy Commission, and the Coastal Commission, originated during the Reagan administration. The California Environmental Quality Act, which required stringent reviews of environmental impact for new development, was signed by Reagan. Like Pat Brown, Reagan loved the Sierra Nevada; his resources secretary was a former Sierra packer who had led trips into the high mountains on mules and horses. Reagan intervened with the Nixon administration to block a proposed highway through the wilderness area and saved the spectacular 210-mile John Muir Trail. Presented with competing bills that designated portions of rivers as "forever wild" to block the construction of future dams, Reagan signed the one with tougher protection. Reagan and Nevada governor Paul Laxalt, also a conservative Republican, formed the Tahoe Regional Planning Agency to regulate development and save the once pristine lake from encroaching pollution.

Jerry dramatically increased the power of the Reagan-era initiatives by appointing environmentalists to head commissions and departments. "People who have been on the outside have had a chance to come inside the government bureaucracy and attempt to apply concepts and ideas in the workaday world of government," he said, citing appointees like Claire Dedrick, a Sierra Club vice president, and environmental advocate Huey Johnson, who replaced Dedrick when she became the first woman on the Public Utilities Commission. Bill Press, director of the Planning and Conservation League, had written a report that recommended abolishing the Office of Planning and Research; he was hired to run the state office. His interview with Jerry took place late in the evening over drinks at Frank Fats. The conversation was mainly about Thorstein Veblen, the economist who coined the phrase "conspicuous consumption."

Jerry's most influential, and controversial, appointee had no environmental background. That did not slow down Tom Quinn as head of the Air Resources Board any more than his lack of political experience had been a bar to running Jerry's campaigns. Reagan had signed the California Air Resources Board into law in 1967. Because the regulatory agency predated the 1970 federal Clean Air Act, California became the only state empowered to enact its own air quality regulations. That positioned California, home of the most cars in the country, to play a powerful role in forcing changes in the automobile industry.

Quinn recruited the expertise he lacked, making two key hires who would shape air policy in California for the next four decades: Mary Nichols, a recent Yale law graduate who had taken on the federal government in a high-profile air pollution case, and Robert Sawyer, a Berkeley engineering professor and sharp critic of the recently created federal EPA. Sawyer's expertise proved critical in guiding the state air board's decisions on how far to push the auto industry to produce cleaner engines. His assurances that car makers could comply with the state's requirements gave Quinn the confidence to push back against protestations that manufacturers could not possibly achieve the emission reductions California demanded.

CAN THIS MAN CLEAN UP CALIFORNIA? asked the *New York Times* headline on an October 1976 profile of Quinn. During his tenure, California imposed exhaust emission standards for motorcycles and restrictions on sulfur and lead content of gasoline; fined cars that didn't meet exhaust emission standards; ordered oil companies to fix leaks in storage tanks; and fined Chrysler $328,000 and ordered the recall of twenty-one thousand cars and seven hundred trucks for smog violations. By imposing its own strict regulations on auto emissions, the Brown administration effectively blocked the industry's attempt to slow down stringent national standards.

Environmental advocates credited Quinn's media savvy as an effective weapon that bolstered the state as it took on powerful industries. He sent in inspectors at two in the morning to the Kaiser Steel Mill in Fontana, where they issued 1,015 violation orders, the largest number ever against a single polluter. "Tom Quinn never appears to be on the defensive," *Sierra* magazine reported, noting that the governor was happiest on the offensive and consistently backed Quinn. "And that, it seems, is the secret of his success with Brown."

California took on a different Goliath to protect its rivers. The state imposed standards that required the State Water Project to curtail the volume pumped out of rivers when the quality of the streams fell below certain levels and endangered the fragile ecosystems. The federal government argued that its Central Valley water project was immune from such standards. California sued to force compliance and won a landmark state's rights decision.

On another front, Jerry stepped in at the eleventh hour to forge a compromise that preserved public access to the California coast and imposed severe limitations on future development. The eleven hundred miles of shoreline had filled up quickly during the boom years of the 1950s and '60s. Power plants spoiled the spectacular landscape. Conservationists became alarmed when Sea Ranch, a town of twenty thousand, sprang up on land that had been bucolic sheep farms along the northern coast. Access to the Malibu beaches was cut off by private homes. In 1972, voters had passed the Coastal Initiative, which created a commission that had temporary control over coastal development and a mandate to prepare a longer-term proposal subject to legislative approval. Without further

Jerry Brown would typically arrive in the office in late morning and often work into the early hours of the next day. (Courtesy of the office of Governor Edmund G. Brown Jr.)

action by the end of 1976, the commission would expire. Jerry negotiated a deal, passed by one vote in the last hour of the legislative session, that created a permanent Coastal Commission with power to review new projects and protect public access to the seashore.

"The most important part of the environmental movement is that there are absolutes that are being communicated," Jerry said in an interview with *Sierra* magazine, which devoted its January 1978 issue to an assessment of the Brown administration. "The oceans, the air, the water have to be respected, and when they're not, then there are negative consequences. And that gives people something to cope with, something against which to define their own behavior, and that's what's missing now. The sense that one can do anything is unreal and childish. It's stimulated by the consumption ethic."

Jerry used scarcity to force both lifestyle changes and innovation. Gas-guzzling Californians had been hard hit by rising prices at the pump that spiked after the 1973 oil embargo by OPEC nations. The Iranian revolution in 1979 created another crisis and fears of shortage that led to hours-long lines at pumps. In May, California became the first state to implement an odd-even gas rationing system, restricting service to license plates ending in certain numbers on certain days. To encourage more long-lasting changes in behavior, Jerry's transportation secretary, Adriana Gianturco, experimented with carpool lanes on the Santa Monica freeway. She was vilified (dubbed the Giant Turkey, among other names), and drivers howled so loudly that the project was scrapped. But even Pat Brown, the master builder, recognized times were changing. "If a great newspaper such as yours does not impress on the people the need for more than one person riding in an automobile, I don't know what will happen," Pat Brown wrote to *Los Angeles Times* publisher Otis Chandler after the paper editorialized against the diamond lanes. "It is more than wasteful, it is a profligate use of a diminishing resource."

A severe drought in 1976 and 1977, the third-worst in state history, became an opportunity for the Brown administration to press for conservation and more efficient technologies. The Department of Water Resources launched a pilot project that placed two hundred thousand toilet and shower conservation devices in six communities. When Prince Charles visited Sacramento for lunch, Jerry served him a sprouts sandwich in a paper bag with a Save Water sticker on it.

"I've spoken of an era of limits and that made people frustrated. Some people got angry; they felt I was antibusiness; they thought I was somehow suppressing expectation, and failing to dream the possibilities that have made this state what it is," Jerry said at a conference on water. "But at some point, we do live in a relatively closed system, and we have to learn to live with the resources that are available." Agriculture needed to change its irrigation methods and look to crops that used less water. Homeowners and businesses needed to rethink their gardens and look to native plants. "I'm not saying it's going to happen overnight, but increasingly I think people in this state will have to become closer in tune with that which nature feels most comfortable with. When one is either in a desert or near a desert, one can't act as though he were in a more rainy area."

Although energy was not a finite resource in the same sense as water, many types of energy depleted natural resources or polluted the air. The state energy commission, led by Jerry's campaign strategist and pollster Richard Maullin, reversed a rate structure that had made energy cheaper the more consumers used. The commission instituted incentives for utilities and consumers to conserve. An early champion of solar power, Jerry vowed California would take the lead in producing energy from the sun, which was more ecological and closer to "our Jeffersonian ideals." By 1980, California had seventy-five thousand solar installations, close to a third of the total in the United States.

Through the San Francisco Zen Center, Jerry met Sim Van der Ryn, an architect who had founded a quasicommune in Sonoma County to experiment with ecological design, the seeds of what would become the sustainability movement. Van der Ryn had taught at Cal in the 1960s, until the trauma of seeing National Guardsmen fire tear gas and rip out flowers in People's Park, which he had helped to create. The man who had fled the Netherlands as a child during the Holocaust fled Berkeley. By the time he met Jerry, Van der Ryn was crusading with Buckminster Fuller for low-flush toilets; he got in trouble with zoning authorities for building a compost privy on his compound without proper permits. When Jerry recruited Van der Ryn as state architect, he turned the job down, wary of rejoining the establishment. Baker Roshi, abbot of the Zen Center, persuaded Van der Ryn to change his mind. "The first few months were very euphoric," the architect said a few years into his service. "I was able to start putting into practice a lot of things I had been thinking about. There was a great power to that."

Van der Ryn insisted on "a separate office that would be a 'David challenging the Goliath' of bureaucracy and its tendency to resist innovation and new ideas." Jerry set up the Office of Appropriate Technology, borrowing a phrase from E. F. Schumacher. With a logo of a mule with his snout in a bag of oats, the office grew to 350 people and a $12 million budget. OAT sponsored trainings around California on solar technology, vegetable gardens, biofuels, drought-tolerant gardens, and bicycle-sharing projects. Van der Ryn developed the first energy standards for state office buildings and pioneered the concept of sustainable buildings. He oversaw construction of a block-long state office complex built around a four-story atrium courtyard topped by skylights and filled with plants. Solar storage, solar-powered water heaters, and a rock bed under the atrium floor absorbed and stored heat during the day to maximize energy efficiency. Louvers on the roof automatically closed in summer, screens deflected sunlight in the winter, and canvas tubes hanging in the atrium recirculated air. In 1981, during a day-long celebration entitled "The State of Things to Come," Jerry Brown christened the building in honor of the cybernetics pioneer Gregory Bateson, who had died a year earlier. Bateson's life, Jerry said, like the building, represented "a quest for underlying unity in all living things."

The governor's actions were watched across the country, not only because of California's power to establish standards and trends, but because of his political ambitions. From the moment Jimmy Carter was elected, the president's political consultants warned of a likely challenge in 1980 from the candidate who had beaten Carter in most primaries he had entered. Traveling to California to study the likely contender, *New York Times* columnist Anthony Lewis described Jerry as detached, ambitious, arrogant, and full of far-fetched ideas. "His budget message included such off-beat energy ideas as building giant windmills, with 100-foot blades, to generate electricity, and using wood chips converted into gas to heat the capitol," Lewis wrote in January 1978, dismissing technologies that would within a decade become commonplace. Others were equally dubious, if somewhat gentler. Jerry showed a *Washington Star* reporter a vial of jojoba bean oil, which he suggested might become an ingredient in cosmetics, another far-out notion. "Of course skepticism has long since fled," she wrote in the profile. "Somehow it seems entirely plausible that Jerry Brown's jojoba bean can solve the problems of California. Of the world, perhaps."

Those who knew Jerry best were not surprised by his forward-thinking focus and interest in technology. "He's always been the one who brought the new bestseller or new idea or place to eat or gimmick or gadget or new important book into my life," said his sister Kathleen. "He has the capacity to build a bridge into the next century."

Jerry found gadgets intriguing and practical science captivating. But he also saw an intimate connection to environmental imperatives, sometimes for destructive purposes, as in the case of nuclear power, but often toward constructive ends. "Ecology and technology are two profound and pervasive themes that affect the human spirit," he said. "What I'm attempting to do is find the synthesis that can link the better parts of both of them."

He was in the right place. The epicenter of the technological revolution was on the peninsula just south of San Francisco, where apricot orchards and vineyards had given way to nondescript concrete buildings full of entrepreneurs whose work would change daily life around the world.

The roots of technological innovation in the Santa Clara Valley went back to 1951, when Stanford decided to use part of its 9,000-acre endowment to establish one of the first university-sponsored industrial parks. For decades, most of the land deeded to the school by Leland and Jane Stanford had been leased to farmers. Facing financial difficulties in the postwar years, Stanford adopted a plan to develop low-slung buildings in a parklike setting and recruit science-based research companies whose work would dovetail with the school's mission and provide jobs to ensure that engineering graduates did not need to go "into exile" in the East. With bucolic scenery, a Mediterranean climate, and easy access to San Francisco, Stanford had little trouble attracting the critical mass of talent and capital that would soon cement the reputation of both the university and the valley.

By 1954, Hewlett-Packard, a small tech company started by two Stanford graduate students, had moved from a Palo Alto garage into the industrial park. Two years later and three miles south, Shockley Semiconductor Laboratory opened in a concrete shed in Mountain View, housing what William Shockley called his "PhD production line." Shockley shared the Nobel Prize in Physics that year for inventing the transistor. A year later, eight of his PhDs moved into another concrete shed twelve blocks away and formed Fairchild Electronics, a bold and unusual defection that became the prototype for what would later be known as start-ups.

The leader of the group known as the "traitorous eight" was twenty-nine-year-old Robert Noyce, as charming as he was brilliant. In 1959, he invented a way of putting all the functions of the small but still clumsy transistors onto a tiny integrated circuit made of silicon. The microchips were so tiny and light that they revolutionized the development of everything from missiles to the Apollo spacecraft. Unlike most companies in the valley, Fairchild did not rely on government dollars to fund its research, although it sold chips primarily to aerospace companies that depended on defense department contracts. Within a decade, Fairchild had twelve thousand employees and sales of $130 million. Its founders, who had been given stock, went from average salaries to enormous wealth, setting a pattern in the valley that would soon be named after the silicon chip.

In its first decade, Stanford's industrial park had grown to about twelve thousand workers at forty-two companies. Hewlett-Packard's research lab was joined by IBM, and both companies raced to use the emerging electronic technology to build a functional computer. As the large influx of federal research funds during the Cold War transformed universities into economic engines for communities, Stanford led the way. Clark Kerr articulated the idea of a "multiversity"; Stanford executed it.

Robert Noyce had a profound impact on the culture of what became known as Silicon Valley as well as its inventions. He eschewed the hierarchical corporate model of the Eastern establishment, finding its layers and status stifling. Noyce abolished private offices, reserved parking spots, chain of command, and dress codes. In Fairchild's first decade, more than two dozen spin-offs were started by defectors, dubbed the "Fairchildren," who took that spirit and culture with them. In 1968, Noyce and Gordon Moore became Fairchildren themselves, leaving to form Intel, which focused on computer memory chips. They gave most of the employees stock options, and deli sandwiches and soda to eat at their desk for lunch.

By the late 1970s, most of the more than four hundred thousand tech jobs in California were in Silicon Valley. Jerry Brown liked to point out in 1978 that 20 percent of the people in California worked in industries that had not existed a decade earlier.

The first Apple computer was produced in a Los Gatos garage in 1976. Four years later, although only about half a million personal computers had been sold, Jerry predicted computers would become common in elementary school classrooms within ten years. He compared the revolution in technology to the Protestant Reformation, "when people began to obtain their own Bibles and make their own direct contact with Christian knowledge and tradition through the Bible, instead of having to go through the priest. Today the same kind of revolution in the secular sector realm is taking place, because through computers, and through telecommunications, people will be able to access directly information which is now within the custody of specialists and various other managers of knowledge."

At his old elementary school, St. Brendan, Jerry signed a bill providing tax breaks for companies that donated computers to schools. He coached the kids on his new slogan, the three C's: computing, calculating, and communicating through technology. "A personal computer is going to be like a pencil, everyone is going to need one," he said. "There will be personal computers that will be the size of a book before the end of this decade, and that book will link people to huge databases that will enable that individual to pick up information on everything from the weather to sports, mathematics to the price of hamburger."

That democratization of knowledge, he predicted, would have practical applications for government. "I see the day when we may have a thousand television channels," he said in early 1978. "You'll plug in University of California lectures, the boardroom of a major multinational corporation, the governor's office, Congress, the supermarket. By pressing a button you'll get more and more information on the decision making going on. That's a fact, and that tends to break down hierarchy."

The sophistication of television cameras, just a decade after arguments as to whether they should be allowed at governors' press conferences, had already changed the balance of power. Any group that came to see the governor and walked out of his office could talk to a television news crew, "and they will have the same access to the people of this state as the governor of California. That's our democratic government, and that's what's changing . . . That information is the equalizer, and that breaks down the hierarchy."

Silicon Valley became an integral and growing part of the California economy. One out of four new jobs during the first seven years Jerry was governor were created, directly or indirectly, by the electronics, aerospace, and related industries. "Here again we see the *energy of character* in the pioneering contribution of our citizens who have miniaturized the computer from huge room-sized machines to dimensions smaller than your fingertip," Jerry said. He contrasted that innovation with obsolete national economic priorities. He outlined a program to invest in new technologies and alternate energy sources, train skilled workers for tech jobs, and look to new markets in third world countries.

"I see the future of America, and California, tied to the ability to store, retrieve and transmit ever greater amounts of data at ever higher rates of speed. This technology is coming along and it's going to happen one way or the other," Jerry said. "I'm going to do what I can to make sure that America does take the leadership position and that California is at the lead of this scientific-technological trajectory."

He saw technological change as the defining hallmark of the era, comparable to the impact of the railroad in the late nineteenth century. The new frontier, which came to dominate conversations in the late 1970s, was outer space. And one of the interesting people Jerry's adviser Stewart Brand brought to meet the governor was Apollo 9 astronaut Rusty Schweickart.

Brand had befriended Schweickart after hearing a speech that became something of a cult classic, "No Frames, No Boundaries," in which the astronaut's emotional description of gazing at the earth from space while circling the planet left half the audience in tears. In early 1977, Brand brought Schweickart to Sacramento, where he spent most of several weekends schooling the governor about space. Schweickart was surprised by Jerry's intensity, intelligence, and interest. More than half of NASA's contracts were with firms in California, and Jerry began to prod the federal agency to move faster. When that didn't work, he created a job for Schweickart. The NASA employee went on loan to the California governor as his chief science adviser, trading a slow-moving and stodgy federal bureaucracy for a boss whose mandate was "Make it happen. Fast."

Jerry Brown, who had built a career on his curiosity and instinct for staying ahead of the curve, became intrigued with space exploration as an exciting, pragmatic solution to the earthly problems of overcrowding, energy depletion, and environmental damage. "Ecology and technology," he said, "find a unity in space." Prominent physicists argued that space colonies would become realistic alternatives to an overcrowded earth. "It's not a question of whether—only when and how," Jerry said. When movie sensation *Star Wars* opened at Grauman's theater in the spring of 1977, Jerry went to see the space epic with Schweickart and Linda Ronstadt.

The movie coincided with a milestone in the nonfictional exploration of space. In the Los Angeles desert, NASA engineers were preparing to launch the first space shuttle on its first free flight. To piggyback on the event, the Brown administration organized a gala Space Day. On August 11, 1977, more than a thousand guests gathered at the California Museum of Science and Industry in Exposition Park near downtown Los Angeles for the program orchestrated by Schweickart and cosponsored by the aerospace industry, which had a big economic stake in the space program. Speakers included leaders of NASA, astronomer Carl Sagan, deep-sea explorer Jacques Cousteau, and Beat poet Michael McClure, who closed the event by reading a new poem, "Antechamber," as footage from a recent space mission ran in the background.

"The Earth map is drenched in the blood of a thousand, a million conflicts in recorded history, but when we look at Earth and the human species from a few hundred miles up, we can't help but sense the oneness

at the Grove a few times at Sheldrake and also at Hillbillies Lodge, as a guest of his friend Mickey Hart, the drummer for the Grateful Dead. Typical of the Grove's eclectic mix, Hart's fellow members of Hillbillies included U.S. Secretary of Defense Donald Rumsfeld, Republican politician George H. W. Bush, and newscaster Walter Cronkite.

In theory, business conversations were strictly forbidden at the Grove. In practice, they were legendary. Herbert Hoover described in his memoir the moment Calvin Coolidge revealed outside his tent that he would not be a candidate for reelection; within an hour, dozens of the nation's power brokers came to Hoover's camp and asked him to run. Richard Nixon, a member of Cave Man camp, cited his Lakeside Chat in 1967 as the turning point in his political rehabilitation. Honored by the invitation to deliver a Lakeside Chat, Pat worked hard preparing his talk for July 29, 1977. Unlike his son, who never had a speechwriter, Pat always relied on others. Former water advisers Bill Warne and Abbott Goldberg offered suggestions. To forecast the future of the still unfinished State Water Project, Pat turned to Ron Robie, head of the Department of Water Resources. The two got along well, and Robie had arranged several times to fly with Pat over the water project. Pat's phone calls invariably opened with the familiar question: "How's Jerry doing?"

The speech was a big hit. Pat's jokes included one of his famous malapropisms, after flying over the flood damage caused when the Eel River overflowed in 1964: "When I view the ravages of this flood—I can tell you, this is the worst disaster that has happened to the people of the state of California since the day I was elected Governor." He talked about how the world had changed since he pushed through the initial project. "A new element has entered the water picture since I left the Governor's office. I am speaking, of course, of the environmental movement. Not surprisingly, California was one of the first states where the environmental ethic surfaced, although it is now a part of the national consciousness."

Pat had weathered the changes in his political fortunes with his usual ebullience, still eager to talk with everyone he met, gifted at making people comfortable. He still played golf poorly, read a lot, and made pilgrimages to Yosemite. He no longer went to church. "I have a lot of Catholic friends, including some priests, but somehow I just couldn't believe in some of that stuff any longer. Take the Assumption of Mary. I just can't bring myself to believe in that," he said.

"A conversation with Pat now is just like a conversation with him in the midfifties, diffuse and warm and funny and self-deprecating," said Fred Dutton, who came back to California for meetings of the Board of Regents, where Pat had appointed him to a twelve-year term. Pat and Bernice remained close to many of his political friends and appointees. Every year, a group of Pat's judges threw a special birthday party. "It's a pleasure to be around you because you take such a delight in life," wrote Superior Court Judge Robert Wenke after Pat's seventieth birthday gathering.

Pat worked with writers on several books, the most notable a look at his death penalty cases. He still felt an inferiority complex about his lack of higher education and vacillated on whether, if he had it do over again, he would have gone to college. "I was always a young man in a hurry," he said. "I see people now who have gone to colleges and universities, maybe four years there would have done some good. I don't know. It's hard to say."

Bernice focused on what she called the three G's—gardening, grandchildren, and golf. Her kitchen drawers were full of coupons she clipped, though there was no need. After preparing meals for a large family for so many years, she still cooked in bulk and froze extra portions. She was often asked to compare the two Governor Browns. "I think they're two different personalities, and I think Jerry has a few of my genes, so he's a little different from Pat," she said. Jerry was reserved, like his mother. "Pat is very outgoing . . . he loves people and, oh, he stops and talks to them, like on trips in foreign countries. He can carry on a conversation with *anyone* and become acquainted and know more about them before you get through."

Never shy about giving his son advice, Pat chastised Jerry for his lack of support for the University of California. "Anything that diminishes that stockpile of intelligence diminishes us. I told Jerry so the other night on my birthday," Pat said in the spring of 1978. "I come on awful strong with him. You should see me sometimes. He doesn't resent it, but he's afraid of it. He shrinks away from it."

As Jerry neared the end of his first term, Pat grew increasingly concerned about the groundswell of anger over rising property taxes, a movement centered in Southern California and gaining strength every month. By the summer of 1978, the whole country would know about California's tax revolt.

Each of the more than five thousand counties, cities, schools, and special districts in California had the power to levy property taxes. Homeowners were billed the tax rate multiplied by the assessed value of their house, a number set by the county assessor. As elected officials, assessors were sensitive to voters. During the years of explosive growth in the 1950s and '60s, when new schools, roads, and services were needed every week, assessors sheltered homeowners from the brunt of the increased cost by assessing businesses at a higher percentage of market value. In the mid-1960s, assessors in San Francisco and several other counties were caught taking bribes to lower assessments. In response, a 1967 state law required counties to reassess all property at 25 percent of full market value. The impact was to shift more of the tax burden from businesses to homeowners, whose bills began to rise.

Efforts to place tax cut initiatives on the state ballot in 1968 and 1972 fell short. Then, as California came out of the recession of the early 1970s, housing prices soared. Driven by inflation, the value of the average home in California went from $34,000 in 1974 to $85,000 in 1978. Municipalities could have lowered tax rates and still collected the same amount of money. They didn't. Most increased overall spending. Over five years in the mid-1970s, total property taxes collected in California almost doubled, to $12 billion. Many people were paying taxes on homes now valued at prices at which they could never have afforded to buy them. By 1977, Jerry's tax bill for his Laurel Canyon home was $2,822—double what it had been just four years earlier.

The governor was initially not eager to wade into the escalating debate over taxation, which he considered primarily a local problem. He repeated his refrain about the need to enter an era of limits. Governments should spend less. Protesters should demand that their cities and schools cut expenses, not look to the state for help.

The tax mess was complicated by a landmark California Supreme Court decision, known as *Serrano v. Priest*, which found that the state's system of funding school districts through property taxes was unconstitutional because homeowners in poor areas were taxed at higher rates—and even then their school districts spent less per student than neighboring communities with more expensive real estate. The court ordered the state to redress the inequities.

In his January 6, 1977, State of the State address, Jerry promised to deal with school and local taxes. "Last night I was reading some of my past statements, and to tell you the truth, I didn't find them all that impressive," he began in typical Jerry Brown fashion. "So this morning I'm just going to share with you some of my thoughts for the coming year. Obviously, number one on the agenda is property tax. It's the issue people have been talking about. We need an immediate solution. We also need a long-term solution." He proposed short-term assistance targeted to those in gravest need, taxpayers whose bills exceeded a certain percentage of family income. For the longer term, he supported a proposal for a so-called "split roll" that would enable municipalities to tax residential and commercial properties at different rates—much as the local assessors had done informally in the 1950s and '60s.

The measures languished amid competing proposals and agendas. Jerry lacked the focus and intensity he had applied to break earlier stalemates. And his relationship with legislative leaders had deteriorated. His absences from the state while campaigning for president, his unusual style, his disdain for the traditional niceties and protocols had all taken a toll. Tom Bane, a Democratic assemblyman from the San Fernando Valley in Los Angeles, the heart of the tax revolt, ran into the governor on a plane. Jerry wondered why Bane never dropped in to talk. The legislator took that as an invitation and stopped by the office. Jerry said to call his staff to set up an appointment for the next day. Bane did, and cleared his calendar. Three weeks later, he was still waiting for a call back. "I realize I am only an Assemblyman, only represent 280,000 people and am only one of eighty votes in the Assembly," Bane wrote Jerry. "It strikes me, however, that your office exhibits a lack of concern for the normal courtesies and considerations due a legislator, not only as a representative of people, but as a human being. Such an attitude is not restricted to your office, but pervades much of your administration."

The legislature went home in 1977 without taking action on taxes. Property taxes kept rising. So did inflation, which pushed incomes up and workers into higher personal income tax brackets. Seventy-five-year-old Howard Jarvis, a bombastic, salty gadfly tax fighter and onetime candidate for U.S. senator and Los Angeles mayor, finally had his chance. For fifteen years, he had tried to force tax cuts, building a small following and a large reputation as a nuisance. His efforts were not taken particularly seriously in Sacramento. But among beleaguered taxpayers, he found plenty of support. Shifting demographics and lawsuits over school finance and desegregation added a racial overtone to the complaints; older, predominantly white homeowners were being asked to pay more for services that would increasingly benefit younger black and brown students. More than a million people signed petitions in support of a sweeping tax cut initiative that would radically change the way California funded public services. Jarvis filed paperwork in November, and the initiative was assigned the thirteenth position on the June 1978 ballot.

Even without the unforeseen consequences that would shape California for decades, Proposition 13 was breathtaking in its scope. Assessments would revert to 1975 levels, and the tax rate would be fixed at 1 percent of market value. Absent significant renovations, assessments could be raised no more than 2 percent a year until a property was sold, which essentially eliminated the ability of schools and local governments to increase taxes. To make future tax increases more difficult, all tax measures would have to be approved by a two-thirds majority vote. The immediate tax cuts—reductions in government revenue—would total more than $7 billion, more than one quarter of the total state budget.

Supporters dismissed as alarmist the predictions of shuttered libraries and parks, tens of thousands of layoffs, and cuts that crippled police and fire departments. Government spent too much money anyway. The state would make up the difference; there was a large surplus. People were in danger of losing their homes because they could not pay their tax bills. Nothing was more sacrosanct.

Jerry, running for reelection as voters decided the fate of Prop 13, did not speak out against the popular initiative right away. When he did, he was circumspect. "I suggest to you that the evil you know is better than the evil you don't know," Jerry finally said more than two months after the proposition qualified. "If you take $7 billion off the table one place, you'll have to probably come up with almost the identical sum someplace else." There were not many places to look; income tax revenue for the entire fiscal year was projected to be $4.5 billion and sales tax would bring in $5 billion.

The governor and legislative leaders tried to craft an alternative that would provide comparable tax relief with less draconian impact, shift more burden to businesses and provide relief to renters, who gained nothing under Prop 13. The ultimate compromise offered much lower savings and could not compete. As the June election neared and the consequences grew clearer, Jerry joined political leaders of both parties, business executives, and union leaders in denouncing Prop 13. He called the measure a consumer fraud and Howard Jarvis a demagogue: "It's a rip-off, a legal morass, and is in reality a long-term tax increase, not a reduction."

A few days before the election, when the passage of Prop 13 seemed all but inevitable, New York columnist Jimmy Breslin visited Jarvis in his Los Angeles living room. "He is a man setting fire to dry grass," Breslin wrote. Jarvis chortled at the response he had provoked. "Every time Brown kicks me, he kicks Brown," Jarvis told Breslin. "If I were Brown, I'd ignore Jarvis. They did it for years, it worked for them. I was regarded as a nuisance, and nothing else." Jarvis laughed. "He seems to laugh a lot these days," Breslin wrote. "And it is a laugh that almost surely is going to be heard in almost every section of the country. And it is the kind of laugh that this movement is merely starting."

The poorly crafted measure not only upended the tax structure, it set a July 1 deadline for implementation, three weeks after the election. Gray Davis, the governor's chief of staff, was on leave to run the November reelection campaign. Tom Quinn met with finance officials to plot a response that might avoid the catastrophic service cuts that schools, cities, libraries, and counties anticipated. Department heads laid out triage plans. The Finance Department predicted job losses that would increase the state unemployment rate, already a point above the 6.2 percent national average. The state's Washington office estimated that California could lose billions in federal funds that required matching contributions from state and local governments.

After a conversation with his son the day before the vote, Pat Brown was dismayed. "He's going to say now that he's going to be able to make the Jarvis plan work, and I said, 'You can't do it.' I said, 'You've got to show some compassion for the people who are going to be thrown out of work and the special programs for the blind and the autistic children and the mentally retarded, all of which will have to be circumscribed.'" Jerry had already faced criticism from liberal Democrats for his perceived lack of compassion, particularly in the treatment of the mentally ill. Pat urged Jerry to temper his acknowledgment of the people's will with a message of empathy. "I told Jerry, I'd say, 'I'm a servant of the people. Whatever they want I'm going to do. But I'm not going to be hypocritical and tell you that it's not going to hurt human beings. It is. And I'm going to do everything I can to see that their hardships are mitigated.'"

Jerry's reelection in November would depend on how he oversaw implementation of the most profound changes to California's financial system in decades. As voters went to the polls on June 6, Quinn went to Linda Ronstadt's house in Los Angeles and made Jerry spend the day going through the plan, point by point. He drafted a mailgram sent to local officials: "If Proposition 13 is approved today, it will create a critical need for close and continuous working relationships between state and local authorities." He set up a Proposition 13 Communications Center in the governor's office to coordinate with local officials in five thousand jurisdictions and field emergency calls about layoffs, cash flow, assessments, and legal interpretations.

Proposition 13 passed with 65 percent of the vote. Jerry Brown declared himself a "born-again tax cutter." Two days later, he addressed the legislature:

> Over four million of our fellow citizens have sent a message to city hall, to Sacramento, and to all of us. The message is that property tax must be sharply curtailed, and that government spending, wherever it is, must be held in check. We must look forward to lean and frugal budgets. It's a great challenge. And we will meet it. We must do everything possible to minimize the human hardship and maximize the total number of state jobs created in our economy. We have only three weeks to act. Three weeks to decide multibillion dollars of fiscal questions.

He pledged to avoid new state taxes, make budget cuts, and use the surplus to help local governments.

About $4 billion of the state surplus went to plug holes in local budgets, averting the most severe cuts. Los Angeles libraries closed on Mondays. Many school districts canceled summer school. Cities ended dial-a-ride services for the elderly. School budgets declined an average of more than 2 percent, the first drop since the Depression. The mood of austerity sapped once proud institutions, which would take years to recover.

"I sometimes have great faith in the people and think that they'll always do the right thing," Pat said sadly. The people had overwhelmingly chosen to "cut the guts out of a great government . . . My faith has been hurt terribly by what happened."

His son was more dispassionate. "This is a hurricane. The people have spoken," he said. "We will make do. We are a pioneer state."

The focus on immediate financial pressures overshadowed more significant long-term structural change. State government assumed control of apportioning tax revenues to the schools and municipalities. That centralized power in Sacramento. Because tax increases now required a two-thirds vote, even a weak minority in the legislature became a powerful player. A grassroots movement that purported to restore authority to the local level had achieved the opposite result.

The intended and unintended consequences of Prop 13 would be unraveled, reknitted, and patched over for decades, shaping not only how Californians spent public money but where they lived, how they learned, and what their neighborhoods looked like. California would drop from near the top of the states on spending per pupil to near the bottom. Municipalities unable to raise property tax became reliant on sales tax and courted retail development, which hurt efforts to build housing. The state became more dependent on the volatile, economically sensitive personal income tax, which precipitated big downturns and upswings. Fees for services increased, exempt from the two-thirds requirement for new taxes. Budgeting by initiative became a popular way to siphon off revenue for a particular cause, further debilitating the budget process.

"When California voters approved Proposition 13, the blockbuster initiative that mandates sweeping reductions in property taxes, it was interpreted around the nation as the beginning of a tax revolt—a modern Boston Tea Party," reported the *New York Times*. Over the next two decades, there were 148 tax-cutting initiatives across the country. By 1994 almost all states had followed California and imposed some new restrictions on taxes or spending.

As soon as Prop 13 passed, Jerry ordered a hiring freeze and compiled lists of potential budget cuts. One of the first items to go was the satellite. The $5.8 million cost over three years was an insignificant expenditure. But Jerry understood the value of symbols. There would be no California space program in the post–Prop 13 world. Three weeks after the election, Rusty Schweickart wrote a colleague to thank him for support, now moot. "Operation successful—patient died but not through lack of effort."

Initial polls after Prop 13 showed Jerry in a tight race with Republican Evelle Younger, the attorney general. Jerry asked Chavez for help; Marshall Ganz and a group of UFW workers were loaned for the rest of the campaign. Then Younger went on vacation to Hawaii. The Brown campaign rushed to make a commercial, with Hawaiian music, showing Jerry hard at work. More significantly, Jerry Brown embraced Prop 13 with such fervor that he was dubbed "Jerry Jarvis" by those who viewed him as politically expedient.

Jarvis became a folk hero, featured on the cover of *Time* magazine. He filmed a television ad that praised Younger, though he stopped short of an endorsement. The Brown campaign asked for equal time, and the man Jerry had called a demagogue happily obliged. Four days after his Younger commercial aired, Jarvis recorded a new spot: "I knew it would work and I knew Governor Brown was the man who could make it work."

Soon, polls showed a majority of Californians believed Jerry Brown had been a force behind the passage of Prop 13. He drew comfortably ahead. The percentage who saw him as an opportunist willing to do anything to get votes had also gone up significantly between March and August. Other views had not changed. The top adjective *Los Angeles Times* poll respondents picked to describe Jerry was "different."

He won in a landslide. "I see myself as an individual who has been given a second chance and a very big job. And I intend to do it," he said the next day. If there were any doubt that his attention remained divided, he added, "What happens after that I don't know."

Pundits from the East Coast, more interested in the "what happens after," saw Prop 13 as an opportunity. "The Jarvis tide will run back east across the country and, if he manages to adjust to it in a manner that appears to be just, equitable and compassionate, he will unquestionably revive his own currently shadowed presidential prospects," wrote the columnist Mary McGrory.

Less than two weeks after the election, two very different dramas captured national headlines and shook California. Jim Jones, leader of a group called the Peoples Temple, had been for many years a prominent part of the San Francisco political scene. Temple members worked on Democratic campaigns, and leading Democrats, including Jerry Brown, routinely attended events that honored Jones. The Peoples Temple was credited with helping George Moscone, a rising star in the progressive wing of San Francisco Democrats, win a close mayoral race in 1975. Moscone appointed Jones to the city housing commission. In 1977, amid allegations of physical and psychological abuse within the organization, Jones suddenly moved his followers to a remote location in Guyana.

Ex-members and relatives remained in the Bay Area, worried about friends and loved ones unable to escape from the cult settlement in the small South American country. Bay Area congressman Leo Ryan flew to Guyana to formally investigate the community known as Jonestown. As he concluded his visit on November 18, 1978, Ryan was assassinated, while Jones orchestrated the murder-suicide of 918 followers, including more than three hundred children.

As San Franciscans struggled to absorb the news from Guyana, tragedy struck at home. Much as Jerry used his appointments to diversify state government, Mayor Moscone had appointed record numbers of women, minorities, and gays to positions in San Francisco government. The gay community in the city had been rapidly growing in size and political clout, and in November 1977, Harvey Milk's election to the San Francisco County Board of Supervisors made him the first openly gay elected official in California. A year later, just days after the news of the Jonestown massacre, a conservative ex-police officer who had resigned his seat on the Board of Supervisors decided he wanted it back. When Moscone refused to reappoint him, Dan White assassinated the mayor, then walked down the hall and shot and killed Milk. The governor ordered flags flown at half-mast.

On January 8, 1979, Jerry was sworn in for a second term and delivered his inaugural address on statewide television, sounding more like a Republican candidate than a Democratic governor. He focused on national economic problems, attacked Congress for failing to control inflation, and proposed an income tax cut. Some of his most loyal supporters and appointees winced at the centerpiece of the address, a call for a balanced budget amendment to the U.S. Constitution, a cause espoused by the conservative National Taxpayers Union.

Undeterred by the difficulty of challenging an incumbent Democratic president, Jerry increasingly aimed his message outside California. Did he want to be president, Washington political consultant Robert Shrum asked? "I wouldn't mind it; I am certainly thinking about it . . . Obviously I have an interest. But the future is uncertain. Perhaps one of my qualities is the ability to live in the midst of uncertainty with a certain degree of . . ." Shrum finished the sentence: "Equanimity." "Yes, and I think the ability to try new things."

Jerry continued to try new things. He visited a small coastal town two hours north of San Francisco where the state had funded a mobile listening station that amplified the voices of migrating whales as they passed by. ("He's not going to talk to the whales?" said a disappointed reporter who had traveled there in hopes of a big story.) He marched again with Cesar Chavez, taking sides in an acrimonious lettuce strike in the Salinas Valley and cheering on thousands of farmworkers gathered for the UFW's biennial convention. And in the most publicized event of his second term, he celebrated his forty-first birthday in Liberia at the start of a trip to Africa with Linda Ronstadt. One of the couple's infrequent forays in public, the vacation landed them on the cover of *People* and *Newsweek*, sparked polls about the propriety of an unmarried presidential candidate going on safari with a rock star, and provided fodder for *Doonesbury* cartoonist Garry Trudeau, who ran two weeks of strips lampooning the noncandidate's ambitions.

Jerry seemed restless in Sacramento, more eager to campaign than to govern. A March 1977 memo from White House chief of staff Hamilton Jordan to President Carter proved prescient: "We should presume a challenge from Jerry Brown for the Democratic Party nomination. I feel strongly that he will probably run against you. By 1980, he will be bored with the job of being Governor. He probably feels that he would be President now if he had gotten into the race earlier."

As he looked for issues that would play well with a national constituency, Jerry turned again to the environment. His cautious approach to nuclear power had frustrated some of his supporters. Once again, he found the right moment. The alarming meltdown at Three Mile Island nuclear power plant on March 28, 1979, came as several nuclear plants sought licenses or permits to begin construction in California. Five weeks after the accident, Jerry spoke at a mass protest in Washington, D.C., seeking a nuclear power moratorium. He opened by thanking Ralph Nader, Tom Hayden, and Jane Fonda,

> prophets in their own time without honor, but prophets today of the future of this country. The antiwar movement was scorned, was looked upon as some kind of subversive effort, and yet history has vindicated those who stepped out first, to stand for truth, to stand for the future, to stand for peace. . . . This is not a Republican issue or a Democratic issue. Nuclear power and its lethal impact for hundreds of thousands of years looms larger than any political personality, any political party, any country. It is

a matter of the species of life that now inhabits this planet. We are living and profiting off the addiction to nuclear power. It has become a pathological addiction in that it has made many feel good, while storing up for generations to come, evils and risks that the human mind can barely grasp.

Two months later, an estimated thirty thousand people shut down California Highway 1 to protest the planned opening of the Diablo Canyon nuclear plant in San Luis Obispo, along the coast between Los Angeles and San Francisco. Organizers grilled Jerry privately for an hour before they allowed him to speak. "I just came by to join your effort to deny the license to Diablo Canyon nuclear power plant," Jerry said, promising to fight any effort by the Nuclear Regulatory Commission to grant the permit. The crowd in jeans and T-shirts exchanged hugs and cheered the politician in the three-piece suit, then listened to Bonnie Raitt, Jackson Browne, Graham Nash, and Peter Yarrow.

Jerry's Hollywood connections became significant as he eyed another run for president. Musicians and movie stars had gained new importance as revenue sources for candidates after federal election law limited individual donations to $1,000 per candidate. Under the 1974 law, celebrities could still donate services of unlimited value. The "rock music loophole" also allowed a portion of concert ticket sales to count toward federal matching funds in a presidential campaign.

The changes coincided with a shift in the politics of the entertainment industry. Warren Beatty's support for George McGovern in 1972 was viewed as a turning point, ending the era of Ronald Reagan and Shirley Temple Black and ushering in the Hollywood politics of Helen Reddy and Jane Fonda. In 1975, Beatty, Paul Newman, Robert Redford, and Neil Diamond financed a Washington-based nonprofit to battle the influence of oil companies. The next year, Jane Fonda and Tom Hayden formed the Campaign for Economic Democracy, which organized around grassroots issues in California and was funded primarily through the entertainment industry.

Hollywood's clout as a political player increased along with its profits and reach. Gross receipts from movies doubled between 1971 and 1979, and record sales tripled. By the end of the 1970s, the average American family went to more movies, bought more records and tapes, and watched 250 hours more television than a dozen years earlier. Politicians who could tap into the celebrity world had a large reach. "Let's face it, people are more into the lives, habits and political preference of today's celebrities," said Gray Davis. "I mean, it might sound ridiculous, but people really care who is Suzanne Sommers's [sic] favorite governor. It wouldn't even have entered anyone's mind five years ago."

The same skills that helped celebrities and their managers attract large audiences translated to the political arena. "There isn't much difference between selling Donna Summer or Jerry Brown," said Richard Trugman, who had done both—he left his job at Casablanca Records to be Jerry's finance chair in the 1978 campaign.

One of the most prominent industry moguls, Jeff Wald, had been a Jerry Brown supporter since the earliest days, along with his wife, the singer Helen Reddy. At the end of 1979, Wald helped arrange two concerts that featured Linda Ronstadt, the Eagles, and Chicago and raised about $300,000 for Jerry's nascent presidential campaign. The first concert was in San Diego, and about 180 contributors paid $150 apiece to take the train from Los Angeles with Jerry and celebrities, taking part in an onboard surprise party for Jane Fonda's forty-second birthday. But most of the audience came for the music, not the politics; when promoters finally let Jerry onstage around one A.M., he was booed. The next night at the Las Vegas concert, the musicians gently told him not to come onstage at all.

His presence in the third row was acknowledged from the stage, however, by Linda Ronstadt, who broke with the program format to note that she hadn't seen Jerry in a while since he had begun to lay the ground-work for his next campaign. "If it hadn't been for the fact that I got to see him on TV I would have forgotten what he looked like," she said. "But he came back yesterday, and he's going to make it all better now." Then she launched into "My Boyfriend's Back." At the end of the song, Jerry jumped up and greeted her with a hug as she walked offstage, a rare public show of affection. "I wanted to lighten up the whole thing a little," Ronstadt said after the concert. "Whenever people write about us, they always wonder if there is a political motive. We just like each other, that's all."

The worlds of Hollywood, politics, and media came together at Lucy's El Adobe, where Jerry and Ronstadt had first met. Dubbed by one magazine "the epicurean epicenter of Hollytics," the restaurant had long been a second home for musicians; now they were joined by Jerry's entourage. When Marshall Ganz worked on campaigns in Los Angeles, he would head over to El Adobe late at night to drink margaritas, talk to the

Casados, and see who was around. The Casados were proud of Jerry's success. Frank Casado was scouting out a location in Washington—just in case. "Where Jerry goes, El Adobe goes," he said.

By 1980, Ronstadt had five platinum records and had just finished a new album, *Mad Love*. The daughter of an English-Dutch-German mother and a Mexican-English-German father, she had been singing since she was four and moved from her Arizona home to Los Angeles when she was eighteen. When Lucy Casado introduced her to Jerry in 1971, both of their careers were just taking off. Ronstadt hit stardom just as Jerry was elected governor; at the end of 1974, *Heart Like a Wheel* became her breakthrough album. She and Jerry were both public figures who valued their privacy, and her Malibu home, with a glass teahouse that jutted out onto the sand, offered a welcome sanctuary. She had asked to go along when Jerry planned a trip to Africa, thinking she could keep it secret, then thinking they could duck the press once they arrived. Instead, they were besieged, and she hid in the bathroom on occasion to avoid photographers and covered her face as she ran out to board small planes.

Unlike others in the industry, Ronstadt had deliberately avoided using her celebrity to lobby for issues or candidates. "I don't want people to take my word for something because they like my music," she said. But she revised her view after thinking about artists in pre-Hitler Germany who had refused to take a stand. Fundraising for Jerry was even more complicated; she had vowed not to do so for fear people would think their relationship was based on her ability to raise money. As Jerry moved to enter the 1980 presidential race, she reconsidered that, too.

"There is no way for me to stay neutral," she said.

> If I won't support him, and I know him best, it looks like an attack. I would like him to be able to speak his ideas. I think they are really important and good and, for the most part, he's right. It's so hard for me, not only as a public figure but also as someone who believes in him, cares about him, is close to him and is on his side. I want to be on his side. I don't see how I can *not* take a stand. It's dangerous territory for me, that's for sure. But if Frank Sinatra is going to do a benefit for Reagan, then I guess I have to do a benefit for Jerry.

Six days before the 1960 election, presidential candidate John F. Kennedy was mobbed by supporters as he left a rally in downtown Los Angeles, accompanied by Pat Brown. The governor predicted the Democrat would carry California by a million votes; instead, Richard Nixon narrowly carried his home state. LOS ANGELES TIMES PHOTOGRAPHIC ARCHIVE, DEPARTMENT OF SPECIAL COLLECTIONS, CHARLES E. YOUNG RESEARCH LIBRARY, UCLA

On August 18, 1962, President Kennedy joined Governor Brown for the groundbreaking ceremony at the site of what would be the San Luis Dam, a joint state-federal project that was key to the development of the State Water Project. JOHN F. KENNEDY PRESIDENTIAL LIBRARY

Democrat Pat Brown treasured his friendship with Republican Earl Warren, in an era when personal relationships often trumped party loyalties. Once a year, Chief Justice Warren returned home for a weekend of hunting on a friend's ranch, and Pat often joined the party. In 1962, the two friends showed off their catch. EDMUND G. BROWN PAPERS, BANC PIC 1968.011-PIC, CARTON 5, COURTESY OF THE BANCROFT LIBRARY, UC BERKELEY

In his socks, student leader Mario Savio speaks from atop a police car surrounded by protesters on the Berkeley campus during the October 1, 1964, confrontation that led to the Free Speech Movement. Recent graduate Jack Weinberg, whose arrest for political advocacy on campus sparked the demonstration, spent thirty-two hours in the police car before he was released.

Bernice, Pat, and Kathleen Brown greet President Johnson on the Sacramento airport tarmac as he deplaned from Air Force One for a campaign stop in September 1964, weeks before he defeated Barry Goldwater in the general election. Johnson was the last Democratic presidential candidate to carry California for almost three decades. CENTER FOR SACRAMENTO HISTORY, SACRAMENTO BEE COLLECTION

Pat Brown, at his desk in the Mansion, hands a key to his oldest granddaughter, Kathleen Kelly.
COURTESY OF KATHLEEN KELLY

Bernice Brown, initially reluctant, grew to embrace her role as First Lady and gradually took on more public appearances and speaking engagements. SAN FRANCISCO HISTORY CENTER, SAN FRANCISCO PUBLIC LIBRARY

Ida Brown, a linchpin for the family, lived on her own into her nineties, enjoying nearby Golden Gate Park and the fog in San Francisco, a city she loved. COURTESY OF KARIN SURBER

Ignoring advice that he should run for a lower office, Jerry Brown jumped into the 1974 guber-natorial race and defeated three veteran Democrats in the primary. On his final campaign swing, he spoke to supporters at the Burbank airport on the eve of the general election. LOS ANGELES TIMES PHOTOGRAPHIC ARCHIVE, DEPARTMENT OF SPECIAL COLLECTIONS, CHARLES E. YOUNG RESEARCH LIBRARY, UCLA

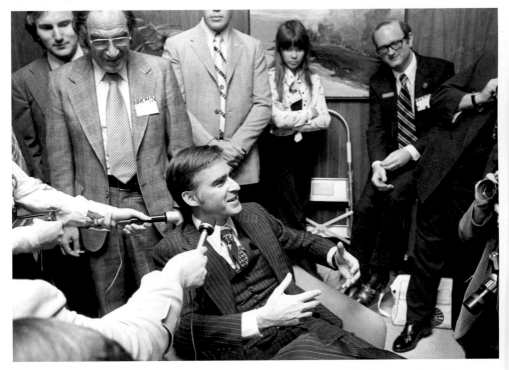

With a rare smile, thirty-six-year-old Jerry Brown talks with reporters before claiming victory on November 6, 1974, the first of four times he would be elected governor. RICK MEYER/LOS ANGELES TIMES PHOTOGRAPHIC ARCHIVE, DEPARTMENT OF SPECIAL COLLECTIONS, CHARLES E. YOUNG RESEARCH LIBRARY, UCLA

Tom Hayden, activist and writer, had spent weeks trailing Jerry during the campaign for an in-depth profile commissioned by *Rolling Stone* magazine. On Jerry's first day in office, Hayden traveled with the governor as he delivered speeches around the state. Jerry shunned the state plane and always flew commercial. CENTER FOR SACRAMENTO HISTORY, SACRAMENTO BEE COLLECTION

After barely more than a year in office, Jerry jumped into the 1976 presidential campaign. He won several primaries, but started too late to catch Jimmy Carter. As his parents looked on, Jerry voted the California delegation for Carter at the Democratic National Convention in New York. ASSOCIATED PRESS

TOP: Jerry Brown met Gregory Bateson, an anthropologist whose thinking would become a major influence on the young governor, in a late-night conversation in June 1975. "The new comes out of the random" was a Bateson saying that Jerry often repeated. He appointed Bateson to the Regents and named the first sustainable state office building after him. COURTESY OF THE OFFICE OF GOVERNOR EDMUND G. BROWN JR.

BOTTOM: Governor Jerry Brown celebrates the re-election victory of Los Angeles mayor Tom Bradley in April 1977, the second of what would be five terms. LOS ANGELES TIMES PHOTO-GRAPHIC ARCHIVE, DEPARTMENT OF SPECIAL COLLECTIONS, CHARLES E. YOUNG RESEARCH LIBRARY, UCLA

Jerry and Linda Ronstadt at an event at the Jonathan Club on the beach in Santa Monica in the summer of 1978. They had met years earlier at Lucy's El Adobe restaurant in Los Angeles, when both their careers were just starting to take off. She became a major star as he was elected governor. They both valued privacy, and despite their very public lives and competing demands, they maintained a relationship through Jerry's eight years as governor. COURTESY OF JODIE EVANS

Jerry celebrated his forty-first birthday at the start of an African trip with Linda Ronstadt, a private vacation that ended up landing them on the cover of several magazines. On April 11, 1979, they visited a United Nations program on sustainable land management in northern Kenya. ASSOCIATED PRESS/MARK FOLEY

Jerry had forged an unusual friendship with Cesar Chavez, founder of the United Farm Workers union. When a union activist was shot and killed during a bitter lettuce strike in 1979, Jerry attended the funeral in Calexico, seated next to Chavez. PHOTOGRAPH © DON BARTLETTI, 1979

TOP: During an early 1980 campaign swing as he prepared to run for president a second time, Jerry rode the subway to Brooklyn for a town meeting. His campaign slogan was "Serve the people. Protect the earth. Explore the universe."

BOTTOM: His attempt to challenge President Carter for the nomination never gained much strength, and he often said later that he should have quit the race when Massachusetts Senator Edward Kennedy jumped in.

In September 1982, a few months before he left office, Jerry returned to St. Brendan, his old elementary school in San Francisco, to sign laws that encouraged use of computers in the classroom. He predicted personal computers would one day be as ubiquitous for students as pens.

Pat Brown had long wanted some piece of the State Water Project named after him. In his last month in office, Jerry acquiesced and joined in the dedication of the Edmund G. Brown Aqueduct. Lauded as the man who had made the project possible, Pat said it was a lot nicer to hear the encomiums rather than have people make speeches when he was dead.

TOP: On his way back from six months in Japan, where he studied and practiced Zen Buddhism, Jerry spent several weeks as a volunteer for Mother Teresa, an experience that made a great impression on the former seminarian.
COURTESY OF THE OFFICE OF GOVERNOR EDMUND G. BROWN JR.

BOTTOM: At a March 1990 event to launch her campaign for state treasurer, Kathleen Brown gives her father a kiss.
COURTESY OF BROWN FAMILY

TOP: In his third run for president Jerry denounced the role of money in campaigns as corrupting, and accepted contributions no larger than one hundred dollars, raising millions of dollars largely through a toll-free phone number. Always looking for free publicity, the campaign staged a "Run for Jerry" on the Santa Monica beach, where the candidate and supporters sported shirts emblazoned with the 1-800 number. LAURENCE KEANE, COURTESY OF ELVIRA LOUNT

BOTTOM: With his political career apparently over after the 1992 presidential campaign, Jerry moved to Oakland, where he assembled a small commune in a warehouse. In the spring of 1996, he worked on the organic rooftop garden, with the modernist loft building in the background. SIBYLLA HERBRICH/SEASONAL CHEF

Jerry Brown poses with students at the Oakland Military Institute, one of two charter schools he founded while he was mayor of Oakland. Even as governor, he remained closely involved in the military academy college prep school, which he modeled on his high school, St. Ignatius. Jerry considered OMI and the Oakland School for the Arts two of his greatest and most lasting achievements. COURTESY OF OAKLAND MILITARY INSTITUTE

On November 7, 2006, as Jerry Brown celebrated his election as California attorney general, he held up a poster from his father's successful campaign for the same office more than fifty years earlier. U.S. Senator Dianne Feinstein joined in the victory celebration. ZUMA PRESS, INC./ALAMY STOCK PHOTO

Jerry and Anne Gust Brown, and Colusa, at the Mountain House ranch in December 2017. Behind them are photos of the original inn and Jerry's great-grandfather August Schuckman feeding his sheep. MATTHEW MORNICK/ COURTESY OF THE OFFICE OF GOVERNOR EDMUND G. BROWN JR.

Jerry Brown on the Colusa ranch that has been in the family for four generations. One hundred forty years after his great-grandfather bought the property, Jerry constructed a solar-powered house and prepared to move back to his ancestral home. COURTESY OF THE OFFICE OF GOVERNOR EDMUND G. BROWN JR.

Asked if she ever thought about being first lady, she said: "Sometimes. It's a pretty funny thought. But if I thought about it seriously, I would probably die laughing. I like my job. And the pay is a lot better." Friends on both sides dismissed the tabloid speculation about a possible wedding, and neither seemed under any illusion their lives could fit together long term.

When Carey McWilliams visited Jerry to write a column that assessed his presidential prospects, their conversation was interrupted twice by phone calls from "Linda," and the writer excused himself after an hour so that the governor could go meet her, as he had been promising on the phone. In an era when push-button phones were just starting to replace rotary dials and every move brought a new number, Linda Ronstadt's addresses and phone numbers spilled over onto card after card in Jerry's oversize Rolodex—three dozen numbers, crossed out one by one as they became obsolete, for recording studios, agents, secretaries, and homes in Brentwood, Hancock Park, and Malibu.

McWilliams found Jerry opportunistic, but with "genuine underdog sympathies"; a good listener who freely acknowledged he did not have all the answers; a skilled media manipulator annoyed with East Coast columnists who failed to understand him or California. "Tense, articulate, interested in ideas, eager for dialogue," McWilliams wrote. "An exceptional politician, he could only have emerged to national prominence in California."

Barely six months into his second term, Jerry filed paperwork to form an exploratory committee for a presidential run. "My own feeling is that people are ready for an alternative, they're ready for a blend of fiscal responsibility and yet a broad vision for the future. That's what we lack right now," he said. His campaign slogan was "Protect the Earth, Serve the People, Explore the Universe."

Tom Quinn went on leave to run the campaign. Quinn thought Carter was beatable, as long as Senator Edward Kennedy didn't enter the race. Four months later, Kennedy announced. Jerry's percentage of the vote in the early primaries was in the single digits. Quinn looked at the numbers and saw no route to victory. In early March, he returned to Los Angeles to take over the family media business. Jerry Brown, his first campaign manager concluded, could not shed the image that he was a flake.

Then came Wisconsin. The Brown campaign had staked its hopes on a strong showing. A few days before the primary, Jerry delivered a major speech in Madison entitled "The Shape of Things to Come." His friend filmmaker Francis Ford Coppola had arranged to use cutting-edge technology to broadcast the speech live to other locations around the state. The technology failed. Audiences watching the remote feed saw strange objects flying out of Jerry's head as his face turned green, with black holes. Coppola was distraught. The Brown campaign was finished.

His candidacy over, Jerry sat down with two *Village Voice* reporters who had recently compared him to Nixon as an ambitious, egotistical politician. Jerry proceeded to analyze his own failure with the detachment of a good Jesuit. He did not pay enough attention to the rituals, he affronted and irritated people on different sides of the spectrum. Prop 13, *Doonesbury*, the African safari, and his call for a balanced budget amendment all reinforced the flaky image.

"I have a certain skeptical approach. I comment in a certain ironic way. That's not a leadership posture. One has to be immersed and of this business, instead of slightly off, slightly standing aside. I think the paradox is that I become so involved in the political process, and reasonably good at it, and yet there is another aspect where I stand aside from the whole process and comment on it. That seems to be a detriment." By his manner, he radiated disdain for "people who are very excited by very conventional ideas which I don't think are really very interesting." His response to those ideas communicated his lack of respect. "In short, I engender some resentment. And you know, it's my fault. I'm in the world but not of it sufficiently." The interviewers did not pick up on the reference to the Jesuit credo that lay at the root of Jerry's dilemma. He had been trained to be in the world, but not of it.

Jerry spent several weekends with key advisers, trying to salvage ideas from the campaign and form an agenda for his last two years. The recession was hurting income tax revenues. The surplus that had cushioned the effects of Prop 13 for the first two years was gone, and the impact of the tax cuts was becoming clearer. In Oakland, twenty-four of thirty-five branch libraries had closed. The legislature passed an $18 million library appropriation bill, which Jerry vetoed. He insisted there be no tax increases. "For the first time since World War II," he told the legislature, "state government spending will clearly not keep pace with inflation."

His relationship with the legislature worsened. His vetoes were overridden by the Democratic-controlled houses more than a dozen times, a new record; before Jerry took office, there had been only two veto over-rides since 1946. At cabinet meetings, the remaining Brown loyalists lamented the negative press that portrayed their governor as brilliant but ineffective. Diana Dooley, who had risen to become the governor's legis-lative counsel and one of the most powerful women in the administra-tion at twenty-eight, had the unenviable task of selling his program to the legislature. "He's a very uncommon person," she said about her boss. "His intellectual capacity is phenomenal, and his appetite for informa-tion is insatiable." To try to ease the acrimony, she and her husband, Dan, chief deputy director of the state Department of Food and Agriculture, hosted backyard parties for the legislators at the end of session. That Jerry attended was considered a victory. "His idea of small talk is to ask a member what bill he's working on," Dooley said. "He just doesn't have what people typically think of as personal relationships with people."

Then Jerry was attacked for the one thing that had never been ques-tioned, his integrity. State workers had entered lists of campaign contrib-utors on a state computer for future political use. A formal investigation found bad judgment but no prosecutable offenses, and no suggestion that the governor had known about the acts. But "Computergate" undermined a core strength of the Brown reputation. That it had happened at all reflected the slow erosion of spirit and control in an office that had started out with such high ambition and exuberance.

Then a tiny pest unleashed a crisis that pitted environmentalists against the agricultural industry and left the governor looking indecisive and ineffective. On June 5, 1980, two Mediterranean fruit flies were discov-ered in San Jose. Medflies ruined fruit by laying larvae under the skin; a widespread outbreak could devastate the agricultural industry. The state began trapping, hoping to contain the flies before they spread from back-yards to orchards. Within a month, twenty-one medflies had been captured and larvae found in orange and loquat trees. To avoid spraying toxic chemicals, state officials released sterile male flies, designed to breed with females and halt the spread of infected larvae. Six million sterile flies arrived from Costa Rica. More came from Hawaii. By the end of September, agriculture officials had released 341 million sterile flies by land and air and quarantined all fruit from trees within a 450-square-mile area. But in October, flies were found in Alameda and Los Gatos, then even farther away in Palo Alto and Morgan Hill. State and federal offi-cials flew to Mexico to plead for more sterile flies.

As a state report later concluded, "Everything that could go wrong, went wrong." Traps weren't out as early as they should have been, there were delays in reporting and identifying the first flies, the invasion was too large to handle with sterile flies.

On December 24, 1980, after 1.309 billion sterile flies had been released, the governor declared a state of emergency. Still hoping to avoid aerial spraying, the most effective eradication technique, state officials tried a multipronged attack all winter. Massive amounts of fruit were stripped from trees and destroyed, sixty-two thousand homes were sprayed every day for six weeks, and sterile flies were released at the rate of 100 million a week. The agricultural industry, losing tens of millions of dollars, pushed hard for aerial spraying. Environmentalists argued that spraying malathion, a potential carcinogen, could cause short- and longer-term health risks. Hundreds of citizens from the affected communities packed a state hearing to plead against aerial sprays. As the number of larvae increased, Jerry announced one last effort to avoid aerial spraying by using the National Guard to strip all fruit in the quarantine area. The next day, the U.S. Department of Agriculture threatened to quarantine the whole state and block the sale of any California produce to prevent the spread of medflies through larvae in contaminated fruit. The governor ordered aerial spraying.

Helicopters took off during the night of July 13, 1981, from a hilltop cemetery, having been denied access to the local airport. Within a week, they had sprayed 160 square miles. Crews went door to door, destroying 17.7 tons of fruit. State police stopped more than a million vehicles at checkpoints and confiscated fruit from more than thirty thousand cars.

The spraying enraged environmentalists, and the delays infuriated the agricultural industry. Amid the outpourings of anger, a few people sent words of cheer and small gifts—which Jerry now accepted. Chris Bragg made a pet rock in the shape of a medfly. Joe Nelson at the state agriculture department sent YOU BUG ME buttons and a medfly T-shirt. "As depicted on the shirts," Jerry wrote in a thank-you note, "the fly is a beautiful creature for being so destructive."

Even Bohemian Grove became a problem for the Brown administration. A coalition of Northern California peace and women's groups formed the Bohemian Grove Action Network and held a twenty-four-hour-a-day vigil at the entrance gate to the grove to protest decisions being made by men in secret that affected the survival of the world. In

June 1981, the Brown administration sued the Bohemian Grove for discrimination because the club would not hire any female staff. Pat Brown was outraged. "Women would ruin it," he said. "Men should be allowed a brief period of time to get away. Getting together without women is part of the complete release from the conformities of society that Bohemians strive for."

Seven years after he had taken office, Jerry Brown's poll numbers had fallen from the unprecedented heights of his first term to near record lows. Forty percent thought he was doing a poor or very poor job while only 26 percent rated him as excellent or good. They had lost faith in him for the very reasons that he had first impressed: By 1981, the Field Poll reported that only 39 percent thought the governor worked hard and just 23 percent thought he was restoring faith in politics. Now he was seen as just another politician who did what he needed to win elections.

Running for a third term seemed precarious. Jerry aimed instead for an open Senate seat, where the baggage of his first two terms might not weigh as heavily. He began his last year in office on a different tone. His State of the State address, unusually long at twenty minutes, was also unusually philosophical, even for Jerry. He looked back at the California pioneers, including his great-grandfather. He read from August Schuckman's diary about crossing the Plains, and then from the State of the State delivered by the first elected governor, Peter Burnett: "Nature, in her kindness and beneficence, has distinguished California by great and decided natural advantages: and these great natural resources will make her either a very great or very sordid and petty State. She can take no middle course."

Jerry concluded with lines that he agonized over until minutes before the speech, words that closely echoed his comments at the prayer breakfast before his first inaugural: "Our obstacles are not the lack of money, or gold, or raw materials," he said. "We have these or can get them. What we need to find anew is the spirit that built this state and sustains us even now."

On March 10, 1982, Jerry announced his candidacy for the Senate, his parents at his side. He again highlighted four issues: jobs and the economy, equity for the elderly and the poor, environmental quality, and scaling back the nuclear arms race. "California during the last seven years has proved that good wages, strong environmental laws, and unparalleled job growth go together," he said.

He faced Pete Wilson, a solid Republican who had been elected to the Assembly three times and then to three terms as San Diego mayor but struggled in earlier efforts to break through as a statewide presence. He was knowledgeable and articulate, but dull. From the start, the race was a referendum on Jerry Brown.

Jerry said that from his losses he had learned patience and a respect for the political processes he had alternately shunned and mocked. He analyzed his failures with less detachment. "I mistakenly thought that I could bypass the normal political process which I had observed my father going through when I was growing up," he told historian Kevin Starr near the end of the campaign. "I thought that because I had been there before I was exempt from it: the handshaking, the lobbying, the showing up before this or that group." He had always found haunting the image of Thomas Jefferson, the only president to insist on walking to his own inauguration, pointedly eschewing the trappings of political royalty. "And so I mistakenly played the iconoclast, thinking that I was working against the cult of personality in government, even to the point of not sending my picture to a six-year-old girl when she requested it."

This time, Jerry welcomed his father's support. Pat campaigned around the state with a dozen stops a day for radio, television, and newspaper interviews. "Jerry is way behind in the polls," Pat wrote to his former finance director Hale Champion in July. "It reminds me of our 1966 campaign. I don't know what we will do, but we will do all we can." He added a handwritten postscript: "Jerry is gaining and *will win!*"

As in 1966, many liberal Democrats were disenchanted. "I might refer you to the latest Field poll which shows that an overwhelming majority of the people in this state do not like your son," Max Palevsky, who had been one of Jerry's earliest supporters, wrote to Pat. "I do not think Jerry has any broad set of political principles—I do not think Jerry believes in *anything* very deeply. Practically without exception, the liberal activists in this state are not backing your son."

As Pat had prevailed upon Fred Dutton to return in 1966, Jerry called Tom Quinn. Quinn drove through a snowstorm from his Reno home to Sacramento and offered help with television spots. He dug up a quote from Wilson about the possibility of cutting Social Security and fashioned an effective ad that urged voters "take another look" at Jerry Brown. He moved up in the polls and pulled almost even. Then the campaign switched to an ad in which a little boy said "I want to go on living" as a nuclear bomb exploded in a mushroom cloud, implying that Wilson would escalate the nuclear arms race. The ad reinforced Jerry's flaky image and backfired. They pulled it after a week, but the damage was done.

Jerry lost by almost 7 points. On election night, he conceded the race had been a referendum on his own performance. He sat eating tortilla chips at El Adobe, still absorbed in watching the last of the television broadcasts, until finally heading home at one A.M. Later that morning, he was cheerful as he met with the press, responding with a half laugh when asked if he intended to run for president again. "I believe the people of California would like a respite from me and in some ways I would like a respite from them. Each of us will withdraw from each other and after a period of time, my services will be available in some interesting capacity." He told his friends he had three plans: to write a book, run a marathon, and maybe get married.

He still had fans. Alex Hutton, who worked in remittance processing in DMV, left a single yellow rose at the governor's office with a note that said, "Hang in there always." Jerry's friends were loyal, none more so than the original Brownies, young people on whom he had taken a chance. "So many of us were nonentities before we joined this governor," said B. T. Collins, a former Green Beret and Vietnam veteran who served in various positions in the governor's office. "He made us something. He gave a lot of people tremendous opportunity to show their stuff." He predicted Jerry would be back. "He's a warrior. Public service is something he's got to do." They would be ready when he returned. "Not many of the old gang will turn their back on him," said Marty Morgenstern, who headed employee relations.

In the governor's race, George Deukmejian had defeated Los Angeles mayor Tom Bradley, returning Republicans to power. There was one more loss for the Brown family on Election Day. A referendum to authorize the final piece of the State Water Project failed overwhelmingly. Proposition 9 would have authorized the state to construct the Peripheral Canal, which was designed to increase the flow of water to Southern and Central California and bypass the environmentally sensitive Delta. Northern Californians saw it as a water grab, the largest growers in the Central Valley rejected the environmental restrictions attached, and many environmentalists objected that the protections were not strong enough. Together they financed an expensive campaign and overcame lukewarm support in Southern California, where users would have been the major beneficiaries.

Pat Brown, who lamented the loss more than his son did, had long wished to see his name permanently connected to some piece of the water project. "It is immodest at the least for me to suggest it, but it is something I really want," Pat had written a friend while Reagan was in office. "I know it is not necessary because history will record the fact that there never would have been a water project if it were not for me."

When Jerry took office, Assemblyman John Knox had submitted a bill to name the aqueduct after Pat Brown. "And Jerry called me up and he said, 'Dad, I think it's a mistake to call the project after you at this time. When you're dead, then they'll name something after you,'" Pat recalled. "I said, 'Hell, I won't know anything about it then!'" But he accepted Jerry's rationale; people had voted down a proposal to name the Sacramento auditorium after Earl Warren. "The people don't like to have you name something after yourself."

Ron Robie, head of the water department, tried again a few years later. "As we discussed yesterday, Governor Edmund G. 'Pat' Brown was the real 'father' of the State Water Project," Robie wrote Resources Secretary Huey Johnson on June 1, 1981. "It was the major accomplishment of his administration. He has not been recognized in any way regarding the Project. Mr. Brown has frequently remarked on this to my deputy directors and I believe it would be appropriate to name the California aqueduct after Mr. Brown in recognition of his accomplishments." He planned a ceremony for two days later. The governor vetoed the idea.

Finally, at the water commission meeting the Friday after the 1982 election, Robie pushed the motion through. He called Jerry, told him there would be a ceremony on December 11, and suggested it would be nice if he showed up.

Pat rented a bus, and most of the family was at the Edmonston pumping plant, which powered water almost two thousand feet up and over the Tehachapi Mountains.

"The aqueduct is symbolic of the whole project, for it is the one facility that bridges the whole state, delivering water from north to south," Robie said in his opening remarks.

"This is a project that transcends any one particular administration, but it certainly does reflect, to a very large degree, my father's interest," Jerry said. "In fact if I would say there's one thing he's talked about more than anything else to me, it's the water project." He referred obliquely to

*Family members arrive at the dedication ceremony for the Edmund G. Brown
state aqueduct, one of Jerry Brown's last official acts as governor in
December 1982. (Courtesy of California Department of Water Resources)*

the failure of the Peripheral Canal bond. "There are battles, some of them
have been won, some of them have been lost. But I think there has been
a forward movement. And as we construct these facilities over time, new
realities intrude, such as the cost of energy, the understanding of the integrated consequences to the ecology and the environment. And yet we
see the initial wisdom of this effort. If we waited until now to build it, it
probably would have never been built."

He and Robie held up a poster of the nameplate that would be
engraved in bronze and mounted on the Edmund G. Brown Aqueduct.
The guest of honor took the microphone, free this time to talk as long
as he wanted.

"I couldn't help but think that it's much nicer to be here today and be
alive to hear those things rather than to hear them after you're gone,
which is usually the way with things that they name after you," Pat said.

He talked about his grandfather praying for water at the Mountain House, about the water cases he handled as attorney general, and about the work that all the people in the room had done to pass the largest bond in California history and make the State Water Project a reality. "We're not through yet," he said, casting the failure of the Peripheral Canal as only a temporary setback. "I hope that the dedication today and the naming of this dam will cause all of us that love our state and love our fellow man, that we will rededicate ourselves to investing in those that are not yet here, the future of California.

"I just want to leave on one note. You'll notice it's the Edmund G. Brown aqueduct. And centuries later, they won't know whether it's the father, or the son."

17

Winter Soldiers

In the summer of 1984, the Democratic convention returned to the Golden State for the first time since 1960, when the party had nominated John F. Kennedy. Unlike that unruly, suspenseful gathering, the 1984 political convention in San Francisco followed a predictable script. Walter Mondale would be nominated to challenge President Reagan, who had brought to Washington the vision of government he had honed in Sacramento.

The lasting memory from the San Francisco convention was a passionate attack on the Reagan vision, delivered with perfect pitch by New York governor Mario Cuomo. America, he said, was not the shining city on the hill that the president invoked, but rather a tale of two cities. "There's another part to the shining the city: the part where some people can't pay their mortgages, and most young people can't afford one, where students can't afford the education they need, and middle-class parents watch the dreams they hold for their children evaporate. In this part of the city there are more poor than ever, more families in trouble, more and more people who need help but can't find it . . . There is despair, Mr. President, in the faces that you don't see, in the places that you don't visit in your shining city."

In the deep cadences of his native Queens, Cuomo rallied Democrats with an attack on "social Darwinism" and a call for government to protect the most vulnerable. "The Republicans believe that the wagon train will not make it to the frontier unless some of the old, some of the young, some of the weak, are left behind by the side of the trail . . . We Democrats believe in something else. We Democrats believe that we can make it all the way with the whole family intact, and we have more than once, ever since Franklin Roosevelt lifted himself from his wheelchair to lift this nation from its knees."

Cuomo's keynote address embraced the values that mattered so much to Pat Brown, the governor who had welcomed Democrats to his state in 1960. Then, all things had seemed possible, as California surged past New York to become the nation's most populous state and Californians united to build water works, roads, and universities. A quarter century later, Reagan's rise had helped propel Republicans back into power in Sacramento. Proposition 13 had eroded public services and exacerbated the growing gap between rich and poor. Poverty was increasing in California faster than the national average rate. The spirit of a greater public good had given way to parochialism that pitted communities against one another and deepened racial divides.

For the first time in decades, no Brown played a formal role in the presidential campaign. Pat attended the convention as an honored VIP, happy to see old friends. Jerry wrote two guest columns for the *San Francisco Chronicle* that hammered familiar themes: the party must find ways to engage the majority of citizens who felt it not worth their time to even vote. He lauded the choice of Geraldine Ferraro as the vice presidential nominee, the first woman on a major party ticket. "In a very basic way, Geraldine Ferraro defines the difference between Mondale and Reagan," he wrote. "One embraces diversity and engages the future. The other fosters privilege and plays the melodies of a bygone age."

Jerry Brown, private citizen, had embarked on what became known among friends as "the wilderness years," a combination of soul-searching, plotting, and penance. After leaving office, he holed up in Laurel Canyon with a parting present from the staff, a new Apple computer. From the start, he and his loyal followers assumed the political exile would be temporary. They formed a political action committee to help Democrats regain control of the U.S. Senate, where Republicans had won a majority in 1980 for the first time in five decades. Jerry started two nonprofit organizations, the National Commission on Industrial Innovation, funded by business and labor organizations, and the Institute for National Strategy, a think tank designed to give him global experience and contacts with influential thinkers.

The strategy was to target the next generation of political leaders. To identify young leaders and arrange introductions, Jerry turned to three men: Occidental Petroleum chairman Armand Hammer, a friend of Pat's with long-standing ties to the Soviet Union; Canadian prime minister Pierre Trudeau; and Richard Nixon. The three became what the director of the institute, Nathan Gardels, called "our tutors." Jerry and Gardels spent a day discussing Russia and China with Nixon at a hotel in Orange County, where the former president was planning his library. Hammer's fixer arranged a trip to the Soviet Union, which included a meeting with the dissident writer Yevgeny Yevtushenko. Jerry sought out literary figures on all his travels; in Mexico, he held back-to-back conversations about American intervention in Central America with Carlos Fuentes and Octavio Paz, writers with sharply divergent politics.

"I'm advancing ideas, but in a very quiet way," Jerry said in early 1985. "I'm interested in building an international network of people who want to shape the future, who feel because of their knowledge, or their ability, or their contacts, that they can make a difference in what happens in the world." The institute published a quarterly and sponsored symposia on subjects such as nuclear proliferation and the future of NATO. Excerpts from a conference on the future of American politics were published in the *New York Review of Books*.

Jerry saw his work as a corrective to the well-financed and organized conservative think tanks that had shaped political thought for a decade and facilitated Republicans' success. "A series of John the Baptists ran around the country, clearing a path for President Reagan," Jerry said, while liberals were slow to respond with organizations that might build support for more enlightened leadership. "That is really the opportunity for those in the private sector. Power is not located in an office. It is diffused throughout society—in institutions, interest groups, the media, campaign contributors, labor unions, and other groups."

His travel was paid for by the institute or by foreign countries. He signed on as an associate with the New York law firm of Reavis & McGrath, which paid him a $50,000 annual retainer to act primarily as a rain-maker. His parents gave him $20,000 each year, as they did each child and grandchild. He earned honoraria of up to $5,000 for speaking engagements.

"I certainly feel the need to be out of active politics for a significant amount of time," he said in January 1985. "I don't know how long, but certainly a long time yet. Not eighty-eight. It's not plausible. My present state of mind is that is just not a reality."

Nonetheless, his political action committee commissioned a top secret survey conducted the same month to assess Jerry's chances as a presidential candidate in 1988. The conclusion by the Washington firm Belden Research: slim to none. The telephone survey of Democratic leaders and activists across the country found the greatest support for Mario Cuomo, largely driven by his 1984 convention speech. Although he was considered a creative thinker with good ideas, Jerry had support in the single digits. Of nine potential candidates, he had the highest unfavorable rating. He was viewed as "eccentric," "a little nutty," too "California," too flamboyant, too liberal, and too opportunistic. "Governor Brown," the report concluded, "will never get the opportunity to prove his worth as the party's messenger of the essential ideas and programs unless he can overcome the pervasive perception that he is not someone to be taken seriously."

Jerry headed to Japan to study Buddhism, reflect, and write.

Thousands of miles away, Jerry did not have to confront the unraveling of many of his signature accomplishments. Though Democrats controlled the legislature, the Republican administration of George Deukmejian gradually undermined the Brown legacy. Deukmejian shut down the Office of Appropriate Technology. Appointments to the state Agricultural Labor Relations Board were unabashedly pro-grower, to balance what Republicans called years of favoritism toward the UFW. The most significant undoing of the Brown era, both in substance and symbol, was the unprecedented recall of three California Supreme Court justices.

In his determination to shake up the white male judiciary, Jerry had appointed his college friend Rose Bird as chief justice, the first woman on the state's highest court. He could not have selected a lawyer the legal establishment would like less. Bird was principled, outspoken, accustomed to breaking gender barriers, and controversial from the start.

Some of Jerry's advisers, concerned about Bird's brusque temperament, had urged him to appoint her as an associate justice and elevate Stanley Mosk or Mathew Tobriner to the court's top job. Bird insisted the obstacles to the revolutionary change the governor wanted would be so great that she could make progress only if she were in charge. Her reception seemed to justify her fears. Mosk, angry that he had been passed over, greeted Bird in 1977 with a line he repeated for years: "I certainly cannot blame you for being here, but I blame Jerry Brown for putting you here." Her intelligence and jurisprudence were never in doubt; in thinly veiled sexist critiques, detractors inside and outside the court attacked her personality and her politics. Ostracized and undermined by colleagues, she was condemned for being insular and unfriendly. In a bureaucracy resistant to change, judges and staff were so upset by her decision to rotate the conference table in her chambers that she moved it back to its original position.

In 1978, Bird was on the ballot for an up-or-down vote and overcame a last-minute smear campaign to narrowly prevail in what normally would have been a routine confirmation. Her efforts to wrest administrative control of the vast court system continued to roil the judicial establishment. Then critics seized on an issue with popular appeal: her opposition to the death penalty. No one had been executed in California in almost two decades, and a revised death penalty statute was undergoing challenges and refinements. Under Bird's leadership, the court found legal grounds to overturn every death sentence it reviewed.

A coalition of conservatives, law enforcement officials, and crime victims tried for several years to force a recall vote but fell short the necessary signatures. In 1986, Bird faced the voters again in a retention election. Two of Jerry's other appointees were on the same ballot, Joseph Grodin, a protégé of Mathew Tobriner, and Cruz Reynoso, the first Latino on the court. Both were esteemed legal thinkers, and both had supported Bird during her stormy tenure. Neither voted in lockstep with the chief justice. But the organized, well-funded opposition lumped the three together as "Jerry's Judges." The three did share a long-standing commitment to farmworkers and the UFW, Bird through her role in negotiating the Agricultural Labor Relations Act, Grodin as a member of the first board created under the act, and Reynoso as a founder of California Rural Legal Assistance. Much of the money raised to unseat the three came from agricultural interests.

The overtly political campaign against Rose Bird, only the second woman in the country to lead a state high court, attracted national attention. "At stake is a choice about fundamental principles and the kind of government we want. How independent should our judiciary be?" Jerry Brown wrote in an op-ed piece. "When I made appointments to the Supreme Court, I did not look for individuals who would take the path of least resistance. I wanted those who were strong and independent, who knew the law and who were willing to apply it with compassion. I did not want justices who followed public-opinion polls." He noted the campaign was essentially a personal attack on Bird, whose decisions differed little from those of her colleagues or predecessors. "She has not embraced the powerful forces of the day or the biases of the moment, but has insisted on the underlying logic of the laws she interprets. She takes the longer view of society and her role in it at the very time when immediate gratification and near-instant response express the ethos of the age."

The campaign against the three was without precedent, and they were hesitant how to fight back. Pat Brown chaired a committee that raised money, but it fell far short of the $10 million spent by recall proponents. For Pat, the fight was personal; his own Supreme Court appointments were among his proudest accomplishments, and he was a passionate defender of a court widely viewed as one of the most progressive and influential in the country. "What's a father to do?" Pat wrote in a letter to the editor of the *Los Angeles Times*. "I said the power brokers would never accept a woman at the top. So what does my son do? He not only picks a woman, but a tough one at that—Rose Elizabeth Bird—and makes her Chief Justice." Pat condemned the recall as a power grab by Governor Deukmejian, an outspoken Bird foe, who would be able to pack the court with conservative allies.

Bird was voted out by a two-to-one margin; Reynoso and Grodin lost in slightly closer tallies. Pat's prophecy came true, and the court slid into years of relative obscurity. Yet the barriers broken by Bird, Reynoso, and dozens of other women and minorities Jerry had appointed to the bench ensured that the California courts would never return to their earlier homogeneous state.

While Jerry combed through his past in search of enlightenment about the future, his father entered his ninth decade at peace. Pat still signed all his letters "Edmund G. 'Pat' Brown, Governor of California, 1959–1967." The Browns had added a third bedroom to the modest Beverly Hills home in anticipation of needing a full-time caretaker in the not too distant future. Pat and his partners still owned the Schuckman homestead in Colusa, which they leased to local ranchers. Though he rarely visited, he felt a sentimental attachment to the Mountain House. "I kind of hope the grandchildren will have some interest in it, will want to return to the soil," he said.

Pat and Bernice still held out hope there might someday be an Edmund G. Brown III, though their only son showed no inclination of getting married. Jerry and Linda Ronstadt had drifted apart, remaining friends. In his typically uninhibited, gregarious manner, Pat still embarrassed both his family and friends with his inquiries and efforts to marry off his son. Bernice scolded him for public comments about Jerry's private life. "This is the thing about Jerry: I think he'll get married when he finds a girl he wants to marry—and when he feels like getting married," she said. She predicted her son would elope because "he thinks big weddings are ridiculous. He once told me, 'When I get married it'll be an accomplished fact when I let you know.'"

Pat had not always had the smoothest relationship with his eldest daughter, who shunned politics and resented the intrusion of her father's life. But as Pat and Bernice approached their fifty-sixth anniversary, he sent Barbara a copy of a letter she had written years earlier, "the best and most beautiful letter we have ever received." Barbara had enclosed comments from her son's teacher, who praised Charlie's contributions to class and interest in government. "I guess that in a way I am attempting to tell you of the strong influence that you have had on me in spite of the different path I choose to follow in my life," Barbara wrote. She had gotten her doctorate and worked as a school and family counselor.

In their major philanthropic effort, Pat and Bernice donated a million dollars to Cal, one of the largest bequests to the university. Pat's beloved university system had so far educated Bernice, her three sisters and one brother, two children, four grandchildren, and several nieces and nephews. The gift funded the Bernice Layne Brown Gallery in the foyer of the Bancroft Library and a new biology building, where the eatery was named Pat Brown's Café.

Pat's annual birthday parties became fundraisers for the Pat Brown Institute, which had grown out of conversations among his friends and former staff members about how to influence government policy. As the institute grew and convened conferences on specific issues, it became a nonprofit organization, eventually housed at California State University at Los Angeles.

The man who worried about his financial well-being when he lost the 1966 election had become wealthier than he had ever imagined. The fervent civil rights supporter did not seem troubled that he earned much of his fortune through the Suharto regime in Indonesia, a repressive, brutal dictatorship characterized by massive corruption. Pat sold his interest in the Indonesian oil firm at a large profit and took pleasure in spending money on his family. Bernice, frugal in all other respects, had pushed Pat into what became a sacrosanct tradition: Each Christmas, they took the extended family on a beach vacation, to Hawaii, or the Caribbean, and once to Tahiti. The trips fostered ties among the four generations and created unusually close bonds among cousins, nieces, and nephews who would otherwise have had only passing acquaintance. Jerry was the family member most likely to miss the outing; when he did show up, Pat always noted his presence with pride. In 1986, their eleventh trip, Pat and Bernice spent ten days in Jamaica with two dozen children, grandchildren, and great-grandchildren. Jerry flew in from Japan for four days. "I don't think Jerry's through in politics by any means," his father said in an interview. "I think he was a good governor. I think he has an attractive political personality. He's good looking. He's studying all the time, traveling all the time . . . Look at the people who've been elected after they were counted out."

In Japan, Jerry immersed himself in the study and practice of Buddhism, a religion that echoed many Jesuit precepts. On a 1986 trip to Japan, Jerry had met a Jesuit priest who was expert in Zen. He sent Jerry to a *roshi*, master teacher, who worked as a hospital administrator and tutored students at night in his backyard meditation room. The roshi invited Jerry to come study. Jerry lived in Kamakura, a seaside town an hour south of Tokyo, where a group of students gathered each night at the *zendo*, temple, in the master's yard. "It is about grasping the immediate, and breaking through the conditioning that limits every human mind," Jerry said. He practiced Zen meditation daily and participated in four one-week retreats, two at a Buddhist center and two with the Jesuits.

He grew a beard and spent his days working on a memoir. "What I'm doing is writing for myself," he told a reporter who tracked him down. "I'm comprehensively looking at my experience, both in politics and before, trying to understand more deeply the principles that best describe what I've tried to do in politics." Jerry wrestled with the same questions about power and leadership that had driven him into the seminary, then into politics, and now into the wilderness. The Jesuit motto "Contemplation in Action" sought to mold men who wielded influence through actions based on insights gained through meditation. "All religious traditions aim at the same thing, and that is the removal, or the minimizing or reducing, of the delusions of the self, the deceptions of the ego that interfere with a clear understanding of who one is and what life makes possible," Jerry wrote. "This is all clouded by delusory thinking."

Three decades after they had entered the seminary at Los Gatos, Jerry sent Frank Damrell a copy of the photo Bart Lally had snapped when he dropped his friends off at Sacred Heart. "Just look at the expression on those faces!" Jerry wrote. "What worlds came and went since then! Despite the intervening years, those first, uncertain steps reflect a common purpose that may still be with us."

En route home from Japan, Jerry stopped in Calcutta, where Damrell's son was working with Mother Teresa. The three weeks Jerry spent in India made an outsized impression and became a stock paragraph in his biography.

Calcutta assaulted his senses, with polluted air and teeming streets. During the daily six A.M. mass, where several hundred nuns sat on a canvas-covered concrete floor, street noise occasionally drowned out the prayers. At the House of the Pure Heart, fifty dying men lay on two rows of metal cots. Jerry bathed patients, fed them, washed soiled blankets, handed out pills. "I experienced a directness and immediacy that I have rarely before encountered," he wrote in a *Life* magazine essay in April 1988. "You see the gratitude or the pain on faces. Nothing is filtered by a need to impress anyone." About a dozen patients died during his three-week stay. Each was wrapped in a white cotton sheet and taken to the small room in back that served as a morgue. Jerry thought about what the nuns at St. Brendan school had said: Pray for a happy death.

"Mother Teresa challenges our whole way of life," Jerry wrote. "She lives as if it were God himself lying there in the street, crying out for help. What does that mean for how we live each day? This is a question I can't get out of my mind today, back in America. I think of politics. After all, that's what I spent a good part of my life doing. Beyond the fascination, the excitement, the ambition, is it possible to really change anything?"

He returned to California on February 8, 1988, the day of the Iowa caucuses, two months shy of his fiftieth birthday. Some of the old Brownies organized a lavish reunion-birthday party, in hopes of jump-starting his political career. They raised tens of thousands of dollars and invited a thousand guests; Jerry vetoed the plan at the last minute. "We tried to hold a 50th birthday party for your son, but he killed the idea. That's what I mean when I say he doesn't know how to deal with people," his former top aide B. T. Collins wrote to Pat in frustration. Jerry further alienated some of his staunchest supporters by briefly taking up the cause of antiabortion activists, saying he was inspired by Mother Teresa's commitment to life.

In his ongoing effort to meld the spiritual with the political, Jerry began to describe politics as "the grammar" of his family life. He layered on that foundation the vocabulary of the Jesuits—Ignatian detachment from creature comforts; being in the world but not of it; the importance of *agere contra*, going against oneself. His time in Japan had convinced him of the universality of those ideas. "To make change, people have to start changing themselves," he wrote. "Start with yourself. That's where all the healing takes place. Things take a lot longer than I used to think they did. I used to think big changes happen overnight, but it only happens in a slow growth pattern. No quick fixes around the corner."

Jerry's next move was as far from Buddhist meditation as Berkeley in the sixties had been from the seminary. He had found something to run for that he could win: the chairmanship of the California Democratic Party. He would engage in the activity he had so condemned, raising money, and transform the ultimate political hack position into a noble undertaking. *Agere contra.* "I know in my bones what politics is—both its evil and its splendor," he wrote, "and I see what it can become: the common endeavor through which people come to trust themselves and thereby create a community that works, not by repressing difference but by honoring our diversity. It is for that which I am offering myself. Not as another candidate climbing the ladder again, but as a person chastened by experience and fully understanding that the opportunity—the greatest opportunity imaginable—is to serve and serve completely."

Party rules required that the chairmanship rotate between a Southern and Northern Californian. To qualify, Jerry switched his registration to San Francisco in time for the November 1988 election. He sold the Laurel Canyon house and, with the help of his parents, bought a $1.2 million historic home in the Pacific Heights section of San Francisco, a restored firehouse built in 1893 for Engine Company 23.

"Yeah, I've got some baggage out there," he said as he campaigned among the twenty-eight hundred delegates who would vote in February 1989. "Guess what? I made some mistakes. I made some enemies. Not every appointment turned out the way it should have. Well, I've been six years doing penance. And I'm asking you to take me back." He promised to transform a little-noticed post into something big ("the most exciting Democratic Party in the country"), just as he had done as secretary of state. He promised a major voter registration drive. He promised to meld the old grassroots spirit of the California Democratic Council clubs with the latest high-tech tactics. "My greatest strength," he said, "is envisioning what hasn't been and bringing it about."

The California Democratic Party was in sad shape, weakened in part by the growing divide between rich and poor. The diversified economy that had slowly emerged after World War II looked healthy on paper: California added three million jobs during the 1980s. But the statistics masked a loss of industrial, middle-class jobs. The split was evident across the state—shining cities on the hill with higher-paying jobs for professionals, and struggling cities in the dust with low-paying service jobs and growing numbers of undereducated, unskilled immigrants. Through the 1970s, the poverty rate in California had been roughly the same as the national average, taking into account regional differences. The lines began to diverge sharply after the passage of Prop 13, with California's poverty rate rising more steeply. In the late 1980s, while the rate declined in most of the country, the number of Californians who struggled on incomes below the poverty level kept climbing. By the end of the decade, more than a quarter of Californians were poor.

The residual impacts of Prop 13 exacerbated the disparities. Affluent communities passed special assessments and bonds to improve their roads, schools, and libraries, while services in poorer communities deteriorated. Blacks and Latinos attended schools that lacked the required courses or quality of teaching to qualify students for admission to the public universities, the traditional route to upward mobility. In 1985, 13 percent of white high school seniors qualified for admission to the University of California, compared to only 4.9 percent of the Latino students and 3.6 percent of the black students. "It appears to me that unwittingly we are evolving into a de facto educational apartheid," Assemblyman Tom Hayden said at a hearing. Tuition and fees had doubled over the past decade, another bar for the working poor. Latinos, the fastest-growing ethnic group, made up one quarter of the population, but only 10 percent of the university enrollment.

Those in the shining cities, who were far more likely to vote, increasingly identified with the Republican Party, which had steadily gained enrollment through the 1980s. No Democratic presidential candidate had carried California since Lyndon Johnson in 1964.

"Some would say this is a vindication. I call it a heroic challenge," Jerry said in his acceptance speech after he easily won election as party chair. "People have raised the question as to whether I have enough nuts and bolts to make it work." Democrats in the room laughed. "And only time will tell." Responding to the Republican glee at the return of Governor Moonbeam, Jerry said theatrically, with his half smile: "For those of you who are worried about this negative aura, remember! I can become the media dark hole that sucks in all the negative feedback and allows our candidate for governor to go into battle unscathed! To victory!"

Political parties, weak or strong, had an institutional longevity comparable only to that of churches and universities, Jerry reasoned. Analyzing his own failures as governor, he concluded he had given experimentation a bad name, in part because there had been weak external support for cutting-edge initiatives. Solar power, wind power, and cogeneration had all been dismissed as flaky ideas, though they eventually became mainstream. A strong Democratic Party, Jerry argued, could move politics off the cautious, poll-driven course that had become the norm. The solution was a party that coupled innovative technology with the neighborhood appeal of old-fashioned political machines, built around the disenfranchised constituencies—immigrants, the poor, and the young.

Jerry hired Marshall Ganz, the former farmworker organizer who had worked on his earlier campaigns, to build an operation for voter registration and organizing. Jerry's main job was to raise money, and there was never enough. During his first year as chair, the party raised a record $2 million—and spent it all. Alan Cranston, the U.S. senator who had helped found the California Democratic Council and rebuild the party in the 1950s, had been at Jerry's side when he won election to the party post and promised his support. He had championed Ganz as the person who could help shape the new iteration of a grassroots party. Within months, Cranston became ensnared in scandal for his efforts to help a major donor, Charles Keating, rescue his failing savings and loan.

Democratic registration slipped below 50 percent for first time in fifty-six years, while Republican enrollment neared 40 percent. Jerry lost interest in the organizing plan. He dismissed Ganz and half a dozen staff and abandoned the voter registration drive as too costly. In November 1990, former San Francisco mayor Dianne Feinstein lost a close race for governor to Pete Wilson. Both were centrists; Feinstein was far to the right of Jerry, and her supporters were not the disenfranchised voters

Jerry had hoped to win back. He was blamed for not having done enough to help her campaign. He gained weight, from a lanky 165 pounds to a portly 215, and worried that he looked round, like his father. He had promised to serve four years and not use the party post as a springboard to run for office. "I said, 'Don't worry, I'll stick to the nuts and bolts,'" he recalled in January 1991, after less than two years. "I want to get off the nuts and bolts."

Two months later, he quit. He expressed disgust with the growing role of money in politics, a particularly acute problem in the vast state of California where campaigns depended on expensive television commercials. He said he would likely run for an open Senate seat the following year. After a few months of reflection, and the reality of a difficult primary against Congresswoman Barbara Boxer, he changed his mind.

In a ten-page letter, Jerry Brown announced to friends and supporters that he would run for president a third time. The campaign would be a quest to reclaim a corrupt political process. He would not accept donations of more than $100. He would raise money through a 1-800 telephone number. "Not for a moment do I believe that I am the only person—or even the best person—to undertake this effort," he wrote in the September 6, 1991, letter. "However by experience, conviction, and circumstance, I am in a position to help open the political door through which many others might walk." At a campaign kickoff with supporters the same evening in the Firehouse, his Pacific Heights home, underneath a banner with his toll-free number, Jerry compared his quest to Václav Havel's party in Czechoslovakia and Pat Brown's organization to restore faith in San Francisco government, the New Order of Cincinnatus. "In a similar vein, what we're awakening here is that spirit of citizenship, that spirit of democracy that's bursting out all over the world."

Jerry made his official announcement in Philadelphia in front of Independence Hall, handing out an eight-page speech with four footnotes. He ended with a reference to Thomas Paine's "American Crisis," the December 23, 1776, pamphlet that opened with the famous lines, "These are the times that try men's souls. The summer soldier and the sunshine patriot will, in this crisis, shrink from the service of their country; but he that stands by it now, deserves the love and thanks of man and woman." Pleading with his weary troops to stay through the bitter winter at Valley Forge, George Washington had used Paine's words to rally the men, and they stepped forward.

"At that moment, America was born," Jerry said. "These were the Winter Soldiers. And they are why we are here in Philadelphia today. Let each of us step forward and enlist as winter soldiers in the cause of America. Join with me. And then, first by the tens, then by the hundreds, then by the thousands and then by the hundreds of thousands, until by the millions, 'we the people' reclaim our democracy."

From the start, the campaign was not so much about winning as being in the game—and carving out a new way to play. Jerry liked to campaign, and he had little to lose. He talked about the "unholy alliance of private greed and corrupt politics" that blurred the lines between the parties and "the hostile takeover engineered by a confederacy of corruption, careerism and campaign consulting." His anger attracted followers disenchanted with the status quo, and it repelled the establishment. "I'm setting up this campaign in such a way that the emphasis is not on the candidate but on the candidacy, and not a campaign but a cause," he said. "I am trying to do my best to be a catalyst for people to sense that they can now make a difference."

Like a reformed alcoholic, he swore off the system he had used, worked, and built. He spoke of expiating his political sins and urged others to repent. He castigated his own flaws; who could more expertly condemn the corrupt system than he who had lived with it his entire life? Of course his judgment had been influenced. He was ashamed of the "wining and dining of corporate elites . . . what an absurdity to get money from tobacco companies and the savings and loan industry to fund get-out-the-vote drives among low-income citizens and other victims of corporate misconduct." He had raised $18 million for campaigns in the last twenty years, he told the Laborers' International Union convention at Bally's Resort in Las Vegas. "You have to beg for money from the very people who have got to be brought under control. I can tell you, when you're sitting around the table and you're having your third glass of wine out of your silver goblets and they serve you the sorbet, you're not going to talk about fighting for anti-strike-breaking legislation and you're not going to pound the table, because you're afraid the crystal will fall over."

At first, he was again dismissed as Governor Moonbeam, a California oddity, and scolded for playing the angry spoilsport. Then he raised millions of dollars. And drew overflow crowds. He opened each rally by asking for a show of hands of those who had never given $1,000 to a politician. He won the Colorado primary, and then Connecticut. "The people of Connecticut said, 'Get lost, we're taking back our country!'" he said the next day to a standing ovation at a union convention, where he touted the Agricultural Labor Relations Act as the sort of labor protection he would bring to the nation. Then he went to New York for a $20-a-person fundraiser at the Ritz Club where he was the opening act for the B-52s.

A new generation in the family took to the campaign trail. Jerry's oldest niece, Kathleen Kelly, traveled to various states as a surrogate speaker, often with her infant daughter. The campaign didn't feel hopeless. The crowds seemed buoyed by the message that individuals could make a difference. "What's dangerous about him to the establishment is he knows how to play the game and he's good at it. He is a master of the process he hates," said Tom Hayden, who was campaigning for a state Senate seat, having made the transition from outside agitator to elected official.

"Because Jerry is so irritating to many people, offensive to many in the press, there is a proclivity to say he's a jerk," observed the political

Campaigning in New Jersey in March 1992 with the New York skyline in the background. (Courtesy of Brown family)

consultant Richard Maullin, Jerry's friend who had worked on his campaigns since the earliest days. "But there is a segment of the electorate that is a natural constituency for him."

That constituency was passionate, if limited. He did well in Maine, Utah, and Washington, though he trailed front-runner Bill Clinton. Running on four or five hours of sleep a night instead of his usual seven, Jerry had lost the excess weight. He was energized. He talked about the dangers of global warming, the need to reduce dependence on fossil fuel, and the path to create millions of jobs by investing in high-speed trains and energy-efficient appliances and lights. He urged investment in new technologies and fuel-efficient cars that would facilitate a lifestyle more compatible with the environment. Mostly he talked about the corrosive influence of money in politics and its connection to the two-tiered society that Mario Cuomo had decried two presidential cycles earlier. "This is a very provocative contradiction that I'm pushing in people's face," Jerry said in an interview with *Rolling Stone*, which endorsed him. "And it's not pleasant. And I don't do it as well as I should. I'm sorry that I'm strident. I would like to be charming and elegant, but I will tell you that as a person enmeshed—in my genes I'm part of this political system—for me to cut out its cancer is almost to cut myself out. And I don't do it with the grace that I had hoped."

In April, a few days before the New York primary, Jerry spent an hour with the *New York Post* editorial board. He stayed beyond the point when aides nudged him to leave, insistent on making his case:

> I have always been for political reform, for protecting the underdog, for environmental protection, for innovation and creativity of all kinds. Am I a perfect person? No. I'm not a saint. I've been in politics twenty years. I grew up with a politician. At the dinner table every night. It was politics. It was labor leaders. It was Jewish leaders. It was black leaders. It was San Francisco Irish politics. That is my upbringing. But I also have a moral commitment to justice . . .
>
> When you see the exile of a whole generation of Americans, be they black, Latino, white, red, or Asian, it's not right. The coincidence of political corruption, mass cynicism at the process, failing competiveness, a loss of decent, high-paying jobs, is combining to unravel the fabric that everyone in this room takes for granted.

A few weeks later, in a tragic illustration of that unraveling, Los Angeles erupted. The most deadly riots in the country began on April 29, 1992, hours after a jury acquitted four police officers in the beating of black motorist Rodney King, a brutal attack that had been videotaped by a nearby resident and broadcast over and over to the world. A shaken Mayor Tom Bradley said the acquittal was hard to reconcile with the beating so many people had seen with their own eyes. He declared a state of emergency. Governor Pete Wilson activated the National Guard. For five days, the violence unfolded on live television. More than sixty people were killed, ten shot by law enforcement officials. More than twenty-three hundred were injured. Looting and arson devastated sections of the city, damage of close to $1 billion. Unlike Watts in 1965, the riots were not contained to one area, nor was the racial tension solely between blacks and whites. Reflecting Los Angeles's evolution into a complex multiethnic mix, Latinos were victims and perpetrators, and much of the violence was between blacks and Koreans. Tensions had been high for months after a Korean merchant shot a fifteen-year-old black girl she suspected of stealing a bottle of orange juice; the girl died clutching the bills to pay for the drink. The merchant was sentenced to a fine and probation.

Jerry cut short campaigning to return home. "There is a systematic, institutionalized injustice across the country," he said, blaming both parties for having failed to respond to unrest in Watts and other cities with investments and jobs. He visited the areas hardest hit and slept on a sofa bed at the home of a black campaign volunteer whose father was a carpet installer; the street was still smoky from fires that burned down nearby stores. At a community meeting, he jabbed his hands in the air in frustration. The violence and despair stemmed, he said, from a political system that deliberately excluded and abandoned groups of people. "The global economy has enshrined the principle of so-called efficiency which requires Americans to be deprived of their high-paying jobs so that people in the third world can be exploited with low-paying jobs to satisfy the needs of those who manage our global corporations . . . The rich are getting richer, the middle class is disappearing, the poor are ground under, and the resulting violence requires more and more of a military response, with a more authoritarian government."

That he had in some ways contributed to this growing gap was just one of the contradictions of Jerry's zigzag political trajectory. As governor, his administration had frozen cost-of-living increases for welfare recipients, cut programs for the mentally ill, and set the state on a path that invested more heavily in prisons than in higher education. In his wilderness years, he lived in part off financial practices he now denounced—as a rainmaker, a board member of a biomedical company run by a longtime campaign supporter, and investor in a tax shelter. Questioned by a *Washington Post* reporter about the dissonance between his personal finances and his campaign rhetoric, Jerry said, "I think you've got a good point."

He did not shy away from the contradictions. Opponents denounced him as hypocritical; supporters saw his unscripted honesty as an asset that allowed him to maintain credibility even as he moved from major fundraiser to critic. He seemed more reconciled with his own past. "What I've learned is that the absolute, the moral principles on which I grew up with, are the anchor," he said. "The anchors that I had growing up are what I believe are the only rudder and the only compass that both keep me going and can keep politics moving in a direction it has to go."

One of those anchors, Bernice Brown, went out on the campaign trail as a surrogate for her son. She had become an accomplished speaker, mixing wit and substance with stories from his youth. One of her favorites was about an irate neighbor who found handprints in the fresh cement of his driveway. The culprit was not hard to find: Jerry had added his initials. He was for full disclosure at an early age, Bernice said. "I've always said Jerry's just ahead of his time," she said. "I don't know if everybody else will ever catch up."

Pat Brown was not strong enough to campaign. On the day before the first major round of primaries in March, Pat made one of his last public appearances. He was honored by a rare joint session of the legislature on what Governor Wilson declared Pat Brown Day. Escorted into the Assembly chamber by the seven legislators still in office who had served while he was governor, Pat was greeted with thunderous applause, hailed as a "California pathfinder," an almost mythic leader from a happier time. Speakers noted his ability to forge bipartisan coalitions, now sorely lacking. In the midst of a crippling recession and multi-billion-dollar budget gaps, they paid homage to achievements that loomed even larger in the rearview mirror. "Pat Brown offers us the spirit with which he governed the state, an unflinching faith in the future of California," Wilson said.

Shortly after he had become a private citizen, Pat had written Ronald Reagan in dismay over his decision to jettison the *Grizzly*, the propeller plane on which Pat had flown around the state, often peering out the window. "A chartered jet flies too high and too fast for you to get a good look at this great, golden state as you fly over," Pat wrote to Reagan. "And that is one of the genuine satisfactions of being governor of this State— soaring over the cities and towns; the farms, the dams and canals; the colleges; the National Guard firefighters on five-minute alert; the highways; all the things that make California the leader among equals in this nation." At the celebratory luncheon on Pat Brown Day, historian Kevin Starr said he pictured Pat someday "soaring over this state . . . a sort of benevolent seraph."

Jerry missed Pat Brown Day. He was immersed in the campaign, committed to the effort to fashion out of politics the sort of movement he had long admired. In many ways, the day-to-day campaign resembled nothing so much as the old days of the UFW boycott. Volunteers, mainly young, traveled on the cheap, slept on couches, and operated on a shoe-string. Creativity was at a premium; people who could make things happen gained power. Volunteers cut stencils and spray-painted their own signs. State coordinators and local hosts were recruited through calls to the toll-free number. "Politics finally has made sense to him, based on his Jesuit upbringing. He can, in essence, be a missionary," said political consultant Patrick Caddell, an adviser to the campaign.

"I think he feels that his goal is to play out a destiny to help set things right," Tom Hayden said about what drove his friend. "He has a very strong sense of the world's being out of whack. And all he knows to try to right it is a combination of spirituality and politics."

For twenty years he had wanted to be president, Jerry told *New York Times* reporter Maureen Dowd. He quoted Sister Alice Joseph about the virtue of perseverance. "Obviously I'm attracted to this or I wouldn't be going through it," he said. "But I've also studied in schools of humility where they put you in your place, whether in the Jesuit order, whether being ridiculed by the press for years, or whether it's working with the dying in Calcutta . . . I have a lot of ambition and a lot of ego. But I think this experience serves me well in a process that is so disorienting as the one we have."

As Bill Clinton became the front-runner, Jerry was the only other Democrat who could afford to stay in the race. He had seven paid staff members, no paid consultants or speechwriters, and little advertising. The campaign was memorable for the sharp, personal clashes with Clinton, many involving the ethics of the Arkansas governor and his wife. The more lasting political relevance was the Brown campaign's innovative use of the toll-free phone, early-generation computers, and the rapidly expanding world of cable television. With lots of time to fill, cable channels offered an effective way to bypass the traditional media and avoid the cost of network television commercials. Cable was the state-of-the-art technology to deliver an unfiltered message, tailored to a niche audience. C-SPAN covered many of Jerry's speeches in their entirety, and he gave the network access to private fundraisers and editorial board meetings.

By the time of the California primary in early June, some ninety thousand people had donated more than $5 million in small amounts, mainly through the toll-free number. But Clinton had almost clinched the nomination. In New York, where Jerry had needed to do well to stay competitive, his announcement that he would choose Jesse Jackson as his running mate torpedoed his chances; Jackson was still controversial for anti-Semitic comments he had made in 1984 about New Yorkers. "We influence, we shape, and we're going to affect the destiny of politics in this country for a long time to come," Jerry told supporters as they awaited results of the California primary. "This is a long-term, day-by-day, slogging through the mud, moving up and taking the mountain. But we'll get there." Clinton beat Jerry by more than seven points in his home state, where they knew him best.

Jerry did win over one voter who would ultimately prove more important than all the rest. In 1990, when he was Democratic Party chair, Jerry had been invited to dinner by Anne Gust, a corporate lawyer who lived a block away from him in Pacific Heights. She wanted to set him up with her roommate. During the evening, Jerry recounted an ongoing legal battle with a disgruntled candidate who had sued because he was denied the right to speak at a Democratic Party forum. Gust said the case sounded ridiculous; he should just move for dismissal. Good idea, he said; why don't you handle it? She did. For free. Instead of dating her roommate, Jerry began to see Gust.

Anne Baldwin Gust had grown up in a political family, too—Michigan Republicans. Her father ran unsuccessfully for Congress and lieutenant governor, on a ticket with George Romney. Anne graduated first in her high school class in Bloomfield Hills and headed west, won over by the beauty and intellectual rigor of Stanford. She majored in political science, which offered flexibility for a prelaw student and enabled her to take art classes and study in Italy. She interrupted her California sojourn to attend law school at the University of Michigan, alma mater of her father, grandfather, and great-grandfather, then moved back to the Bay Area to work as a litigator and then a corporate lawyer. She was on a fast track at Brobeck, Phleger & Harrison; the San Francisco firm wanted to make her the first female partner in Silicon Valley. The prestige and title didn't mean much to her. She walked away just short of becoming partner, weary of the grind, the focus on billable hours, and a culture that viewed sensible decisions—wearing pants, commuting in late morning to miss rush hour—as acts of defiance. By the time Jerry ran for president, she had quit (against his advice) to become a counsel at the Gap, where she found a mentor in the man who had recruited her, Gap founder Donald Fisher. In 1992, Gust registered as a Democrat for the first time so that she could vote for Jerry in the California primary.

California was the last contest. In July, Jerry Brown arrived in New York for the Democratic National Convention with a detailed, thirty-four-page "We the People" platform and 614 delegates, representing some four million votes. They shunned cocktail parties and receptions at which they would not have been welcome and held a picnic in Central Park, in the rain. The Hotel McAlpin, where the buoyant Brownies had stayed in 1976, was long gone. Jerry worked out of the office of *Rolling Stone*, spent a night helping at a homeless transition shelter, and stayed the rest of the time with his friends the writers Joan Didion and John Gregory Dunne. He was no longer the thirty-eighty-year-old wunderkind in demand by every network anchor, but a fifty-four-year-old ex-governor very much at odds with those who controlled his party. Minicams from around the world buzzed around the dissident when he appeared in public, at odds with what was, for his friends, an elegiac occasion. It was all over.

In the Madison Square Garden Convention Center, where Cesar Chavez had nominated him sixteen years earlier, Jerry was persona non grata. His platform, which opposed NAFTA and endorsed single payer healthcare and campaign finance reform, was rejected sight unseen. He would not be allowed to speak unless he agreed to endorse Clinton, a deal Jerry rejected. "In a democracy, debate, vigorous, robust difference, is healthy," he told his California delegates at breakfast as the convention opened. "And what we want is not conformity, not uniformity, but unity, based on the spirit of this party. Stand up. Act up. Take back America!" Jerry decided to address the convention during the twenty minutes allotted to place his name in nomination, a move the party leaders could not contest.

"Whatever the odds, whoever the adversaries, however long it takes, we will create the power for the powerless, for there is no other reason for a Democratic Party to exist," he said in his address. "For many, many years I believed we that could change politics through a series of changes. Some small, some large. But all incremental, within the framework of politics as we know it. Progressive appointments. More money for college scholarships. Good environmental laws. Urban assistance programs. Yet when I was governor, I'm sorry to acknowledge, wages toward the end started to fall. Factory jobs started moving abroad. And the numbers of the poor began to grow. Ten years later, South Central Los Angeles exploded. How I tried to make that system work as governor of California!"

He had embarked on the campaign for president, he said, "to give people, especially those who stopped believing, a real choice, and an equal opportunity to participate. That's why we limited donations to a hundred dollars. We wanted people who had no access. They didn't know any particular person with power. We wanted them to take ownership of this cause."

Bernice and Kathleen Brown were there to cheer Jerry on. "My God, he went the distance!" said Kathleen. "I admire his guts and I admire his staying power. This was about ideas, about his passion to reform the political process and the Democratic Party. And, from his perspective, he had to go to the end."

When Jerry took the podium in Madison Square Garden to deliver his defiant address to the national convention, he waited till the chants of "Jer-*ry*, Jer-*ry*, Jer-*ry*" died down and then thanked all his supporters. "I want to thank," he began, and then choked up, "one other person, who's not here tonight"—he blinked and swallowed hard, struggling through the sentence—"and is missing his first—convention—since the Depression." Then his voice regained its strength, as the audience cheered. "A man who beat President Nixon in 1962 and almost stopped Ronald Reagan in 1966, and in my view is the greatest Democrat in this country! My father, Pat Brown! Dad," he said, looking into the camera and raising his arm in salute, "thanks a lot for all you've done."

After the speech, Jerry called home to see what his father thought of the address. Pat had been having fewer and fewer good days. He had fallen asleep and missed the speech.

18

A Different Shade of Brown

The guest speaker looked poised, sipping coffee in salmon blazer and black skirt, as Pamela Harriman delivered her introduction at the Woman's National Democratic Club luncheon in April 1992. Harriman, whose Georgetown home had become a social mecca and fundraising machine for Democrats-in-exile during the 1980s, opened with an anecdote. "I happened to be seated at dinner next to one of our nation's most influential political writers the other night. And of course the conversation turned to national politics. Out of the blue, he said, 'I've met the woman most likely to be president in my lifetime.'" Harriman paused, grinned as applause and a few whoops rippled through the room in anticipation, then slowly delivered her punch line to accentuate each syllable: "Her name—you guessed it—was Kath—leen—Brown."

Kathleen wrinkled up her face, a combination laugh and wince that conveyed modesty, excitement, embarrassment, and ambition all at once. The guests had been invited to lunch with the California state treasurer. The subtext was a chance for Washington power brokers to meet the youngest and most promising Brown, with her father's charm, her mother's style, and her brother's political instincts. She had not quite realized what she was walking into. She might have dressed differently, or written a different speech.

"I am a proud Californian, fourth generation, so I kind of take in stride a lot of this East Coast bad-mouthing of California," she began, with gentle jabs at journalists who delighted in endless stories about California's imminent demise and New Yorkers who viewed the state as little more than an exporter of fruits, nuts, and oddball trends. "I don't even mind it when they say, 'Oh, that California, they just brought America hula hoops, channelers, Ronald Reagan, and . . . Jerry Brown. It's okay. It speaks to our diversity. It speaks to our ability to generate and manage new ideas and new trends."

In a talk imbued with her father's spirit, she focused on California's exceptionalism, its resilience, and its role in defining America's future. The recent recession had caused multi-billion-dollar budget deficits and staggering jobs losses, particularly severe because of retrenchment in the defense spending that underlay so much of the state's economy. But the downturn forced a diversification that repositioned California well. Defense spending was now less than 10 percent of the overall state economy. California had added six million people in the past decade, many of them young. "It means that our state constantly changes, constantly evolves, and we reinvent our self almost in whole each decade, because twenty percent of our population is new," Kathleen said. "It means we can't be stuck in our old ways; it means we have got to be future-looking."

She pointed to the cutting-edge environmental standards for cars and appliances that California had enacted years ago—initially denounced by corporate America as implausible, eventually emulated worldwide. California led the country in its diversity, an advantage in the emerging global economy. The state was home to more Filipinos, Koreans, Vietnamese, Mexicans, and Russians than anyplace outside their home countries. Demographers predicted the state would be "majority minority" in less than a decade. "I suspect that if we were to seek clues as to what our nation's future is going to be all about," Kathleen said, "we would do well to look at California."

East Coast journalists' schadenfreude notwithstanding, California had rebounded after each boom-and-bust cycle since the Gold Rush. To make the point more personal, Kathleen finished with a story about her son, whom she had dragged cross-country from Los Angeles to New York and then back. After his first day at yet another new school, she asked the fifteen-year-old how he was doing. "Mom," he said, "what fails to destroy me will only make me stronger." Where, she asked in surprise, had he learned that? "Uncle Jerry." The audience laughed.

Though the teenager got the Nietzsche quote from his uncle, the sentiment was pure Kathleen. She described herself as a relentless optimist, a risk taker who believed that the worst misfortunes were great opportunities in disguise. Her path to the Washington podium was as nonlinear as her brother's political career, and the influence of family loomed even larger. She had the benefit and the burden of not only her father's history, but her brother's.

Like Jerry, Kathy had grown up in politics, with more exposure and less ambivalence. Ever since Election Day 1958, when cameras flashed and the thirteen-year-old daughter of the governor-elect found herself looking "extremely goofy" in the paper the next day, she realized she lived in a fishbowl. Her father's unhappiness at the lack of history requirements in her junior high school became front page news about curriculum reform. She made the state police drop her off blocks from school to minimize embarrassment. She traveled the world, a teenager dining with heads of state. She enjoyed VIP seats at Olympic events. Always competitive (her earliest campaign slogan was "Give the Crown to Kathy Brown"), she won election as class vice president her first year in Sacramento junior high and lost a race for secretary the next, to her father's chagrin. "I suppose I am prejudiced but I think she is a wonderful girl," he wrote in his diary.

Pat doted on Kathy, and she returned the affection. If he told everyone they should run for public office, he told his youngest daughter twice as often. "Everyone thinks that Kathy is Pat's favorite," Bernice said. "But that's only because he always liked the baby and she was the last so she'll always be the baby."

Born a few months too early to officially count as a baby boomer, Kathy grew up in an era just beginning to accept that women could have careers. A mother at twenty, she had left Stanford and put a professional life on hold while her husband attended law school. She juggled childcare with finishing her degree long distance. Back in Los Angeles, her plan to become a social worker was derailed when the graduate school at UCLA refused to place a pregnant woman in a work assignment.

Like her father, she connected with people on a personal, human level. She remembered names and faces and facts. At a phone bank fundraiser for Stanford, if a hundred alumni were making calls, the prize for the one who raised the most money would go to Kathy. When she campaigned for her brother, she focused on issues that interested her, education and women's rights. She talked about the need to revamp textbooks that showed women only as nurses, never doctors. Her speaker biography listed her hobbies as photography, tennis, skiing, tap dancing, macramé, and reading historical novels.

Within weeks of Jerry's victory in November 1974, Kathy Brown Rice announced she would challenge J. C. Chambers, a sixteen-year incumbent and archconservative on the Los Angeles school board. She planned a $50,000 radio and mail campaign and was endorsed by both California senators, five congressmen, and dozens of state legislators. Governor Pat sent out a fundraising letter and Governor Jerry took time after a Regents meeting to campaign with his sister at the Farmers Market, a Los Angeles landmark. Kathleen dealt with the family issue with the forthrightness common to all the Browns: "I was raised in a family where public office is one of the highest callings we can aspire to," Kathleen said. "I would not expect anyone to vote for me because my name is Brown, but I would not expect them to hold it against me."

The siblings' styles drew inevitable comparisons, usually in Kathleen's favor. At twenty-nine, she had been hosting dinner parties for years, and the Rice house in the upscale neighborhood of Hancock Park was a social hub. Jerry felt comfortable bringing dates there, out of the public glare. And he preached limits to his sister even as he enjoyed her hospitality.

Kathleen Brown easily defeated an incumbent in her first campaign in 1975, becoming the youngest person ever elected to the Los Angeles school board. (Courtesy of George A. Rice)

"He always comes here and says I should lower my standard of living," Kathleen told an interviewer.

Her 1975 campaign coincided with a concerted effort to groom more women candidates in California, where they were all but absent from elected office. One woman sat on the Los Angeles City Council, one each on the school board and community college board, one in the forty-three-member congressional delegation, and two in the state Assembly. No woman had ever been elected to the state Senate.

Kathleen won the school board race in a landslide. No one kept records, but she was believed to be the youngest member ever on a board viewed as a stepping-stone to higher office. "I'm twenty-nine and a half, and I don't intend to stay on the board of education until I'm eighty," she said when asked about her aspirations. She was sworn in on July 1, 1975, along with Diane Watson, who would become the first black woman (and second woman) elected to the state Senate, and Julian Nava, who would become the first Mexican American to serve as U.S. ambassador to Mexico.

Kathleen sat on the board during a period of wrenching change in the nation's second-largest school district, reflecting demographic and political trends that reshaped not only the Los Angeles schools, but all of Southern California.

The dominant issue facing the board in the mid-1970s was whether and how to comply with a court order to desegregate schools that were starkly divided by race. The case dated from 1961, when Mary Ellen Crawford, a black teenager, was denied admission to South Gate High School, near her home and 98 percent white. She was sent to the more distant, all-black Jordan High. Two years later, the ACLU filed a class action suit on her behalf, citing a precedent-setting case out of Pasadena in which the California Supreme Court had ruled that segregation violated the state constitution, regardless of whether or why racial separation occurred. In federal court, plaintiffs had to prove that a school board officially sanctioned segregation. The lower threshold in California courts meant an area like Los Angeles could not use its long history of exclusionary zoning and racist covenants as an excuse to maintain segregated schools.

"For more than a decade this court has adhered to the position that school boards in this state bear a constitutional obligation to attempt to alleviate school segregation, regardless of its cause," Supreme Court Justice Mathew Tobriner wrote in a June 28, 1976 decision that affirmed the order to desegregate Los Angeles schools. In the thirteen years since the Crawford case had been filed, Tobriner wrote, the school board had stonewalled and made no effort to improve the second-rate conditions, faculty, and curriculum in the ninety-two schools that were more than 90 percent black.

Like many things in Los Angeles, the sheer size of the district complicated an emotional, highly charged political process. The Los Angeles Unified School District had six hundred thousand students in six hundred schools, spread out over 714 square miles. The far-flung geography compounded the isolation of the different communities and the logistic difficulty of integration. The predominantly white schools amid the postwar tract homes of the San Fernando Valley were separated from the heavily black areas to the south by the Santa Monica Mountains.

The election of Kathleen and Diane Watson restored a liberal majority on the board, sympathetic to the goal of integration and willing to comply with the court order. Kathleen's position fluctuated, as did the board's, veering from voluntary to mandatory busing plans and back. She respected the right of black children to quality education, and the anger of white parents who felt their children were being punished for societal injustice. "So here I sit as a board member, trying to balance these rights, these interests, and these very, very legitimate concerns," she said at a board meeting in 1977. "I don't think that integrated education ought to be a punishment. I have said I don't think it should be a penance. I think that it should be the best quality education that this district and public education can provide."

In September 1978, a thousand buses carried more than forty thousand students to new schools. Within six months, about thirty thousand students, 15 percent of the district's white enrollment, had withdrawn from the public schools. White students, a majority in the district just a few years earlier, now made up just 20 percent of the lower grades. Despite the court order, Kathleen voted with the majority to end the integration trial in hopes of stemming further white flight. She defended the switch as a bow to reality. "I think reasonable people can have honest differences about what in the end will achieve the goal of an integrated society," she said. "I have lost, in some ways, my tolerance for those who shouted at us at the hearings, for those who said, 'Hell no, we won't go.' I don't buy that. But I also have strong feelings about those who, in the name of righteousness, have shown a certain arrogance to basic human and paternal feelings, whether they are brown, black, or white."

The political ramifications long outlived the busing fight. Los Angeles's traditionally liberal Jewish community splintered, leaving a conservative faction in the San Fernando Valley. Bobbi Fiedler, one of the leaders of the opposition to busing, was elected to the school board, went on to unseat a Democratic congressman in 1980, and then led efforts to turn the San Fernando Valley into what would have been the nation's sixth-largest city. State legislation temporarily derailed the secession campaign but did little to dampen the underlying sense of a separate identity in the suburban communities north of Mulholland Drive.

The second demographic trend with far-reaching consequences during Kathleen's tenure on the board was the burgeoning number of non-English speakers, mostly Mexicans, who would soon become the largest ethnic group in Los Angeles. Although essentially left out of the Crawford case, Mexicans were the fastest-growing ethnic group in the city and the schools. Latino students outnumbered whites for the first time in 1977 and two years later made up almost 40 percent of the district's enrollment. While classrooms in the San Fernando Valley had more and more empty desks, Union Avenue Elementary School near downtown struggled on double sessions to educate more than two thousand kids in a school built for half as many. The majority were recent immigrants from Mexico who spoke little or no English. Asians were a relatively small but growing percentage of students in the district, as Southern California became the prime destination for immigrants from Southeast Asia. Because mass immigration was often triggered by crises abroad, the sudden, unpredictable waves of non-English-speaking refugees overwhelmed the schools. When thousands of Vietnamese refugees moved into a Los Angeles neighborhood in 1979, the local schools faced severe overcrowding.

As the Los Angeles school district grappled with the difficulty of educating an influx of English learners from an increasing number of countries, the state assumed control of public education financing in the wake of Prop 13. The combined fiscal and educational challenges crippled the district, leading even more middle-class parents to opt for private schools. By 1979, the Los Angeles district had so few white students that integration became largely moot. The same year, voters approved a constitutional amendment that relieved districts of the responsibility to desegregate through mandatory busing, abolishing the stricter threshold that had been imposed by the California Supreme Court.

Kathleen was easily reelected in March 1979, amid speculation she would soon run for higher office. Interviewers began to ask whether she planned to become the first woman elected governor in California. Then on Memorial Day 1979, her husband told her he was leaving her. She stayed in the house for days, then fled to her childhood home on Magellan Avenue in San Francisco, where her sister lived. But just as she would later describe the resilience of California, Kathleen bounced back. In July, she went on a blind date with Van Gordon Sauter, the manager of television station KNXT and a frequent conservative commentator on the local CBS affiliate. Sauter had seen Kathleen on television and wondered how anyone so attractive could have such bad politics. Incensed over a recent decision to ban candy bars from school vending machines, he called school board members "chronic bedwetters and mystical social engineers." Kathleen agreed to the date as an opportunity to argue with the man who regularly lambasted her positions in editorial commentaries. Sauter, dressed in his customary bow tie, blue blazer, khaki pants, and shoes without socks, told her over dessert at Le St. Germain on Melrose that they would marry. A year later, they did.

Two weeks before the wedding, Sauter was named president of the CBS Sports Division in New York. After considering options that included commuting on weekends, Kathleen decided to resign from the school board and join him in New York. "It was a matter of love," she said after moving into a Park Avenue co-op. "It was also a matter of priorities, and a belief that I'm only putting my career on hold." Her oldest daughter stayed with her father, while the two younger children moved to New York. "If someone had told me two years ago today that I would be remarried, living twelve stories in the sky in this town, had quit my job on the board of education and abandoned my political career in California, I would have asked them what they were smoking," Kathleen said. "But my life changed."

She settled into the role of corporate executive's spouse, with a weekend home in Connecticut. Tom and Meredith Brokaw lived downstairs and became close friends. Kathleen organized neighbors to fight a proposed high-rise around the corner. She described herself as "the house radical . . . bringing my California environmental understanding to New York." She thought about opening a Tex-Mex restaurant to have a place to drink margaritas. Instead, she enrolled at Fordham Law School. Riding the subway downtown to the Manhattan district attorney's office for a summer internship, in the popular New York uniform of Walkman and running shoes, she had a sense of wonder. "I looked uptown at that skyline and said, 'I cannot believe this, a Magellan Avenue kid . . . I work in New York City and I'm going to be a lawyer.' It was pretty special."

In New York, Kathleen gained new appreciation for the expansiveness of California, in space and people. She could drive through several states in the Northeast in less time than it would take to drive the length of Los Angeles County, without traffic. She found New Yorkers quick to make judgments about outsiders. "People here don't have time for newcomers, so they make fast connections based on who you are, whom you're married to, whom you know," Kathleen wrote after five years in the city. Her life didn't fit into the neat boxes. "In California, there's more openness to new people and new ideas."

In early 1987, she returned home. Sauter, who had risen to head of CBS News, was ousted during a management shuffle. After six years away from California, Kathleen was eager to revive her political career, and the family moved back to Los Angeles. Kathleen had started work as a bond lawyer in the New York office of O'Melveny & Myers and she transferred to the firm's home office in Los Angeles. The junior attorney's small cubicle was strategically located next to the office of senior partner Warren Christopher, once an adviser to her father, now an influential city leader.

By fall, Kathleen had made her first move. She was named by Mayor Bradley to a seat on the Board of Public Works, a plum appointment that involved overseeing trash, sewers, lights, and contracts for major construction projects. By early 1988, she had all but declared as a candidate for state treasurer, a post that fitted her interests and expertise in municipal finance and looked like a winnable race after the death of longtime incumbent Jesse Unruh.

Big Daddy Unruh, the shrewd, flamboyant Democrat who had run the Assembly and feuded with Pat Brown, had never ascended to the governor's office he coveted, denied the chance when Pat ran for a third term and then defeated in 1970 by Ronald Reagan. Instead, in 1974, Unruh was elected state treasurer, and over the next thirteen years he transformed the post into a powerful political and financial platform. As treasurer, he found no shortage of opportunities to act on the adage he popularized: "Money is the mother's milk of politics." He oversaw investment strategies for the

$17-billion-a-year state portfolio and sat on boards that invested another $50 billion in state pension funds. Wall Street firms competed for the business, and Unruh was quick to leverage campaign contributions for Democrats. He became what the *Wall Street Journal* called the most powerful public finance official outside the federal treasury. When Unruh died in office in August 1987, Deukmejian appointed as his successor Thomas Hayes, a little-known Republican who had been auditor general. His first campaign would be the race for a full term in 1990.

At the national Democratic convention in the summer of 1988, Pat Brown hosted a poolside brunch at the Atlanta Hilton for the California delegation. At eighty-three the oldest member of the delegation, Pat introduced his daughter as "the most astute politician in the family." Back home a week later, Pat sent Kathleen a story about the event. "I intend to send you all my clippings—you can save them, treasure them or throw them out," he wrote his daughter. "In every speech I make, I tell them that you will be Governor one day. Sometimes I even mention that you are also running for State Treasurer (!)"

Pat was at his daughter's side when she made her formal announcement on March 5, 1988. "It seems everywhere I go there are people there to tell me they were touched by some positive activity of my father's or my brother's administration," she said.

Her campaign coincided with Jerry's term as chair of the state Democratic Party. He joined his parents in cosponsoring Kathleen's first fundraiser, a $1,000-a-person dinner at Chasen's, a Hollywood favorite of the older entertainment crowd, with booths named after regulars like Frank Sinatra, James Stewart, and Groucho Marx. A few weeks later, Kathleen held a $500-a-person fundraiser at the old Governor's Mansion where she had grown up, long uninhabited and now a state historic site. She used a line that she would proffer dozens of times in the coming months: "I'm a different shade of Brown."

Kathleen was comfortable with the political nuts and bolts her brother eschewed: raising money, mingling with crowds, talking one on one, closing deals. "Kathleen is more natural, I think," Pat said. "She says things that she believes and she says them well. Jerry is more serious. He's more intense in his political views." Asked about a report that at Jerry's fiftieth birthday party, Pat called Kathleen the "real politician in the family," Jerry responded, "Well, she is. Anyway, what makes you think I want to be known as a politician?"

"She finds the time to do nice little things, thank people, and people complained that Jerry didn't do that," Bernice said. "Jerry creates very strong feelings, one way or the other. People are either devoted to him or they don't like him at all. Everybody likes Kathy, Democrats and Republicans."

Family and friends from earlier years still called her Kathy; those who knew her professionally called her Kathleen. She cited as role models the wives of two television anchors, Meredith Brokaw and Jean Rather, and Texas governor Ann Richards, who had jumped to the top office after serving as state treasurer. Being a Brown, Kathleen said, was a two-edged sword. "The first test in politics is to get your name known, to rise above the noise level of the crowd . . . I have an advantage there. Once people identify and become familiar with me as a Brown, my task is to color Kathleen Brown in. I am not my father. I am not my brother. I hope I am the best of both of them. And why not?"

Roger Ailes, who ran her opponent's campaign, derided Kathleen as "Sister Moonbeam," interested in the treasurer's job only as a stepping-stone to the governorship. Kathleen called Ailes "the mudslinging media guru who made Willie Horton a household name," referring to the infamous ad against Democratic presidential candidate Michael Dukakis. She ran a $1.5 million blitz of television commercials in the final two weeks. Hayes ran a last-minute ad that asked "Remember Jerry Brown?" Kathleen eked out a narrow victory, carrying the Bay Area, Los Angeles, and coastal counties to win by fewer than 232,000 votes out of more than seven million.

Despite her slim margin and bare-bones political portfolio, she became a national name overnight on the strength of her personal charm and political pedigree. *Washington Post* columnist David Broder noted that California Republicans had appeared on seven of the last ten national tickets, while no Democrat from the most populous state ever ran as the party's presidential or vice presidential candidate. With Kathleen as state treasurer, Broder wrote, "California will finally have a statewide Democratic official with the potential to be on the national ticket."

California law required that state officials be sworn in by a judge or prosecutor. The Los Angeles district attorney deputized Pat Brown for a day so that he could do the honor. A welcome rain broke weeks of drought and a crowd of a couple hundred stood under umbrellas outside what would be Kathleen's new office. Dozens of relatives came, and some of

Pat's old staff members. After Pat administered the oath of office, someone asked why he had never sworn in his son. Pat laughed. "He never asked me. He didn't need me. You know Jerry."

Timing was everything, Pat Brown often said. Kathleen might have been anointed as the next gubernatorial candidate regardless, but timing turned the process into a virtual coronation. She took office the same year Republican Pete Wilson became governor, as California struggled through a deep recession at the end of a decade that had not been kind to the Golden State. The number of Californians who rated their state as "one of the best places to live" dropped from an average of 75 percent in earlier years to 60 percent in 1989. Even a 1989 hometown World Series, pitting the Oakland Athletics against the San Francisco Giants, turned from celebration into tragedy. Millions watched on national television as the 6.9 Loma Prieta earthquake disrupted game 3 with an interminable fifteen seconds of shaking that left sixty-seven people dead, caused $7 billion in damage, and flattened parts of two major freeways.

By 1990, a decade of living under Prop 13 had left overcrowded schools, broken-down parks, and crumbling roads. Many supporters of the tax cut initiative had not favored reduced services—they just wanted property tax relief and believed government could find other ways to pay for programs. The state surplus that cushioned the first few years evaporated. The loss of billions of dollars in property tax revenue, compounded by dramatic drops in income and sales taxes during the recession, led to deficits and budget cuts.

Education suffered most severely. In 1990, California spent $4,000 per pupil, about half of what New York State spent on its students. Schools and public colleges that had once drawn so many to the state now posted test scores among the lowest in the country. Los Angeles schools struggled to educate students who spoke a hundred different languages, and the trends with which Kathleen had grappled a decade earlier had spread across the state. Voters approved another milestone (or millstone, some would contend), Proposition 98, designed to guarantee a minimum level of spending on kindergarten through community college students. The formulae that stemmed from that 1988 initiative were so complex that only a handful of people even understood them. The increased reliance on "ballot box budgeting" left state officials even less flexibility.

The first budget Governor Wilson signed in July 1991 included $7 billion in tax increases and $7 billion in spending cuts. Over the next year, the state lost tens of thousands more jobs. In 1992, a sixty-four-day budget deadlock forced the state to issue IOUs in lieu of tax refunds for the first time since the Depression. The state's credit rating plummeted, which increased the cost of borrowing. As manager of the state's $24 billion investment portfolio, Treasurer Brown had a pulpit from which to criticize the state's precarious fiscal condition, and its Republican governor.

Californians had approved term limits; if Kathleen ran for reelection and served a second term as treasurer, the governor's race would be wide open in 1998. But the pressure for her to challenge the incumbent grew. The Draft Brown movement gained momentum in June 1992, when Californians made history by electing women in Democratic primaries for both of the state's Senate seats. "It's a great day to be a girl!" Kathleen proclaimed at a luncheon fundraiser she hosted for Dianne Feinstein and Barbara Boxer, who would go on to represent California in Washington for many years. Kathleen traveled the state helping women candidates for local offices. Magazines wrote about her with headlines like BORN TO RUN. Her friends were quoted saying it was destiny. Kathleen appeared to be less convinced. "It's kind of scary—people talking about me running for governor, putting their cards in my pocket," she told Gail Sheehy in the fall of 1992 when the writer visited the treasurer's office.

Crime rates, unemployment, and tuition fees at the university all went up. Wilson's ratings sank to an all-time low. Three quarters of the people polled by the *Los Angeles Times* in March 1993 believed the state was on the wrong track. In a hypothetical matchup, Kathleen led Wilson by 22 points. The *Economist* portrayed the governor as a brooding king in his castle. "Outside the walls the kingdom, after many years of plenty, has fallen on unhappy times. Natural disasters—drought, flood and fire—roll across the land. The people feel accursed. Support is ebbing away to a fair princess, whose brother and father both ruled the land before her."

In the months that followed, in the candidacy that became an inevitability, Kathleen Brown struggled to find her voice, to define a rationale under the constant glare of electoral combat. She changed campaign managers midstream and seemed to doubt her own political instincts. But she did not waver in her core values, among them, family. "I am incredibly proud of my brother's and my father's legacy in this state," she said. "They touched something, each in their own distinctive way, very powerful, that is part of what I think the California dream is about, the California psyche is about, and to be part of that legacy is pretty daunting."

She forfeited a prime-time speaking slot at the 1992 convention because she supported her brother and refused to endorse Bill Clinton. "I'm not into repudiating family," she said. "I'm a Brown and I'm proud of it and I'm not going to do anything that would not make me feel good to be a Brown at the end of the day. Family transcends politics."

She grimaced good-naturedly about her mother's response when asked on national television which of her offspring was smarter. "I think Jer—well, I—Kathy is smart. Don't misunderstand. But Jerry's brilliant," Bernice said on *60 Minutes*.

Kathleen disregarded advisers who saw Jerry as a liability and prevailed upon her reluctant brother to join family members on February 8, 1994, when she announced her candidacy on the steps of the San Francisco police station where their Grandfather Layne once worked. "I wanted him there and it was important to me. He's my brother," Kathleen said. "I said, 'Hey, this is family.'" In the end, he unexpectedly bounded on the dais and kissed his sister. The public confusion mirrored the more worrisome confusion behind the scenes—a candidate buffeted by conflicting advice and unsure whom to trust. At the end of every day, Kathleen gave her cell phone to her press secretary, Michael Reese. Jerry had a habit of calling in the early morning hours. Kathleen didn't want to be awakened, but she wanted to hear his thoughts. So Reese took the calls.

Pete Wilson was a seasoned politician, a veteran of multiple statewide campaigns with a strong, experienced team. By the time the campaign got under way, the unpopular tax increases had improved the state's financial stability. Kathleen might still have won an election that was a referendum on the Wilson record. Instead, he skillfully focused the campaign on issues that put her on the defensive—crime and immigration. Once again, a candidate piggybacked on that powerful California weapon, the initiative.

At the December 9, 1993, funeral of Polly Klaas, the twelve-year-old Petaluma girl whose kidnapping and murder became a national symbol of wanton crime, Wilson endorsed a Three Strikes ballot initiative. The measure that became Prop 184 was the strictest such law in any state, doubling sentences for second offenders and making life sentences mandatory no matter the severity of the third offense. Four days after Klaas was mourned by thousands and eulogized by Wilson, Kathleen outlined a detailed agenda to combat crime. She hoped her plan would neutralize her personal opposition to the death penalty.

It didn't. By June, when it was clear that Republicans were effectively exploiting the death penalty issue, Kathleen returned to her childhood home, the Mansion at Sixteenth and H. She stood in the room where her father had wrestled with life-and-death decisions and told reporters that no daughter who had grown up watching the agony of Pat Brown could in good conscience support the death penalty. She recalled walking into the house through crowds of chanting demonstrators each time an execution approached. She talked about sneaking downstairs when her father went to sleep to read the black binders filled with the details of each case, the photos and letters from families of victims and death row inmates. Pat Brown had commuted twenty-three sentences and allowed thirty-six executions to proceed. He took office believing capital punishment was a necessary evil and left believing it was morally wrong, an ineffective deterrent, inequitably enforced.

"There is no way that I, Kathleen Brown, could possibly change my personal views on capital punishment for they are too rooted in the values that were passed on to me by my father," she said. "A change would represent a repudiation of what he taught me, of what he endured for his beliefs, and for what he instilled in me about the fundamental responsibilities that come with holding public office."

She pledged to uphold the law of the state, regardless of her personal beliefs. Ultimately, she supported the Three Strikes proposition, too. But her opposition to capital punishment, and the record of her father and brother, enabled Wilson to capitalize on what should have been a weakness—crime rates had risen for a decade under Republican administrations. Instead, Wilson played to voters' stereotypes of women as weak on criminal justice issues. His media consultant, Don Sipple, did commercials for gubernatorial candidates in California, Texas, and Illinois, all running against women, that underscored the same theme. "Kathleen, you lack the courage," Wilson said in a debate.

Fears about crime, the number one issue in polls, tied into an equally potent issue, immigration. From the Chinese Exclusion Act to the Japanese internment to mass Mexican deportations during the Depression, immigrants had often served as a convenient scapegoat in times of stress. For the still overwhelmingly white California electorate, frustrated with a sluggish economy, burdened by new taxes, worried about crime, and apprehensive about becoming a minority, Mexicans who had immigrated illegally became an appealing target.

California had always had an above average percentage of foreign-born residents, starting with the Gold Rush that drew immigrants from around the world. From a high of 38 percent foreign-born population in 1870, the share declined gradually to a low of around 10 percent from 1950 through 1970, still almost twice the national average. When immigration quotas were abolished in 1965, the numbers climbed rapidly in California, much faster than in the country as a whole. By 1990, more than one out of five Californians had been born in another country. Those 6.5 million people accounted for nearly one third of all immigrants in the United States.

Because of geography and opportunity, California also led the country in the number of immigrants who arrived without legal papers, eager to escape poverty and violence and to work at minimum wage jobs that still paid far more than they could earn back home. Of the six million people who moved to California in the 1980s, the best estimates suggested more than a quarter were undocumented immigrants. Most crossed the relatively porous border from Mexico, in flows that correlated closely with the vicissitudes of economic opportunity. In the early 1980s, when the California economy was relatively stagnant, about a hundred thousand undocumented immigrants arrived each year, working primarily in agriculture, gardening, construction, and service jobs. In the second half of the decade, the California economy picked up, wages in manufacturing jobs in Mexico declined, and the value of the peso dropped dramatically. The number of illegal border crossers surged, peaking at around two hundred thousand in 1989.

Some of the bump was attributable to the unintended consequences of the 1986 Immigration Reform and Control Act, signed by President Reagan, which granted a path to citizenship for unauthorized immigrants who had been in the country for more than five years. In all, about 2.7 million immigrants were able to legalize their status. Some sent for relatives, who might get tired of long waits for legal papers and cross on their own. The law also offered special provision for farmworkers, who qualified for legalization if they had worked in the fields in the past year. California farmworkers granted legal status often were able to move out of the fields into higher-paying jobs; their replacements were typically undocumented.

By the 1990s, hundreds of thousands of jobs had disappeared during the recession, unemployment had risen, and the number of Mexicans coming to California had declined sharply. That did not stop Republicans from seizing on a politically potent issue. Pete Wilson proposed the federal government deny citizenship to children of undocumented immigrants and cut off health and education benefits. In an open letter to the White House and paid advertisements in national newspapers, he wrote, "Illegal immigration is eroding the quality of life for legal residents of California."

His approval ratings went up, with a third of voters saying his position on immigration influenced them favorably. In a September 1993 *Los Angeles Times* poll, 86 percent of Californians said illegal immigration had become a problem, third only to the economy and crime. Kathleen's lead over Wilson in polls narrowed.

In June 1994, the most famous and influential California proposition since Prop 13 qualified for the ballot. Under the Save Our State initiative, better known as Prop 187, undocumented immigrants would not be able to attend public school or receive nonemergency healthcare or welfare benefits. It would require service providers to report any suspected undocumented immigrants to the attorney general and the immigration service, and would make the creation or use of false documents a felony.

Kathleen opposed the fundamentals of Prop 187 as soon as they surfaced. In a town hall speech in Los Angeles in the fall of 1993, she talked about her great-grandfathers, August Schuckman, an immigrant who built a life and raised a family in Colusa, and Joseph Brown, who emigrated from Ireland and found opportunity in San Francisco. "Immigration and immigrants add immeasurable value to California and to our economy and should be celebrated as one of California's greatest assets," she said. "Perhaps more than any other force, immigration—legal and illegal—has shaped and will continue to shape California's destiny. I want to be unequivocal on this point: Immigrants are among California's greatest strengths."

She acknowledged that the porous border caused problems, but pointed out over and over that immigrants came to work, not, as Wilson insisted, to obtain public services. She denounced as cruel the proposal to deny children admission to schools or hospitals. "Visiting the crimes of an adult upon a child is barbaric, and proposals that do so are based on the coldest and most cynical political calculations."

Wilson closely tied his campaign to Prop 187 and funded a commercial that became infamous across the country: "They Keep Coming." Grainy footage showed shadowy, sinister figures dashing across the Mexican border as the narrator ominously intoned, "They keep coming.

Two million illegal immigrants in California. The federal government won't stop them at the border, yet requires us to pay billions to take care of them."

The commercial resonated with an electorate that remained disproportionately white. Whites made up 57 percent of the population, but an estimated 80 percent of the voters. Latinos made up a quarter of the population, but only about 8 percent of the voters. Prop 187 would play a major role in changing that arithmetic.

On the eve of the election, seventy thousand people marched through Los Angeles to protest Prop 187, one of the largest demonstrations the city had seen. Most were ethnic Mexicans, many young, many proudly waving Mexican flags. The flags sparked a backlash, and in the short run, the demonstration may have won more votes for the anti-immigrant initiative. But in the long run, the severe and unconstitutional provisions of Prop 187 spurred a new generation of Latinos to become politically active, encouraged immigrants to become citizens, and instilled a lasting antipathy toward the Republican Party. Prop 187 would be widely viewed in retrospect as an inflection point that drew Latinos into civic participation, bolstering and reshaping the Democratic Party.

Many California households had become a mix of citizens, legal immigrants, and undocumented residents. Workshops sprouted to organize opposition to the anti-immigrant initiatives and to encourage immigrants to continue using services in the wake of reports of lowered attendance in schools. Latino activists began to define the next civil rights movement as one that would focus on preserving the rights of immigrants, regardless of their legal status. Even before Election Day, some saw Wilson's decision to tie his fate to Prop 187 as a move with long-term political consequences. "That is a major statement that's going to reverberate through the Republican Party and the rest of the country over the next couple years," *Newsweek* deputy Washington bureau chief Howard Fineman said presciently on C-SPAN on the eve of the election.

Toward the end of the campaign, Kathleen mentioned Prop 187 in every speech, not because she entertained any illusion that doing so would win her votes but because it seemed such a moral imperative. "It was a fight for California," she said a week after the election. "For the new California that we're going to be living with, no matter who's governor."

The Brown campaign ran out of money and was essentially off the air during the final weekend, an unforgivable sin in the world of California campaigns. By then, Kathleen had found her voice, too late to change the outcome but in time to reconcile her sense of her own place in the Brown dynasty and California. "You take what you've got and you make the best you can out of it. I think that is what I got from my mother and my father and the life that I've had," she said. "It was: Remember who you represent. Remember who you represent when you walk out the door. And I think that's what leaders are supposed to do."

When Gail Sheehy asked dozens of friends to define Kathleen's passion, her husband, Van Sauter, offered the clearest response: "She has a mystical feeling about California. Her belief in this state and the people's potential is profound. I don't want to sound New Age touchy-feely, but she has almost a sense of responsibility for speaking to its best sentiments, its economic and social potential. It comes directly from her father. Not diluted. *From the father.*"

Prop 187 passed 59 to 41 percent, with unusually high turnout in counties with large white populations. Forty percent of the people surveyed said the initiative was what drew them to the polls. Support ranged from a low of 29 percent in San Francisco to a high of 77 percent in Colusa. Immediately challenged in court and ultimately ruled unconstitutional, the provisions of Prop 187 never went into effect. An earlier U.S. Supreme Court decision had established the rights of undocumented children to public education, and a federal judge also concluded the initiative was an illegal attempt to regulate immigration, a federal prerogative.

Pat Brown was fading. When Kathleen had visited during the campaign, as often as she could, they would have the same conversation over and over. He asked what she was running for, and they talked about the race. Their first conversation after the election, she told him she had lost. He asked by how much. She gave him the numbers: Wilson won 55 percent of the vote; she won 40 percent. The old politician's mind clicked into focus. "That's a loss!" he said, and he never asked her about it again.

During the election, Kathleen had thought about her father and his unbridled effort in 1964 to defeat Proposition 14, the measure to undo the Rumford Fair Housing Act. How he called people bigots for supporting the initiative, even when his handlers discouraged him from talking about race. "There was pressure on me not to talk about 187," she said, as she readjusted to life as a private citizen. "But that was ridiculous. The tradition of politics I believe in is one where you stand for things. That's the way I was raised. I was never tempted to soften my stand, even when I slipped in the polls. I wanted to give people a sense of standing up, of being counted. Let that be my legacy."

Whatever her legacy in the political world, she loomed large as a role model in the extended Brown family. In a clan descended from generations of strong, smart, determined women, Kathleen was the first female offspring of August Schuckman to succeed as a high-powered professional on her own terms. She ushered in a generational change.

Kathleen Kelly idolized both her aunt Kathleen, twelve years her senior, and her grandmother Bernice. Cynthia and Joe Kelly's oldest child wanted to go to Stanford, like Kathleen. When she ended up at Cal, Kelly took French, because Bernice had studied French. Bernice returned the affection, paying special attention to her oldest granddaughter. She bought Kathleen her first bikini, miniskirt, and go-go boots. When Pat and Bernice went on a month-long trip to China in 1980, among the first westerners in the country, Bernice insisted Kathleen Kelly come along as a college graduation present.

Kelly admired her Uncle Jerry, too, and had worked in the governor's office for a high school externship. She did a project about redlining for Marc Poché, Jerry's friend since college, and Poché became a mentor. He encouraged Kelly to pursue her interest in the law. By the time she was in her final year at law school, Jerry had appointed Poché a judge on the appellate court. He gave Kelly a clerkship her last year of school.

For Pat Brown, Jerry's initial failure to pass the bar still loomed large. He worried that an internship would distract his granddaughter from her studies. When she found out she had passed the bar, her grandfather was the first person she wanted to tell. Kelly tracked him down at dinner at Chez Panisse in Berkeley. She excitedly told him the news, only to hear dead silence. After a minute, Bernice got on the line and anxiously asked Kelly what was wrong. Pat was crying.

Kathleen Kelly was the same age as Anne Gust, and as Jerry spent more time with Anne and brought her to family functions, the two women became friends. Anne went on the last of the big Brown family trips to Hawaii. Jerry showed her the California of his youth—Camp Curry in Yosemite; the Boy Scouts' Camp Royaneh on the Russian River. She met the childhood friends, with whom Jerry had happily reconnected when he moved back to San Francisco—the Magellan Avenue boys and the St. Ignatius crowd. The S.I. Class of '55 had lunch in North Beach the first Friday of every month, and Jerry went whenever he could. Even at the early dinners with his old friends, when Anne was quiet, her intelligence and sharp wit were readily apparent. Anne was the first woman, Jerry told the wife of his Magellan Avenue friend Pete Roddy, with whom he was never bored.

As Pat faded, Bernice took particular comfort in Anne's presence, in her life and in that of her bachelor son. Anne was outside the room when Jerry visited with his father toward the end. How's your marriage going? she overheard Pat ask. To her relief, for once, Jerry did not feel compelled to set the record straight.

Pat Brown died on February 16, 1996. His youngest daughter was first to arrive at the house, and Kathleen began to make decisions. She picked the cheapest casket she could find in the catalog. When Jerry arrived, he found a cheaper one: a plain pine box with a Star of David. Llew Werner, one of Jerry's aides from long ago, offered to arrange a police motorcade, a twenty-one-gun salute, and a flyover for the funeral. Jerry objected to the pomp and circumstance. He was overruled.

Hundreds waited in line to pay respects at the wake in Los Angeles, some old friends, some total strangers. "He touched so many lives and helped so many people," Bernice said. Days later, hundreds more filled St. Cecilia's Church in their old Forest Hill neighborhood in San Francisco. Jerry had planned the funeral mass.

Kathleen Kelly recalled in her eulogy that her grandfather would ask her boyfriends three questions: Are you Catholic? Are you Irish? Are you a Democrat? "This is just where Grandpa loved to be," she said. "Right up front, surrounded by his family and dear friends, the clergy, distinguished dignitaries, the press—and hundreds of voting Democrats."

Jerry spoke about what his father had told him was his proudest achievement. Not the water project, or the university. The law that extended old age pensions to noncitizens. It meant so much to people. He "just didn't understand that business of 'lower your expectations.'" Jerry said. "Expanding and building. That's what his life represented."

Anne Gust had been warned by Jerry's sisters about Bernice's reserve. The Browns were not an expressive family. Not like her own large clan where relatives said "I love you" to one another all the time, without a second thought. As Bernice Brown mourned the man she had met when she was thirteen and married sixty-five years ago, she turned to Gust and told her she loved her.

19

Oakland Ecopolis

In 1878, the year Ida Schuckman was born, four-year-old Gertrude Stein moved to Oakland. The rural city of thirty-five thousand boasted one Main Street and the terminus of the transcontinental railroad, which had arrived almost a decade earlier. Gertrude grew up on a ten-acre lot in East Oakland, in a wood-frame house surrounded by trees and gardens. In 1935, she returned to Oakland for the first time in more than four decades, a celebrated writer on a national lecture tour. Stein sought out her childhood home, only to find the orchards and oaks replaced by a drab subdivision in a city that had grown almost tenfold. In her dismay, she penned one of the most famous quotes about Oakland, a nostalgic lament invariably misconstrued as a put-down: "There is no there there."

By the time Stein died in 1946, Oakland had been transformed again by the largest shipbuilding industry in the country. The round-the-clock operation in the East Bay during World War II drew thousands of workers, many of them Southern blacks, who joined a thriving community that became known as a Harlem of the West. For a time, Oakland prospered as a relatively integrated, multicultural city. But in the 1960s, freeways sliced through the city, working-class neighborhoods were demolished, and a ring of suburbs sucked out industry and middle-class homeowners.

Stein would scarcely have recognized Oakland in the twilight of the twentieth century: Art Deco masterpieces abandoned downtown, mansions in the hills, poverty and violence in the flatlands. But perhaps the writer who flourished in the salon life of Paris would have felt at home at 200 Harrison Street, a small commune in a modernist warehouse that hosted Cosmic Rave Masses, a Martin Buber study group, sustainability workshops, and yoga classes. The building was the home of We the People and its founder, Jerry Brown, who had come to Oakland seeking community and political redemption.

Jerry had made good on his vow to the Winter Soldiers to continue his movement in some form. A month after the Democratic convention, he incorporated We the People on August 20, 1992, "to promote better government in the United States, educate Americans concerning the American political system and issues facing the nation, and promote honesty and integrity in government through reforms in the electoral and governmental system." When he looked for a home for his work in progress, he looked across the bay to Oakland, where land was cheap and problems plentiful. Big enough to receive national attention and small enough to make an impression, Oakland, too, was a work in progress. "You can't take America back from Pacific Heights," he said when the news of his move from San Francisco was bannered across the front page of the *Oakland Tribune*. "You know, Oakland really is the All-American city."

Jerry bought a lot near Jack London Square, the waterfront complex named for the city's most famous son, and hired an architect to design a 17,500-square-foot commune that included a three-hundred-seat auditorium, a kitchen and dining area, and ten living units, most with private bathrooms. He planned a rooftop vegetable garden that would employ students to harvest and sell crops, a food co-op, and a law office to help low-income residents. He defined his most important battles as reversing inequality and environmental destruction. "Oakland is a reality that in itself represents the diversity of America, the potential of America, and the suffering of America," Jerry said. "It's all here. And what happens to Oakland, in all probability, happens to the United States."

In his quest to create communal living, Jerry consulted Cesar Chavez, who had turned his attention from labor organizing to cooperatives, which he saw as the only viable alternative for working people. Jerry revisited the isolated UFW headquarters in the San Joaquin Valley in early 1993. After mass, over breakfast in the cafeteria-style dining room, Chavez lamented his failure to persuade his own family to eat communally. He advised Jerry not to allow refrigerators in the apartments.

"For Chavez, some form of *common life* was the most natural way for human beings to live," Jerry wrote in a eulogy a few months later after Chavez died unexpectedly in his sleep, only sixty-six years old. "He had an overwhelming sense that modern life was disordered and that human beings were being cut off from the soil and a harmonious balance of friendship and nature. He recoiled from the pervasive waste and poisoning that we call our affluent modern life . . . in a mechanical age full of plastic and loneliness, he stood against the crowd: unbossed, undoctored and unbought."

By the summer of 1995, the construction of the $1.3 million, two-and-a-half-story building on Harrison Street was complete, a gray corrugated metal façade with a sweeping entrance ramp that led into the largely white interior. "People are moving to the suburbs to be protected from minorities, poor people and poor schools," Jerry said. "We need cooperative caring as opposed to excessive competition." He had always liked communal living arrangements that included dining halls, whether in the seminary or International House. In Oakland, the residents included Jacques Barzaghi, the adviser and friend who had never been far from Jerry since they first met in the early 1970s, and two strangers, the computer consultant who wired the building and the woman who sold them kitchen equipment. She prepared dinner most nights for whoever was around. One of the frequent guests was Anne Gust.

From a soundproof radio booth in the Oakland commune, Jerry broadcast a daily live two-hour show on which he interviewed an eclectic assortment of guests he sought out for their intelligence and expertise. "We are going to take apart the conventional wisdom—the dumb ideas that are wrecking the country, the lies politicians tell, the greed of the corporate high and mighty, the phoniness of the wannabe liberals," he said on his initial broadcast in 1994. "There are no sacred cows on this show." He got a good luck call from "Kathy in D.C.," better known as his sister.

At first the show was carried by Talk America network, which meant local listeners could tune in only to a late-night rebroadcast on a Sacramento station. In July 1995 the program moved to KPFA in Berkeley, the oldest listener-supported radio station in the country. The Pacifica Radio station, like sister stations WBAI in New York City and KPFK in Los Angeles, was known for its leftist politics. "For the work I want to do in Oakland, this provides an excellent opportunity," Jerry said.

"The focus is not political; it's more social. I want to create new institutions."

As he always did, he sought guests he found interesting. A typical show ranged from current events to history, boldface names to obscure literary references. With Gore Vidal, Jerry talked about power and the Kennedys, recalling the cynical pragmatism he had sensed from their forays into California. "The word they loved was 'tough,'" Jerry said. "They liked Jesse Unruh in California because he was 'tough.' Pat Brown, he was 'soft.'" The Kennedys, Vidal agreed, "never got beyond the pleasures of winning. They were blank." The idea of emptiness behind a façade of elegance and grace reminded Jerry of an Archibald MacLeish poem about the circus that he often quoted, and he paraphrased the end: "They looked up at the sky. And they saw nothing at all."

We the People anticipated the advent of podcasts with a website that enabled listeners to download interviews with such thinker-activists as Helen Caldicott, Noam Chomsky, and Ralph Nader. "These people are not looking at society in the conventional way, but in a deeper and more honest way," Jerry said. "And the insights from these very different people lead me to a critical position. We're living in an unsustainable situation that is taking us in the direction of catastrophe—social, moral, and ecological. And it is my interest, perhaps my vocation, to resist that, and to work with others to provide positive alternatives . . . I'm doing what I know how to do and what I have the opportunity to do. It's part politician, part student, part activist, part seeker."

In a talk to the International Transpersonal Association, a group that supported research that integrated spirituality into modern culture, Jerry expanded on his effort to forge new paths to address income inequality, on the death of democracy ("D-E-A-D dead"), and on the limited influence of politicians. "As much as I dislike politics, I have devoted my life to it—out of some form of enlightened masochism or some other deep motive that I have not yet been able to plumb . . . I am not sick of it, and I am not cynical about it. But I'm not naïve about it." The key to meaningful political action was in community. "I have moved to a warehouse in Oakland. I have thirteen bedrooms and nine bathrooms. I'm ready for community! I believe anything that allows people to work together in a direct honest way is the seed of change—cooperatives, base communities, liberation theology, engaged Buddhism."

He repeatedly sidestepped speculation that he had moved to Oakland to restart his political career yet again, though he had confided his plans to close friends before even moving across the bay. "I obviously enjoy running for office," he acknowledged in an interview. "That's pretty clear." He continued to attack the political system in his on-air commentaries: "Most contributions are bribes," and "You think you can collect ten million or twenty million dollars and not let it affect your judgment? Your behavior is influenced, and that is the vice that is destroying us." He called the 1996 presidential race between Bill Clinton and Bob Dole a choice between "the evil of two lessers." He said the two parties no longer offered alternative visions: "In a real sense, Democrats represent only a softer, fuzzier version of harder-edged Republican policies." He wrote an opinion piece when he changed his registration to Decline to State, the California equivalent of Independent. "You can say I have separated myself from the Democratic Party, but I say the Democratic Party has forgotten its Democratic and populist roots."

Jerry began to show up at Oakland churches, benefits, community forums, and City Council meetings. He invited labor leaders and ministers to his loft for wine and cheese. He spoke during debates about waterfront development. By Thanksgiving 1996, the *Oakland Tribune* ran a front page story that speculated about a 1998 run for mayor. Political insiders were dubious. "Let's face it. I think his time has passed," said City Council member Ignacio de la Fuente, a mayoral contender himself. Jerry lobbied openly for an appointment to the city's Port Commission and was rejected. The former governor was reduced to the sidelines, figuratively and literally, cheering on a City Council ally as he headed into executive session on a controversial issue.

Jerry was clear about his ambitions in the summer of 1997 when he contacted Ernest J. Yanarella, a political science professor at the University of Kentucky who had written about sustainable cities. Jerry asked Yanarella to help formulate a green plan for Oakland that might serve as a centerpiece of a mayoral campaign, a potential prelude to one last race for higher office. Yanarella and three graduate students formed "the Green Team" and worked up a draft for Jerry's vision of Oakland Ecopolis, a word derived from the Greek *oikos*, house, and *polis*, city.

On October 28, 1997, in the kitchen of We the People, dressed in what had become his trademark black collarless shirt, Jerry announced his candidacy for Oakland mayor. He pledged to use all he had learned in politics and government to help revive the troubled city. "Government at this level is no different than at any other level," he said. "All the things that I worked on in Sacramento, or failed to work on, are at stake right here. This will be another opportunity to make the democratic process work."

Once again, he viewed himself as a catalyst: "While I don't purport to have the answer to this very difficult problem of racial polarization and class difference, which is getting worse, I see this one city as a place where these problems can be dealt with. Because there is enough balance among the different groups—white, African American, Latino, Asian—that out of that conversation with enough goodwill it's my hope that we can get at the problem of learning, the problem of shared culture, the problem of advancing in our society. That's all I can do. And I intend to walk neighborhoods and walk streets and talk to people and see opportunities to make things work, on the ground."

Mexicans, Chinese, Filipinos, and other Latino and Asian immigrants had turned Oakland into one of the most ethnically diverse cities in the country, about 43 percent black, 28 percent white, 14 percent Hispanic, and 14 percent Asian. The more established black community, though a shrinking percentage of the population, had maintained political control of City Hall, and to a lesser degree the school district. Jerry was taking on the political machine in his somewhat improbable quest to become the city's first white mayor in two decades. "It is a tight little club that someone has to break up," he said. "Many people remember good times in California, and more often than not, they associate those times with either myself or my father."

Jerry's lofty vision of Oakland as "an ecopolis of the future—a city that is both in harmony with the environment and in harmony for itself," was short-lived. He posted on his website the academics' draft proposal, which referred to Italian hill towns, not as a model for Oakland but as inspiration. The reference triggered derision about the latest incarnation of Governor Moonbeam, and the plan was shelved. The candidate instead adopted a more conventional platform: less crime, better schools, more business.

His timing, again, was excellent.

For much of the past century, Oakland had been dominated by Republican families like the Knowlands, owners of the *Oakland Tribune*. Joseph Knowland was elected to the House of Representatives and his son William to the Senate, a rising star until he lost the 1958 race for governor to Pat Brown. Oakland's white elite lived in Mediterranean villas in the hills, with views of the bay and San Francisco. The middle class lived in the foothills, the working class in the flatlands. When ship-building subsided after the war, there were jobs with the railroad, nearby factories like Nabisco and Coca-Cola, the canneries clustered around the port, and Kaiser Permanente, offshoot of the first health maintenance organization, founded by Henry Kaiser to provide healthcare for workers at his shipyards. During the postwar years, Oakland's black population grew from 3 percent in 1940 to 12 percent in 1950 and 23 percent in 1960.

During the 1960s, Oakland became a prime example of the displace-ment and unrest that followed "urban renewal," code words for leveling the homes of poor people. New highways that cut across the city destroyed neighborhoods, displacing thousands of families, most of them black. The political unrest and struggle to maintain a sense of community gave birth to the Black Panthers, founded in Oakland in 1966 by Bobby Seale and Huey Newton. They conducted armed patrols to protect residents who found the almost all-white police force more of a threat than protection. Before they became a national force, embroiled in controversy and violence and targeted by FBI Director J. Edgar Hoover, the Panthers focused on community services in Oakland. They ran community health clinics and a free breakfast program for children. In 1973, Seale ran a cred-ible race for mayor. Two years later, Black Panther Elaine Brown won 40 percent of the vote in a City Council campaign, and in 1977 the Panthers helped Lionel Wilson become the first Democrat, and the first black, elected mayor. In 1983, Robert C. Maynard bought the *Oakland Tribune*, becoming the first black editor and owner of a major daily news-paper in the United States.

The 1980s in Oakland were bleak. Neighborhoods were riven by gang wars and a drug trade that flourished with the crack cocaine epidemic in the latter part of the decade. The 1989 San Francisco earthquake caused extensive damage in Oakland. Two years later, the worst fire in California history ripped through the Oakland Hills, killing twenty-five people and destroying thousands of homes. Sandwiched between the two natural disasters was the 1990 recession, deepening the city's economic woes. Downtown became a ghost town. Oakland became known for its high homicide rates and low educational test scores, which drove out more middle-class families as well as longtime business anchors.

By the time Jerry announced his candidacy, Oakland's downtown was beginning to show signs of life, thanks to the strong economy fueled by the dot-com boom centered nearby. In 1998, the year Jerry ran for mayor, Google was founded and Apple introduced the first iMac. The percentage of households with computers was still a minority, but more than double the 15 percent in 1990. Just thirty miles north of Silicon Valley, San Francisco became a haven for entrepreneurs, venture capitalists, and Internet start-ups. Soaring real estate prices sparked new interest in Oakland, a short BART ride away with prime office space at half the cost. The area was still deserted after work, but free land and $90 million in city subsidies had attracted government agencies. Earlier development had skipped over Oakland and saturated the outlying suburbs; now worsening traffic and high gas prices spurred interest in Oakland's easy access to mass transit. Crime was down, although Oakland's homicide rate was still double that of New York City. At most of the high schools, less than 10 percent of tenth graders read at grade level. Those statistics didn't deter the Gen Xers overrunning the Bay Area and interested in affordable urban housing. Eager to shed its status as poor cousin of the city across the bay, Oakland was poised to embrace a national figure as its champion.

Jerry canceled his subscription to the *New York Times* and took the *Oakland Tribune*. He held dozens of small house meetings around the city. He collected contributions of no more than $100 each, and he lent his campaign $108,000 during the month before the June 1998 primary. His slogan was "Oaklanders First," with a drawing of the tree that gave the city its name reproduced on green campaign T-shirts. "Dealing with racial division, school improvement, friendly streets, and a beautiful, interesting downtown and an interesting city—that is big stuff. But we can have some impact on that," he said at a campaign event. "If you want to have study groups about Serbia, I think that's good. But I don't think you can have an impact. The big leverage point for us as human beings is to deal with what is within our grasp, and that is what's closest in hand."

On Election Day, June 2, 1998, four television satellite trucks arrived at the We the People loft in the early afternoon to snag good positions for live broadcasts when the polls closed. A dozen journalists from publications including *USA Today* and the *Korea Times* showed up in the evening as the block party began, with barbecued ribs, the Oakland band the Naked Barbies, and dancing in the street. Around ten fifteen P.M., after chants of "Jer-*ry*, Jer-*ry*, Jer-*ry*," the mayor-elect came out to address the crowd. Jerry had beaten ten other candidates, captured more black votes than the six black candidates put together, and avoided a November runoff by winning 60 percent of the vote. "I think the people voted for change," he said. "People want to see the bars come down from the windows, and better schools. They want to see this city stop wasting money."

A few hours later, he was on ABC's *Good Morning America*, followed by appearances on CNN and CNBC. Vice President Al Gore called with congratulations. Oakland readied for its celebrity mayor, returning to elected office after a sixteen-year hiatus. "It's like sitting in the stands or being down on the field," he said. "One, you're watching the team; and the other, you are the captain of the team."

Jerry immediately turned his attention to qualifying a measure for the November ballot that would change Oakland's charter to a strong mayor form of government; instead of presiding over the City Council, he would run the city when he took office in January. "It's the city where we can rejuvenate an active political movement in this country—that's my commitment," he told a California Labor Federation Convention meeting in Oakland a month after the election. "Look at the forgotten places, the urban apartheid embedded within this successful economy, and you will find numbers of people living in neighborhoods where forty percent of them are below the poverty line. That situation has doubled in the last twenty years. This is the test of Democratic leadership and the commitment to a society that really works for people. That's what I've been talking about, and now I have a chance to deliver."

As he had as governor, he made four promises when he took office on January 4, 1999: to reduce crime, bring ten thousand residents to downtown, use charter schools to spur school reform, and emphasize artistic culture. "Integrated, international, artistic, both rich and poor at the same time, a place of creativity and hope—there is Oakland: a microcosm of the unfinished American agenda," he said. "Today I make a solemn pledge to be a catalyst for change."

Whatever his impact on Oakland, a subject that would be debated long after he had moved on, Oakland had a profound impact on Jerry Brown. He experienced the frustration of local officials battling dictates from a distant bureaucracy. The city altered his views about schools and prison.

He became convinced local governments should have more power. All those ideas would reshape the state in years to come.

From his earliest days in politics, Jerry had thought about people who would be affected by his actions, in particular the majority who didn't even bother to vote. Now he met them. "I'd never met people who had a gun put in their back. Not once, or twice, but frequently," he said. "You face a specific dead body on a well-traveled street, or the vacant lot that will soon become a condo tower, or the school down the street where half the kids don't graduate. No theory here. Not much comfort from partisan rhetoric. Just hands-on reality with names and faces. Management at the human scale versus pontification from on high."

He became a common sight on the streets and around Lake Merritt often walking Anne Gust's black lab, Dharma, stopping to talk with drug dealers, parolees, homeless people, and business owners. He liked the vitality of the street life. He walked over to investigate a drive-by shooting he saw from his apartment. He browbeat federal housing officials to cancel Section 8 vouchers for a neighborhood crack house. He helped a bar owner get a karaoke permit. He carried printouts of daily crime stats in his pocket.

From the governor who had argued inaction was often the best course, he became the mayor who rammed through development projects as fast as possible. "You have to be able to produce," he said. "This is what the world is about." From the outraged talk show host on left-wing radio he became the pragmatic mayor who invited the Navy and Marines to conduct military training exercises in Oakland to prepare troops for urban combat. The exercises brought the city several million dollars, and pickets outside Jerry's house.

He fought laws that he had created. A section of the Political Reform Act of 1974 blocked elected officials from taking action that might benefit any area within twenty-five hundred feet of property they owned. That meant Jerry could not support a downtown redevelopment project near his loft. He sued to obtain an exemption and won. "I think it's a very salutary experience to make laws and unmake them, all in the same lifetime," he said. "Because you see every law has unintended consequences."

Unlike the tiresome nuts and bolts of politics, the unfamiliar details of governing a city presented a captivating challenge. "I want to tell you why I'm so focused on potholes," he told a group of Bay Area government officials. "They're small, they're physical, people don't like them. And you can eliminate them in a short period of time. I am interested in down-to-earth stuff, like more policemen on the streets, fewer potholes to drive over."

Oakland Ecopolis gave way to the more politically acceptable phrase "elegant density." He maneuvered to get the first floor of a brick office building next door to City Hall set aside for a café. He used connections to attract businesses to space that had been hard to fill: the Italian men's clothing store where Jacques Barzaghi bought suits; a well-known San Francisco restaurateur. The opening of an Oakland Gap became a high-profile media event, attended by Jerry and Anne Gust, whose connections had facilitated the new store. "The suburbs are cheaper, cleaner, safer, and they have better schools. The city has to trump that, and it can do so with culture, accessibility, and a flow of human activity that is ultimately more satisfying and fulfilling," Jerry said. "And I believe that having people live closer to where they work will begin to illustrate a different form of development."

His high profile bolstered the city's morale, reassured investors, and helped expedite action. Gray Davis, Jerry's former chief of staff, had just been elected governor. When city officials went to retail conventions, they no longer had to beg for meetings; people wanted their picture taken with the ex-governor who had slept on a futon, driven a Plymouth, and dated Linda Ronstadt. "They all want an autograph," said city attorney John Russo.

Maya Angelou and Angela Davis turned down Jerry's offer to be library director, but Harry Edwards, a star sports sociologist at Cal, accepted the job of head of Parks and Recreation. Edwards was an expert on race and sports, a former Black Panther, and the college athlete who inspired the Black Power salute by two American sprinters at the 1968 Mexico City Olympics. He wanted, Jerry said, "to shake things up and bring charismatic leadership to energize the young people of Oakland."

The mayor's most successful and controversial accomplishment was the "10K plan," to bring ten thousand people to downtown Oakland, a goal he pursued with unabashed support for developers. "Every single project that has surfaced in the first one hundred days has been opposed," he said in his first State of the City address. "Many of these reasons are fine, but if we let them decide the day, we're moving back to stagnation." He had no patience for those worried about the impact on the people who could never afford the new apartments and might find their substandard housing razed if property values soared. He did not hesitate to take on his liberal critics. "There's this kind of negative cheering section that says, anything that happens, 'whoaaaa, that's going to disrupt something. We're going to be displaced.' They get a name for it. They'll call it gentrification. Or they'll call it . . . something." Some people began to call it Jerrification. They were unimpressed with his defense ("If gentrification means neighborhood improvement, well, what's wrong with that? Please show me some neighborhood that doesn't want to improve"), which sidestepped the question of where poor and working-class people would live.

One of the keys to Jerry's downtown plans was Phil Tagami, a young developer making his mark in the city where he had grown up. Jerry and Tagami had met a few years earlier through Matthew Fox, a defrocked Dominican priest who started his own divinity school. Tagami was an autodidact who had skipped college; he enrolled in classes at Fox's University of Creation Spirituality. When Fox needed a new home for the school, Tagami found a building two blocks from the downtown BART station. The neighborhood was dicey, but the piano company and Meals on Wheels program downstairs paid their rent on time. Jerry helped raise the money for the school to buy the building. Fox had pioneered what he called the Techno Cosmic Mass, a religious rave designed to attract young people to the church. In 1996, the rave mass debuted in Jerry's loft. When crowds outgrew the auditorium, Tagami found an abandoned Art Deco dance hall downtown. He helped them fix up the long-vacant Sweet's Ballroom, once the most famous venue during the Big Band era, hosting jazz greats like Duke Ellington and welcoming black and Latino musicians.

"Economic development is somebody who has some money and somebody who has an idea," Jerry said. "They put them together and take some risk." Tagami had ideas. Jerry had access to money. Both were willing to take risks. Tagami had started a construction company when he was twenty-two and learned to renovate old buildings. He developed contacts in city politics, working on campaigns for Mayor Elihu Harris, Jerry's predecessor, and Councilman de la Fuente. In 1998, Tagami got his big break. City officials picked him over major national developers to renovate an elaborate Beaux Arts building across from City Hall, boarded up for more than a decade and dubbed by the *San Francisco Chronicle* "a beached whale."

With $12 million in city loans and private investment, Tagami turned the beached whale into the Rotunda, a stunning space that opened in 2000 as one of the city's most desirable office complexes. Tagami had restored the building to its early grandeur, with gold-leaf-trimmed columns and wrought iron railings that encircled an open center court-yard, seven stories of offices under an elliptical glass dome more than 120 feet overhead.

The Rotunda established Tagami as a major player, and by then he was an important ally of the new mayor. Jerry appointed Tagami to the Port Commission. "Jerry and I talk about Oakland every day," Tagami said. "He pelts questions at me. It's no-holds-barred. It could be parks, it could be union dues, it could be the port, it could be planning. It's a dialogue." Jerry's style and intellectual curiosity had not changed. He solicited multiple opinions and wanted as much information as possible. Not knowing is not good, Jerry often said to the developer. If he asked Tagami a question, he'd take his answer to a dozen other people. If he concluded Tagami's views had merit and were supported by data, he came back to talk some more.

Lowering crime rates was essential to the 10K plan, to attract people and businesses. Jerry consulted former New York City police chief Bill Bratton and modeled a reporting system after the changes Bratton had pioneered. Every morning, a crime stat report broken down by fifty-seven beats was on the desk of the mayor, city manager, police chief, and City Council members and posted online for the public. Overall crime decreased, though homicides remained high.

In probing the numbers, Jerry unraveled a problem that went far beyond Oakland. "They have this thing called the determinate sentence which I happened to have created twenty-five years ago," he said at a conference sponsored by the Milken Institute, a nonpartisan think tank in Santa Monica. As governor, Jerry had signed strict sentencing laws that took discretion away from judges and parole boards. "It was a big mistake. What you do is you just go to prison. You sit there with no rehabilita-tion. You're just getting punished. And then they let you out. Ninety percent do get out. And then as soon as you get out, you have no skill, and you're kind of irritated at everybody anyway. So you're then violated, and back you go, about eighty percent. Then after you're there for a little while, then you come back, and it's just a pinball. So it's a total scandal. It's a failure."

For years, the recidivism rate in California had been so high that it skewed the national average. Each year, California prisons released about seventy thousand inmates. Within three years, about 60 percent would be back in prison, the majority for violating conditions of their parole. Decades of get-tough policies, antigang sanctions, rigid sentences, and the Three Strikes law had overcrowded prisons, where inmates absorbed more about how to be part of a criminal enterprise than how to avoid it.

The overwhelming majority of the homicide victims in Oakland were young black men, many of them among the one in fourteen adult men in the city who were on parole or probation. "It's a treadmill. It's a merry-go-round. It's a scandal," Jerry told a state commission, calling prisons "postgraduate schools of crime." He instituted a protocol under which teams of Oakland police and parole agents met with every parolee as he was released and offered job training, substance abuse counseling, and a support network for reentering the community. The concept was not universally embraced by the police. "There is tension," Jerry said, "and I would say this is a different kind of culture that has to be slowly introduced into the police force."

Even as he focused on potholes and crime statistics, Jerry still yearned to create the intellectual community he had sought in different guises since his seminary days. The opening page of the mayor's website quoted the "Charter of Calcutta," adopted in 1990 at a conference in the Indian city, which proclaimed "The city can save the world!" The Arts section of the website quoted a letter John Adams sent his wife about ensuring that their sons studied poetry, painting, and music. We the People offered public yoga and tai chi classes. Jerry raised money for a project he called "research by people," which would bring scholars in residence to focus on "reclaiming the ethical basis for civic action." Oakland, and the loft, were the perfect setting for "deep intellectual exchange and civic engagement—all in a context of hospitality and friendship."

The result was the Oakland Table, two six-week sessions in 2000 and 2001 that Jerry described as a more open version of the Berkeley Faculty Club—"a group of people sitting around a table, reading books, talking about ideas, in friendship pursuing truth." The first Oakland Table focused on the city as place, with a 450-page binder of readings available at the public libraries; the second was on the history of hospitality. "Why am I doing this?" Jerry said. "The primary reason I'm doing this is because I find it interesting."

The Oakland Table featured the philosopher, historian, and social critic Ivan Illich, who had been a significant influence on Jerry Brown since the two met in 1976 at the Green Gulch Zen retreat in Marin County. Illich was a radical ex-priest living in Mexico, a scholar and writer best known for his work *Deschooling Society*, a critique of modern education. In the summer of 1983, six months out of the governor's office, Jerry and the director of his nonprofit institute, Nathan Gardels, had lived at Illich's compound in the small village of Ocotopec, outside Cuernavaca. For six weeks, they studied Spanish and spent time with Illich, whose work focused on the nature of technology and modern institutions and the ways in which they were destroying common sense.

"When I try to understand Ivan Illich, I am forced back upon my experience in the Jesuit Novitiate in the 1950s," Jerry wrote in a eulogy in 2002.

> There, I was taught Ignatian indifference to secular values of long life, fame and riches. It is only through that mystical lens that I can grasp the powerful simplicity of the way Illich lived. Ivan Illich was the rarest of human beings: erudite, yet possessed of aliveness and sensitivity. He savored the ordinary pleasures of life even as he cheerfully embraced its inevitable suffering. Steeped in an authentic Catholic tradition, he observed with detachment and as a pilgrim the unforgiving allure of science and progress. With acute clarity and a sense of humor, he undermined, in all that he wrote, the uncontested certitudes of modern society.

Illich's work influenced Jerry's deep skepticism about the educational establishment and his views about schools, perhaps the most failed institutions in Oakland. Across California, the public school system that had once drawn families to the Golden State had never regained its strength after Prop 13. In Oakland, the failure and dropout rates were among the worst in the state. Jerry pushed through a charter change that added three mayoral appointees to the seven-member elected Oakland school board. But he grew frustrated when the board passed over his preferred candidate for superintendent. The state took over the financially troubled district. Jerry turned his attention to founding two charter schools that would eventually include grades six through twelve, a military institute and an arts academy.

He modeled the Oakland Military Institute as a secular version of St. Ignatius, with strict discipline, structure, and academic requirements. He asked the local bishop to recommend his best principal and hired her as a consultant. In addition to the expected opposition to charter schools from labor unions and local school administrators who would lose state aid, OMI was denounced by some of the mayor's liberal supporters who objected to the military emphasis, personnel, and funding. Turned down by the local and county school boards, OMI was approved only after the intervention of Governor Davis, the first charter to be approved by the State Board of Education. Jerry immersed himself in the details, from the school flag to the funding, $2 million from the U.S. Defense Department and $1.3 million from the California National Guard. He chose as its motto the Jesuit saying he had learned at the novitiate—*Age quod agis.* Do what you are doing. The first class of 166 seventh graders entered in August 2001, spending ten-hour days on a campus of portable trailers named for traits they were to master, Fort Justice and Fort Cooperation. Eighty percent of the students were black, most came from poor families, and all were way behind in school. The mission was to produce graduates who would go on to four-year colleges.

"I think public schools are not instilling the kind of strong character that we need and I don't think there's the discipline nor do I think there's the inspiration to learn," Jerry said. Criticized for walking away from the public schools, he argued that the charters would pressure the whole district to improve. Successful charter schools would "make the superintendent and board come together and work through the incredible byzantine set of rules and regulations and relationships that have made it dysfunctional for over two decades."

For someone who hated rules and being told what to do, a military academy might seem an odd choice. Jerry's explanation shed light on his passion for the school and his own upbringing. He compared the military academy to the seminary he had attended: "I had the experience of being in a framework where right was right, wrong was wrong, the people in charge are in charge, and you do what they tell you. Very structured. And if you have somewhat of a chaotic mind, structure is actually kind of pleasant. You can fight against it. But it's very comforting to know there's all sorts of boundaries that you can push against, but they're still there. And I think some of these kids in very chaotic neighborhoods, they need real structure. So that was the idea of the military school."

OMI was followed a year later by the Oakland School for the Arts, opened with far less controversy. "I don't think a mayor in California has ever done that," Jerry said about his two charter schools. "I consider that a major achievement. I think it will probably be my most lasting achievement." He often stopped by classrooms unannounced and grilled the students on what they were learning. He handed out diplomas at graduation. Before he left office, he would sell the Harrison Street property and use the proceeds to donate more than half a million dollars to each school.

Jerry was easily reelected to a second term, and by his inauguration in January 2003, attention had shifted to the state's collapsing economy. Oakland, facing the loss of millions of dollars in state aid, planned to cut police overtime and close libraries and recreation centers. But the city's turmoil paled in comparison with the impending upheaval in the state's political landscape.

In Sacramento, Jerry's former chief of staff, Gray Davis, was in trouble. During Davis's first term, the dot-com boom had swelled state revenues, and the governor and legislators spent freely. They restored money that had been cut from budgets during the past sixteen years under Republican governors. Prop 13 and the state's progressive tax structure made California's budget heavily dependent on the income of the top 1 percent of earners and subject to big, sudden, volatile swings in capital gains. When the recession hit California in 2000 and the dot-com boom collapsed, revenues that had poured in a few years earlier dried up just as fast. By then, the state had committed billions of dollars to ongoing programs. The budget deficit grew to $38 billion. At the same time, California faced an energy crisis that drove a utility into bankruptcy, caused

Jerry Brown designed the logo for the charter school he founded, using the Jesuit motto he learned in the seminary: Do what you are doing.

rolling blackouts, and all but paralyzed a state that depended on massive amounts of energy to power lights and move water. Eventually, investigators would unravel what became known as the Enron scandal, energy companies' blatant and illegal manipulation of the complicated, flawed energy grid California had adopted under Pete Wilson. But that would come too late to salvage Gray Davis's career or his reputation as a weak, indecisive leader.

In July 2003, the state's bond rating dropped to near junk status, the lowest in the nation. To plug the budget hole, Davis tripled the vehicle licensing fee, an unpopular move in a state with 28 million cars and trucks. Popular AM talk radio hosts fired up voters to boot Davis out of office just months into his second term. Congressman Darrell Issa funded a petition-signing drive: "Mad about the car tax? Sign here to recall Gov. Gray Davis."

The recall was the third piece of the changes ushered in by Hiram Johnson and the Progressives in 1911 to provide direct democracy, along with the initiative and referendum. Only three petitions to recall state officials had reached the ballot since then, all aimed at state senators. Unlike most of the eighteen states with similar provisions, California required no specific grounds for a gubernatorial recall, just a petition signed by 12 percent of the people who had voted in the last statewide election, the lowest threshold of any state. On the same ballot, voters would decide whether to recall the governor and choose among candidates who would take office if the recall passed. Anyone could run for governor; all it took was ten thousand signatures, or sixty-five signatures and a $3,500 fee. Once the Recall Davis petition qualified, dozens of people jumped into the free-for-all. One hundred thirty-five names appeared on the October 2003 ballot, including Lieutenant Governor Cruz Bustamante, commentator Arianna Huffington, *Hustler* publisher Larry Flynt, and Angelyne, a billboard diva who cruised Los Angeles in a pink Corvette. Only one hopeful, however, announced his candidacy on the *Tonight Show.*

"With this big entrance of Arnold Schwarzenegger . . . it is going to be like a tidal wave," Jerry said on Fox News television hours after the bodybuilder and action movie star jumped into the race. "He's like a tsunami coming at us." Jerry saw little chance that Davis could retain his job.

Asked whether he, too, would enter the race, Jerry said, "No. It's not my time right now." He had a different path to Sacramento in mind.

Schwarzenegger, a moderate who would have had difficulty winning a primary among the state's conservative Republican voters, dominated the short, spectacular campaign. He had no difficulty with name recognition and offered an exuberant alternative to the staid, cautious Davis. "*Hasta la vista*, car tax!" Schwarzenegger declared, updating his famous line from *Terminator 2* as he watched a crane drop a 3,600-pound wrecking ball on an Oldsmobile painted with the words "Davis Car Tax." Married into the Kennedy clan, he attracted Democratic support through his wife, Maria Shriver, who took a leave from her television news job to campaign for her husband. Schwarzenegger vowed to end the dysfunctional culture in Sacramento. "Money goes in. Favors go out. The people lose," he intoned in his Austrian accent on one of his television spots.

"Though Schwarzenegger ran as a Republican, he was the candidate of voter rebellion who came from outside the party machinery," Jerry said on election night, speaking as something of an expert on running as an outsider and crusading against the role of money in politics. Davis was overwhelmingly recalled, and Schwarzenegger coasted to victory in the October 7, 2003, election. Jerry knew better than the governor-elect what he would soon face, trying to stabilize a financially precarious budget with little room to maneuver. "The governor, in reality, has discretionary spending capability of about one half to one percent," Jerry said. "The idea that a governor of California has any real decision-making capacity is highly exaggerated."

One of Davis's last acts in office was to appoint Kathleen Kelly to the San Francisco Superior Court, where she was sworn in by her uncle, Oakland mayor Jerry Brown. Her application had been stalled for years amid concern that there might be a political backlash against Davis as a result of her family's well-known opposition to the death penalty.

Kelly's greatest advocate, perhaps most responsible for the appointment, did not live to see her granddaughter sworn in. Bernice Layne Brown doted on all her grandchildren, but pretty much everyone believed Kathleen Kelly was her favorite. Kelly had devoted her career to juvenile justice, working for the San Francisco city attorney. Convinced that her oldest granddaughter belonged on the bench, Bernice felt so strongly about it that she lobbied Davis herself. Bernice, the precocious student who grew up to be the governor's wife, was simultaneously content with her own life and full of the highest aspirations for her granddaughters whose options were so vastly different in the twenty-first century.

Bernice had been in poor health for several years, confined to a wheel-chair and blind, but her mind had remained sharp. She died on May 9, 2002. "She was the steady hand behind my father, and made everything work in the family," Jerry said. "She had a very strong will." He arranged the funeral at St. Brendan's Church, near their old Magellan Avenue home, although his mother had never had any use for religion. In her eulogy, Kathleen Kelly recalled the frugality that led Bernice to use assorted souvenir dishes from golf tournaments instead of fine china and to pinch the stems out of strawberries with tweezers so as not to waste any fruit—and the generosity Grandma showered on her offspring, especially during their annual Christmas trips.

Jerry spoke of how his mother had broken down in tears when he went into the Jesuit seminary, one of the two times anyone remembered Bernice losing her composure. He had only just learned that from his aunt Connie. He returned to a familiar theme—the comfort of structure. "The thought I kept having was she created the order so I could indulge in disorder. The order was so powerful and all-pervasive that I never had to worry about how much chaos and disorder I would create."

By the summer of 2003, just six months into his second term as mayor, Jerry began to talk about running for attorney general in 2006. "I would say that nothing in my past shows that my ambition is limited," he said to filmmaker Stephen Talbot, who was working on a documentary about the Oakland mayor entitled *The Celebrity and the City.* Jerry paused. "I'm too old to change that."

After a six-year hiatus, he rejoined the Democratic Party in August 2003. A year later, he moved out of the We the People commune, and moved in with Anne Gust. They lived in a loft in the old Sears Roebuck building on Telegraph Avenue, which had been renovated into fifty-four live/work units around an open atrium. From the rooftop patio they could see a Korean barbecue restaurant, a check cashing store, a metal plating shop, and a crack house.

Around the same time, Jerry parted ways with his longtime friend Jacques Barzaghi, who had worked in City Hall since Jerry took office. Pressure to jettison Barzaghi had increased since an investigation triggered by a sexual harassment claim revealed that all nineteen women who worked around him complained about inappropriate comments or gestures. The city settled the case for $50,000 and he was demoted to a nonsupervisory job. With a loyalty that surprised few of his longtime friends, Jerry stubbornly refused to believe the complaints. "Jacques is a catalytic element in the mix of advisers I have," he said. "I understand he's not everybody's favorite person, but he's quite remarkable." In July 2004, when Barzaghi's sixth wife called police to report she had been pushed down the stairs, the Brown-Barzaghi alliance finally came to an end. He was fired, and left town.

In Oakland, the debates would continue over who profited most from the symbiotic relationship between the city and its celebrity mayor who would soon be moving on. Community groups criticized his focus on downtown and market rate housing, arguing that other neighborhoods got shortchanged and the crisis of affordable housing had worsened. He antagonized black supporters and roiled City Hall when he abruptly fired the black city manager, acting in a manner the city attorney compared to "an eight-year-old with an ant farm: Turn it upside down and shake it to see what happens." The military school struggled, with high staff turnover and mixed results. Crime went down and the police force increased from 620 to about 800 officers, but homicides spiked at the end of his tenure, and the police department weathered a major scandal. Property values rose, good for some, difficult for poor people more likely to face eviction.

Jerry came close to his goal of ten thousand new people downtown, and stores and restaurants began to follow. He attracted an estimated $1 billion in investment. He gave the city spirit. They had a famous mayor who walked around the worst neighborhoods by himself and reported drug dealers and slumlords. An *Oakland Tribune* columnist at a journalists' convention in Ohio reported that her peers were excited to see Oakland on her nametag and asked about the mayor, not the crime rates.

In the end, Jerry left Oakland with what he needed. Two decades after the consultants had said Jerry would have to be taken seriously in order to have a political future, he finally was. A dozen years after he had been a political has-been fighting to deliver a speech in Madison Square Garden, he had become a player once again.

Always interested in disseminating his message unvarnished, Jerry jumped on the latest trend and became one of the first politicians to blog. In its first six days in early 2005, the Mayor's Blog got twenty thousand hits. Jerry blogged about new solar power installations, charter schools, and parolees. He described the inauguration of Antonio Villaraigosa, the first Mexican American mayor of Los Angeles, and the groundbreaking for a Whole Foods that would be the first major supermarket in downtown

Oakland in decades. He quoted Schopenhauer, who said "extracting truth from oneself required putting one's mind on a rack and subjecting it to relentless interrogation." He mused about Mortimer Adler, Saint Paul, and Allen Ginsberg. And he announced more personal news.

"I've been absent from the blogosphere, but for a good cause," he posted on April 15, 2005. "I got engaged and will be married on the steps of City Hall in June." He had proposed to Anne Gust on her birthday, after cooking her chicken and peas for dinner. She was in no rush and assumed they would have a long engagement. Jerry had other ideas.

In the same blog post, he announced professional news: "I am writing this from the press office in the Los Angeles Convention Center, where California Democrats have gathered for their annual convention. I am here seeking support for my candidacy for state attorney general."

His two big pieces of news were not unrelated. Anne would become both his wife and key adviser, inseparable partner at home and work. Jerry had said many years earlier that marriage was incompatible with his job because he did not have time to focus on both. He solved the problem by eliminating the distinction. He viewed the marriage commitment as the creation of "indissoluble bonds" that extended to the political world that had been for so long his natural habitat.

Anne had greater assets than Jerry, and her financial adviser had suggested a prenuptial agreement. Jerry rejected the idea out of hand; the notion that the indissoluble bonds of marriage might be anything less than indissoluble was not even worthy of consideration.

In the end, the wedding took place across from City Hall, in the Oakland Rotunda. Anne would have preferred a small wedding; better yet an elopement. It was Jerry who wanted a gala celebration, befitting the mayor of the city and the Irish-German Catholic son of San Francisco. Anne acquiesced because it seemed so important to him. She agreed to handle the caterer; everything else was up to him. He planned the ceremony, down to the Gregorian chants. His friend Diane von Fürstenburg designed Anne's dress.

On June 18, 2005, Edmund G. Brown Jr., sixty-seven, and Anne Baldwin Gust, forty-seven, were married by Senator Dianne Feinstein, with a guest list that included pretty much all the political royalty in California. The closest friends and family sat in the courtyard; the rest of the almost six hundred guests were assigned, in descending order of importance, to the rings of terraces on higher floors.

After the festivities, a small group took a bus across the Bay Bridge to St. Agnes Church. In the same San Francisco chapel where Pat and Bernice had exchanged vows seventy-five years earlier, Jerry and Anne were married in a religious ceremony performed by Father John Baumann. Baumann had entered Sacred Heart Novitiate in 1956 with Jerry Brown and ended up in Oakland, where the two men reconnected after many years. Baumann ran a faith-based organizing group. He understood Jerry's bond to the church, his attachment to the structure and rituals, and the importance of the Jesuit traditions. When Jerry called and asked him to perform the ceremony, Baumann went to talk with him and meet Anne. Jerry had a stack of books about marriage he was reading, including *The Constitution of the Jesuits.*

On their honeymoon, the Browns canoed down the Russian River. Then Jerry took Anne to meet his old Berkeley professor Sheldon Wolin, who lived in a tree house in Mendocino.

Jerry's last entry in the blog was on June 22, 2005. "Fourth day of marriage. Bliss endures."

20

Son of Sacramento

On January 8, 2007, Jerry Brown stood at the foot of the grand staircase in the rotunda of San Francisco City Hall and pointed to the spot a few feet away where he had sat sixty-three years earlier to the day. He was not yet six when he watched his father sworn in as district attorney and wondered aloud if the man he had beaten would show up to be sworn out. "I'm very glad to come back to the place where I guess I got my first glimpse of political, should we call it, power, responsibility, opportunity," Jerry said. "Anyway, I got the first sense right on these steps."

At sixty-eight, Jerry Brown was following in his father's footsteps once more, deliberately, and with pride. Jerry had easily defeated a Democratic opponent in the primary and a Republican in the general election to assume the second most powerful job in California, that of attorney general. Pat Brown had always said it was the best job he ever had. That, Jerry told friends, was part of the reason he had run.

Judge Kathleen Kelly stood on the steps of City Hall with the man who had sworn her in to office three years earlier. Now it was her turn to do the honors. "Uncle Jerry, I know I speak for the entire Brown family proudly gathered here today when I say that you've inspired and challenged each of us," Kelly said. "And even though a casual conversation with you often feels like an oral argument before the Supreme Court, we are so grateful for the profound impact that you've had on all of our lives."

Uniformed cadets from the Oakland Military Institute stood at attention along the banisters of the grand staircase. Gregorian chanters sang the Latin hymn "Te Deum." Jerry reflected on his swearing-in as governor more than three decades earlier, noting that his seven-and-a-half-minute inaugural address remained his most popular speech. "No one remembered what I said, but they remembered how few words I took to say it. I want to keep in that spirit."

He spoke about the need for common sense and mentioned, as he did often, that at one time people thought common sense was an organ, behind the pituitary gland. He promised to follow the edict his father had laid down sixty-three years earlier: Prosecute, not persecute. "I want to make sure that our laws that protect working people are vigorously enforced," Jerry said. He rattled off relevant laws on overtime, workers' compensation, minimum wage. "All these are meant to create living, fair conditions in the workplace, or in the fields."

He singled out environmental protection, particularly landmark actions championed by Governor Arnold Schwarzenegger to combat global warming. The state had been sued, and it would fall to the new attorney general to defend the efforts to shift the state to a more sustainable energy future and to limit emissions of greenhouse gases.

"The law is not a game," he concluded. "It's not a business; it's a calling."

When Pat Brown left the attorney general's office, his staff gave him a life-sized mosaic by Beniamino Bufano, an Italian American sculptor who had settled in San Francisco during World War I and focused much of his work on themes of peace. The mosaic given to the first Attorney General Brown showed a woman embracing a multitude of children of different colors with the inscription ONE WORLD, ONE PEOPLE, ONE DESTINY, ONE JUSTICE. Pat Brown had kept the mosaic in his office as governor and pointed to those words as his guiding principle on civil rights. His son inherited the artwork, which would now become a mantra for another attorney general.

"I think about my father now," Jerry said after his inauguration. "The law is not just about change, it's about tradition."

One major change since the last time Jerry had held statewide office was Anne Gust Brown. By the time she held the Gust family Bible as her husband took the oath of office, his wife of eighteen months had established herself as a full and omnipresent partner in Jerry Brown's political career. Her role was in some ways only logical. "I am married to a person who likes to work seven days a week," she said. "He loves what he does and finds it not only his vocation but his hobby."

When they got engaged in the spring of 2005, Anne had already decided to leave the Gap, where she had worked since 1991 in a variety of senior positions, the last five years as chief administrative officer. She loved the work, but was ready for a change. Jerry was beginning to plan his campaign. "I might have gone on more boards, things like that, but Jerry really did want me to get involved with helping him on running his attorney general campaign and then helping in the attorney general's office," Anne said. "It's been fascinating and fun in terms of the work, and it's strengthened our relationship, too."

During the many years they dated, even when they lived together, Anne had a separate life and career. When they married, she had had some trepidation about the amount of time she and Jerry would spend together as they merged personal and professional lives. But Jerry wanted and needed a partner, and Anne plunged in. She was smart, confident, incisive, and completely devoted to Jerry's best interest. Anne had started as his campaign finance chair, then quickly established herself as the de facto campaign manager. Once again, Jerry had turned to someone outside the traditional political establishment, whose instincts he trusted and who understood him well. Jerry described their working relationship as a natural extension of their marriage: "There are a lot of businesses where a husband and wife run the business. We live together. We work together. We go to the gym together . . . It's a life that we're leading, and it so happens that at this moment in time it includes this campaign."

Anne provided the structure that Jerry always sought. Where he was nonlinear, she remained on point. She was a corporate executive accustomed to organizing and running things. She worked hard and stayed on task. Friends described her as tough, fierce, funny, decisive, unforgiving, analytical, and quick to size up a situation, with an intelligence and wit to match her husband's. She credited Jerry with teaching her almost everything she knew about politics.

After Jerry won the election, the couple visited offices in the state Justice Department to plan the transition. "Some of you may have noticed my wife, Anne, accompanying me as I have made the rounds of the various offices," Jerry wrote in an email to his future employees. "I find her advice pretty invaluable and very practical." By the time he was sworn in, she had been appointed an unpaid special adviser. "If you can't get in to see her," Jerry said at his inauguration, "you probably won't be allowed to get in to see me." She functioned as a chief of staff, bringing legal acumen and management experience to an office of eleven hundred lawyers. "It is a broad title," Jerry said when he made the appointment. "And she certainly will have a broad mandate, because her experience is very broad."

Like his father, he declined to move to Sacramento, commuting when necessary and working primarily from the Bay Area. The Browns remained in Oakland, though they moved out of the loft into a glass-and-wood-filled home in the Oakland Hills. The Skyline House, inspired by Japanese design, embodied qualities they both prized: beauty, serenity, and privacy.

Only the garage was visible from the road; secluded between city-owned tree-filled lots, the house spilled down the hillside in five levels, with unobstructed views of San Francisco Bay. The builder, Sallie Lang, had apprenticed under a Zen priest turned builder whose Oakland company had spent seven years constructing an elaborate compound for Oracle founder Larry Ellison. Lang incorporated design elements and techniques she learned from that experience. With shoji sliding doors, local elm slabs over the mantelpiece, and handmade iridescent tiles on the bathroom floor, Lang combined Japanese warmth and detail with American sturdiness.

Anne saw the house online and insisted they take a look, despite Jerry's skepticism about moving out of the loft. "My husband fell in love with it as soon as he walked down the steps into the 'great room' with its panoramic view of the bay," she said.

What both father and son liked about the attorney general job was its independence and breadth. The general did not have to negotiate with a legislature. He had room to creatively defend or interpret California laws and initiate litigation on behalf of the state's residents. Because of California's size, cases often set precedent and affected other states. In his first email to the staff, Jerry singled out the priority with which he would become closely identified: "to implement—in a practical and effective way—California's global warming legislation." Soon after he took office, Jerry had a new partner. Governor Schwarzenegger tapped Mary Nichols to head the Air Resources Board, the same post she had held under Jerry Brown in the 1970s. When Nichols arrived in Sacramento to start work, one of the first calls came from her former boss. The state's top lawyer wanted to come talk about strategies to combat climate change.

After a rocky start, Schwarzenegger turned to Sacramento veterans like Nichols, mainly Democrats, to further his agenda. The whirlwind nature of the recall had meant he took office with little preparation, facing the same crises that had helped drive his predecessor out of office. The internationally famous Terminator lived up to his Hollywood persona: he installed a cigar tent outside the governor's office, called Democratic legislators "girlie men," and vowed to "blow up the boxes." Yet the Californian whose philosophy the Austrian immigrant governor took to heart was Kevin Starr, the erudite, bow-tie-clad historian who served as state librarian.

In a *Los Angeles Times* op-ed that ran after the recall, Starr urged a return to the "Party of California," arguing the greatest California governors had transcended partisan politics. "The core principle of the Party of California is that the state—its history and heritage, its environment, its economy and, above all, the well-being of its people—is worth imagining, worth struggling for; California represents a collective ideal connected to individual and social fulfillment," Starr wrote. "Everyone belongs to the Party of California. Everyone is welcome." Schwarzenegger circulated the essay among his senior staff as a road map for the administration.

In many areas, such consensus proved elusive. Schwarzenegger was stymied on fiscal issues by Democrats, who controlled the legislature, and out of sync on social issues with an increasingly conservative Republican Party. Budgets, which required a two-thirds vote and thus needed bipartisan support, degenerated into bitter fights, and the governor failed to address structural problems that plagued the state's finances and drove boom-and-bust spending. He called a special election in November 2005 and placed four initiatives on the ballot—to impose certain spending caps, amend teacher tenure, restrict the use of union dues for political campaigns, and create a redistricting commission. He spent $8 million of his own money and lost all four. The election set a new record for spending on ballot initiatives, more than $313 million.

By contrast, the environment proved an area of common ground where California again forged national policy. Three months after former Vice President Al Gore's documentary *An Inconvenient Truth* set box office records, the California legislature passed the Global Warming Solutions Act, championed by Democrat leaders and Schwarzenegger. California became the first state to enact a long-range plan to reduce the emissions of carbon dioxide, methane, and other greenhouse gases, so named because their release traps heat from the sun to create a greenhouselike effect that hastens a dangerous rise in temperatures. The law directed the Air Resources Board to enact a plan that would reduce greenhouse gas emissions to 1990 levels by the year 2020, about 15 percent less than would otherwise be expected. The goal was to wean the state from coal and oil in favor of nonpolluting, sustainable energy sources.

The plan adopted by the board strengthened the 1970s-era car emission standards, provided incentives for electric vehicles, and required the state to generate one third of its power from cleaner fuels by 2020. The mechanism at the heart of the program was "cap and trade," which placed limits, or caps, on overall emissions, required businesses to obtain permits for carbon emissions, and set up a market for companies to buy and trade permits. The market built in financial incentives to reduce emissions, gave businesses flexibility, and generated revenue that the state could apply to other projects to combat global warming. Cap and trade would become a model for other states and countries.

Jerry called global warming "the biggest problem facing the state . . . a totally unique threat because it's somewhat subtle, and it's building up year by year." The attorney general defended the law against several challenges and teamed up with the governor on other environmental initiatives. They sued the Bush administration when federal officials stalled in granting California a waiver so the state could require stricter emission standards for cars.

"This lawsuit today is not about politics; it's about science, it's about human welfare and it's about innovation," Jerry said. He pointed to previous waivers the state had been granted, going all the way back to President Reagan's administration. The waiver was eventually granted by the Obama administration, and the standards took effect for 2009 model cars. California again forced automakers to produce more environmentally friendly cars for the entire country.

The Schwarzenegger administration initiated several significant policies that would over time change how the state dealt with juvenile offenders, water management, and political boundaries. But the governor's accomplishments were largely overshadowed by his ongoing failure to deal with mounting budget crises. In part, the failure stemmed from inexperience, in part from the convoluted, patchwork nature of California government, and in part from the recession that began soon after Schwarzenegger began his first full term in January 2007. As with the downturn in the early 1990s, the Great Recession after the financial crisis hit California harder than the rest of the country and lasted long past its official

June 2009 end. The recession affected every facet of life in the Golden State, causing record unemployment, a collapsed housing market, and multi-billion-dollar budget shortfalls. Because a spectacular real estate boom had preceded the crash, the impact was particularly severe in construction and related industries, including financial services. California lost 1.37 million jobs, a drop of 9 percent. In parts of the state, entire subdivisions were abandoned as families could not pay the mortgages that never should have been approved. The economic collapse would hasten the hollowing out of the middle class and exacerbate income inequality that had been building for decades.

For Jerry Brown, the Great Recession presented both short- and long-term opportunities. As attorney general, he took legal action against scammers who preyed on homeowners facing foreclosure. He sued Fannie Mae and Freddie Mac for blocking an energy efficiency program. He prompted the U.S. Justice Department to successfully sue Standard & Poor's, which had issued high credit ratings to bonds backed by risky subprime mortgages. In a high-profile case overseen by Anne Gust Brown, California sued Los Angeles–based Countrywide Financial Corporation, one of the largest subprime mortgage lenders, for deceptive practices that led homeowners to take out risky loans the company then resold in secondary markets at huge profit. California took the lead in a multistate settlement with Countrywide that provided billions of dollars in relief to homeowners facing foreclosure.

The longer-term opportunity that the recession posed for Jerry would come in 2010, when angry, disillusioned voters would seek a candidate who held out the promise of restoring faith in government—an echo of the 1974 post-Watergate, post-Vietnam era that had launched his political career.

The recession devastated a California budget heavily dependent on personal income tax, and plummeting revenues exacerbated partisan gridlock. In 2008, after missing the deadline by several months, the state adopted a budget balanced by accounting maneuvers and internal borrowing that worsened the deficit. By the end of 2008, Schwarzenegger ordered mandatory furloughs for state workers. State offices closed two Fridays a month. The comptroller issued $2.6 billion worth of IOUs to prevent the state from running out of cash. Billions of dollars of tax refunds and payments to local service providers and contractors were delayed. By the summer of 2009, the state had cut about $30 billion over two years, affecting schools, healthcare, prisons, and recreation. The University of California instituted layoffs and furloughs, delayed hiring, and raised tuition 32 percent.

In September 2009, a Public Policy Institute of California poll showed record levels of distrust in state government. Although the recession was technically over and the housing market had stabilized, the state's unemployment rate hit 12.2 percent, the highest point in seventy years. Like everything about California, the crisis assumed mythic proportions. Commentators compared California to Greece, a "failed state." California was ungovernable. Schwarzenegger talked about "fiscal Armageddon" as his popularity reached new lows. Only 30 percent of the people viewed him favorably, and the legislature rated even worse. Kevin Starr compared the state to France in 1958 when General Charles de Gaulle came out of retirement to unite a fractured country and founded the Fifth Republic. Starr knew California's retired governor in waiting. They had gone to the same high school.

Jerry Brown had mapped out a potential path back to power years earlier, and rumors about a gubernatorial bid began almost as soon as he became attorney general. "The thought has certainly crossed my mind, but I haven't really come to any conclusion," he said in an interview, less than eight months after taking office. By 2009, he had mused about the idea for months to friends. As he had urged his father to do in 1958, he spent several days meditating. He returned to the Abbey of New Clairvaux, the Trappist monastery in the small Northern California town of Vina where he had gone after winning the gubernatorial primary in 1974. Jerry came home with a clearly articulated rationale for his decision: I am a son of California, this is what I was meant to do. I have the experience. I know how to make things happen. Everything I've done in my life has been building to this.

"I have a sense of the historic character of California," he said in the spring of 2009. "My family came here as pioneers. We came during the gold rush. We still have the land that my great grandfather farmed." He had recently taken his ninety-seven-year-old aunt Connie to visit the Mountain House and her mother's nearby grave. "I want to summon Californians to a renewed, shared commitment to the state's real greatness and that's not about one party or the other . . . the most successful governors—Hiram Johnson, who led the reform era, and Earl Warren, who was there during World War II and was put on the U.S. Supreme

Court, I would also say my father. These were the people who built the state, who were innovators and who were not ideologues or people who were pigeonholed into one partisan box."

On September 29, 2009, Jerry filed papers to run for governor, which enabled him to raise money at a higher contribution limit than as a candidate for attorney general. He had long ago jettisoned the idea of a $100 contribution limit as impractical, and few of his supporters seemed troubled by the shift back to a more conventional politics. His likely opponent, eBay founder Meg Whitman, was the fourth-wealthiest woman in California, with a net worth of more than $1 billion and a willingness to spend a chunk of her personal fortune in a campaign to run the world's sixth-largest economy.

"The next governor must have the preparation and the knowledge and the know-how to get California working again," Jerry said in his formal announcement, released by video on March 2, 2010. "At this stage in my life, I'm prepared to focus on nothing else but fixing the state I love."

The phrase "at this stage in my life" became his mantra, a sentiment that seemed to make voters comfortable in a year when they rejected professional politicians and looked to outsiders for solutions. He turned the potential negatives of his age and political pedigree into a plus, casting Whitman as another Schwarzenegger-like wealthy political neophyte incapable of governing effectively. At seventy-two, Jerry Brown had no focus beyond the state's best interest, no national ambitions, and plenty of experience. "It's a meat grinder," he told a union convention. "And you need somebody who's been trained in the arts of self-abnegation and mortification. That's something I learned at the seminary; we were told that the good Jesuit novice seeks his greater abnegation and continuing mortification. Mortification is from the Latin word 'death.' You must die to yourself. That's a good requisite if you're running for governor. 'Cause when you get there, they're not going to be too happy."

Often the first question was "Why do you want this job?" When Jerry visited Google a month after his announcement, CEO Eric Schmidt posed that query. Interviewing Jerry in an auditorium full of Google employees, Schmidt laid out the problems: the deficit, the boom-and-bust cycles, the pending battle over reapportionment, the requirement that budgets pass by a two-thirds majority. Why run? "I'm drawn to the task, perhaps as to the fire," Jerry said. "I've studied this government for most of my life." Studies had shown wisdom came with age, Jerry said, to which Schmidt quickly pointed out he was talking to a young crowd. "It's something to look forward to," the candidate quipped.

The second question: How do you win, running against a moderate Republican with unlimited cash? "I run a very frugal operation," Jerry said. "The plan to win is not to waste scarce campaign funds." Schmidt vouched for the frugality, noting that Jerry picked up the phone himself when the Google executive called the campaign office. He had raised $15.5 million, Jerry said, and needed millions more for television spots that cost $100,000 each. The key voters would be the Decline to State, those not registered in either party. Since his first run for governor in 1974, the share of the electorate who registered as independents had gone from 3 to 20 percent of all voters. "They're the ones who will ultimately decide who the next governor is," Jerry said. "They are not reading journals; they're watching TV."

Democrats had controlled the state legislature for decades. But in the history of the state, only four Democrats had been elected governor. One was recalled, and two were named Brown. While the large metropolitan areas and much of the coast generally voted Democratic, big swaths of the state inland and in the Central Valley tended to support Republicans.

Addressing another young audience at GreenNet 2010, a San Francisco conference on the role of clean energy start-ups in Silicon Valley innovation, Jerry was direct in explaining his motive and vision. He wanted to be governor because

> only the executive can convene, can create the civic engagement. What kind of a California do we want? California has been in its history a place of dreams, a place of change, a place of immigration. Ultimately the future of this state is in the imagination, the creativity, the capital, that follows that in practical ways. I am optimistic. I've seen how people get depressed and frustrated when we're at the bottom of a recession. And then very quickly, we start to come back. It may take a little longer, but California will come back. It's the continuity, it's the foresight, and it's the embrace of the tremendous diversity and innovation that is California.

When Jerry became a candidate, he asked the Department of Finance for a courtesy briefing. The budget director was out of town and participated by phone, so his chief deputy, Ana Matosantos, sat in on the meeting. Jerry kept asking questions. Matosantos kept answering. They talked for hours. From then on, he would periodically call the thirty-three-year-old finance whiz, who had grown up in Puerto Rico and attended Stanford, turned off by Harvard on her first visit when students introduced themselves by citing their SAT scores. She had intended to become a lawyer, but a fellowship in Sacramento hooked her on public policy and municipal finance. Matosantos viewed the budget as a four-dimensional puzzle: math, policy, politics, and people. They all had to line up, like a Rubik's cube. Like Jerry's, her mind worked at a high rate of speed. She had a relentless determination, the kind of person who learned to fly as a teenager to overcome her fear of boarding an airplane.

Jerry called with questions for Matosantos on Easter. And on Father's Day. By then Matosantos had moved up to the top job, the youngest-ever California finance director. Jerry focused on education, the biggest chunk of the budget, and the financial relationships between the state and the counties, cities and local governments. He would need a plan that met his three clearly articulated campaign promises: No more gimmicks, no new taxes without voter approval, restore decision making to the local level wherever possible.

As the campaign progressed, the old crew returned. Actor and author Peter Coyote, who had headed the state arts council in Jerry's first term as governor, taped ads. Tom Quinn helped with strategy and insisted Jerry prepare for the debates. Quinn, who had recruited Mary Nichols to the Air Resources Board in 1975, now recruited her to play Meg Whitman in debate practice. Nichols watched videos, bought a blond wig, and stood on a box to mimic the Republican candidate's height. Like most everyone involved in the campaign, Quinn and Nichols quickly recognized that Anne Gust Brown was in charge, though the candidate sometimes ignored even her advice.

Anne had refined her role, through the experience of the attorney general race and three years of working closely with her husband. "I think a lot of the campaign stuff, it's kind of common sense," she said in an interview in the campaign's Oakland headquarters, around the corner from what had been the old We the People loft. A strategic thinker, she had little difficulty applying her acumen to political campaigns. "Because, as someone who likes politics and watches it, you kind of know what can

At a Halloween rally a week before the 2010 election, the candidate makes a comment that elicts laughter from former Brownies Diana Dooley (left) and Sherry Williams (far right), who worked for him in the 1970s. (Courtesy of Sherry Williams)

resonate and not. I also know Jerry well enough to know what sorts of things he would agree to or not agree to."

While much of the campaign focused on fiscal issues, immigration again played a central role. Sixteen years earlier, Pete Wilson had ridden the anti-Mexican fervor of Prop 187 to victory over Kathleen Brown. During his second term, Californians passed a proposition outlawing bilingual education and another banning affirmative action in admissions to public universities. By 2010, those efforts had backfired. This time, reflecting a decade of demographic shifts, the question of how California treated immigrants worked in the Democrat's favor.

The number of Latinos in California, overwhelmingly Mexican, had doubled in the past two decades to about 14 million, 38 percent of the population. In Los Angeles in particular, Latinos formed the core of a resurgent labor movement that had become a powerful political force, helping elect Antonio Villaraigosa as the first Mexican American mayor of the city. In March 2010, John Pérez became the fourth Latino speaker of the California Assembly, the third to come out of the Los Angeles labor movement. Democratic activists who had gotten their start decades earlier protesting Prop 187 continued to tie Republicans to the increasingly unpopular measure, which became shorthand for "anti-Mexican." As the number of ethnic Mexicans in the state edged close to the number of whites, they became increasingly woven into the fabric of California life, as partners, colleagues, students, and neighbors. Support for anti-immigrant measures diminished even in difficult economic times.

"I cannot win the governor's race without the Latino vote," Meg Whitman said at Cal State Fresno, in the heart of the Central Valley, where the candidates made history in the first gubernatorial debate hosted by a Spanish television channel, Univision, and broadcast bilingually.

Whitman said she would have voted against Prop 187 had she lived in California (the fact that she had not registered to vote until 2002, when she was forty-six years old, also became a campaign issue). But her positions did little to win support among the more than five million eligible Latino voters. When an undocumented student asked if she supported the Dream Act, which would provide a path to citizenship for children brought into the country illegally, Whitman waffled, then said no. "She wants to kick you out of this school because you are not documented and that is wrong, morally and humanly," Jerry said, promising to support financial aid for undocumented students at state universities and colleges.

Whitman's admission that she had for nine years employed an undocumented Mexican housekeeper, whom she fired as she began to campaign for governor, amplified her image as not only anti-immigrant, but hypocritical and heartless. Jerry jumped on Whitman's hypocrisy in urging that the state pursue and prosecute employers who hired undocumented workers. "I strongly oppose state police, state sheriffs, the attorney general's office, going after undocumented people," he said. "That is not the business of the state at all."

Jerry's adherence to his father's "one world, one people, one dignity, one justice" creed influenced his actions on an issue that gained him support with another politically engaged constituency, the gay community. A June 2008 Supreme Court ruling had made California the second state, after Massachusetts, to issue same-sex marriage licenses. Thousands of couples joyfully wed, only to have their marriages thrown into limbo five months later when voters narrowly approved Proposition 8, a constitutional amendment that banned same-sex marriage. Gay marriage supporters sued, and months of litigation in state and federal courts followed. Both Governor Schwarzenegger and Attorney General Brown refused to defend Prop 8. Jerry argued that a majority vote could not deprive Californians of an inalienable constitutional right. He based his refusal to defend the law on the only precedent in California history, a landmark case close to his father's heart. In 1964, Governor Pat Brown and his friend Attorney General Tom Lynch had refused to defend Proposition 14, the initiative to overturn the state's fair housing laws, which was eventually thrown out as unconstitutional. In August 2010, in the midst of the gubernatorial contest, a federal judge ruled Prop 8 was unconstitutional. Jerry's refusal to defend it ultimately became a key reason the U.S. Supreme Court voided the initiative.

Whitman had begun airing radio ads more than a year before the election. She spent $19 million in 2009 and launched her first million-dollar television buy in early 2010, saturating the airwaves for months. Despite polls that consistently showed Whitman with a narrow lead, Jerry resisted pressure from Democrats to launch a counteroffensive. The Brown campaign husbanded its relatively limited resources to use after Labor Day, a decision widely credited to Anne's influence. By mid-September, soon after Jerry's television commercials began to air, he pulled slightly ahead. "There were a lot of pundits across the state who said we wouldn't be around if we didn't spend money," said Joe Trippi, a national media consultant who was volunteering his services. "Well, we're around and we're competitive, and a lot of that is due to Anne."

Whitman broke national records for a self-financed campaign, spending $144 million of her personal fortune. The Brown campaign raised $40 million. Three quarters of that went to television buys, and the strategy of waiting till Labor Day enabled Jerry to outspend Whitman on TV in the final month. As Election Day neared, polls showed him pulling away.

Oakland, the city that had been key to the improbable return of Jerry Brown, had the unusual honor of hosting his victory party. Jerry, for whom symbols were always important, had chosen an election night venue that held great significance, for the past, present, and future.

The Fox Theater was an exquisitely crafted 1928 masterpiece, the last of its kind to open before the Depression. The theater, which had seated almost four thousand for vaudeville shows and first-run movies, was closed in 1965. Within a decade, the Fox became so run-down that it was slated for demolition. Supporters rallied to place the theater on the National Register instead, but the landmark remained in disrepair. Homeless people camped out in the lobby beneath the colored tile dome. Squatters cooked meals that blackened the intricate Moorish patterns in the plaster ceiling. When the city bought the decaying theater in 1996, the Fox stood as a symbol of Oakland's desolation. Mayor Jerry Brown had seen the Fox as one of the catalysts that could help revitalize downtown. His friend Phil Tagami came up with a plan to restore the theater, where Tagami's parents had once gone on early dates. Jerry helped put together $90 million in public and private money. Key to the project was his arts charter school, which moved into space above the theater; its rent helped pay off the loans. In early 2009, restored to its original elegance, the Fox reopened as a twenty-eight-hundred-seat concert hall.

Like Jerry, the building was a unique melding of old and new. "The new comes out of the random," was a quote from Gregory Bateson that Jerry often repeated. "I've been thinking a lot about that," he said during the campaign. "Some people think I am a little random. But unless you open the possibilities, you rarely come up with something new."

On Tuesday, November 2, 2010, thousands crowded expectantly into the Art Deco theater, ready to party. When the results showed Jerry easily beating Whitman, Anne Gust Brown took the stage. "Here we are in this beautiful Fox Theater, that was renovated under the mayorship of my wonderful husband, Jerry Brown!" she said to cheers. She spoke for only a minute before calling onstage, and kissing, the man about to become the oldest governor ever elected in California.

"You know, I did this thirty-six years ago!" Jerry said, speaking extemporaneously as usual. (Anne tried with limited success to get him to stay on the X where the television cameras wanted him to stand.) "And I tried during the campaign never to mention the word 'experience' or tell too many old stories because after a while, people are looking for something new. But I'm a little something old. So that's why I wanted to be here at the Fox Theater, the home of the Oakland School for the Arts."

Jerry had choreographed his victory celebration with care. Standing at attention onstage were cadets from the Oakland Military Institute, now in its tenth year, sending a quarter of its graduates to the University of California. Behind them stood the chorus from the Oakland School for the Arts. "I wanted the military to represent my sense of honor, and duty, and leadership, and camaraderie, and I wanted the arts school to exemplify creativity and imagination," Jerry said. "Because all that is what California needs over the next four years. And I want everyone here tonight and throughout California to know, this is why I'm doing it. I built these schools because I want to build for the future . . . Will this help the next generation? That's going to be my watchword."

He condemned the polarization in Sacramento and in Washington, yet acknowledged the existence of real divisions that needed to be recognized and addressed. "I take as my challenge forging a common purpose, but a common purpose based not just on compromise, but on a vision of what California can be. And I see a California leading once again in renewable energy, in public education, and in openness to every kind of person, whatever their color is. We're all God's children. While I'm really into this politics thing, I still carry with me my sense of, kind of that missionary zeal to transform the world."

21

Second Chances

Fond of peppering his comments with Latin phrases and classical references, Jerry Brown began to occasionally compare himself to Cincinnatus. Laymen likely missed the analogy to the Roman dictator called
out of retirement to rescue the Republic in 439 B.C. Fewer still caught the
echo of the Order of Cincinnatus, the Depression-era group of young San
Franciscans dedicated to honest government, founded by Pat Brown.

As Jerry returned to Sacramento, the spirit of Pat Brown hovered over
the capitol, this time welcomed by his son as a lodestar rather than a
burden. In his office, Jerry hung framed posters from Pat's early campaigns,
photos of Pat meeting with John F. Kennedy, and a nine-foot marlin
caught by his mother that had been displayed on the wall of Pat's office in
the Mansion. Jerry's victory had vindicated the family, avenging after
more than four decades his father's loss to Ronald Reagan. Governor Pat
had kept track of how many more days he needed to beat Earl Warren's
ten years and nine months in office. On October 13, 2013, Jerry's staff
presented him with a cake inscribed 3,927 DAYS AND COUNTING. He had
broken the record his father coveted, adding longest-tenured California
governor to his improbable résumé.

Jerry embraced his father's vision in substance as well as sentiment.
With faith in elected officials near an all-time low, and California branded
a failed republic, Jerry set out with missionary zeal to make government
a force for good. He had undergone something of a conversion; rather
than preaching that small is beautiful, he argued that the traditional functions of government were more essential than ever to protect people in
perilous times.

In 1975, Jerry had arrived in Sacramento determined to blow up the status quo, to disrupt the comfortable, clubby world of older white male politics. In 2011, he came to mend a dysfunctional system that had brought California to the brink of financial collapse. "Those pillars that I certainly endeavored to pull down to some degree have already fallen down," he said. "Now I feel that we've got to build them up and to create structures and foundations on which we can build this ever-changing, complex, diverse world."

Both times, his goal was to restore faith in a government that alienated the people it was supposed to serve. That became a theme of the inaugural address he finished editing in the car with Tom Quinn, his first campaign manager, en route to the ceremony on January 3, 2011:

> This is a special moment as executive power passes from one governor to another, determined solely by majority vote. It is a sacred and special ritual that affirms that the people are in charge and that elected officials are given only a limited time in which to perform their appointed tasks. For me this day is also special because I get to follow in my father's footsteps once again—and 36 years after my first inauguration as governor, even follow in my own.
>
> Then—1975—it was the ending of the Vietnam War and a recession caused by the Middle East oil embargo. Now, as we gather in this restored Memorial Auditorium, dedicated to those who died in World War I, it is our soldiers fighting in Iraq and Afghanistan, and our economy caught in the undertow of a deep and prolonged recession. With so many people out of work and so many families losing their homes in foreclosure it is not surprising that voters tell us they are worried and believe that California is on the wrong track.
>
> Yet, in the face of huge budget deficits year after year and the worst credit rating among the 50 states, our two political parties can't come close to agreeing on the right path forward. They remain in their respective comfort zones, rehearsing and rehashing old political positions. Perhaps this is the reason why the public holds the state government in such low esteem. And that's a profound problem, not just for those of us who are elected, but for our whole system of self-government. Without the trust

of the people, politics degenerates into mere spectacle, and democracy declines, leaving demagoguery and cynicism to fill the void.

Jerry looked to his own past for strength. He summoned the courage of his great-grandfather and again read from the diary August Schuckman had kept on his difficult journey across the Plains in 1852. Then the governor invoked his father once more as he called for a return to the "Philosophy of Loyalty" laid out by the nineteenth-century California pioneer Josiah Royce: The needs of the community come first. "A long time ago, my father spoke to me about his philosophy of loyalty. I didn't really grasp its importance. But as I look back now, I understand how this loyalty to California was my father's philosophy as well. It drove him to build our freeways, our universities, our public schools, and our state water plan."

In his own way, Jerry, too, inspired loyalty. His inauguration drew his oldest friends and many of the original Brownies, who celebrated at a reunion the night before. Some came to stay. Marty Morgenstern, who had been director of employee relations in the first Brown administration, came out of retirement to join the cabinet as secretary of the Labor and Workforce Development Agency. Diana Dooley, hired by Morgenstern in 1975 as an assistant when she was twenty-four, had become a lawyer specializing in healthcare administration; she took over the Health and Human Services agency and worked in the building named after Gregory Bateson. Mike Picker, who got his start in the mailroom, became president of the Public Utilities Commission. Michael Kirst, a Stanford professor who chaired the state Board of Education during Jerry's first two terms, went back for a second tour. Dan Richard, who had worked as a deputy in science and energy, moved back to California to chair the High Speed Rail Authority. The Brownies found it hard to turn down a governor trying to rebuild the state in a time of crisis. Besides, Jerry had taken a chance on them decades ago when they were very young, and his faith shaped their lives.

Jerry brought to his new job political instincts refined over decades and a clearer analysis of the tactics necessary to govern effectively. He needed two distinct skill sets: an "inside game" of persuasion within the capitol to cut deals, and an "outside game" to inspire the public. "There are all these things that I've devoted my whole life to in one sense. And now I'm trying to make them work," he said, midway through his term. "Unlike when I was here [before]. I said, 'Oh boy, I can be president. I can beat this guy. Who's running for president? Ford? Carter? I can beat these guys. So let's go.' But it was kind of ridiculous. I was only thirty-eight and I had only been governor less than two years. But I'm an enthusiast. Now I find each of these things extremely fascinating; every one of these topics, I don't care what it is."

While there remained flashes of the unpredictable spontaneity and the revolutionary spirit that characterized Jerry 1.0, on the whole, the tenor of Jerry 2.0 was comparatively conventional. Jerry engaged in the political rituals he had spurned the first time around. Where he had once condemned his father for immersing him in that world since childhood, he now paid credit. "I thought I had a 'purer' view and was above politics," he said, "But here's the truth: It's like a little duck who learns to swim by following the mother duck. Obviously I was imprinted early with these skills and propensities." He courted legislators with drinks and dinners, no longer the young upstart, now often twice their age. Most key aides were subordinates who treated him with deference and worked with a discipline that had been absent the first time around when Jerry was surrounded by peers—in age, intellect, and, to some degree, ambition. "I have a group of people, many of whom were here with me last time, and they are now working I think at a higher level of knowledge and intensity and effectiveness," Jerry said.

He still preferred a conversation to a photo-op. Occasionally abrupt or socially awkward, he did not, however, radiate the disdain he had once displayed. When he unintentionally slighted people, his wife pointed out his missteps. She added money when he failed to leave a tip and chastised him when his interior monologues interfered with social niceties. He had a dog, which helped soften his image. Kathleen Brown worked in municipal finance in California for Goldman Sachs; when her brother was elected, she transferred to the company's Chicago office to avoid conflicts of interest and left her corgi with Jerry and Anne. Sutter Brown soon became the wildly popular First Dog, with his own Facebook page and Twitter account, a familiar sight in and around the capitol and the nearby loft where the Browns stayed in Sacramento. The Oakland house was still home, though Jerry held events in the old Mansion and hoped to move in once renovations were complete.

Anne Gust Brown had a small office near her husband's in the horse-shoe, the warren of offices that made up the governor's quarters in the capitol. She was an unpaid special counsel, a title she found more comfortable than first lady. "Jerry and I work closely together on any big issues," she said in an interview with a Sacramento TV station. "If he needs help on them or an extra pair of hands, I help dig into things . . . If he's off having to do something else I can move the ball forward on other projects."

Anne brought a business perspective, and the structure Jerry needed. "I'd say he thinks like more of a long-term visionary and I'm more 'Let's make sure every train is running on time,'" Anne said. Others turned to her for help when Jerry became too deeply immersed or sidetracked. "We do have to corral him sometimes because he's a man who is really amazing in how much he thinks about things, and topics going back to prehistoric times to now, he reads almost anything you can imagine, very complex things, he's just always exploring, new ideas and new ways. And a lot of times we have to sort of manage him to, what it is we have to decide today. And I can be pretty good at that. Not perfect."

Where Jerry was attracted to communal life in part because he worked through issues by verbal interactions, Anne needed solitude to think through problems. She walked the Oakland Hills or went for runs. Once in a while she persuaded Jerry to get away. His first summer as governor, they went hiking in Yosemite. When they did travel, he liked to stay with friends—not only because he was frugal, but because he preferred to see places through the eyes of locals rather than as an ordinary tourist.

"I have a husband who thinks that his job is like a vacation," Anne said. "He's like, 'What do you mean get away from work? This is like a vacation.' And I said, 'No, honey, really that is so not true and there's not a person on the planet who believes that other than you.' He loves what he does. So to come home and talk about it incessantly is just nirvana for him. I on the other hand am not in that camp. I've actually had times when I've said to him, 'Jerry, stop now, shut up, really, do not talk about this. We're going to read books.' . . . He lives this twenty-four seven. And loves it."

Jerry returned to govern 38 million Californians, 50 percent more than had lived in the state his first time around. California was emerging from the third and most serious recession in two decades. The recent loss of a million jobs had heightened the disparity between rich and poor. Three decades earlier, the top 1 percent in the state earned about 10 percent of the income. In 2011, the top 1 percent earned 22 percent, or $2 trillion. The shift had come at the expense of the middle class. "We're not in a caste system yet," Jerry said, "but we're forming our own little version as it gets harder and harder for people without previous positioning to rise in our society."

The concentration of wealth contributed to the extreme volatility of state finances: The top 1 percent paid more than 60 percent of the state's income tax, much of which was dependent on capital gains. Jerry confronted a $26.6 billion deficit, larger than the entire state budget had been when he became governor the first time. The need to stabilize state finances became the overwhelming focus of his first few years. Options were limited, in part because big chunks of the $120 billion budget were protected by dozens of initiatives that set aside money for specific programs, without adding new revenue. "You have a chess game of government with fewer and fewer moves," Jerry said.

The yawning gap between revenues and expenditures enabled Jerry to shepherd through deep cuts that would have otherwise been politically unthinkable. In a move important both symbolically and practically, his first budget abolished local redevelopment agencies (RDAs), which had grown from a small program to combat urban renewal into a major drain on state finance. In areas that cities designated as blighted, the RDA could keep any new property tax revenue raised from that area—in effect, siphoning off tax dollars that would have otherwise been distributed to local schools and counties. RDAs had exploded after Prop 13 capped the property tax rate at 1 percent; some cities designated entire downtowns as blighted. By 2008, one out of every eight property tax dollars went to one of about four hundred RDAs across the state. Jerry had used redevelopment money extensively in Oakland, including the restoration of the Fox Theater; now he argued the program was a drain the state could no longer afford. His ability to prevail in eliminating the popular local program spoke to the dire financial times and the relative leadership vacuum.

Jerry's indispensable partner in the multidimensional budget puzzle was Ana Matosantos, the young Schwarzenegger administration finance director who had briefed Jerry two years earlier. Like many of Jerry's cabinet members, she found out that she had been reappointed to her old job from someone else. Jerry was as uncomfortable being thanked as he was thanking others. Matosantos jumped at the chance to join the revolution, much as an earlier generation had done in 1975. She loved matching wits with Jerry and watching his mind work on issues big and small. When the budget leaked out, forcing the administration to hold the press conference a day early, Matosantos was baffled by the governor's insistence in the middle of last-minute preparation that he needed a showy chart. Afterward he explained: The goal was to avoid news stories that began "In a hastily called press conference . . ."

Never one to waste a crisis, Jerry used the budget to significantly reshape the relationship of state government to the counties, cities, and school districts. In addition to dissolving the redevelopment agencies, his plan to stabilize state finances relied on a shift with the deceptively nondescript term "realignment."

More than three decades later, almost all major fiscal policies in California could be traced back to the realignment of services after Proposition 13, the seismic shift that occurred while a young Governor Jerry Brown was running for reelection, in between two campaigns for president. Prop 13 mandated that the state allocate property taxes collected at the local level. Under the omnibus law adopted to comply with that requirement, the state assumed a greater share of funding social services and health programs formerly the purview of local governments, which no longer had the ability to set their own tax rates. The law froze the system in time, apportioning funds based on what counties had spent on services before Prop 13; in effect, it institutionalized existing inequalities.

For better or worse, financial crises often spurred sweeping change that would have otherwise been difficult to achieve. When Pete Wilson became governor in 1991 and faced a huge deficit, part of his solution was to transfer certain health and mental health programs back to the counties. That helped soften a tax increase—money dedicated to fund those programs—and enabled the state to plug a $2 billion hole. Counties gained stable funding and greater flexibility; the state developed formulas that corrected some of the inequities and shifted a greater portion of ongoing costs to the counties. That was Realignment One.

State money generally came with mandates. Just as states often balked at federal mandates, the fifty-eight far-flung, disparate counties in California often protested that one-size-fits-all directives from Sacramento were inefficient and impractical and robbed them of the ability to craft programs that best met their constituents' needs. Jerry had campaigned on the promise to move as much decision making as possible to the local level. He argued those closest to problems could devise the most effective solutions. His experience in Oakland and with Catholic doctrine deepened the sense of personal responsibility that he had grown up with. He preached the importance of subsidiarity, a Catholic principle essential to achieving the common good. Starting with the basic unit of the family and moving up through neighborhood, school, city, and state, decisions should be made at the lowest level possible and the highest level necessary. Subsidiarity required a balance, imposing state oversight on local decision making.

In Oakland, Jerry had been confronted daily with the dysfunctional criminal justice system, caused in part by laws he had once championed. Prison spending, 3 percent of the budget when he left office, was 10 percent when he returned. More dollars were spent on prisons than on higher education. For moral, economic, and legal reasons, the prison system became a logical place to begin applying the principle of subsidiarity.

California's penal system began with its most notorious prison, San Quentin, opened in 1854 with cells built by inmates who had been housed on a floating prison ship anchored nearby. James "Bluebeard" Watson, who killed seven of his twenty-two wives, was buried in the San Quentin cemetery. Woody Allen filmed scenes at San Quentin for *Take the Money and Run*. Charles Manson spent much of his prison time in the Q. Johnny Cash played his "At San Quentin" concert in the prison yard. For many years, the whole prison system was San Quentin and Folsom, which opened in 1880 and also was made famous by Cash.

For several decades after its creation in 1944, the Department of Corrections grew modestly. A total of twelve prisons housed about thirty thousand inmates. With the exception of the Depression years, the number of prisoners relative to the overall population declined as the state grew—until the first governorship of Jerry Brown. Determinate sentencing encouraged the legislature to create new crimes and impose longer sentences, actions Jerry supported. He boasted in 1982 that 19,000 people would go to prison that year—more than double the number when he took office. New crimes and harsher sentences proliferated even faster during the Deukmejian administration, and prison population tripled. A $94 million prison expansion plan Jerry had pushed through ballooned to

$3 billion under his successor. The era of "tough on crime" legislation, Three Strikes, and the emphasis on punishment, not rehabilitation, ushered in the cycle of high recidivism that Jerry discovered many years later on the streets of Oakland.

Even with almost triple the number of prisons, conditions deteriorated rapidly in California's thirty-four facilities. Double bunking became common, then three prisoners were put in cells designed for one. Health-care was so inadequate that inmates were dying at the rate of one a week. A series of lawsuits forced the state to forfeit unprecedented control: A special federal master was put in charge of mental health programs, and a federal judge took over the healthcare system. In 2006, the prison population peaked at 173,000. In a fight that went up to the U.S. Supreme Court, judges ordered California to limit the number of inmates to 137.5 percent of the capacity of the prisons. When Jerry took office, that translated to thirty thousand fewer prisoners.

In his first budget, Jerry proposed what became known as Realignment Two: California shifted responsibility for most lower-level felons to the county jails and probation departments. The goals were to save money, comply with court orders, and reduce recidivism rates. The theory was that counties could make more intelligent, informed decisions about what combination of treatment and punishment would most likely rehabilitate offenders and keep them from committing further crimes. Instead of being placed on parole, low-level felons released from prison would be supervised by local probation officers, who would determine sanctions for any violations. Only those charged with serious crimes would be returned to state prison. In addition, offenders convicted of nonviolent crimes with no record of serious or sexual crimes would serve time in county jail instead of state prison.

The state prison population dropped dramatically after realignment, but not enough to comply with the court orders. As popular opinion shifted away from the punitive sentiment of the "get tough" years, Jerry campaigned for two propositions that further eased prison overcrowding. The first reduced penalties for many nonviolent drug and property crimes to misdemeanors. The second restored greater discretion in sentencing to judges and parole boards and allowed inmates to accumulate credits that could speed up their release. "This is a very interesting topic, a very important topic, that touches safety, fear, religion, forgiveness, redemption, the whole definition of who we are as a civilization," Jerry said as he campaigned for the second proposition.

Both passed, as did a softening of the Three Strikes law. By the end of 2015, the state's incarceration rate had fallen 30 percent from its peak, to the lowest level since the early 1990s. "I've been able to create problems that I then later was able to solve," Jerry said. "That's a very good feeling." Or, as he said in his typical candid fashion at a San Diego forum to encourage businesses to hire ex-felons: "I helped screw things up, but I helped unscrew things."

Studies in the years after realignment suggested that the sweeping changes had little if any immediate impact on overall crime rates in California, which continued at historic lows. The impact on recidivism was murkier and would take longer to unravel, as counties adjusted to new responsibilities. Initial studies suggested counties that placed more emphasis on programs geared to help ex-felons reenter society had significantly lower rearrest and conviction rates.

A young Jerry Brown had complained about money wasted on prison mental health programs where inmates took part in "group gab sessions about what your mother did or didn't do to you." He had praised tough sentencing laws as "based not on sociology or Freudian theory but on simple justice." An older Jerry Brown invoked his father's core view of government and its power to be a force for good. "We always were told to pray for the souls in purgatory," he said at a Black Legislative Caucus event on Martin Luther King Jr. Day in 2017, echoing one of his father's favorite sentiments. "My father would think about, who's the most forgotten soul in California? Who is that person? I want to make sure I'm there to help. And I can tell you that many of the people behind bars today are forgotten."

Jerry spent hours reviewing and debating applications for clemency and commutations. He granted a record number of pardons, which restored rights to ex-felons. As he neared the end of his tenure, Jerry had issued 1,115 pardons and 51 commutations since taking office again in 2011, far more than any other governor in modern times. As governor the first time around, he issued 404 pardons and one commutation. "We all do bad things. A little humility in the face of people who have done bad things is called for," he said. "People who commit crimes can change. Some people change right away, some people don't change for five years. Some people, it takes them forty years."

Jerry's interest in correcting his own youthful missteps that affected the criminal justice system extended to judicial appointments. He had a second chance to reshape a powerful institution that had suffered when his attempts the first time backfired: the California Supreme Court.

"I'm the only governor who appointed judges that were unelected," he said at his fiftieth Yale Law School reunion. He had chosen them, he said, because as a clerk to Justice Mathew Tobriner, Jerry found the Supreme Court dull, not "yeasty" enough, one of his favorite words. "There was too much inertia. I wanted a little more dynamism. I thought, at least in 1964 when I was there, that there should have been more activism. So I looked for some judges who would shake thing up a bit." But when Rose Bird, Joe Grodin, and Cruz Reynoso were thrown off the court, their replacements ushered in decades of conservative decisions. "So I guess that says that you do have to maintain a certain range. And if you get outside that range in a system that has elections, then you may create the exact opposite of where you were going."

Three vacancies during Jerry's first term gave him an opportunity to rebuild the state's highest court a second time. He chose a group diverse in their ethnicity if not their pedigree; all three were young Yale Law School graduates, the first two having already established reputations as legal intellectuals—Goodwin Liu, Mariano Florentino Cuellar, and Leondra Kruger. Jerry urged his appointees to read the work of Grant Gilmore, who argued that judges should revise statutes in accordance with historic developments. Jerry wanted the court to return to its preeminent position during the Earl Warren and Pat Brown years, when pioneering decisions on issues such as abortion rights and free speech at shopping malls granted Californians protections rooted in the state constitution and the political culture of the West.

California's oldest governor also had a second chance to influence the state's fiscal policy through a popular referendum. His effort to avert Proposition 13 during his first term by supporting an alternative tax cut proposition had come only as a last-minute attempt to defeat the Jarvis measure—too little, too late. Three decades later, ballot box budgeting had become common, along with the practice of building up large funds to spend on initiative campaigns.

As he wrestled to balance state finances, Jerry had a major advantage over his predecessors: The year he was elected, voters approved a proposition that allowed the legislature to pass budgets with a simple majority, undoing the two-thirds requirement that had been written into the 1879 constitution. Polls showed that frustration with Sacramento gridlock had become so extreme that even Republicans supported the change, although it meant their party would lose much of its leverage, since Democrats could easily muster a majority vote.

Tax increases still required a two-thirds majority; that translated to at least four Republican votes in the 2011 legislature. Jerry appealed for bipartisan support to extend temporary taxes by placing a proposal on the November 2011 ballot. When that failed, he was forced to go the petition route instead. Proposition 30 on the November 2012 ballot would raise the sales tax a quarter of a cent and set higher income tax rates for the wealthiest residents in order to restore funds to school districts, public colleges, and universities. California, the state that had launched tax cut fever, would vote on a tax increase. Jerry rejected efforts to craft solutions that would avoid a popular vote. He believed that the consent of the governed was critical.

Back on the campaign trail, Jerry relied again on his own instincts. He enlisted support from business groups, coordinated with labor allies, and crisscrossed the state speaking on college campuses. Jerry made a clear, stark case to the audience that would be most affected: Either these new taxes pass, or there will be another $600 million in cuts to education. *Tertium non datum.* There is no third way. To balance the budget and satisfy the bond market, the budget had "trigger cuts" that would by law go into effect if Proposition 30 failed. He kept close tabs on a student voter registration drive that took advantage of a new online option. More than six hundred thousand voters signed up online, about a third of them under twenty-five.

"Proposition 30 is an opportunity for the people themselves not only to fix California, but to send a message to the rest of the country that we as a people can invest together in our schools, in our community colleges, and in the great University of California," Jerry said at a rally on the UCLA campus. "A lot is riding on this election. A lot for you as students, but also for the people of California."

A lot for his own political future as well. He portrayed the campaign as the second act of an Aristotelian-structured drama, built around the suspense of a hero's attempts to extricate himself from danger. He framed the decision as a moral, economic, and political choice, another step in the return to the Philosophy of Loyalty of Josiah Royce, a willingness to rise above self-interest for the greater good. He quoted, by chapter and verse, the Gospel of Luke: Of those to whom much is given, much is required. In an era of profound inequality, only individuals making more than $250,000 and couples earning more than $500,000 would pay more income tax.

While Jerry made the case around the state, labor unions, especially those representing teachers, mobilized members to spread the message and worked with the campaign to build an infrastructure in every community. Still, Anne Gust Brown worried. Compared to a traditional election, polling in an initiative campaign was notoriously unreliable. External polls showed support for Prop 30 was wobbly at best. Anne used multiple tracking polls, online as well as by phone, as many as five at once. In the end, Prop 30 passed easily, with 55 percent of the vote. Although the taxes were temporary, they were easily extended by a second referendum four years later.

The vote represented an inflection point in California. For decades, harkening back to Prop 13, an older, white electorate had been unwilling to pay for state services that increasingly benefited a growing young Latino and Asian population. Prop 30 reflected both an increased commitment to the Party of California and a shift in the electorate. Although whites still voted at disproportionately higher rates, the Latino share of the vote had jumped from 6.6 percent in 1980 to 23.5 percent in 2012. The electorate was beginning to match more closely the people who depended on public schools, colleges, health care, and social services.

"You helped make that happen, as did so many others in colleges and schools across the state," Jerry told political science majors in a graduation speech at Cal, referring to the passage of Prop 30. "And, lo and behold, voter surveys indicate that many more people in California feel good about the direction of their state. For an important moment, democracy came alive. I am not saying that the big issues are going to be settled easily, that greenhouse gases will soon be curbed or that inequality will be quickly reversed. But I do affirm, based on my experience, that people can exercise power wherever they are in society. Certainly not on every occasion, but at crucial moments, imaginative and bold people make a difference."

22

Fiat Lux Redux

Amid thousands of acres of fields, vineyards, and wetlands, the first new research university in the United States since the millennium arose in a region best known for poverty and sweet potatoes. The University of California, Merced, deep in the Central Valley between Modesto and Fresno, became both harbinger and symbol of changing times.

During the Great Recession, the city of Merced had made national headlines as a foreclosure capital of the United States. Homes lost half their value. Unemployment, a perennial problem in the largely agricultural area, was among the highest in the state. The recession and concomitant budget cuts complicated construction of the first University of California campus built since Pat Brown was governor. Planned over the course of twenty years and four gubernatorial administrations, the school was designed to bring higher education to a region badly in need. The Central Valley had both the lowest median income in the state and the greatest degree of income inequality.

When the first freshman class entered UC Merced, only the library and one housing complex were open. Four years later, the Class of 2009 made history: The first graduates persuaded First Lady Michelle Obama to deliver her first commencement speech on their campus. They had wooed her with hundreds of letters, valentines, and videos that stressed their commitment to public service, a message she found so inspiring she agreed almost at once. Attorney General Jerry Brown was in the crowd of twelve thousand that gathered on the field in hundred-degree heat on Commencement Day. Remember where you came from, Michelle Obama told the graduates. Like most of them, she said, she, too, had been the first in her family to earn a college degree. "You must bend down and let someone stand on your shoulders so they can see a better future," she said. "Make your legacy a lasting one. Dream big."

The firsts continued. The university anchored an economic boom; unemployment in Merced dipped to 8.5 percent, the lowest level since the 1980s. The 750 apartment units under construction nearby would help house the ten thousand students expected by 2020, when UC Merced would double in size. A Laotian immigrant who had arrived in the Central Valley as a toddler became the school's police chief, the first person of Hmong descent to lead a university safety agency. A Mexican American who had been brought to Merced as a five-year-old was awarded a doctorate in biology, the first undocumented immigrant in the Valley to earn a PhD.

For high school students in Central Valley communities where the primary option had historically been community college, a university education became an accessible aspiration, if not yet a tradition. Siblings of the first graduates enrolled at UC Merced. The school's young alumni, far from the wealthiest cohort, donated to their alma mater at higher rates than their counterparts at the legacy campuses. During the first decade that UC Merced was open, applications to all University of California schools from Central Valley students doubled, and admissions jumped 78 percent.

UC Merced drew students in about equal thirds from the Central Valley, Southern, and Northern California. Some were startled to see cows grazing nearby. Others came to hike the Sierra foothills and take part in programs at Yosemite, less than two hours away. About 60 percent came from low-income families, 70 percent from families in which neither parent had graduated from college. Although those numbers were higher than at other campuses, they reflected trends across a university system in transition. More than half the students at UC Merced were Latino; about 20 percent were Asian. The campus looked a lot like the rest of California. Its success or failure would go a long way toward shaping the future of the state.

Around the time Jerry was reelected in 2014, California passed a demographic milestone as significant as the one Pat Brown had celebrated in 1963 when the Golden State became the nation's most populous: Latinos passed Anglos to became the largest ethnic group in the state.

The approximately 15 million Latinos in California were predominantly ethnic Mexicans. Compared with statewide averages, they were significantly younger, lived in larger, extended families, and had more children. Latinos in California earned less, were more likely to work in blue-collar jobs, and were less likely to own their homes. In 2015, more than one fourth of the Latinos in California lived in poverty, twice the rate among whites.

As California's economy rebounded, the state restored some of the earlier draconian cuts to social services. But even as the state's wealth climbed, the gap between rich and poor remained cavernous. California had the most of everything, including poverty. In 2016, one in five Californians lived below the poverty line, adjusted for the higher cost of living in the Golden State. Another one in five lived perilously close to it.

Jerry favored policies that directed money to people rather than providers. The state adopted an earned income tax credit for the poorest families. California aggressively expanded its Medi-Cal program when the Affordable Care Act went into effect, reducing the percentage of residents without health insurance from almost 20 percent to a historic low of under 7 percent. By some measures, the combined social safety net kept more than 8 percent of Californians out of poverty.

California became the first state to phase in a $15-an-hour minimum wage. Jerry called the modest increase "economic justice," though he preferred to dwell on the second half of that equation. "Economics is about dollars and cents. It's very mechanical. It's rather heartless. Justice is about giving people their due. Those aren't the same things," he said as he signed the bill to raise the minimum wage. Justice "derives from morality, from fraternity, from the Bible, from prophetic traditions, and everything that gives meaning to our lives." He acknowledged both the import and the insignificance of the new law, at a time when so many struggled. "It's about creating a little, *tiny* balance, in a system that every day becomes more unbalanced."

In the long run, efforts to bridge that inequality would depend to a large extent on education. Among Californians with a college degree, the poverty rate was 8.2 percent; for those without a high school diploma, it was 35.5 percent. Put another way, workers with a bachelor's degree earned about 70 percent more than those with a high school diploma. Poverty rates were highest among the largest, least well-educated group of young adults, Latinos.

The disparity was rooted in California's public schools, which had never regained their former luster after Prop 13. More than half the students were Latino. They scored significantly lower on standardized tests than the state averages, which were low to begin with. The percentages of Latinos graduating from high school and college had been increasing, but still lagged far behind those of whites and Asians. In 2017, only 12 percent of Latinos over the age of twenty-five had a bachelor's degree. African Americans were twice as likely to have degrees, whites and Asians four times as likely. Latino students who pursued higher education were most likely to enroll in community college and least likely to be eligible for admission to the University of California. While the vast majority of high school graduates attended some college, studies suggested fewer than a third would ever earn a bachelor's degree under the current system, relegating most to lower-paying jobs and leaving California in need of more than a million college graduates.

In an effort to improve the odds and break the cycle, Jerry initiated the first significant overhaul of school funding in four decades. The change grew out of a paper co-written by Stanford professor Michael Kirst, who had advised Jerry on education issues since 1974. They met when Kirst was invited to a brainstorming retreat at a Los Angeles convent to help the gubernatorial candidate formulate positions. When Jerry was elected, he appointed Kirst to chair the state Board of Education. Jerry had not focused much on education his first time around. That changed after Oakland. He remained closely involved in the two charter schools he founded. Based on his own experience, his Jesuit education, and the influence of scholars like Ivan Illich and Paul Goodman, Jerry formed strong opinions that ran counter to the prevailing emphasis on standardized tests. As attorney general, he protested a U.S. Education Department requirement to link teacher pay to test scores: "There are so many unknowns about what produces educational success that a little humility would be in order."

As an example of learning that could not be captured on standardized tests, Jerry occasionally cited one of his high school English assignments: Write your impression of a leaf. "Boy, did I have trouble with that," he told a teachers' convention almost six decades later. "After I wrote the damn essay I realized, I didn't even have an impression of a green leaf. I'd never thought about green leaves. And now for the rest of my life, every time I pass a tree I think of that exam. What is my impression? Do I have one? Do I need to develop a new aspect of my character or my sensibility? So, that's a good teacher. And that's a good test."

When Jerry appointed Kirst to chair the state Board of Education again in 2011, his mandate was to deemphasize standardized tests, develop alternate measures to evaluate schools, and help reshape the way the state funded primary and secondary education. Kirst's 2008 paper, which proposed an education funding formula weighted to drive more dollars to districts with students who needed the most help, formed the basis of a radical change.

Like so many parts of the budget, the tangled roots of education financing went back to Prop 13. In the wake of the tax cut measure, the state had taken over allocating funds to more than a thousand school districts. The formulas grew progressively more complex as the state apportioned aid based on an increasing number of categories, each tied to a specific program or mandate. Each time a constituency felt its needs were ignored, it lobbied for a new categorical aid. The regulations took up hundreds of pages. More than a third of the total aid was earmarked for specific purposes.

The idea behind what became the Local Control Funding Formula was basic: Money should be allocated in accordance with students' needs. The execution was complex and controversial. The new formula adopted in 2013 gave districts flexibility to determine priorities by abolishing almost all the categorical aid requirements. Each district received a base amount per pupil; those with higher percentages of low-income students, English learners, or foster children received an additional increment per student. Districts with high concentrations of students in those categories received more. In the initial years, about one third of the students were low-income and one quarter were English language learners. In 2016, that translated into 1.3 million students who entered school speaking sixty-five languages, the overwhelming majority Spanish.

Jerry saw the new formula as integral to his quest for subsidiarity and dismissed concerns that relaxing specific mandates might weaken education for students who most needed help. "Now, local districts might screw up. I understand that," he said at a think tank gala in Los

Angeles. "But if the parent screwed up things, and if the principal's no good, if the principal can't lead, if the superintendent isn't very good, if the local school board isn't so good, what makes you think that the legislature can fix it? Think about that. If the culture is such that we're not stressing discipline and learning and curiosity and all the things we have to do to train our people, it's not going to happen. So I do think we have to set goals, we have to have accountability, but we have to respect the fact that those closest to the problem are the ones most capable of dealing with it."

One of the goals was to provide more equal access to the University of California. The gaps had shrunk consistently over the past decade. Yet of all the Latino students in the high school class of 2015, only 8.5 percent had the requisite grades and coursework to apply to the university, compared with 13.9 percent of all students. In big swaths of the state like the Central Valley, with high concentrations of English language learners and poverty, the disparities were greater. Students from socioeconomically disadvantaged homes were less than half as likely to be eligible to apply.

Even after years of budget cuts and turmoil that had hurt its reputation and reach, the university continued to be a primary route to upward mobility. With more than a million UC alumni in California, a big chunk of the population had a direct or indirect tie to the university. By 2015, more than 40 percent of UC undergraduates were the first in their family to attend college. About the same share came from families with incomes of less than $50,000. Within five years of graduating, those students earned more than their parents' combined income. The university was not just "the engine of growth," Jerry said. "It's also the foundation of citizenship in our community. So I can't think of anything much more important than a vibrant, accessible university system."

There were those who would never forgive Jerry Brown for how he had treated the university the first time around, not because of his disrespect or challenge to the entrenched bureaucracy but because his lack of support had inflicted real, lasting harm—at a time when the state was flush with money. Much antipathy lingered. (When Jerry had sought to place his gubernatorial papers from the 1970s in the Bancroft Library at Berkeley, which housed the Pat Brown papers, the library declined to provide funds to accession the collection.) Jerry recalled what then university president David Saxon had said during an argument in the 1970s: The university was here before you arrived, and we'll be here after you're gone. The governor tried, this time, to be more diplomatic, cognizant that Saxon's words had proved true. "Before when I used to go to the Regents, I'd go armed and I was attacking. But it's totally marginal, you can't influence," he said. "You've got to be more subtle, you need more allies. You need a long-term game plan. So I have a longer term game plan than I had thirty years ago, even though I've got less time because I'm seventy-four, I'm not thirty-six."

Jerry acknowledged his long, complicated history with the institution, memorialized in his infamous suggestion decades earlier that the faculty should accept a lesser raise and make up the difference in psychic income. "I know the university never lived that down," he said at a January 2013 Regents meeting. "I don't make those statements anymore. That left a scar in my relationship with many professors. So today, this is a generous spirit. An opening. A willingness to work together."

This time, the state struggled with deficits, not surpluses. After years of eroding support, by 2010 the state paid less than half the cost of educating undergraduates at the university—compared with 78 percent two decades earlier. The year Jerry took office, revenue from student tuition for the first time surpassed state aid.

During financial crises, the university was an easy target for Sacramento. Unlike most state-funded services, it had the ability to raise money from other sources. The campuses could shift further toward independently funded research. The Regents could raise tuition and admit more out-of-state students, who paid a premium. During and after the Great Recession, the university did all of that. University officials argued they had little choice. The university had lost $900 million during the two worst years of the Great Recession, almost a third of its annual state appropriation.

The constitutional independence of the university stoked a vicious cycle. Because the Regents could make financial and educational decisions without approval from the governor or the legislature, Sacramento felt less invested. The less invested, the less support, the more the university turned to outside sources, the less it cared what state officials thought, the greater the frustration on both sides. Many still remembered when university fees were a nominal amount, not even called tuition. They felt betrayed by the big jump. Yet even with tuition of more than $12,000 a year, the schools had no trouble attracting students. In fact, as more high school seniors qualified for admission, demand continued to far outstrip the available spots.

The 1960 Master Plan had been built around the promise of access and quality. Financial pressures had reduced access, especially for California students seeking admission to the more competitive campuses. At Jerry's alma mater, Cal, one third of the freshmen who entered in 2014 were from out of state—eighteen hundred places that were denied to Californians. Jerry's battle with the Regents came down to this: He argued they had sufficient funds to restore and even expand access for Californians without compromising quality—a term he questioned, though he failed to offer his own definition.

The governor did not, as some expected and others urged, take on a badly needed update of the fifty-year-old Master Plan, which had long outlived its subtitle: "1960–1975." Unlike Jerry's clearly articulated plans and rationale for funding public schools or realigning criminal justice services, his vision for the state's higher education systems remained somewhat nebulous. While he had backed off from the idea of "psychic income," he still believed that teaching at a UC was a "calling," not merely a well-paid job. He valued a liberal arts education that exposed students to a broad array of knowledge and functioned as a "foundation of citizenship." He lamented that students did not read T. S. Eliot. He still frequently consulted the work of Sheldon Wolin and Carl Schorske, as well as that of intellectuals he admired who had functioned largely outside the academy, including Illich and Gregory Bateson. As he had through a variety of venues, from the seminary to the Zen center to the Oakland Table, Jerry sought places to nurture a spirit of collective inquiry. He thought the University of California should play that role for a new generation of Californians.

"We're dealing not just with UC," he said to the Regents. "We're dealing with California, we're dealing with America, we're dealing with the West. How are we going to make it as us old white guys age?"

Much of his effort to spark change focused on the university's financial decisions. At a Regents meeting the week after the passage of Proposition 30 stabilized state finances, Jerry was polite, but direct: "Let's get real. I'm proposing five percent more in your budget. You're proposing eleven point six. How do you make up the gap?" He impressed upon them the political reality. "I don't have a Nobel Prize but I know the political climate of California as well as anybody else . . . the five percent we're going to give you is pretty much what you're going to get . . . I'm trying to say this as diplomatically and as warmly and fuzzily as I can."

The technological revolution imposed urgency to find new paradigms, he warned, or the schools would go the way of the post office, struggling to survive. He told the Regents about walking through newsrooms of the once powerful California newspaper empires as he lobbied for Prop 30. There were rows and rows of empty desks.

Over the next year, he attended committee meetings and board sessions, and spent hours talking with faculty and administrators. He asked questions: When did a six-year graduation rate become the norm, and why? Is it financial pressure, or a social norm, or the attitude of the university? Why did graduation rates at different campuses vary widely? He asked them to reevaluate teaching loads and research and ratios between undergraduate and graduate students. He voted against salary packages for new chancellors. He pressed for experimentation with online classes to expand the reach.

"How do we maintain, enhance, this wonderful institution called the University of California?" he asked at a Regents meeting. "I'm a person who's been around a long time, I care about this university. I love learning. I love research. But I'm a realist. And we've got to figure out how to make it work. Together. I want to understand better how you distribute the costs. Let's unpack the various costs and let's look at what they are.

When UC president Janet Napolitano flatly declared at the end of 2014 that without additional state aid, they would need to raise tuition, Jerry forced a showdown. He refused to support a tuition increase and countered with the creation of the "Committee of Two"—he and Napolitano would examine all facets of the university's spending practices to come up with new ideas. The result was a four-year pact, consistent with the principle of subsidiarity, that included a tuition freeze, increased state funding of 4 to 5 percent per year, and broad discretion in how the university spent that money. When the legislature subsequently tried to tie funds to specific programs, Jerry vetoed the earmarks. He rejected enrollment quotas and instead required the university to submit annual reports on various metrics, including transfers from community colleges, four- and six-year graduation rates, low-income students as a percentage of the population, and spending per degree granted. Both UC and CSU also agreed to use part of their state funds to develop online classes.

By the fall of 2015, the university's 248,000 students at ten campuses included more California undergraduates than ever, the single largest increase since the GI Bill. For the first time in a decade, each campus enrolled more Californians than before the Great Recession, when schools turned to out-of-state students for revenue. In addition to state and federal aid, the university used a portion of tuition revenue and fees to provide aid to low-income students. Almost 60 percent of the undergraduates paid no tuition, and another 15 percent had partial waivers.

In 2015 and 2016 analyses that assessed which top colleges in the United States played the greatest role in economic upward mobility by offering affordable education to poor and middle-class students, the top five spots were all UC campuses.

In the fall of 2017, 45 percent of the freshman class were the first generation in their family to attend college. UC launched a "First Gen" campaign on social media and on campuses. The first week of classes, more than eight hundred faculty who had once been in the same position wore FIRST-GEN T-shirts and buttons. They worked to educate colleagues as well, to reframe long-held, outdated assumptions about what successful students looked like and how they acted in class.

"This is a very powerful state and this is a very powerful university," Jerry told the Regents. "We have to lead. I like that idea. We want to lead. I'm not saying exactly how to do that. I'm telling you I am engaged in this challenge. With you. Not against you. Let's move carefully, let's look at all the collective wisdom here, and through this wonderful process, let's make the best decisions we can possibly make. And I pledge that my mind is open. I believe that if you know where you're going, you're already dead. So I confess: I don't know where I'm going. But I know I'm going to get there."

23

Past as Prologue

The task of introducing the nation's oldest governor as he took office for an unprecedented fourth term fell to the person who knew him best, first lady Anne Gust Brown. She had grown comfortable with her role, if not the title, much as decades earlier the naturally reserved Bernice Brown had developed a public persona that matched her elegance. Anne, the first attorney in the role, admired the grace with which Bernice had applied her formidable intelligence to raising a family and supporting her husband's career.

At Jerry's 2011 inauguration, bright lights shining in her eyes, Anne had said little in her introduction beyond noting the dignitaries in the audience she could not see. During the ensuing years, she had been the governor's indispensable partner, key to the successes, failures, and ongoing struggles. On January 5, 2015, she took the microphone with assurance, her opening as memorable as it was spontaneous, delivered from notes jotted down that morning:

> How to introduce Jerry Brown? He's obviously someone known to all of you, and he's been in the public eye forty years. I guess I can only say, what does he mean to me? When I first met Jerry Brown, the thing that struck me immediately was his mind. Oh my god, this mind that runs at a hundred miles per hour! It is restless. It's seeking. It's probing. It's creative. And frankly, for all of us who work with him, it's exhausting. But it is so stimulating, that mind of his. What many of you may not know as well is his heart and his soul, which I've come to know so well over

these years. And that I would say is very firmly grounded in tradition, and principle, and in the past.

She spoke of his recent passion for tracing family roots, an effort to connect his own past, present, and future. "I think that Jerry more than anyone looks to the past for guidance, to his ancestors," she said. "For California, especially in this kind of place, this combination makes him a perfect governor. He's someone we know will enthusiastically and creatively forge a new and bold future for us. Yet he will do so grounded enough in wisdom of the past that we won't drive off a cliff."

Taking his oath in the Assembly chamber, Jerry thought back to January 5, 1959, the day he first entered the ornate room. In cassock and collar, seated next to his eighty-one-year-old grandmother, Ida Schuckman Brown, Jerry had felt out of place, suddenly transported from the seclusion of the Jesuit seminary. "To me, the boisterous crowd, the applause, the worldliness of it all was jarring," he said in his inaugural address. "That was fifty-six years ago, yet the issues that my father raised at his inauguration bear eerie resemblance to those we still grapple with today." He ticked them off: discrimination, quality education, air pollution, water resources, economic development, overcrowded prisons.

In an era when term limits reinforced politicians' short-term focus on the next election, Jerry fixed his gaze on a far-off horizon. In part that was age, in part his nature, in part nurture. From his father, he had absorbed the imperative to think big. Each man in his own way looked beyond the relentlessness of those chronic conditions and took on challenges others avoided as too risky. Pat Brown had been determined to provide water, schools, and freeways for millions of people who would arrive long after he was gone. Jerry focused on how to prepare a different generation of Californians to succeed in an uncertain future, and how California might lead the way to make sure the world had any future at all.

"I see California as both a trendsetter but also as the state that deals and grapples with the big issues," he told a group of student journalists. "And the big issues are inequality, climate change, and promoting and handling the innovation that both adds to our quality of life, but also undermines our sense of our traditional identity. That puts us in kind of a hothouse of experimentation, and I think California has to both look to its past and also pave the way for its future."

Though he paid the bureaucracy more respect in his second tour as governor, he had little patience for bureaucrats and still not much interest in nuts and bolts. "There is a certain amount of just taking in the laundry," he said, as he focused on stabilizing state finances. "And a certain amount of innovation. I would say I am doing a lot of the laundry here, but I don't think I have in any way given up on the vision of doing big things."

Some big ideas came in response to events. California finally enacted a law that would regulate and monitor pumping of groundwater, after years of drought prompted so much drawing down of well water that land in the Central Valley sank. Other big ideas were public works projects in the tradition of Pat Brown. Jerry championed a version of the Peripheral Canal that had failed to pass in 1982—two massive water tunnels that would bypass the ecologically fragile Delta and modernize the system for moving water from the north to Southern and Central California. Navigating the geographic, political, economic, and environmental divides necessary to make the project financially viable, Jerry faced the same splits his father had confronted. At best, he would leave office long before ground was even broken.

After deliberation, Jerry embraced a Schwarzenegger initiative, construction of a high-speed train route from Los Angeles to San Francisco. Even during the budget crisis, he found ways to finance the start of what would be a costly, decades-long project, if the entire route came to fruition. Jerry and Anne took part in the groundbreaking for the first section on the day after he was inaugurated for his second term. He dismissed skeptics and naysayers as Lilliputians who lacked vision, much as many had opposed the construction of the BART system in San Francisco decades earlier.

Jerry used BART as an example of the visionary thinking that shaped California, often in unforeseen ways. Each weekday morning, dozens of students at the Oakland School for the Arts emerged from the 19th Street Station, which had become a catalyst for the revitalized downtown. The construction of BART was financed with a 1966 bond issue championed by Pat Brown. "My father, I don't think, was thinking about Oakland," Jerry said. "We have to be able to have a politics where we make investments where the full realization is not going to happen for ten or twenty or forty years But that sense of continuity from the past to the present, but being a part of the future. That's what it means to be a Californian. Because we are from a pioneering tradition. We need to keep that pioneering going, that experimentation, that innovation, creativity, but at the same time we need to be rooted, in a tradition. And that's the way I conceptualize things."

He pointed to massive, transformative projects undertaken in the midst of economic hardship—the transcontinental railroad, started during the Civil War; the Golden Gate Bridge, built during the Depression. More recently, the Great Recession had not impeded the $2.5 billion NASA project to build, launch, and operate a rover to explore Mars. In the summer of 2012, Jerry joined scientists at the Jet Propulsion Laboratory in Pasadena to watch a live feed as their creation took its first walk on Mars. "This is not the first Space Day I've declared," he joked, reminiscing about his early interest in space in 1977. In an era when government had

One of Jerry Brown's proudest accomplishments his first time in office was the creation of the California Conservation Corps, which he called "an embodiment of the Jesuit seminary, the kibbutz, the Marine Corps, and the utopian community, all in support of ecological values." In 2016, he presided over the fortieth anniversary celebration, where he was presented a golden work boot. (Courtesy of California Department of Water Resources)

lost legitimacy, he told the scientists, their lab embodied the power of vision and collaboration, hallmarks of the state. "California from the beginning has attracted the bold and the imaginative," he said. "The Gold Rush, they came from all over the world too, to extract wealth from the ground, from the rivers, the mountains. Now people come here to extract wealth from the collective imagination of all those that are here."

In raw numbers, migration to California had slowed. Most of the population growth in recent years came from the children and grandchildren of immigrants. That shaped another important demographic change with uncertain consequences. In the land that had always lured people from near and far, for the first time since the Gold Rush, a majority of Californians had been born in the state.

Anthony Rendon, who in 2016 became the fifth Latino to serve as Assembly Speaker, exemplified those trends and their political implications. He was a third-generation Mexican American, born in 1968. He grew up in Los Angeles, where his father worked for a mobile home company and his mother was an aide at a Catholic school. Rendon graduated from Whittier High School, Richard Nixon's alma mater. He had terrible grades and knew almost no one who had gone to college. After working graveyard shifts at a warehouse for a couple of years and watching students get off the bus at Cerritos Community College as he headed home, he enrolled. He discovered philosophy, became an avid reader, graduated from Cal State Fullerton, and then earned a doctorate in political philosophy from the University of California, Riverside. After more than a decade as an environmental activist and educator, Rendon ran for Assembly in 2012 to represent a Southeast Los Angeles county district made up mainly of poor, predominantly Latino cities. So few voted that he won the Democratic primary with eighty-seven hundred votes in a district of half a million people. His wife was a second-generation Asian American; her parents fled Vietnam and ended up in Sacramento, where she worked in the fields through high school.

Rendon was the twelfth Assembly leader since 1995, when a term limits initiative had ended the long, powerful reign of Democrat Willie Brown. The strict limits—six years in the Assembly and eight in the Senate— meant lawmakers started eyeing their next office almost as soon as they arrived. Legislative leaders often had almost no experience in Sacramento. Lobbyists gained enormous power. In a move billed as a way to encourage stronger, more stable leadership, voters approved relaxed limits in 2012, the year Rendon was elected. He could potentially serve as Speaker for as long as eight years.

With Rendon's election as Assembly leader, Latinos for the first time led both houses. Senate president pro tem Kevin de León, two years older than Rendon, had been raised in San Diego by his Guatemalan immigrant mother. First in his family to graduate high school, he traced his political activism to the marches against Prop 187.

The governor joked about the generational and ethnic passing of the guard. "My little ilk of old German Americans is kind of fading into the sunset, and Kevin and his ilk are kind of taking over, and that's all right," Jerry said at the dedication of an urban park in downtown Los Angeles in the midst of immigrant neighborhoods—on the edge of Chinatown, and a little south of Chavez Ravine, the site of Dodger Stadium, where more than a thousand Mexican American families had been displaced in the 1950s for a public housing project that was never built. Jerry traced the waves of immigrants who had settled on what was once Native American land—Spaniards, then Mexicans, then Anglos. "And now, the Mexicans are coming back. And the Mayans are coming back. And the Guatemaltecos are coming back."

Although immigration had slowed and even showed a net decrease in recent years, California, by virtue of its size, still led the nation in almost every demographic category related to the foreign born. (To get a sense of scale: Los Angeles County alone, with more than ten million people, was larger than forty-one states.) Mexico remained the leading country of origin, followed by China and the Philippines. Asian immigrants were the fastest-growing group. In recent years, more than half of new arrivals had come from Asia. Of the more than ten million immigrants in California, the best estimates suggested roughly half were citizens and another quarter were legal residents.

The rest, as many as three million, were living in the United States without permission. About two thirds had lived in California for more than a decade. Many had crossed the border illegally as children; some discovered their status only as teenagers. Others had paid thousands of dollars to *coyotes* who helped them evade patrols and cross the Mexican border. Among more recent arrivals, most had simply overstayed their visas. Undocumented Californians had married and raised families, worked for years under fake credentials, paid taxes and Social Security. Most farmworkers were undocumented. Labor unions actively organized undocumented janitors, day laborers, and restaurant workers. Many families had blended status. Census data estimated that 1.9 million children lived in a house with an undocumented family member. By the time Jerry returned to Sacramento, in much of California it would have been hard to find many people who did not know someone who lacked legal residency papers.

Change happened fast in California, ever since the frenetic pace of the Gold Rush era. The state that had only a generation earlier led the way in demonizing illegal immigrants now pioneered efforts to help them lead normal lives. As it had on environmental regulation, California struck out on its own, ahead of and sometimes in conflict with the federal government. Home to as many as one fourth of the roughly 12 million undocumented immigrants in the United States, California grew impatient as Congress failed for more than a decade to enact reform. With little controversy and some bipartisan support, the state adopted a series of laws to extend and protect the rights of all immigrants.

"While Washington waffles on immigration, California is forging ahead," Jerry said in the fall of 2013, as he signed a measure limiting cooperation between local police and immigration officials. It seemed to him a matter of common sense, that ancient organ often found wanting in politics. "I'm not waiting."

Latino legislators who had been stymied for years in trying to authorize driver's licenses for undocumented immigrants encountered a governor who insisted they revive the shelved measure at the end of the 2013 legislative session. It passed easily, with Republican votes as well as Democrats. "No longer are undocumented people in the shadows," Jerry said as he signed the bill on the steps of Los Angeles City Hall. "They are alive and well and respected in the state of California."

The lines formed before dawn outside state Department of Motor Vehicles offices on January 2, 2015, the day the law went into effect. Over the next six months, half the licenses the state issued went to undocumented immigrants. California opened four new offices and hired a thousand workers to cope with the demand. The ability to drive legally, without fear of having a car impounded, or worse, was life-changing for many people. There were fewer uninsured drivers in the state and fewer hit-and-run accidents. Within three years, California had issued more than a million of the special licenses.

Each year brought more steps to narrow the distinction between those with papers and those without. Children from low-income families were eligible for subsidized healthcare, regardless of their residency status. Undocumented immigrants could obtain licenses in most professions, including electricians, architects, and contractors. In 2014, California became the first state to allow undocumented immigrants to practice law—although federal law prohibited any firm from hiring them. Californians paid in-state tuition at the public colleges and universities, regardless of immigration status. The 2011 California Dream Act made all undocumented immigrants eligible for state financial aid that covered full tuition at public universities. Subsequent laws waived fees at community colleges and allowed undocumented students to serve in student governments.

"Professor [Sheldon] Wolin coined the term 'fugitive democracy' to indicate that the power of people—democracy—is episodic, not continuously present," Jerry told students at Cal, quoting his former professor. "But at key moments, bureaucratic and corporate power gives way to an aroused citizenry. Look how the hostility to immigrants expressed in the passage of Proposition 187 in 1994, gave way to what is now a majority in California who support immigration reform."

Jerry's most pressing crusade, to which he devoted his most passionate attempts to arouse the citizenry, was a battle where the past, present, and future converged, for California and its fourth-term governor. Throughout his political life, Jerry had been drawn to environmental issues, which he saw as comparable to the sort of moral absolutes that had attracted him to the Jesuits. While Pat and Jerry Brown shared a sense of responsibility to plan for the future, Jerry's future was more cerebral. Pat wanted his name on the California aqueduct. Jerry wanted a place in history for helping save the planet. "You have to be able to imagine what isn't, that's what real leadership is," he told a group of county officials. "It's not just managing what is, but it's imagining what might be and taking the steps to get there."

His cause became climate change, which threatened to remain unacknowledged until it was too late to reverse catastrophic damage. His interest went back decades. In 1992, he had attended the world climate summit in Rio as a guest of environmentalist David Brower. A decade later, as mayor of Oakland, he joined three congressmen at the World

Summit on Sustainable Development in Johannesburg, to demonstrate an American presence at a meeting skipped by President George W. Bush. With Americans focused on terrorism in the wake of the September 11 attacks, Jerry warned of a different threat: man-made destruction of the environment. "This is the moment for prophets, for vision. Otherwise, the people will truly perish," Jerry wrote after the Johannesburg summit. "This is unpleasant stuff. It is so unpleasant that conventional leaders would rather comfort us with reassuring words about the power of markets and the inevitability of medical and technical breakthroughs."

Over the years, the environmental movement in California had been bipartisan, largely white, and middle- to upper-class. As the state's demographics shifted, so did environmental concerns. Climate change became "not about polar bears, but people," in the words of Assemblyman Eduardo Garcia, a Democrat from an inland area who began to play a leading role. Garcia was a generation younger than the Latino leaders of the legislature. Born in 1977, during Jerry Brown's first term as governor, Garcia grew up in the Coachella Valley east of Los Angeles, an area of rich agricultural land. His parents were farmworkers who made it out of the fields; his father became a gardener, then worked for the city of Indio, date capital of the world. His mother started a housecleaning business. A mediocre student, Garcia went to community college for four years, eventually transferring to graduate from the University of California, Riverside. He taught English to farmworkers, to help them get jobs in a hotel, or a better shift. An internship shooting video at Coachella City Hall had piqued his interest in politics, and he ran for City Council in 2004 and was elected mayor two years later. His issue was creating parks. He didn't have any when he was growing up. Parks became his rallying cry when he was elected to the Assembly in 2014, too. He represented a district that stretched from Coachella south to the Mexican border, where Garcia had spent every Saturday as a child visiting his grandparents.

The landmark cap-and-trade bill signed by Arnold Schwarzenegger, which had become a centerpiece of California's efforts to reduce greenhouse gases, expired in 2016. Although the Democrats held a two-thirds majority in both houses, conservative legislators from oil-rich districts opposed renewal. The sponsors needed votes from the Latino caucus. Eduardo Garcia saw an opportunity to draw attention to environmental issues in parts of the state too often overlooked. Like his district, where seven out of ten children had asthma. Or the Central Valley, where thousands had no access to clean drinking water. In exchange for support of cap and trade, he wanted greater input into policies enacted by the powerful, independent Air Resources Board. He wanted to ensure that an institution that had been viewed as the domain of Westside Los Angeles liberals became responsive to the needs of the state's poorest residents and its growing Latino majority.

One of the provisions of the Garcia bill, packaged with an extension of cap and trade through 2020, increased the legislative oversight of the Air Resources Board by adding two ex officio members. To the surprise of her staff, ARB chair Mary Nichols not only accepted but embraced the change. She saw it as a way to "move California's air pollution and climate program ahead by another decade and bring into the discussion a whole new set of players that have not felt like they had a seat at the table up until now."

She spoke at Vista Hermosa, the first park built in a hundred years in a densely populated, heavily Latino Los Angeles neighborhood, as she watched Jerry Brown sign the bills into law. She saw the event as public recognition of a coalition that would be important to California's future, a symbolic passing of the torch to the next generation, who would carry on the commitment in their own way. Jerry's rhetoric reflected the shift, too. "I want to say something about low income people, people of modest means, who live in the Central Valley, who live in Riverside, San Bernardino, Imperial County," he said. "They're the ones who eat the dirtiest air. And we're not going to clean up that air until we reduce pollutants in the way this bill is purporting to do, and will do . . . The great problem with these big issues is that you wait too long, because you can't see it, [and then] it's too late to do anything about it."

Worried about legal challenges to the cap-and-trade program, which could be construed as a tax, Jerry next pushed for a further ten-year extension, which needed to pass by a two-thirds vote. His all-out lobbying included the unusual step of appearing in person before legislative committees debating the measure. "I'm not here about some cockamamie legacy that people talk about," he told a room packed with lobbyists and lawmakers at the state Senate hearing. "This isn't for me—I'm going to be dead! It's for you, and it's damn real!" Then he sat in the audience and took notes on concerns expressed by environmentalists, who faulted the bill for concessions to the oil industry, which they saw as part of an ongoing pattern. Some objected to cap and trade because it allowed large polluters to continue unabated, if they purchased sufficient permits.

Jerry turned a problem—the defection of some Democrats who felt provisions were too favorable to large polluters—into an advantage: Eight Republicans supported the measure. "That is a breakthrough. The iceberg of denial is cracking. These are real Republicans," Jerry said. Republican support nationally would also be key to further action on climate change. He urged the business community to pressure Republicans for more bipartisan support.

He also viewed Republican support as significant in a time of deep partisan divides, a reaffirmation of the Party of California, and he gave full credit to his Republican predecessor for setting cap and trade in motion. Schwarzenegger shared the podium for the bill signing on Treasure Island, the San Francisco skyline in the background. It was the same place the first cap-and-trade bill had been signed. "To ratchet into another eleven years, this is pretty great," Jerry said as he signed the law.

> The fact that California can welcome an immigrant from Austria and make him governor, that's another miracle. We're on the move, because we're California. This is not one of those ordinary legislative things. We're dealing with climate change, and next to the nuclear threat, which is the other existential danger, nothing is more serious than extinction. There are tipping points . . . the gravity of this topic is so great that it's hard to talk about, people think you're a little wacky. People think you're Cassandra.
>
> Eleven years from now, when this thing expires, I'll be in my nineties. If I'm around. So this is not about me, it's not about Arnold, it's not about these younger legislators here. It's about the world. And California is leading that world in dealing with the principal existential threat that the world faces. What could be more glorious?

He spoke in July 2017, a time when many who shared his beliefs found it difficult to rejoice. In his first months in office, President Donald Trump had championed policies and values that ran counter to much of what California had come to represent. Trump appointed climate change deniers; he sought to build a wall on the U.S.–Mexico border, to ban certain immigrants from entering the country, and to deport others. The Golden State became the counterforce, a hopeful beacon in an era of uncertainty. Jerry Brown assumed the role for which he had prepared since childhood, that of the most powerful Democrat in the United States.

Those Jerry had derided a few years earlier as East Coast "dystopian declinists" when they called California a failed state now hailed it as the promised land. In reality, the state where everything was outsized still faced huge challenges, even before Trump's ascendancy. The aging infrastructure of Pat Brown's era was crumbling. A compromise plan to raise the gas tax to fund highway repairs would fix only a fraction, and the plan was threatened by a move to rescind the tax by a ballot initiative. The housing market had become so tight that to buy a median-priced house in San Jose required a household income of more than $200,000. To replenish the state's stock of affordable housing would take decades. Homeless people formed tent colonies in every city, in record numbers, with no solutions in sight. Half the children in the state qualified for subsidized medical care. Climate change was playing havoc with water supplies and fire danger.

Jerry delivered his State of the State message a few days after President Trump's inauguration. He broke with the tradition of laying out an agenda for the coming year to deliver instead an impassioned rebuttal to the divisive, xenophobic politics of Washington, D.C. It was one of his most powerful speeches.

> This is California, the sixth most powerful economy in the world. One out of every eight Americans lives right here and 27 percent—almost eleven million—were born in a foreign land. When California does well, America does well. And when California hurts, America hurts. We don't have a Statue of Liberty with its inscription: "Give me your tired, your poor, your huddled masses yearning to breathe free . . ." But we do have the Golden Gate and a spirit of adventure and openness that has welcomed, since the Gold Rush of 1848, one wave of immigration after another.
>
> For myself, I feel privileged to stand before you as your governor, as did my father almost sixty years ago. His mother, Ida, the youngest of eight children, was born in very modest circumstances, not very far from where we are gathered today. Her father arrived in California in 1852, having left from the Port of Hamburg, aboard a ship named *Perseverance*. It is that spirit

of perseverance and courage which built our state from the beginning. And it is that spirit which will get us through the great uncertainty and the difficulties ahead. So as we reflect on the state of our state, we should do so in the broader context of our country and its challenges. We must prepare for uncertain times and reaffirm the basic principles that have made California the Great Exception that it is.

He quoted John Donne ("No man is an island"), the Dutch jurist Hugo Grotius ("Even God cannot cause two times two not to make four"), and Woody Guthrie ("This land is made for you and me"). His most eloquent passages sought to reassure undocumented immigrants, including more than seventy-two thousand enrolled in California's public colleges and universities: "First, in California, immigrants are an integral part of who we are and what we've become. They have helped create the wealth and dynamism of this state from the very beginning." He recited some of the laws protecting the undocumented. "We may be called upon to defend those laws and defend them we will. And let me be clear: We will defend everybody—every man, woman and child—who has come here for a better life and has contributed to the well-being of our state."

Jerry paid careful attention to words. When writing, he labored over each sentence. He took issue with words that were becoming popular among Democrats in the Trump era. "Resistance," he said, meant underground fighters in World War II who gave up their lives fighting the Nazis. "Sanctuary" had a particular religious meaning. He was clear and outspoken about the difference between right and wrong. Building a wall to keep people out was wrong. Deporting immigrants who had built lives in California and contributed to a state that had been built by immigrants was wrong. Denying climate change was wrong; suggesting it was a Chinese hoax was preposterous.

When Donald Trump announced in June 2017 that the United States would attempt to renege on its commitment to the Paris climate change treaty, Jerry Brown became the de facto American political leader on global warming, by virtue of his long-standing commitment to the issue and the economic importance of California. He already had standing as an international leader in the climate change fight. A partnership between California and the German province of Baden-Württemberg had led to the formation of the Under2 Coalition, committed to keeping the rise in average global temperature to under the two degrees Celsius that scientists saw as a benchmark for irreversible catastrophic change. In Sacramento on May 19, 2015, a dozen leaders from states and provinces had signed the initial memorandum of understanding, dubbing themselves the Under2MOU. They committed to reduce greenhouse gas emissions to certain targets and to share technology and scientific research as well as monitoring and reporting. The goal was also to demonstrate at the United Nations climate change summit in Paris the role that states and provinces could play. By the end of 2017, the group included more than two hundred states, nations, and regions representing more than one billion people.

"I come from a mere state, or what people like to call a subnational unit," Jerry said at the Eastern Economic Forum in Vladivostok. "Nevertheless, we have an impact in the world. Our gross domestic product is about $2.5 trillion. We're a land of innovation: Google, Facebook, Jet Propulsion Laboratory, Hollywood. We're a land of disruption, where we never set in and accept a status quo, but we disrupt and create and build a future that works for everyone."

Jerry had traveled abroad extensively before Trump's election. On a trip to China after the election, Jerry was treated like a head of state. The governor continued discussions with President Xi Jinping about how to share best practices and provide assistance as China formed its own cap-and-trade market. Across Europe, Jerry was greeted with motorcades at the airport, standing ovations, and effusive welcomes. At the World Economic Forum in New York, he was introduced as the "man of the moment in this country who is taking the reins of the horse and driving the action forward."

He delivered a call for action with all the urgency he could muster. "Human civilization is on the chopping block," Jerry told a room full of lawmakers and students in Stuttgart. "We have to wake up the world. We have to wake up Europe, wake up America, wake up the whole world to realize that we have a common destiny."

"At the highest circles, people still don't get it," he told religious leaders at the Vatican. "It's not just a light rinse . . . We need a total, I might say brain washing. We need to wash our brains out and see a very different kind of world."

Looking grim, he spoke of the dire future. He listened carefully at meetings and took notes, his eyebrows furrowed in concentration. He never smiled. He derided a reporter who asked him if he enjoyed the foreign travel. Yet he left audiences inspired and energized. They thanked him for his honesty and clarity, and they seemed to respond to his faith, and his excitement.

"There's a lot of stuff we do in politics—schools, crime, water, highways . . . I don't want to call them little," he said in Oslo. "They're important. But it's not like changing the very basis of how life exists. That's very exciting. It elicits creativity, energy, building." He compared the current moment to the challenges described by the historian Arnold Toynbee in his chronicles of the rise and fall of ancient civilizations. "What drives civilization? What drove the Vikings? What drove the Christians? What drove Greece or Rome? You have a challenge. And then you have a response. Challenge, and response . . . These are opportunities to either destroy humanity or to enlighten and improve it."

Blunt in his criticism of Trump, Jerry did not dwell on the president, other than to say that his dismissive comments on climate change would only help rally support for much-needed action. Trump as the bogeyman was a simplistic distraction that risked becoming an excuse for delay. The biggest obstacle was "the oil, the cars, the way of life, the packaging, the waste, the whole way our society is organized." The 32 million cars in California traveled 330 billion miles a year. He invoked the image of a rocket launched into orbit: The energy required to escape the gravity field of Earth was once unthinkable but is now routine. That was the level of psychic energy required to confront the existential threat of global warming, to turn the three hundred thousand electric cars in California into 32 million.

In an interview in Norway, he returned to the connection between his theological and environmental beliefs. "Nature, the rules of nature, physics, biology, chemistry, ecology, those are rules. They're laws. We may not fully understand them, you understand little bits of them. And you can't argue with them. It's not like politics. Politics is based on the principle, let's make a deal. You can't make a deal with nature. Nature is sovereign. And we have to get on the side of nature instead of attempting to destroy it, which will be destroying ourselves . . . And that's why I do see it having the importance that I earlier ascribed to theology and religion when I went to study to be a Jesuit priest."

Friends who had been in the seminary with Jerry—those who stayed and those who left—saw the Jesuit principles as his core operating system.

He sometimes carried around his old Jesuit rulebook and pulled it out to quote one of the rules. He pushed the Oakland bishop, a Jesuit, to perform more elaborate rituals each year on the feast day of Saint Ignatius. He often used the phrase *agere contra*. "I've been fighting self all my life," he said, accepting an award from the Asia Society and comparing the Jesuit saying to one of Mao Tse-tung. "And unless you do that, you can't make any progress."

At a climate change conference at the Vatican, a local reporter asked Jerry if he was Catholic. Jerry resisted the question. He answered instead how his faith had shaped his work:

> I think the formation that I've undergone growing up in the Catholic faith, the Catholic religion, puts forth a world that's orderly, that has purpose and that ultimately is a positive. And that's very helpful when you look at a world that looks very much the opposite, in terms of the wars, the corruption and the breakdown. And so even though from an intellectual point of view it looks very dark, in another sense I have great faith and confidence that there is a way forward. And I would attribute that in some way to my Catholic upbringing and training.

He had long ago broken with the Catholic Church by favoring abortion rights and same-sex marriage. In 2015, he was confronted with another issue on which Church leaders lobbied hard—whether to sign a bill allowing physician-assisted death in certain cases. In an unusually personal message, the seventy-seven-year-old governor explained his decision to sign the bill. "The crux of the matter is whether the state of California should continue to make it a crime for a dying person to end his life, no matter how great his pain or suffering." He had read all the material and arguments carefully and had talked with a Catholic bishop, two of his own doctors, and former Jesuit classmates. "In the end, I was left to reflect on what I would want in the face of my own death. I do not know what I would do if I were dying in prolonged and excruciating pain. I am certain, however, that it would be a comfort to be able to consider the options afforded by this bill. And I wouldn't deny that right to others."

He described his belief system as "optimism of the will, pessimism of the intellect." Throughout his public life, that unusual mix had been an essential part of his appeal. He spoke forthrightly about bad news, whether budget cuts or impending nuclear doom, and yet with a confidence about the power of society to tackle what he called not problems but conditions, enduring in nature.

In a conversation with author and historian Studs Terkel shortly after 9/11, Jerry had reflected on how his Jesuit training shaped his worldview in times of crises and despair. "I have a skeptical eye," he said. "At the same time, I have a bedrock confidence in the way our society is organized, in the way I was brought up. It gives me a certain hope, although my critical intelligence tells me that we're in one hell of a lot of problems in the contemporary world. I'm never satisfied that where I am is where I always need to be, a feeling reinforced in the Jesuit order."

In California, Jerry's unique blend of alarm and reassurance became a tonic in the wake of the 2016 election that left the Golden State shaken. Hillary Clinton had beaten Trump in California by a margin of two to one, easily carrying even traditionally more conservative Orange County. In the weeks after the election, Californians responded with marches, protests, fear, confusion, and anger. Students at schools not known for their political activism marched around campus chanting "Not my president." Immigration activists huddled with lawyers. Legislative leaders in Sacramento issued proclamations of "resistance." Undocumented students wondered if they would be able to stay in school, or find jobs.

Jerry Brown was quiet in the initial aftermath. Timing was everything, Pat Brown taught his son. Jerry waited for the right moment.

On December 6, 2016, the president-elect announced the head of the Environmental Protection Agency would be the Republican attorney general of Oklahoma, who denied that climate change existed. Five days later, on a Sunday talk show, Trump said "nobody really knows" whether climate change was real and spoke about withdrawing from the global warming agreement reached in Paris a year earlier.

The next morning, almost twenty-five thousand scientists gathered in San Francisco for the start of the annual American Geophysical Union conference, the largest international gathering of earth and space scientists. Their mood was glum. On Tuesday, organizers got a phone call from the governor's office. Jerry Brown wanted to come address the meeting the next morning. They scurried to spread the word about the last-minute addition to the program.

About twenty-five hundred tired scientists straggled into the Moscone Convention Center in time for the nine thirty A.M. special guest and greeted him with a standing ovation as he took the stage in dark gray suit, blue-and-white-striped shirt, and no tie. He still wrote his own speeches, but his best performances, like this one, were largely extemporaneous.

"We're facing far more than one or two or even thousands of politicians," he said, arms waving, hands punching the air for emphasis. "We're facing big oil, we're facing big financial structures that are at odds with the survivability of our world. It will be up to you as truth tellers, truth seekers, to mobilize all your efforts to fight back."

He grew more animated as he went on, and the crowd responded. He mentioned the president-elect by name only once, referring to rumors that Trump might shut down data-collecting satellites. "Back in 1978 I proposed a land satellite for California. They called me Governor Moonbeam because of that. I didn't get that moniker for nothing. And if Trump turns off the satellites, California will launch its own damn satellites!"

He detailed some of California's recent successes: strict vehicle emission standards that had become the national standard; energy efficiency standards; a goal of 50 percent renewable energy by 2030; new limits on short-lived climate pollutants. He told the scientists their work mattered now more than ever.

"A lot of people say, 'What the hell are you doing, Brown? You're not a country.' Well," he said, pausing for the scientists' laughter to subside, "we're the fifth- or sixth-largest economy in the world, and we've got a lot of firepower. We've got the scientists, we've got the universities, we have the national labs, and we have the political clout and sophistication for the battle. And we will persevere. Have no doubt about that."

The Mountain House

Jerry Brown recognized many of the faces in the crowd gathered on the Williams town square the first Saturday in November 2014. His sisters, Barbara, Cynthia, and Kathleen, who had come from their respective homes in Sacramento, San Francisco, and Los Angeles. Half a dozen of his extended family from nearby Colusa. The mayor of Williams. The local congressman, who had started in the Assembly in 1975, the year Jerry first became governor. Staff members who had driven an hour north from the capital to cheer for their boss the weekend before Election Day.

The candidate was a little disappointed by the turnout, sorry he hadn't done more than the one robocall and mailing. In the old days, his rule of thumb had been to hand out ten flyers to get one person to an event. Not that it mattered. He held such a large lead in his reelection bid that he had barely campaigned. He had not come to Williams seeking votes. Jerry had planned the final event of his final campaign as a tribute to his great-grandfather August Schuckman.

Jerry was introduced by August's oldest living great-grandchild, ninety-year-old Patricia Schaad. She still lived in Williams, not far from the Mountain House, where she had spent childhood evenings on the porch with August's son Frank, her great-uncle. She had been raised by her grandmother Emma, but inspired by Great-aunt Ida. Emma told her grandchildren to be content; Ida said go after what you want. Schaad had wanted badly to attend Cal. With no way to afford the university, she rode a bus thirty-five miles to Yuba Junior College. When the bus stopped picking up kids in Williams, she found a place to stay in Colusa. Schaad was the first woman student body president at the community college.

She married, had a son, grew bored, and went back to school. She drove an hour each way to Chico State, which offered teacher training programs to meet the shortage in the postwar years. Schaad taught for many years at the Williams school she had attended.

On November 1, 2014, she welcomed her cousin back to his ancestral home. "Governor Brown places great value on his Schuckman descendants and the property and is in the process of establishing a residence out there," she said. "We will be proud to have him as part of our community and are proud to have him in Williams today."

Jerry had been spending a lot of time in the hot, barren land where his great-grandfather had settled a century and a half earlier. "I don't want you to feel this is some walk down memory lane," he told the crowd at the Williams rally. "But it's really important that we know where we came from, if we want to figure out where we're going. Certainly, I've always been one to try to keep my eyes on the stars but keep my feet on the ground. And I can think a lot, and care a lot, about Williams and our Mountain House ranch, and all the different places of California, and I also can look to the future."

For almost half an hour, he jumped from past to future and back, his speech mirroring the way his mind made associations. From the history of Williams, the town called Central before the railroad came, to his plan for high-speed rail. From the diary of August Schuckman's journey across the Plains to Governor Moonbeam. From the frugality of his ancestors to the need for a state rainy day reserve fund. "This is a very big complicated state, that has an extremely rich and diverse history. We only are here for a while, and we pass on, and that's the story. But what do we leave as we go?"

He veered into what might have been mistaken for a non sequitur. "By the way," he said, one of his favorite phrases, "I did another charter school, which is called the Oakland Military Institute . . ."

Though he spurned the word "legacy" as irrelevant until he stopped working, which would be when he was dead, the Oakland charter schools he founded would be there when he moved on. He had stayed closely involved, selecting the superintendent, monitoring progress, attending graduations, and raising millions of dollars for them each year. Jerry pointed to his windbreaker, which bore the insignia he had designed for the Oakland Military Institute—the California bear flag with the motto AGE QUOD AGIS. He told the story of how as a Jesuit seminarian he preferred to pose philosophical questions when he should have been picking grapes. *Age quod agis*, the novices would tell him. Do what you are doing, Brother Brown. Pick the grapes.

Four years earlier, Jerry had wound up an intense campaign with a traditional fly-around of the state, firing up supporters in half a dozen cities from San Diego to Oakland. The relaxed Williams rally in a town square festooned with balloon arches and red-white-and-blue bunting seemed a throwback to another era. Jerry spoke without notes, waving one hand instead of the usual two, because he clutched a red folder. He pulled from it a copy of his great-grandfather's diary from 1852 and read the section about oxen and horses that died on the journey, and the discarded wagons that littered the Plains.

"The spirit of August Schuckman is still here," Jerry said. "It's still in Williams, it's still affecting California, by all his descendants, which now number in the hundreds. I think it is well to keep in mind, as we look to the future, to understand what we owe to those who got us this far, and what we owe to those who are going to come after us."

In his younger years, Jerry had been to the family ranch only once, with his father in 1961 when the land was in limbo. Frank Schuckman had died and the ranch was up for sale. Jerry's main memory was of the State Police driver waiting for sheep to cross the road. A year later, Pat and his brother Harold had bought the land, with financial help from friends. The family kept a majority stake in the small corporation. When Pat died in 1996, Jerry told his mother he wanted the shares. Bernice signed them over to her son. None of his sisters cared.

It would be another decade before Jerry began to think of Williams as the place he wanted to live. In the 1990s, Jerry and Anne went up to the ranch every year or two to hike in the hills. Sometimes they stopped by to visit Janet Staple and her husband, Jack, the family historian. In his second term as Oakland mayor, Jerry brought his friend Phil Tagami to see the land. Jerry had begun to contact first cousins he had never known, Pat Schaad and her four half sisters, who had stayed in Colusa. Jerry and Tagami spent a day with the Staples, hearing stories about the Mountain House and family legends. Jerry hosted dinners for the cousins at Louis Cairo's steakhouse in Williams. He visited the cemetery where the Schuckmans were buried, including his grandmother Ida. He met the ranchers who leased the Mountain House land to graze their cattle.

Jerry began to regularly invoke the spirit of the Schuckman pioneers in his speeches. "I went up to my land, west of Williams, and I hiked on the very hilltops that my great-grandfather did just shortly after the Gold Rush," he said the day after Proposition 30 passed in 2012. "And I like to reflect on how tough it was then, what they faced. What we have to do now, it's really not as difficult. So we should be able to make California even better."

The second Mountain House, built by Frank Schuckman, had burned down long ago, but several barns were still standing. Tagami, the Oakland developer who had started out in construction, began to sketch out design concepts that might work with the rolling, oak-covered hills. He filled the first of what would be a dozen binders. At one point, after Jerry overheard a discussion in his gym locker room about a Buddhist monastery looking for land, the Mountain House was going to have its own temple. The land had a monastic quality that reminded Jerry of the seminary.

Jerry did research. He went to Wyntoon to talk with the Hearsts about their isolated family compound in Northern California. William Hearst came to visit the Mountain House. Jerry collected early histories of Colusa, including one written by Will Green, August's neighbor in 1860. Arrowheads and shards of pottery used to grind acorns sent Jerry in search of the Indian history of the land. He talked to geologists about the soil. He and Anne spent time with their nearest neighbors. He flew over the sparsely populated land and memorized the names of all the towns. "What the land was, what it is, what it could be"—that was his mantra.

"It's a hostile environment in many ways," Jerry said. They were careful to keep their dog, Sutter, away from rattlesnakes. "It's a hostile environment, and people come to terms with it."

That spirit of coming to terms with conditions, and the quiet isolation, reminded him of the seminary and silent retreats. Tagami built two small wooden cabins so Jerry and Anne could stay overnight, off the grid. The land had no water or power. A water witch found two bad wells, then eventually two good ones.

The land led Jerry to the people. Beyond the cousins with whom he had become reacquainted in Colusa, Jerry became curious about his family's more distant roots. He called his sister Kathleen. In 1996, Kathleen had embarked on what became a decades-long genealogical quest. She began in Ireland, finding marriage records for her great-great-grandparents

Michael and Judith Brown. She traced their offspring through the Irish enclave of Framingham, Massachusetts, to San Francisco, visiting neighborhoods to recreate their lives. On her mother's side, Kathleen found records back to the Gold Rush. She visited the shack in the mining town of Vallecito that had been Cuneo's general store, with an 1866 inventory that included pickaxes, canned oysters, and French champagne. To understand the Schuckmans, Kathleen and her husband, Van, retraced August's steps along the Oregon Trail, using his diary as a guide. They stood alongside the Platte River at Fort Laramie, arriving by chance on the same date August had been there, 159 years earlier. In the wind and heat, they stared at the names pioneers had carved into the rocks. "It was an eerie experience," Kathleen wrote.

"About a century and a half after all this, I received a 10 pm telephone call from brother Jerry," Kathleen wrote in a scrapbook for the family. "He was meeting the next morning with Hannelore Kraft, the Minister-President of North Rhine–Westphalia, and he wanted me to send him all the information that I had collected over the last 2 decades by the next morning."

That didn't happen. Instead, the call led the two couples to journey to Ireland and Germany in the summer of 2013. In Tipperary, they met third cousins and scrambled over the ruins of the stables where their great-great-grandfather had lived. In Germany, one of their guides was the retired executive who had entertained Kathleen when the teenager visited with her parents in 1963. In the tiny town of Wüsten, August Schuckman's home, their trip was big news. Herta Schuckman arrived with an envelope of genealogical charts; she was the widow of the grandson of August's youngest brother. Jerry sat in the pew of the church where August and Augusta were married in 1863.

In Bremen, they found Udo Schuckman, the great-grandson of August's older brother. A split in the family after World War II had left eleven-year-old Udo's family impoverished when his half brother sold the family brick business. An employee found letters August had sent to his brother when he arrived in California. He sent them to Frank Schuckman, in the hope he might take pity on his relatives and send money. That was how August Schuckman's diary came to California.

"We are unbelievably fortunate that the letters of August were preserved for nearly 100 years by his German family and that a loyal and kind family employee took the time and effort to translate them and send them to

California," Kathleen wrote. "It is a remarkable family story that stirs the soul and the imagination and is a priceless gift for future generations of Schuckman descendants."

Jerry invited all the German relatives to Colusa. "Never mind that there is nothing there but some empty barns," Kathleen wrote, "but hope springs eternal that in his spare time he will create a homestead for the family. It is a worthy goal."

It was more than a goal. One year later, Jerry organized the first Schuckman family reunion at the Mountain House. About thirty people camped out in tents. His sister Barbara rented an RV. A few others stayed in nearby hotels. They spread out a six-foot-long family tree and people filled in blanks. The Colusa cousins met some of their city relatives. The second year, the reunion was twice as large and more elaborate. Tagami built raised platforms for the tents. Distant relatives came from several states. From the encampments came the idea of building a home.

At the end of the Williams rally the weekend before his final election, Jerry brought his siblings and their families out to the ranch. From a locker in the small wood cabin he extracted a bottle of bourbon and poured shots in plastic cups. Then they walked the land, debating the best place to build the third Mountain House. Right where the old one had been, they decided. Jerry and Anne found a local architect who designed a solar-powered, sustainable home that curved around the small knoll of oak trees.

As he neared the end of his final term, and celebrated his eightieth birthday, Jerry was often asked about his next act. He again referred to the Roman general Cincinnatus, who had come out of retirement to save the empire. "Like Cincinnatus, after saving the Republic, he went back to the plow. That's exactly where I plan to go."

He talked vaguely about a salon, perhaps a variation on the Oakland Table. The Mountain House might be a place to pursue his climate change crusade. His friends joked about Camp David West, a phrase Jerry himself had used. At the monthly lunches of the St. Ignatius Class of '55, which Jerry often attended, his classmates found the fascination with Colusa a little baffling. Pete Roddy, Jerry's first friend on Magellan Avenue, swore he would never go up to the rattlesnake-infested land.

"People will come here," Jerry said, unconcerned. "It has a certain historic presence. Enough happened here that has been told to enough people." He envisioned one of the old barns as a place to display family artifacts, like the land patent signed by Abraham Lincoln. Little had survived from August's wife, Augusta. Ida had kept her mother's white porcelain teapot, then passed it on to her only daughter, Connie. Connie guarded the teapot on a high shelf in a dark closet. It passed on to her daughter Karin, who would pass it on to her daughter.

Jerry went to Easter sunrise service at a cross in the road that topped an intersection near the Mountain House. He and Anne attended Memorial Day services at the Williams cemetery, after visiting his grandmother's grave. When first dog Sutter Brown died, he was buried on the ranch. The new first dog was named Colusa. Phil Tagami, whose sister ran an olive oil company, helped arrange the planting of 125 mature olive trees of three varieties, pendolino, frantoio, and leccino. The first Mountain House olive oil was bottled at the end of 2017, with a picture of August Schuckman on the label.

In all his campaigns, Jerry never won the staunchly Republican county of Colusa. Williams had become more heavily Latino in recent years, drawing families that worked in the nearby fields. In 2014, Jerry carried Williams 142–105. In the Venado precinct, home to the Mountain House, Jerry lost, 23–21.

In his office, he kept a cow skull on the table, dug up at the ranch. On the wall, the old wooden Rancho Venado sign that once graced the Mountain House gate hung above a panorama of the land when his grandmother was a child. Below it was a photo of August Schuckman feeding sheep. Visitors to the governor's office sometimes found every surface covered with documents related to the Schuckmans. "It has a history. I'm putting it back together," he said. "I think the history of this family might explain life to me in some important ways."

Each year, the governor spoke at induction ceremonies for the California Hall of Fame, an event hosted at the state museum. Each class spanned the range of professions and eras, an eclectic snapshot of those, like August Schuckman, who had been drawn to find their fortune in California. Many of the names were part of Jerry's past: Pat Brown, Cesar Chavez, Joan Didion, Francis Ford Coppola, Gregory Bateson, Gary Snyder, Kevin Starr, Earl Warren.

In his last few turns hosting the ceremony, Jerry reflected on his ancestors. "When we think Hall of Fame, we think innovation, but we think partly of our past, our tradition," he said at the 2015 ceremony. "I was just musing, as I was listening, on my own forebears." He talked about how much the Mountain House meant to him. "It is nice to walk in the very footprints of your grandmother, and your great-grandfather. It's very meaningful to me."

Then, in classic Jerry Brown fashion, he pivoted to Robert Frost's description of how he wrote a poem. Jerry had used a variation of the quote in his first campaign for president, four decades earlier. Its significance changed with the years. The search for wisdom through questions remained constant.

"I am very inspired by something Robert Frost put in the introduction to his collected poems," Jerry said. "He said a poem begins with a question, and then, like a piece of ice on a hot stove, rides on its own melting, and then ends in wisdom. Now, I don't know if everyone feels they're like a piece of ice on a hot stove. But I've always viewed my political career in those terms. And I just keep rolling across that stove. Luckily, it was a solid piece of ice, so it hasn't completely melted."

Acknowledgments

This is a family story, and I'm grateful to all the members of the extended Brown family, from Colusa to Los Angeles, who shared memories, documents, and pictures. They set aside many hours amid busy schedules, unconditionally, without really knowing, as the governor put it, where exactly I was going with this.

Dozens of friends, classmates, and public officials past and present were similarly generous with both their time and trust. They helped me color in the lacunae in the documents and provided much-needed background and explanations. They schooled me in everything from local county history to realignment. My thanks to them all.

The book relies extensively on primary sources. A narrative that spanned more than a hundred fifty years required research that ran the gamut from rare manuscript archives to Twitter. I'm grateful to all the keepers of records, official and unofficial, from handwritten nineteenth-century ledgers in the Colusa County Recorder's office to twenty-first century video clips, and to all those who hunted down old letters and photos in garages and basements. Big thanks, posthumously, to Pat Brown, for keeping almost every scrap that documented his life, from high school on.

The visual presentation owes a big debt to Karin Surber, who has preserved so much of the early Brown family photo archives. My deep appreciation to Wendy Vissar for all her guidance and expertise in selecting and assembling images for the book.

Among the many archivists who offered help, I'm particularly indebted to Susan Luftschein in Special Collections at the University of

Southern California, Brother Dan Peterson at Santa Clara University, and Iris Donovan and Michael Lange at the Bancroft Library at the University of California, Berkeley.

To wander the stacks of the Huntington Library was both an immense pleasure and an invaluable resource. There's no better place to research the history of California, and no milieu more conducive to writing; it's a privilege to be a reader. I'm deeply grateful to Bill Deverell for all the knowledge and wisdom he imparted on our walks in the Huntington gardens. Those conversations were an indispensable part of my education about California history.

The carefully researched, lengthy interviews conducted by the Oral History Center of the Bancroft Library are a remarkable resource. The voices captured in the extensive project documenting the Goodwin Knight and Edmund G. Brown eras were particularly valuable for my work. I'm grateful to all who participated in that project as interviewers and interviewees.

In writing about the more recent past, the reports of the Public Policy Institute of California provided reasoned, well-researched, cogent analyses on a wide range of issues that helped me understand and contextualize both demographic trends and governmental actions.

I'm indebted to all the journalists who documented California and its political life over the decades, starting with the era when four newspapers competed in San Francisco. In addition to the growing digital archives, the Newspapers & Microforms Library at UC Berkeley is an invaluable resource for that history. Thanks to my former *Los Angeles Times* colleagues Mark Z. Barabak, Dan Morain, and George Skelton for sharing their insights in person as well as in print, as they have done since I first moved to California and they helped me understand my new home.

Every week, more primary source material is digitized and available online. Thanks to all those who posted transcripts and videos of meeting, speeches, and events, and special thanks to the Internet Archive and all who contribute. It gives me hope for future historians, who will lose the ability to see and touch the past on paper; the trade-off of universal access balances that loss.

A few more assorted thanks: In addition to those listed as interviewees, Judy Gerrard, Janice Lauppe, Allen Schaad, and Walt Seaver provided information about the Schuckmans and facilitated my research in Colusa. Evan Westrup facilitated my work and found ways to accommodate me in an always crowded schedule. LeRoy Chatfield encouraged the project, made early connections that got it off the ground, and provided valuable advice throughout. My agent, Gloria Loomis, championed the idea from the start.

Writing is a solitary pursuit, but publishing a book is a team effort. I feel fortunate to be a Bloomsbury author, with the support and encouragement of everyone from Cindy Loh to Jessica Shohfi. Thanks to Patti Ratchford for the amazing cover, to Laura Phillips for her meticulous oversight of the production process (and her patience with all my changes), to Emily DeHuff for her careful copyediting, to Sara Mercurio, the most ardent publicist and advocate an author could want, and above all to Nancy Miller, whose thoughtful editing, sure hand, and great oversight made this a far better book.

Finally, I owe a great deal to several friends who read versions of the manuscript in progress and offered suggestions that sharpened everything from sentence structure to overarching themes. I'm very lucky to have such good friends willing to invest so much time, and even more fortunate that they are such gifted editors. Thanks to Sam Enriquez, Nick Goldberg, and Geoff Mohan. And above all, thanks to my husband, Michael Muskal, who lived with this project as long as I did, my first and last reader, a talented editor, and an exceptional best friend.

Bibliography

Books

Adams, Ansel, ed. *California, the Dynamic State*. Santa Barbara: Mcnally and Loftin, 1966.

Adams, Ansel, and Nancy Newhall. *Fiat Lux*. New York: McGraw-Hill, 1967.

Brower, David, ed. *Wilderness: America's Living Heritage*. San Francisco: Sierra Club, 1961.

Brown, Edmund G. *Public Justice, Private Mercy: A Governor's Education on Death Row*. New York: Weidenfeld & Nicolson, 1989.

Brown, Edmund G. Jr. *Dialogues*. Berkeley: Berkeley Hill Books, 1998.

Cooper, Erwin. *Aqueduct Empire: A Guide to Water in California*. Glendale, CA: Arthur H. Clark Company, 1968.

Dallek, Matthew. *The Right Moment*. New York: Free Press, 2000.

Didion, Joan. *Where I Was From*. New York: Alfred A. Knopf, 2003.

Eaton, Herbert. *The Overland Trail to California in 1852*. New York: G. P. Putnam's Sons.

Federal Writers Project of the Works Progress Administration. *California in the 1930s: The WPA Guide*. Berkeley: University of California Press, 2013.

Green, W. S. *The History of Colusa County*. San Francisco: Elliott & Moore, 1880.

HoSang, Daniel. *Racial Propositions: Ballot Initiatives and the Making of Postwar California*. Berkeley: University of California Press, 2010.

Hundley, Norris. *The Great Thirst: Californians and Water*. Berkeley: University of California Press, 2001.

Kerr, Clark. *The Gold and the Blue: A Personal Memoir of the University of California, 1949–1967*, vols. 1 and 2. Berkeley: University of California Press, 2001.

Leary, Mary Ellen. *Phantom Politics: Campaigning in California*. Washington, D.C.: Public Affairs Press, 1977.

Mathews, Joe, and Mark Paul. *California Crack-up*. Berkeley: University of California Press, 2010.

McWilliams, Carey. *California: The Great Exception*. New York: Current Books, 1949.

———. *Southern California: An Island on the Land*. New York: Duell, Sloan & Pearce, 1946.

O'Mara, Margaret. *Cities of Knowledge*. Princeton: Princeton University Press, 2005.

Pack, Robert. *Jerry Brown: The Philosopher Prince*. Briarcliff Manor, NY: Stein and Day, 1978.

Rapoport, Roger. *California Dreaming: The Political Odyssey of Pat and Jerry Brown*. Berkeley: Nolo Press, 1982.

Rarick, Ethan. *California Rising: The Life and Times of Pat Brown*. Berkeley: University of California Press, 2005.

Rogers, Justus. *Colusa County: Its History*. Orland, CA: 1891.

Schell, Orville. *Brown*. New York: Random House, 1978.

Schrag, Peter. *Paradise Lost*. New York: New Press, 1998.

Self, Robert. *American Babylon*. Princeton: Princeton University Press, 2003.

Starr, Kevin. *Americans and the California Dream, 1859–1915*. New York: Oxford University Press, 1973.

———. *Embattled Dreams: California in War and Peace, 1940–1950*. New York: Oxford University Press, 2002.

———. *Golden Dreams: California in an Age of Abundance, 1950–1963*. New York: Oxford University Press, 2009.

Walker, Franklin. *San Francisco's Literary Frontier*. New York: Alfred A. Knopf, 1939.

Walsh, James, ed. *The San Francisco Irish, 1850–1976*. San Francisco: Irish Literary and Historical Society, 1978.

Ware, Joseph. *The Emigrants' Guide to California*. St. Louis: J. Halsall, 1849.

White, Richard. *"It's Your Misfortune and None of My Own": A History of the American West*. Norman: University of Oklahoma Press, 1991.

Wolin, Sheldon, and John Scharr. *The Berkeley Rebellion and Beyond.* New York: New York Review Books, 1970.

Interviews

John Baumann, June 10, 2016

Anne Gust Brown, April 12, 2018

Chris Brown, December 2, 2016

Geoffrey Brown, March 30, 2018

Jerry Brown, April 11, 2015, April 19, 2017, October 20, 2017, and December 27, 2017

Kathleen Brown, January 27, 2016, February 14, 2017, and February 13, 2018

Marion Burman, May 2, 2016

Donald Burns, January 13, 2016

John Burton, March 27, 2018

Barbara Brown Casey, February 22, 2016, and October 10, 2016

LeRoy Chatfield, January 9, 2017

Eli Chernow, October 22, 2016

John Coleman, February 24, 2016

Denis Collins, December 2, 2016

Diane Cummins, October 21, 2017

Frank Damrell, January 12, 2016, May 25, 2016, and November 2, 2017

Dan Dooley, October 5, 2016, and February 28, 2018

Diana Dooley, October 11, 2016, and November 3, 2017

Jodie Evans, December 20, 2016

Doug Faigin, May 16, 2017

Raymond Fisher, November 18, 2016

Marshall Ganz, June 17, 2017

Nathan Gardels, June 10, 2017

John Geesman, February 28, 2018

Lucie Gikovich, April 12, 2018

Joyce Godon, May 13, 2015

Johnna Grell, March 27, 2018

Joseph Grodin, January 27, 2017

Hans Johnson, March 16, 2018

Mitchell Johnson, January 12, 2016

Joseph Kelly, June 2, 2016, and October 18, 2017

Kathleen Kelly, July 27, 2017, and October 18, 2017

Michael Kirst, July 20, 2017

Anthony Kline, February 24, 2016

Bart Lally, May 13, 2016, and June 24, 2016

Daniel Lowenstein, February 10, 2017

Gloria Lujan, February 4, 2017

Barbara Marcus, February 24, 2017

Ana Matosantos, January 12, 2017, and February 28, 2018

Richard Maullin, October 21, 2016, and June 13, 2017

Walter McGuire, January 26, 2017

John McInerny, June 24, 2016

Harold Meyerson, October 14, 2017

Marie Moretti, November 30, 2016

Martin Morgenstern, January 13, 2016, and October 27, 2016

Dowell Myers, July 5, 2017

Mary Nichols, September 26, 2016

June O'Sullivan, May 13, 2015

Michael Picker, January 13, 2017

Marc Poché, August 18, 2016

Bill Press, February 3, 2018

Tom Quinn, October 13, 2016, October 17, 2016, and May 2, 2017

Michael Reese, March 22, 2017

Stephen Reinhardt, September 13, 2016

Joyce Rey, March 2, 2017

Baxter Rice, April 5, 2016, and May 24, 2017

George Rice III, May 27, 2017

Dan Richard, May 25, 2017

Ron Robie, October 12, 2016

Peter Roddy, June 20, 2016

Van Gordon Sauter, March 14, 2018

Patricia Schaad, February 22, 2016

Bobbi Jo Seaver, May 13, 2015

Janita Smith, May 13, 2015

Janet Staple, May 13, 2015, May 24, 2016, and October 11, 2016

Kevin Starr, June 23, 2015

Faye Straus, March 25, 2016

Karin Surber, March 25, 2016, and October 19, 2017

Phil Tagami, September 22, 2017

Peter Taylor, November 7, 2016

Stephen Tobriner, March 21, 2017

Larry Tramutola, March 21, 2017

Llew Werner, September 7, 2017

Chuck Winner, April 27, 2017

Notes

Unless otherwise indicated, oral histories cited are from the Bancroft Regional Oral History Center collection, "Interviews of the Goodwin Knight–Edmund G. Brown, Sr., Gubernatorial Eras," Bancroft Library, University of California, Berkeley.

Archives abbreviations

BANC: Bancroft Library, University of California, Berkeley

CDC: California Democratic Council Papers, Southern California Research Library, Los Angeles

EGB: Edmund G. Brown Papers, Bancroft Library, University of California, Berkeley

HUNT: The Huntington Library, San Marino, California

JB: Edmund G. Brown Jr. Papers, Special Collections, University of Southern California Libraries, Los Angeles

JES: California Jesuit Archives, University Library, Santa Clara University, Santa Clara

JFK: John F. Kennedy Presidential Library, Boston, Mass.

NARA: National Archives and Records Administration, Washington, D.C.

OH: Oral Histories from the Regional Oral History Center, Bancroft Library, University of California, Berkeley

TIME: Dispatches from Time magazine correspondents: second series, 1956–1968, Houghton Library, Harvard University, Cambridge, Mass.

UCLA: UCLA Library Special Collections

WRCA: Water Resources Collections & Archives, Orbach Science Library, University of California, Riverside

Other abbreviations

LAT: Los Angeles Times

NYT: New York Times

PPIC: Public Policy Institute of California, San Francisco

SFC: San Francisco Chronicle

SFE: San Francisco Examiner

TRIB: Oakland Tribune

The Mansion

Sources: "Visiting with Huell Howser: The Governor's Mansion," July 8, 1996; Library of Congress, Historic American Building Survey; "Stewards of the Mansion," California State Parks; Pat Brown, Bernice Brown, Connie Carlson, OH; Author interviews with Kathleen Brown, Jerry Brown

003 "an extremely individual house" Joan Didion, *The White Album* (New York: Simon & Schuster, 1979), pp. 70–71

004 "Every day I come down the stairs" Author interview Oct. 20, 2017

1: The Pioneer

Sources: Patents and deeds, Colusa Clerk-Recorder; Land Entry Files, U.S. Bureau of Land Management, NARA; Shipping and immigration records, NARA; U.S. Census; Great Registers, Colusa County; Green, *The History of Colusa*; McWilliams, *California the Great Exception*; Rogers, *Colusa County*; Starr, *Americans and the California Dream*; Papers of Kathleen Brown, Jane Staple; *Wagon Wheels*, Vol. 20, No. 1, Feb. 1970; Williams Cemetery; Author interviews with Ash, O'Sullivan, Schaad, Seaver, Smith, Staple, Surber

006 "now engrossing the attention of the civilized world" Felix Wierzbicki, *California As It Is, and As It May Be* (Tarrytown, NY: Reprinted, W. Abbatt, 1927), E173.M24 no.126, HUNT, p. 1

006 "It is not necessary to be gifted" Ibid., p. 8

006 "a new and great community" Josiah Royce, *California, from the Conquest in 1846 to the Second Vigilance Committee in San Francisco* (New York: Alfred A. Knopf, 1948), p. viii

007 on the ship the *Perseverance* New York Passenger Lists, 1820–1897, Microcopy No. 237, Roll 79, NARA

007 a record number of pioneers William Hill, *The California Trail* (Boulder: Pruett, 1986), p. 18

008 But he kept a diary Diary courtesy of Kathleen Brown and Janet Staple

010 Colusa was a small town Rogers, *Colusa County*

011 "Those who came here came to stay" Ibid., p. 89

011 Home for August by 1860 1860 census; Peter Thomas Conmy, "Will Semple Green, Colusa Pioneer," Oakland, CA, 1955, Call # 19465, HUNT

012 He chose the quickest route New York Passenger Lists, 1820–1957, Records of the U.S. Customs Service, RG 36, NARA; Passport Applications, 1795–1905, M1372, Roll 106, NARA

013 boarding the SS *Hansa* New York Passenger Lists, 1820–1897

014 August continued to prosper Property deeds, Colusa Recorder; "Production of Agriculture in Stoney Creek," 1970, California State Library History Room

014 a well-known inn and tavern called the Mountain House Much of the description of life at the Mountain House is drawn from the writings of Gilbert Allen, grandson of August Schuckman, courtesy of Janet Staple

017 to keep her English grammar book Writing of Harold Brown, courtesy of Chris Brown

2: The Paris of America

Sources: U.S. Census; Great Registers, California State History Room; Pat Brown, Harold Brown, OH; Unitarian Church of San Francisco archives; Papers of Kathleen Brown; Starr, *Americans and the California Dream*; Temple, Josiah Howard, *A History of Framingham* (Town of Framingham, 1887); Walker, *San Francisco's Literary Frontier*; Frank Brown, Harold Brown, Pat Brown, Constance Carlson, OH; Author interviews with Ash, Kathleen Brown, Straus, Surber

018 "There is in the whole world no city" Henry George, "What the Railroad Will Bring Us," *Overland Monthly*, October 1868

019 "**There were suddenly all these opportunities**" *TIME*, Bill Glasgow, Aug. 29, 1958, Box 248

020 **on the clipper ship** *Anglo American* Boston Passenger Lists, 1820–1891, NARA

020 **aboard the** *Aeolius* Ibid.

022 **the bulk of his $1,200 estate** Probate records, Colusa Courthouse

023 "**The wheel of fortune**" George, "What the Railroad Will Bring Us"

023 **For ten dollars** *SFC*, Nov. 6, 1908

025 "**We are all anxious about you**" Nov. 8, 1917, courtesy of Karin Surber

026 **take your girl to the Palace** Mervyn Galvin to Pat, Aug. 1974, EGB, Carton 19, Folder 22

3: The Yell Leader

Sources: Bernice Brown, Frank Brown, Pat Brown, Constance Carlson, Tom Lynch, Albert Shumate, OH. Author interviews with Casey, Joseph Kelly, Straus, Surber

028 "**The citizens of San Francisco have**" *Lowell Alumni Roster, 1856–1930*, LD7501.S2 L8, HUNT

031 **he laid out his vision for the congregation** Dr. David Sammons, April 26, 2016, revsammons.wordpress.com/2016/04/26/dutton/

033 "**In no other state**" Quoted in Starr, *Americans and the California Dream*, p. 314

036 POLICE CAPTAIN'S DAUGHTER ELOPES *SFC*, Nov. 1, 1930

037 **The Gaylord had been built** United States Department of Interior, National Register of Historic Places

037 **write down his thoughts** Notes, Jan. 10, 1931, EGB, Carton 2, Folder 12

4: The Roosevelt Democrat

Sources: San Francisco City Directories; Starr, *Embattled Dreams*; Kevin Starr, *Golden Gate*; *California in the 1930s: The WPA Guide*; Frank Brown, Pat Brown, Carlson, Lynch, OH; "Lawyer for Quasi-Public Associations: the Biography of Mathew O. Tobriner," 1961 oral history, UCLA; Author interviews with Casey, Grodin, Joseph Kelly, Schaad, Tobriner

039 **Tobriner had grown up** Tobriner oral history

040 Tobriner delighted in recalling author interviews with Tobriner, Grodin; Pat Brown OH

042 bill collection work Various bills, EGB, Carton 40, Folder 21

042 net income for the year Brown 1938 tax return, EGB, Carton 40, Folder 23

042 The two lawyers roomed together Tobriner Oral History, UCLA

043 "all of the pressure that I can think of" Pat to Mr. and Mrs. Norval Fast, July 6, 1939, EGB, Carton 40, Folder 23

043 "I cannot understand why my name" Pat to Olson, Dec. 12, 1942, EGB, Carton 40, Folder 29

043 exchanged vows on May 27 Church records, St. Agnes, San Francisco

044 they leased furniture for $20 a month Bills, EGB, Carton 3, Folder 44

046 "I do not see how anything" Pat to Ken Dawson, Feb. 7, 1941, EGB, Carton 40, Folder 25

047 "to determine which side is right" Pat to Dawson, Mar. 20, 1941, ibid.

047 "it is my desire to serve" Pat to FBI, Dec. 16, 1941, EGB, Carton 40, Folder 26

047 "wherein I would be making a real contribution" Pat to Downey, Jan. 13, 1942, EGB, Carton 40, Folder 29

047 "does not know that there is a war going on" Pat to Civil Service, Mar. 16, 1942, ibid.

048 "the feeling of alienage" Pat to Knox, Mar. 23, 1942, ibid.

048 Harold wrote home with detailed accounts Harold to Edmund, Jan. 31, 1943, EGB, Carton 2, Folder 13

048 "it is kind of tough" Pat to Frank, Jan. 8, 1943, EGB, Carton 41, Folder 4

048 "I felt very sorry" Pat to Harold, Apr. 26, 1943, EGB, Carton 2, Folder 13

049 total federal spending was $728 million Walton Bean, *California: An Interpretive History* (New York: McGraw-Hill, 1988), pp. 425–26

049 "we should live each day to the fullest" Pat to George Keefe, Jun. 23, 1943, EGB, Carton 41, Folder 2

049 Japanese-operated farms McWilliams, "Moving the West Coast Japanese," *Harper's*, September 1942

050 Yoneo Bepp War Relocation Authority files, NARA; Blue and Gold, Cal 1927 Yearbook

050 "the reason for the movement" Pat to Bepp, Nov. 3, 1942, EGB, Carton 40, Folder 27

051 **"virtually a 'concentration' camp"** Bepp to Pat, Jun. 14, 1942, EGB, Carton 40, Folder 28

051 **"as much of an American as I am"** Pat to WRA, Jan. 29, 1943, EGB, Carton 41, Folder 4

051 **"my contribution to the war effort"** Bepp to Pat, Jul. 13, 1943, EGB, Carton 41, Folder 3

051 **"marking their ballots for them"** Pat to Bepp, Jan. 26, 1943, EGB, Carton 41, Folder 4

052 **"he has the energy"** *SFC*, Oct. 21, 1943

052 **"Born and reared in San Francisco"** 1943 campaign literature, EGB, Carton 691, Folder 32

052 **"I am confident that"** EGB to George Keefe, Aug. 19, 1943, EGB, Carton 41, Folder 2

053 **"It felt as if the whole world"** Belcher to Pat, Nov. 6, 1943, EGB, Carton 60, Folder 11

053 **just a stepping-stone** Glasgow, Sep. 1, 1958, *TIME*, Box 250

053 **"I listened to the election returns"** Levy to Pat, Nov. 5, 1943, EGB, Carton 60, Folder 7

053 **"Norton Simon's dice games"** Klein to Pat, Nov. 16, 1943, EGB, Carton 60, Folder 8

054 **"Belated congratulations"** Laye to Pat, Nov. 19, 1943, EGB, Carton 60, Folder 10

054 **"I am very proud"** Frank to Pat, Dec. 27, 1943, EGB, Carton 2, Folder 16

055 **"The prosecutor must not become the persecutor"** *San Francisco News*, Jan. 8, 1944

5: Forest Hill

Sources: Pat Brown, Bernice Brown, Connie Carlson, Fred Dutton, Tim Lynch, OH; Author interviews with Jerry Brown, Casey, Coleman, Johnson, Joseph Kelly, Lally, Rice, Roddy, Starr, Straus, Surber

056 **"a country home within the city"** Newell-Murdoch Co., Forest Hill pamphlet, San Francisco Heritage

057 **Pat wrote to his son** Pat to Jerry, Jul. 21, 1948, EGB, Carton 41, Folder 5

058 **"I have two teen-age daughters"** Pat to Frank Mackin, Aug. 12, 1948, EGB, Carton 693, Folder 15

c59 **to make arrangements for Pat** Pat to Yosemite Superintendent, EGB, Carton 39, Folder 3

c59 **during the wartime years** Starr, *Embattled Dreams*

c60 **"the gambling situation"** Pat to George Keefe, Aug. 9, 1945, EGB, Carton 39, Folder 2

c61 **"I want to be Attorney General"** Pat to Patrick Cooney, EGB, Carton 60, Folder 34

c62 **("She says she has enough trouble")** Pat to Keefe, Jun. 23, 1943, EGB, Carton 41, Folder 2

c62 **Lockheed employed ninety thousand workers** Starr, *Embattled Dreams*, pp. 124–25

c63 **veterans made up half the students** Ibid., p. 191

c63 **"Warren-ize yourself"** Mackin to Pat, Jul. 27, 1948, EGB, Carton 693, Folder 15

c64 **made his pitch** Pat to Leslie Claypool, political editor, *Daily News*, Feb. 7, 1950, EGB, Carton 60, Folder 31

c64 **a thirteen-page confidential letter** Pat to Clarvoe, Mar. 1, 1950, EGB, Carton 60, Folder 29

c66 **"Pat Brown's children run the gamut"** *SFE*, Jan. 9, 1951

c67 **"highest, most articulate idea of itself"** Pelfrey, *Brief History of the University of California*, p. 3

c67 **"interested in being a priest"** Burt Chandler to Pat, Jul. 15, 1951, EGB, Carton 3, Folder 25

c68 **"to mold manhood"** St. Ignatius High Catalog, 1951–52 and 1952–53, Ecx 9, JES

c68 **the annual Silver Medal Debate** Ibid.

c69 **"It trains the student to read between the lines"** *The Ignatian*, 1955, Ecx 12, JES

c69 **"was about ready to explode"** Pat to Fraynes, Oct. 29, 1971, EGB, Carton 13, Folder 6

c71 **"a glad-handing politician"** Pat to Chandler, Jul. 8, 1954, EGB, Carton 695, Folder 1

c73 **"In a conversation with Governor Knight"** notes, EGB, Carton 76, Folder 29

c73 **he subscribed to the *Catholic Lawyer*** Various documents, EGB, Carton 75, Folder 34

c74 **"California is a tremendous state"** Pat to Chandler, Dec. 4, 1950, EGB, Carton 60, Folder 30

6: The Governor and the Seminarian

Sources: Beadle books, Rector Files, Minister logs, photographs, correspondence, Jesuit Archives; Bernice Brown, Pat Brown, Warren Christopher, Fred Dutton, Marc Poché, OH; Pat Brown Oral History, JFK; Ben Swig Oral History, BANC; Walter Blum, *Benjamin H. Swig: The Measure of a Man* (San Francisco: Lawton and Alfred Kennedy, 1968), 493043, HUNT; Author interviews with Baumann, Burman, Coleman, Collins, Damrell, Joe Kelly, Lally, Poché, Rice

076 **"Everybody at home is very well"** Pat to Jerry, Mar. 15, 1956, EGB, Carton 67, Folder 14

076 **"A tremendous opportunity"** Jerry to Harold, Apr. 14, 1959, in Harold Brown OH

076 **"devoted to religion"** *San Jose Mercury-News*, January 1971

076 **"the party for you"** 1956 Convention program, Alexander Pope papers, Box 184, HUNT

077 **"I must confess"** Pat to Nolan, Aug. 22, 1956, EGB, Carton 695, Folder 22

078 **On his first full day at Sacred Heart** Rector's book, Aug. 15, 1956, JES

080 **"As in any 'boot-camp'"** "Points for Parents," JES

080 **"beginning to feel the loss"** Straukamp to Pat, Aug. 30, 1956, EGB, Carton 67, Folder 12

080 **"The change in routine"** Jerry to Harold, Apr. 14, 1959, in Harold Brown OH

080 **"with a truly American throng"** Speech, Oct. 27, 1956, EGB, Carton 695, Folder 13

081 **"a magnetic personality"** Pat to Jerry, Oct. 2, 1956, EGB, Carton 67, Folder 12

081 **"an excellent performance"** Jerry to Pat, May 11, 1957, EGB, Carton 67, Folder 9

082 **"necessary evil"** Pat to Jerry, May 20, 1957, ibid.

082 **"one of these days"** Pat to Jerry, Mar. 1, 1957, EGB, Carton 67, Folder 10

083 **"enjoyed politics"** Pat to Jerry, Jul. 11, 1957, EGB, Carton 67, Folder 8

083 **"being Attorney General"** Pat to Jerry, Apr. 26, 1957, EGB, Carton 67, Folder 9

083 **"Dear Dad"** Jerry to Pat, Jul. 3, 1957, EGB, Carton 67, Folder 8

084 **"cross the Rubicon"** Pat to Jerry, Jul. 11, 1957, ibid.

035 **"you have to decide"** Dutton to Pat, Jul. 27, 1957, EGB, Carton 79, Folder 3

035 **"slides in the bedrooms"** Pat to Kathy, Jul. 18, 1957, EGB, Carton 67, Folder 16

036 **"early announcement"** Dutton to Pat, Aug. 23, 1957, EGB, Carton 79, Folder 12

036 **"most important year"** Pat to Jerry, Aug. 13, 1957, EGB, Carton 67, Folder 8

037 **"a great state"** Speech, Oct. 30, 1957, EGB, Carton 721, Folder 19

037 **"the 4 major papers"** Rogers to Dutton, n.d., EGB, Carton 79, Folder 15

038 **campaigned year-round** "Overall Conclusions," Dutton, n.d., EGB, Carton 102, Folder 8

038 **"indispensable arm"** Harris to Dutton, Oct. 28, 1957, EGB, Carton 79, Folder 14

038 **outlined for Harris areas they should poll** Dutton to Harris, Nov. 25, 1957, EGB, Carton 79, Folder 5

039 **"as natural as an old shoe"** Curry to Brewer, Jun. 4, 1958, EGB, Carton 200, Folder 18

091 **"very, very real"** Pollard, Sep. 5, 1958, *TIME*, Box 252

091 **Pat was hurt** Pollard, Sep. 5, 1958, ibid.

091 **"a finished masterpiece"** Jerry to Harold, April 14, 1959

091 **"an inspiring picture"** Ibid.

092 **"early election returns"** Minister's Diary, Box 4, Nov. 4, 1958, JES

093 **"caused some uneasiness"** Rector to Rome, Jan. 1959, Rector Files, Box 20, JES

093 **Father William Burman** Vice Provincial to Rector, December 1958, JES

093 **"the greatness of California"** Pat to Jerry, Dec. 23, 1958, EGB, Carton 261, Folder 1

094 **"the only time we will have an opportunity"** *LAT*, Jan. 1, 1959

095 **decisive political leader** Dutton to Pat, Oct. 31, 1958, EGB, Carton 79, Folder 3

095 **"challenging budget"** Diary entry, Jan. 28, 1959, EGB, Vol. 25

095 **"Worried very much"** Diary entry, Mar. 13, 1959, ibid.

095 **"passed with highest marks"** Mar. 23, 1959, Hearst News Service

096 **"It amazes me sometimes"** EGB to Bert Dunne, Feb. 10, 1960, EGB, Carton 200, Folder 21

096 "some real thunderheads" Pat to Jerry, Jan. 21, 1959, EGB, Carton 192, Folder 22

096 "The tough part is ahead" Diary entry, April 21, 1959, EGB, Vol. 25

096 "a stimulating life" Diary entry, Jun. 24, 1959, ibid.

096 The juniors were admonished Rector to Father Provincial, Sep. 29, 1959, JES

097 "lend them a willing ear" Burman to Rector Connally, Jan. 29, 1960, JES

097 "visited my son" diary entry, Dec. 20, 1960, EGB, Vol. 26

098 "no vocation" Rector John F. Connally to Father Provincial Carroll M. O'Sullivan, Dec. 30, 1959, Rector Files, JES

098 "I see no hope" Ibid.

098 Finnegan made the same request Rector to Father Provincial, Jan. 1, 1960, Rector Files, JES

098 "attitudes toward religious life" Rector to Rome, July 3, 1960, JES

099 "the most forgotten soul" Pat Brown oral history interview, Jul. 27, 1972, Banc 83/97, Box 1

7: Fiat Lux

Sources: California Master Plan; *California, the Dynamic State*; Kerr, *Gold and the Blue*; Patricia Pelfrey, *A Brief History of the University of California* (Berkeley: University of California Press, 2004); Adams, *Fiat Lux*; Bernice Brown, Pat Brown, OH; Author interviews with Jerry Brown, Casey, Damrell, Lally, Poché

100 "a laboratory" Rockefeller to Robert Gordon Sproul, n.d., ihouse .berkeley.edu/about/HistoryBook.pdf

100 I-House opened Ibid.

101 Schorske had turned down Cal "Carl E. Schorske: Intellectual Life, Civil Libertarian Issues, and the Student Movement at the University of California, Berkeley, 1960–1969," an oral history conducted in 1996 and 1997, OH

102 "Fine boy but too intense" Diary entry, Mar. 8, 1960, EGB, Vol. 26

102 "I knew exactly what I wanted to do" Pat to William Flynn, Jan. 20, 1970, EGB, Carton 17, Folder 18

103 Phoebe Apperson Hearst Kerr, *Gold and the Blue*, Vol 1, p. 112

104 A 1959 survey Kerr report, Apr. 10, 1959, EGB, Carton 334, Folder 2

105 the chancellor warned UCLA Newsletter, Jan. 1959, EGB, Carton 333, Folder 21

106 **"stark necessity"** Kerr, *Gold and the Blue*, Vol. 1, p. 172

106 **"the knowledge industry"** "Clark Kerr - The Godkin Lecture at Harvard," Mar. 1, 1963, posted by UCLACommStudies, www.youtube.com/watch?v=H67 fOGXFgko

107 **"my university"** Kerr, *The Gold and the Blue*, Vol.1, p. 162

107 **"the most striking introduction to democracy"** Nathan Glazer, "Notes on Southern California: A Reasonable Suggestion as to How Things Can Be," *Commentary*, Aug. 1, 1959

107 **"only in California"** *California, the Dynamic State*, p. 13

108 **"very impressed"** Kaplan to Pat, Nov. 12, 1960, EGB, Carton 201, Folder 22

108 **"some fine talks"** Tobriner to Pat, Mar. 30, 1961, EGB, Carton 210, Folder 16

108 **"to probe deeply"** Tobriner to Yale Law School Dean, Apr. 4, 1961, ibid.

109 **"a real Californian"** Lurie to Pat, Mar. 20, 1961, EGB, Carton 209, Folder 17

109 **"the purpose of education"** "University of California, Berkeley. Charter Day, 1962. President John F. Kennedy," Mar. 23, 1962, archive.org/details /cubanc_00005

110 **"a bold and challenging idea"** Adams to Kerr, Mar. 27, 1963, BANC, University Archives, CU-5.93, Box 1, Folder 1

110 **"the intimate and effective relationship"** Ibid.

110 **"To look at the University of California"** Adams, *Fiat Lux*, p. 7

8: Down but Not Out

Sources: "Squaw Valley 1960: How It All Began," www.olympic.org/news /squaw-valley-1960-how-it-all-began; Elizabeth Rudel Gatov, Fred Dutton, Pat Brown, Oral Histories, JFK; May Layne Bonnell, Pat Brown, Jack Burby, Hale Champion, Fred Dutton, Richard Kline, Wallace Lynn, Cecil Poole, OH

112 **a fifth of liquor waiting** Memo, Dutton to Pat, Jul. 5, 1960, EGB, Carton 727, Folder 2

112 **"Your Party, and mine"** 1960 Convention program, Alexander Pope papers, Box 184, HUNT

114 **"Toughest decision I will make"** Diary, Oct. 15, 1959, EGB, Vol. 25

114 **"Wrote statement at 3:30 am"** Diary, Oct. 17, ibid.

115 **"And there was Pat"** Poole oral history, 1977, OH

116 **"I often wonder"** Bernice Brown oral history, May 17, 1979, OH

116 **"I have no doubt"** Tobriner to Pat, Mar. 17, 1960, EGB, Carton 201, Folder 7

116 **"My greatest fault"** Diary, Apr. 18, 1960, EGB, Vol. 26

116 **"very tough—no sleep"** Diary, Mar. 10, 1960, ibid.

117 **"Chessman will be executed"** Diary, May 2, 1960, ibid.

118 **"the best brains"** diary, Mar. 12, 1960, ibid.

118 **Pat's bewilderment** Tom Lynch, OH

119 **"I pleaded, urged"** diary, Jul. 12–13, 1960, EGB, Vol. 26

119 **"fatal mistake"** Ibid.

119 **"a nice guy"** Champion to Dr. Eugene Lee, Sep. 30, 1960, EGB, Carton 727, Folder 3

119 **"realities of the present"** Dutton to Pat, Jun. 1960, EGB, Carton 257, Folder 5

119 **five million passengers** Meeting minutes, Feb. 1, 1961, EGB, Carton 396, Folder 1

120 **"The industry which causes air pollution"** Hahn to Pat, Apr. 14, 1959, Hahn papers, Box 3.2.1.2.1, HUNT

122 **"I've become deeply interested"** Press release, Jun. 3, 1960, EGB, Carton 201, Folder 22

123 **"I was a little uneasy"** Kay Pinkham to Pat, Nov. 7, 1960, EGB, Carton 201, Folder 22

123 **"Why should I trouble anybody?"** *SFE*, Oct. 16, 1966

123 **"I knew I loved her"** Diary, Oct. 30, 1960, EGB, Vol. 26

124 **"He would be tough opposition"** Diary, Nov. 10, 1960, ibid.

124 **fundraiser at the Hollywood Palladium** Nov. 18, 1961, White House Audio Collection, WH-057-003, JFK

126 **"Let's buy this place"** Pat to Harold, Aug. 9, 1960, EGB, Carton 200, Folder 18

126 **a sale of the property all but closed** Probate file, Frank Schuckman, Colusa Courthouse

126 **"old sentimentalist"** Gertrude Rosenback to Pat, Dec. 20, 1962, EGB, Carton 227, Folder 3

126 **"that old Mountain House"** Pat to Rosenback, Feb. 5, 1963, ibid.

126 **confidential Harris poll** Harris poll, August 1962, Nixon Library, White House Special Files, Box 67, Folder 9

127 **"I have never lost California"** Text of Nixon-Brown Discussion, Oct. 1, 1962, Nixon Library, White House Special Files, Box 62, Folder 4

128 "a shoddy campaign" Oct. 25, 1962, Pope Papers, Folder, Pope Personal, HUNT

128 "reduced him to the nut house" Nov. 7, 1962, Dictabelt 6A, President's Office Files, JFK

129 "two happy old buddies" Champion oral history, interviewed April 14, 1978, OH

9: "Water for People. For Living"

Sources: Cooper, *Aqueduct Empire*; Hundley, *Great Thirst*; *California Water Atlas*, California Office of Planning and Development; "California water issues, 1950–1966: an oral history"; Ralph Brody, Pat Brown, Abbot Goldberg, William Warne, Harvey Banks, Hugh Burns, Ron Robie, OH; Warne and Robie Papers, WRCA; Harvey Grody, "From North to South: The Feather River Project," *Southern California Quarterly*, Vol. 60, No. 3, Fall 1978; Peveril Meigs III, "Water Planning in the Great Central Valley, California," *Geographical Review*, Vol. 29, No. 2 (April 1939)

130 "the water problem" Pat to Dan Beebe, Jan. 12, 1959, EGB, Carton 334, Folder 24

132 Muir pleaded "The Struggle for the Valley," *California Historical Society Quarterly*, September 1959

134 half the country's fresh fruit Cooper, p. 176

134 two valley towns Walter Goldschmidt, *As You Sow* (New York: Harcourt, Brace 1947)

136 passed seventy laws Cooper, p. 421

137 "essential to the future" Speech, Sept. 10, 1958, Pat Brown OH, "California Water Issues"

138 "doing the Lord's work" In particular, see Abbott Goldberg OH

138 "our destiny of greatness" Jan. 22, 1959, address to the legislature

139 "sufficient planning" Pat to Walter Gleason, May 16, 1959, EGB, Carton 583, Folder 3

140 "unequivocal loyalty" McBride to Ralph Brody, Aug. 7, 1959, EGB, Carton 588, Folder 6

140 "Water bill passed" Diary, Jun. 17, 1959, EGB, Vol. 25

140 "growth and prosperity" Bill signing, Jul. 9, 1959, EGB, Carton 588, Folder 6

140 "Your place in history" Charles Corker to Pat, Jun. 9, 1959, ibid.

140 "My place in history" Pat to Corker, Jun. 12, 1959, ibid.

141 "the need for more water" Dutton to Brody, Oct. 14, 1959, EGB, Carton 335, Folder 28

141 "I had qualms" Feather River dam groundbreaking, Sep. 29, 1959, EGB, Carton 336, Folder 8

141 "water or no water" Norris Poulson, Jun. 27, 1960, EGB, Carton 364, Folder 10

142 "the cash register" Interview transcript, Oct. 28, 1960, EGB, Carton 365, Folder 5

142 "endless argument" Sacramento Host Breakfast, Sep. 3, 1960, EGB, Carton 364, Folder 23

142 "a great step" Warren to Pat, Dec.10. 1960, EGB, Carton 201, Folder 7

142 "frustrating fight" Pat to Warren, Dec. 14, 1960, ibid.

143 he wrote memos Warne to Pat, Jun. 12, 1959, EGB, Carton 334, Folder 24

144 "growth and development" Speech, Jan. 13, 1961, Warne papers, Folder 1961

145 Kennedy arrived from Yosemite Remarks in Los Banos, Aug. 18, 1962, White House Audio Collection, WH-121-002, JFK; /www.jfklibrary.org /Asset-Viewer/Archives/JFKWHA-121-002.aspx

146 look back a decade later Warne to Pat, Apr. 10, 1973, EGB, Carton 30, Folder 15

10: The Turbulent Term

Sources: Kerr, *Gold and the Blue*, Vol. 2; Free Speech Movement Digital Archive and Oral History Project, BANC; Wolin, *Berkeley Rebellion and Beyond*; Governor's Commission on the Los Angeles Riots, McCone Commission Report, #633745, HUNT; Becker, Champion, Dutton, OH; Dallek, *Right Moment*; Author interviews with Jerry Brown, Kathleen Brown, Joe Kelly, Kline, McInerny, Rice

147 an address to conservationists Transcript of the seventh biennial wilderness conference, Apr. 7–8, 1961, in Brower, *Wilderness*, 496996, HUNT

148 "geography of hope" Wallace Stegner, "Wilderness Letter," 1960 and 1980, web.stanford.edu/~cbross/Ecospeak/wildernessletterintro.html

148 "most beautiful place" Pat to Art Seidenbaum, Jan. 29, 1970, EGB, Carton 17, Folder 22

148 "We painfully realize" Adams, *Wilderness*

1.8 an electronic counter James J. Rawls, "Visions and Revisions," *Wilson Quarterly*, Vol. 4, No. 3 (Summer 1980)

1.8 "more spectacularly endowed" *California: The Dynamic State*, p. 224

1.9 a city a week Ibid., pp. 50–53

1.9 "It stood to lose what it most loved" Adams, *Fiat Lux*, p. 16

1.9 "little pockets" Roy Bell OH

149 "California plans big" *California: The Dynamic State*, p. 222

150 "more glitter and glamour" *Sacramento Bee*, Jan. 8, 1963

150 "I didn't dance" *SFE*, Jan. 12, 1963

150 "I have a deep sense of urgency" Pat to Warren, Jan. 11, 1963, EGB, Carton 227, Folder 5

150 "aimed at the people" Burby to Pat, Apr. 26, 1963, EGB, Carton 259, Folder 19

151 "I no longer believe it is possible" Burby to Pat, Dec. 4, 1962, ibid.

151 a leisurely European trip News reports, EGB, Vol. 22 and Carton 225, Folder 17

152 "the place went wild" *Stanford Daily*, Oct. 31, 1963

153 "that time is now" "Paving the Way for Freedom Summer," *Stanford Magazine*, July/August 1996

153 "my Brown brain" Kathy to Lurie, Sept. 1964, EGB, Carton 27, Folder 5

154 "quite fascinating" Jerry to Lurie, Feb. 19, 1964, EGB, Carton 259, Folder 9

154 "as soon as possible" Jerry to Pat, Oct. 2, 1961, EGB, Carton 201, Folder 10

155 "property will win" Stegner, *California, the Dynamic State*, p. 220

156 "a long way to go" Pat to Kathleen, Nov. 9, 1964, quoted in Rarick, *California Rising*

157 events were unfolding Chronology and quotes that follow drawn from documents and recordings on the Free Speech Movement Digital Archive, www.lib.berkeley.edu/MRC/FSM/fsmtranscripts.html and Kerr, *Gold and the Blue*

157 "I say: Thank God" Commencement speech, Jun. 3, 1961, Santa Clara College

158 "This is not a matter of freedom of speech" quoted in Kerr, Vol. 2, p. 189

160 "suddenly goes smash" Wolin, Mar. 11, 1965, *New York Review of Books*

161 "violations of state law" Form letter, n.d., EGB, Carton 461, Folder 6

161 "its own moral downfall" Wolin, NYRB, March 11, 1965

161 "a thoughtful mind" Tobriner to Pat, Oct. 22, 1963, EGB, Carton 227, Folder 5

162 "It's a big day" *SFE*, Jun. 15, 1965

162 Jerry found it riveting He first told the story publicly at his fiftieth Yale Law School reunion in 2011; also author interview Oct. 20, 2017

162 four communities in the center of the city "Poverty Areas in Los Angeles County," Welfare Planning Council Working Paper No. 51, Apr. 1964, EGB, Carton 500, Folder 10

163 young, poor, and disillusioned Demographics and descriptions from the McCone Commission Report, archive.org/details/ViolenceInCity

164 "between fear and hope" Aug. 19, 1965, EGB, Carton 134, Folder 49

164 By Monday Testimony to McCone Commission, EGB, Carton 500, Folder 15

164 "slipped all restraints" Warne to Pat, Aug. 16, 1965, EGB, Carton 500, Folder 10

165 "universal bitterness" Becker to Pat, Aug. 30, 1965, ibid.

165 "The white backlash" Pat to Pearson, Aug. 20, 1965, ibid.

165 "an awful lot to be thankful for" *LAT*, Nov. 26, 1965

166 front page news *San Francisco Call-Bulletin*, Mar. 8, 1965

166 "our problems are many" "Ronald Reagan Announces for Governor: 01/04/1966," Jan. 4, 1966, posted by CONELRAD6401240, www.youtube.com /watch?v=0VNUOO7POXs

167 "The Watts problem" Dutton to Pat, May 24, 1966, EGB, Carton 751, Folder 17

167 saw the primary results as a warning Dutton to Moyers, Jun. 10, 1966, Minnesota Historical Society, Hubert Humphrey Vice Presidential Papers, Box 1057, Folder California, 1966

169 Viva Pat Brown Cruz Reynoso papers, Box 67, UC Davis Special Coll

170 "a rough campaign" Telephone conversation 10299, EGB and LBJ, Jun. 13, 1966, LBJ Library

170 "rallying point for Communists" "The Morality Gap," San Francisco Cow Palace, May 12, 1966

170 "a right held by all our citizens" *LAT*, Oct. 7, 1966

171 "double everything" *Palo Alto Times*, May 4, 1966

171 "developed an environmental conscience" *Oxnard Press Courier*, Oct. 12, 1966

171 Pat looked unusually grim Pat Brown at PG&E, Nov. 2, 1966, archive .org/details/csth_000055

172 "the boy next door" Ronald Reagan, Nov. 3, 1966, archive.org/details /csth_000060

172 "The people of California have been very, very good to me" *LAT,* Nov. 9, 1966

172 in a daze Swig to Warren, Nov. 25, 1966, Warren LOC Papers, Box 119, Folder 4,

172 "a Jolly Good Fellow" "Governor Edmund Pat Brown #1," archive.org /details/casacsh_000068

172 set up a lunch date Christopher to Pat, Nov. 30, 1966, EGB, Carton 252, Folder 8

173 "Nina and I voted" Warren to Pat, Nov. 10, 1966, EGB, Carton 252, Folder 13

173 "it just couldn't be done" Pat to Warren, Dec. 9, 1966, ibid.

11: The Browns of Los Angeles

Sources: Joe Wyatt, Ed Pauley papers, UCLA; CDC Papers; Bernice Brown, OH; Joseph Cerrell oral history, JFK; Dan Lowenstein oral history, UCLA; Bill Norris, *Liberal Opinions: My Life in the Stream of History* (2016); Author interviews with Jerry Brown, Kathleen Brown, Chernow, Damrell, Fisher, Lowenstein, Lujan, Maullin, Quinn, Rice, Surber

174 "a paradox: a desert that faces an ocean" McWilliams, in *West of the West: Imagining California* (San Francisco: North Point Press, 1989), p. 7

177 "The Other America" "50 Years Ago: Martin Luther King, Jr., Speaks at Stanford University," Apr. 14, 1967, kinginstitute.stanford.edu/news/50-years -ago-martin-luther-king-jr-speaks-stanford-university

178 "We are still in control of our destiny" Sep. 30, 1967, CDC, Box 32

178 McCarthy met with the steering committee Jan. 12, 1968, CDC, Box 29

179 "hoopla and streamers" *LAT,* Feb. 9, 1968

179 King spoke again about the two Americas Transcript, CDC convention, Mar. 16, 1968, CDC, Box 32

179 "I have been trying for weeks" *LAT,* May 23, 1968

180 "the lights went out for me" Dutton, *LAT,* Oct. 28, 1981

180 voted for the progressive Henry Wallace *SFC,* Apr. 12, 1948

180 "I like it quiet" *SFC,* Jan. 12, 1973

181 "pride, love, involvement" Connie to Ed and Bern, Jan. 23, 1969, EGB, Carton 2, Folder 31

181 "two years out of public service" Pat to friends, Dec. 1968, EGB, Carton 16, Folder 10

181 "I am trying awfully hard" Pat to Harold, Jun. 26, 1967, EGB, Carton 2, Folder 13

181 "some degree of material security" Pat to Bill Flynn, Apr. 29, 1967, EGB, Carton 3, Folder 4

181 "When I looked at that Santa Barbara campus" Pat to Storke, Oct. 20, 1969, EGB, Carton 12, Folder 24

181 By 1965, the Los Angeles Unified School District Lowell Janes Erikson, "The LA Community College District Crisis, 1981–87," LA Valley College, 1997

184 "students are not infantile" *LAT*, Nov. 26, 1969

184 "a religious cult" *LAT*, Jun. 30, 1970

184 "the problems we should try to solve" *LAT*, Dec. 30, 1970

186 "inherently corrupting" *LAT*, Mar. 3, 1970

186 "I wanted my grandmother to be here" *Desert Sun*, Mar. 3, 1970

186 requested the necessary state filing forms Judy Carter to Secretary of State, Mar. 2, 1970, EGB, Carton 17, Folder 21

186 "I was a good governor" Pat to McBride, Mar. 18, 1969, EGB, Carton 10, Folder 13

186 "Anything you can do to help" Pat to Marsh, Apr. 22, 1970, EGB, Carton 17, Folder 17

189 "the first application of systematic terror" Wolin, NYRB, Jun. 19, 1969

189 "a lily-white system of public schools" *LAT*, Apr. 8, 1970

189 "I don't intend to remain secretary of state" *LAT*, Aug. 23, 1970

190 "I want to thank my mother" UPI, Jan. 4, 1971

190 "breath of fresh air" Bird to Jerry, Jan. 10, 1971, JB, Box B-22-4

190 "the Tall Sycamore" *California Journal*, February 1971

191 "a rich man's preserve" *Sacramento Bee*, Sep. 5, 1971

192 could add 1.2 million first-time voters Maullin to Jerry, Nov. 30, 1971 JB, Box B-24-4

192 "collective voice of students" Notes, Apr. 24, 1971, JB, Box B-22-4

192 "What impressed me" Byrnes to Jerry, Oct. 13, 1972, JB, Box B-24-4

192 the most common reason cited Field Poll, Fall 1973, JB, Box B-32-6

192 "I don't quite enjoy the crowds" *San Jose Mercury-News*, January 1971 by Henry Farrell, political editor

193 Notes for a speech Notes, May 19, 1971, JB, Box B-22-4

193 red-penciled staff drafts Various letters, 1972, JB, Box B-23-7

193 "a reason to live" *LAT*, Mar. 19, 1972

193 "I can be alone" Ibid.

193 ("if that wouldn't be too outrageous") Jerry to Karen, Apr. 17, 1971, JB, Box B-22-4

194 "congratulations, and happy birthday" Pat and Bernice to Jerry, Apr. 7, 1971, ibid.

154 "I have been almost totally absorbed in my work" Jerry to Karen, Apr. 17, 1971

12: The Candidate

Pat Brown, Eckbo, Houghteling, Lowenstein, Pew, OH; Author interviews with Jerry Brown, Evans, Faigin, Fisher, Kline, Maullin, Picker, Quinn, Reinhardt, Werner, Winner

196 "It's largely an ad hoc job" Mary Jean Pew oral history, "Women in Politics, Vol. 3" Oct. 24, 1973, BANC

197 "I have a son" Pat to Cronkite, Sep. 26, 1973, EGB, Carton 19, Folder 2

198 "Without secret money" Town Hall speech, May 15, 1973, JB, Box B-22-4

198 ("He wanted to be a great president") Interview, 1971, Donated Oral Histories Collection, 2113, Box 014, UCLA

193 "I was booed unmercifully" Pat to Nixon, Apr. 26, 1973, EGB, Carton 3, Folder 34

193 "I threw in a name" Tape 445, June. 13, 1973, Nixon Library

199 "It is by far the most powerful body" Press release, Aug. 3, 1973, JB, Box B-32-6

200 "I don't want a bunch of sycophants around me" *LAT*, Mar. 19, 1972

200 "California has its problems" Jan. 28, 1974, JB, Box B-22-4

201 A Central Valley farmer sent $500 Dave Bryant to Pat, EGB, Carton 2, Folder 17

201 "more like his mother" Pat to Jim Gregg, Jun. 26, 1974, EGB, Carton 1, Folder 19

202 "There's still the notion that a woman is best suited" Pew oral history

203 He spoke extemporaneously Transcript, Feb. 9, 1974, JB, Box B-32-3

204 Jerry placed third CDC Paper, Box 41, UCLA

204 "the night my father lost" *Los Angeles Magazine*, Fall 1974

205 "I'm not one of the pampered rich" Mary Ellen Leary, *Phantom Politics*, p. 169

205 "If ambition could crack steel" "The Mystic and the Machine," *Rolling Stone*, Dec. 19, 1974

206 "people aren't ready for it" Ibid.

207 [Garrett] Eckbo . . . helped design Wonderland Park, Eckbo Oral History, OH

207 "It's rather isolated" "The Governor's Son," *Family Weekly*, Jan. 11, 1976

207 "It takes a very strong sense of yourself" *LAT*, Nov. 7, 1974

208 "an uncertain trumpet" *Rolling Stone*, Dec. 19, 1974

208 "We have the resources" Ibid.

208 "pointed to the Mansion" C. A. Maino to Jerry, Dec. 17, 1974, JB, Box E-28-2

209 "turn out this way" Finnegan to Pat, Nov. 9, 1974, EGB, Carton 20, Folder 19

209 "the impact you have" Pat to Finnegan, Feb. 13, 1975, ibid.

209 "The Jesuit ideal" *Esquire*, November 1974

210 "a fine boy" *SFE*, Jan. 12, 1972

210 "I love to read" *SFC*, Jan. 12, 1974

210 "tremendous human poise" Dutton to Pat, Jul. 19, 1974, EGB, Carton 30, Folder 9

210 "so deservedly proud" Houghteling to Pat, Jul. 8, 1974, ibid.

13: The New Spirit

Allard Lowenstein papers, Wilson Library, UNC; Bernice Brown OH; Author interviews with Burns, Dan Dooley, Diana Dooley, Evans, Fisher, Gardels, Gikovich, Kline, Lowenstein, Maullin, McGuire, Morgenstern, Poché, Press, Quinn, Robie

212 "I often have to turn" Invitation, Dec. 19, 1974, JB, Box A-29-4

212 "a crisis of the spirit" Prayer Breakfast, Jan. 6, 1975, archive.org/details /cbpf_000111

213 "What have we learned?" Inaugural address, Jan. 6, 1975

214 "there's a darker side" *Firing Line*, Oct. 11, 1975

214 "I like people" *Family Weekly*, Jan. 11, 1976

214 "every time I leave my cell" *Time*, Oct. 21, 1974

215 "damn good joiner" Pat to George Hart, Jul. 26, 1971, EGB, Carton 18, Folder 6

215 "I don't have the time" *Family Life*, Jan. 11, 1976

215 "We were always paraded" *Time*, Oct. 21, 1974

215 "attracted and repelled" *NYT Magazine*, Aug. 24, 1975

215 "see its limitations" *Playboy*, April 1976

215 "the family business" Ibid.

215 "always felt uncomfortable" Draft speech on democracy, May 14, 1973, JB, Box B-22-5

215 "blizzard of state paperwork" Memo, Feb. 26, 1975, JB, Box A-29-5

215 "symbolize the restraint" *Firing Line*, Oct. 11, 1975

215 returned hundreds of gifts Press release, Feb. 24, 1975, JB, Box A-29-4; Bill Stall form letter, JB, Box E-28-1

217 "I appreciate the 'loan'" Berrigan to Jerry; Jerry to Berrigan, 1976, n.d., JB Box E-33-10

217 "a misplaced cult" Form letter, Dec. 1, 1976, JB, Box E-31-7

217 "very, very busy" Pat to Jerry; Pat to Leonard, Jun. 25, 1976, EGB, Carton 8, Folder 30

217 "conventional wisdom" *Playboy*, April 1976

218 "He is contentious" *NYT Magazine*, Aug. 24, 1975

220 "like an energy source" Interview, Nov. 23, 1990, Lowenstein Oral History Project

220 "like a windshield wiper" KNBC Newscenter4 Viewpoint, Aug. 5, 1976, JB, Box E-31-6

220 "energy and talent" Nov. 23, 1990, Lowenstein project interview

220 "Dear Governor Brown" William Raiford to Jerry, Feb. 11, 1977, JB, Box F-36-3

220 "Jerry doesn't need approval" *NYT Magazine*, Aug. 24, 1975

220 "Green sea turtles" John T. Knox oral history in "Statewide and Regional Land-use planning in California, 1950–1980," OH; *LAT*, Sep. 27, 1977

220 "my theological training" News conference transcript, Jan. 14, 1975, JB, Box A-29-5

224 "understand my philosophy" Ibid.

224 "money that goes to people" News conference transcript, Jul. 1, 1975, JB, Box A-29-4

224 "**the great disparities**" Ibid.

225 "**an overblown expectation**" *Firing Line*, Oct. 11, 1975

225 "**before you dump something over**" News conference transcript, Mar. 11, 1975, JB, Box A-29-4

225 "**a few great decisions**" Jerry to Jack Valenti, Jun. 21, 1972, JB, Box B-24-6

226 "**delusions of grandeur**" Regents meeting, July 1975, JB, Box E-27-4

226 "**Look at Gandhi**" Joseph Kraft, *Baltimore Sun*, Mar. 20, 1975

226 Saxon had a saying Gardels interview

226 "**the squid process**" Jul. 1, 1975, news conference

226 At Regents meetings Transcripts, Jan., Mar., June, July 1977, JB, Box F-37-7

227 "**He learned the Socratic approach**" *SFE*, Jun. 26, 1977

227 "**They don't know the Lord's Prayer**" Transcript of conversation, Jun. 24, 1975, in *Coevolution Quarterly*, Fall 1975

227 "**unable to decide**" Bateson to Bill Coblentz, Regents, Sep. 27, 1977, JB, Box F-37-6

227 "**added a new dimension**" Carol Wilder, "Remembering Gregory Bateson," *Kybernetes*, Vol. 42, No. 9/10 (2013): doi.org/10.1108/K-11-2012-0117

227 "**not a sign of glory**" Notes, Jan. 29, 1977, JB, Box E-28-2

228 "**He's a phenomenon**" *60 Minutes*, Mar. 7, 1976

228 "**Junior Enigma**" *LAT*, Jul. 6, 1975

228 "**confront the confusion**" *Atlantic*, January, 1978

228 "**catalytic series of seminal works**" Ferlinghetti to Jerry, Dec. 4, 1975, JB, Box E-31-6

229 "**a great deal of interest**" Grunwald to Jerry, Dec. 27, 1975, JB, Box E-28-1

229 "**You haven't paid very much attention**" Pat to Jerry, Jul. 7, 1975, EGB, Carton 5, Folder 30

229 "**the problems of a former governor**" Mellon to Pat, JB, Box D-6-7

229 "**the surplus of rhetoric**" *SFE*, Jun. 9, 1975

230 "**reduce the sum of human misery**" *NYT*, Aug. 24, 1975

230 "**Jerry is more private**" Bernice Brown oral history, May 17, 1979

231 "**Hope you build a house**" Mrs. H. M. Cullers to Jerry, Sep. 16, 1976, JB, Box E-33-10

231 "**the idea of starting a family farm**" Jerry to Cullers, Nov. 29, 1976, ibid.

14: Jerry and Cesar

Sources: Jacques E. Levy Research Collection, Beinecke Library, Yale University (JEL); Tapes of UFW board meetings, UFW Archives, Walter P. Reuther Labor Library, Wayne State University; Author interviews with Jerry Brown, Chatfield, Ganz, Nathan, Press, Reinhardt

232 "position of power" *Playboy*, April 1976

234 "tool of the special interests" Assembly hearing transcript, Oct. 10, 1972, JB B-22-5

234 "In the future" Younger to Jerry, Sep. 21, 1972, JB, Box B-24-6

236 "treat all workers alike" Inaugural address, Jan. 6, 1975

237 "Dear Governor" Tape of Modesto rally, Mar. 1, 1975, Reuther Library, Wayne State

237 On Saturday morning Chronology from Levy interviews (JEL) and tapes of UFW meetings

237 "We wanted damn contracts" Tape of UFW board, Mar. 26, 1975, Reuther Library, Wayne State

237 "We walked out" Ibid.

238 "secret ballot elections" News conference transcript, Apr. 10, 1975, JB, Box D-6-7

239 "provide the framework" News conference transcript, Jun. 5, 1975, JB, Box A-29-4

239 "an idea is more powerful" *Firing Line*, Oct. 11, 1975

239 "Cesar needed a movement" Interview, n.d., Paradigm Productions

240 "he played it straight" Levy interview with Nathan and Cohen, Jun. 19, 1975, JEL

240 "as much impact in New York" *California Journal*, August 1975

240 "no deus ex machina" *Firing Line*, Oct. 11, 1975

241 "to be a movement leader" *Village Voice*, Jul. 2–8, 1980

241 "I represent a generation" *San Diego Union*, May 3, 1976

241 On the flight to Maryland Description and quotes, Schell, p. 10

242 "What can a president do?" Schell, p.13

242 "a leader can set a tone" *LAT*, Apr. 5, 1976

242 Someone ripped a button off his suit *Rolling Stone*, Jul. 15, 1976

242 "I can really win" *Newsweek*, May 31, 1976

242 "Jerry's contemplative" Nick Thinmesch, May 18, 1976, EGB, Carton 22, Folder 10

243 "This is my vocation" *SFE*, Jul. 25, 1976

244 "restore honesty" University of Oregon rally, May 1976, "Jerry Brown Campaigns in Eugene, Oregon, 1976," posted by Knight Library, www.youtube .com/watch?v=pVogT5tAmhY

244 diverted to Rhode Island Tape of UFW board meeting, Jun. 13, 1976, Reuther Library, Wayne State

245 "Every eight years" Jun. 1, 1976, tape by Andy Warhol, for *Interview* magazine

246 they organized an event Tape of Jul. 24, 1976 UFW board meeting, Reuther Library, Wayne State

246 "the power establishment" Interview, n.d., Paradigm Productions

247 "just a beginning" *LAT*, Jul. 15, 1976

247 "they know more than Jerry" *LAT*, Jul. 16, 1976

15: To the Moon and Back

Sources: Rusty Schweickart, NASA Johnson Space Center Oral History Project, 1999; O'Mara, *Cities of Knowledge*; Tom Wolfe, "The Tinkerings of Robert Noyce," *Esquire*, Dec. 1983; Leslie R. Berlin, "Robert Noyce and Fairchild Semi-conductor, 1957–1968," *The Business History Review*, Spring 2001; Stewart Brand, *Space Colonies, A Coevolution Book*; *Coevolution Quarterly*; Lindisfarne Tapes, Schumacher Center; Simon Sadler, "The Bateson Building," *Journal of the Society of Architectural Historians*, Vol. 75, No. 4 (December 2016); Author interviews with Jerry Brown, Press, Richard, Robie

248 "more interested than most things" "Loser Tells All," *Village Voice*, Jul. 9–15, 1980

249 "environmental crisis" Governor's Budget Message, Jan. 10, 1975

249 "our true wealth" 1979 State of the State address, JB, Box F-22-7

251 "a chance to come inside" *Sierra* magazine, June 1978

252 "Can this man clean up California?" *NYT*, Oct. 17, 1976

252 "the secret of his success" *Sierra* magazine, June 1978

253 "there are absolutes" Ibid.

254 "If a great newspaper" Pat to Chandler, Jun. 25, 1976, EGB, Carton 21, Folder 10

254 "an era of limits" "Conference on Western Water Issues," Caltech, May 17, 1979

255 "very euphoric" Lindisfarne talk, June 1978, archive.org/details/Sim VanDerRynII.C7

255 "a separate office" Sim Van der Ryn, *Culture, Architecture and Nature: An Ecological Design Retrospective* (New York: Routledge, 2014), p. 104

256 "a quest for underlying unity" "Outlook" CA Department of General Services newsletter, July–August 1981

256 and full of far-fetched ideas *NYT*, Jan. 16, 1978

256 "Jerry Brown's jojoba bean" *Washington Star*, Jun. 5, 1977

256 "He's always been the one" *Washington Post*, Jan. 6, 1980

256 "Ecology and technology" *LAT*, Aug. 30, 1977

258 In its first decade O'Mara, *Cities of Knowledge*

258 computers would become common Interview with Faculty Association of California Community Colleges, March 1982, JB, Box B-31-3

258 "everyone is going to need one" Ibid.

259 "a thousand television channels" *Esquire*, Feb. 1978

259 "information is the equalizer" Ibid.

259 "the *energy of character*" "Growth in an era of limits," Dec. 3, 1981, JB, Box C-6-10

259 "the future of America" *LAT*, Feb. 19, 1978

260 "ecology and technology" August 1977, *Space Colonies*, p. 146

260 "not a question of whether" Ibid.

260 "the Earth map is drenched" *LAT*, Aug. 12, 1977

261 "Going into space is an investment" *Space Colonies*, p. 146

262 "I hope Brown is still around" *Chicago Sun-Times*, Aug. 15, 1980

16: The Fall

Sources: Starr, "Lakeside Talk on History of Bohemian Club," June 4, 1977; Frank Levy, "On Understanding Proposition 13," *Public Interest*, No. 56, Summer 1979; Meyerson, "Proposition 13: Screwing the Poor," *Dissent*, Aug. 29, 1978; Meyerson, "Brown's California—After Proposition 13," *Dissent*, Winter 1979; "Playboy Interview: Linda Ronstadt," *Playboy*, April 1980; Author interviews with Meyerson, Quinn, Richard, Robie

263 "the best men's club" Lakeside talk, Jun. 4, 1977, EGB, Carton 758, Folder 56

264 "no other club like it" Pat to Kathleen, Jul. 24, 1957, EGB, Carton 67, Folder 16

264 "Nothing human is alien" *Newsweek*, Nov. 25, 1975

265 "a new element" Lakeside talk, Jul. 29, 1977, EGB, Carton 758, Folder 52

265 no longer went to church *LAT*, Mar. 5, 1978

266 "A conversation with Pat now" Dutton oral history interview, Apr. 15, 1978

266 "delight in life" Wenke to Pat, May 1, 1975, EGB, Carton 21, Folder 5

266 "young man in a hurry" Oral history interview, Jan. 11, 1978, OH

266 "two different personalities" Oral history interview, May 17, 1979, OH

266 "anything that diminishes that stockpile of intelligence" Pat Brown oral history interview, Jun. 5, 1978, OH

267 Jerry's tax bill Alexander Pope papers, Box 161, HUNT

268 "only an Assemblyman" Bane to Jerry, Jul. 20, 1977, JB, Box F-36-3

269 "the evil you know" *LAT*, Jan. 28, 1978

270 "a rip-off" *LAT*, May 23, 1978

270 Breslin visited Jarvis "Prop. 13: The Shot Heard Around America," *LAT*, Jun. 5, 1978

270 "show some compassion" Pat Brown oral history interview, Jun. 5, 1978, OH

271 going through the plan Various memos, June 1978, JB, Box A-24-8

271 "over four million" Address to the legislature, Jun. 8, 1978

271 school budgets declined Meyerson, *Dissent*, Winter 1979

271 "cut the guts out" Pat Brown interview, Jun. 13, 1978, Media Resources Center Collection, UC Berkeley, archive.org/details/cabemrc_00002

272 "The people have spoken" *LAT*, Jun. 7, 1978

272 "a modern Boston Tea Party" *NYT*, Jun. 12, 1978

272 "Operation successful—patient died" Schweickart to B. T. Collins, Jul. 5, 1978, JB, Box F-36-10

273 "I knew it would work" NBC News, Oct. 10, 1978

273 "given a second chance" *LAT*, Nov. 9, 1978

273 "The Jarvis tide" *LAT*, Jun. 7, 1978

274 "I have an interest" *Politics Today*, July/August 1979

275 ("He's not going to talk to the whales?") "Jerry Brown Talks to Whales," 1977, archive.org/details/cbpf_000082

275 "he will be bored" Jordan to Carter, March 1977, Office of the Chief of Staff Files, Hamilton Jordan's Confidential Files, Container 34a, Carter Library

275 "prophets in their own time" May 6, 1979, Washington, D.C., JB, Box C-2-7

276 promising to fight "A Question of Power," 1986, "Public Opposition to Diablo Canyon Nuclear Plant - Historic Clip," posted by eon3, www.youtube .com/watch?v=4kvSlVblE4I

277 "it might sound ridiculous" *Washington Post*, Feb. 25, 1979

277 "there isn't much difference" *Politics Today*, July/August 1979

277 he was booed "Squeezing Money out of Rock," *New York* magazine, Feb. 11, 1980

277 "My Boyfriend's Back" "Linda Ronstadt Sings My Boyfriend's Back to Jerry Brown," posted by jpspanishfan3, www.youtube.com/watch ?v=U-QmdzBYDWA

277 "we just like each other" *LAT*, Dec. 24, 1979

278 "Where Jerry goes" *Politics Today*, July/August 1979

278 Ronstadt had deliberately avoided using her celebrity *Playboy*, April 1980

279 if she ever thought about being first lady Ibid.

279 "genuine underdog sympathies" Mar. 10, 1979, Carey McWilliams papers, Box 8, UCLA

279 "ready for an alternative" Announcement, July 30, 1979, EGB, Carton 228, Folder 23

280 "a certain skeptical approach" "Loser Tells All," *Village Voice*, July 2–8, 1980

280 "not keep pace with inflation" State of the State address, Jan. 8, 1981

281 At cabinet meetings Cabinet meeting notes, Apr. 24, 1981, JB, Box C-2-7

281 "a very uncommon person" *Sacramento Bee*, Sep. 20, 1979

281 a tiny pest Medfly chronology from documents in JB, Boxes C-2-7, A-21-10

282 "a beautiful creature" Jerry to Nelson, Sep. 24, 1981, JB, Box F-8-2

283 "Women would ruin it" *Wall Street Journal*, Jun. 1, 1981

283 only 26 percent Field Poll, Aug. 20, 1981

283 "the spirit that built this state" State of the State address, Jan. 7, 1982

283 "California during the last seven years" Press release, Mar. 10, 1982, Brower papers, Carton 45, Folder 4

284 "I mistakenly thought" *SFC*, Sep. 15, 1982

284 "behind in the polls" Pat to Champion, Jul. 19, 1982, EGB, Carton 25, Folder 17

284 "do not like your son" Palevsky to Pat, Apr. 27, 1982, EGB, Carton 2, Folder 6

285 "a respite from me" UPI, Nov. 6, 1982

285 "Hang in there always" Hutton to Jerry, Nov. 19, 1982, JB, Box F-2-1

285 "He made us something" "Exodus of the Eclectic," *California Journal*, January 1982

286 "It is immodest" Pat to Denis Peckinpah, Aug. 16, 1971, EGB, Carton 12, Folder 4

286 "Jerry called me up" Pat Brown oral history interview, Apr. 24, 1979

286 "As we discussed" Robie to Huey Johnson, Jun. 1, 1981, Robie Papers, Box 14, WRCA

286 Pat rented a bus Video of aqueduct dedication, Dec. 11, 1982, video courtesy of Ron Robie

17: Winter Soldiers

Sources: Kathleen Cairns, *The Case of Rose Bird* (Lincoln: University of Nebraska Press, 2016); Author interviews with Anne Gust Brown, Evans, Ganz, Gardels, Geesman, Kathleen Kelly, Meyerson

289 "the shining city" "Mario Cuomo's 1984 Convention Speech," Jul. 16, 1984, posted bv 3rdeyestrategies, www.youtube.com/watch?v=kOdIqKsv624

290 "the difference between Mondale and Reagan" *SFC*, Jul. 15, 1984

291 "I'm advancing ideas" *SFE*, Jan. 14, 1985

291 "John the Baptists" *World Policy Journal*, Jun. 14, 1984

291 "out of active politics" *SFE*, Jan. 14, 1985

292 telephone survey Belden Research, Feb. 1985, EGB, Carton 31, Folder 28

292 "I blame Jerry Brown" Mosk, Apr. 2, 1998, in Peter J. Belton oral history, "A Senior Staff Attorney Reflects"

293 her decision to rotate the conference table Cairns, p. 107

293 "At stake is a choice" *LAT*, Mar. 2, 1986

294 "What's a father to do?" *LAT*, Oct. 28, 1986

294 "return to the soil" *California Journal*, June 1984

295 "when he feels like getting married" *SFC*, Oct. 20, 1978

295 "the strong influence" Barbara to Pat, Jan. 14, 1974, EGB, Carton 28, Folder 19

296 "I think he was a good governor" *California Journal*, June 1984

296 "It is about grasping the immediate" *East Bay Express*, Mar. 22, 1991

296 "writing for myself" *LAT*, Jan. 20, 1987

296 "the delusions of the self" *East Bay Express*, Mar. 22, 1991

297 "the expression on those faces!" Courtesy of Frank Damrell

297 "the pain on faces" *Life* magazine, April 1988

297 "he killed the idea" Collins to Pat, March 1988, EGB, Carton 27, Folder 16

298 "To make change" *Whole Earth Catalog*, Winter 1988

298 "I know in my bones" Op-ed, *Sacramento Bee*, Dec. 1988

298 "I've got some baggage" *LAT*, Dec. 18, 1988

299 "de facto educational apartheid" *Education Week*, June 19, 1985

300 "a heroic challenge" ABC News, Feb. 12, 1989, www.youtube.com/watch?v=DLBEXNCxKEE

301 "nuts and bolts" *LAT*, Jan. 12, 1991

301 "not for a moment" Jerry to friends, Sep. 6, 1991

301 "that spirit of democracy" "We the People," Sep. 6, 1991, www.c-span.org/video/?21224-1/people

302 "Join with me" Oct. 21, 1991, David Brower Papers, Carton 93, BANC

302 "to be a catalyst" *Whole Life Times*, October 1991

302 "wining and dining" Jerry to the Winter Soldiers, Fall 1992

302 "beg for money" *SFC*, Sep. 13, 1991

303 at a union convention "Brown Campaign Speech," Mar. 25, 1992, www.c-span.org/video/?25312-1/brown-campaign-speech

303 "a master of the process" *NYT*, Apr. 2, 1992

303 "Jerry is so irritating" *NYT*, Mar. 9, 1992

304 "very provocative contradiction" Jan. 14, 1992 interview, in *Rolling Stone*, Mar. 5, 1992

304 spent an hour with the *New York Post* editorial board "Jerry Brown Editorial Meeting with New York Post," Apr. 2, 1992, archive.org/details /CSPAN3_20160410_140000_Jerry_Brown_Editorial_Meeting_with_New _York_Post

305 "institutionalized injustice" *LAT*, May 2 and 3, 1992

305 "the rich are getting richer" May 30, 1992, American Community Summit, www.c-span.org/video/?26329-1/brown-campaign-speech

306 "you've got a good point" *Washington Post*, Apr. 17, 1992

306 "the absolute, the moral principles" *New York Post* meeting, Apr. 2, 1992

306 "just ahead of his time" Associated Press profile, Mar. 27, 1992

306 "an unflinching faith" *LAT*, Mar. 3, 1992

307 soaring over the cities Pat to Reagan, an open letter, Pat Brown oral history, OH

307 "benevolent seraph" *LAT*, Mar. 3, 1992

307 "be a missionary" *LAT*, Mar. 30, 1992

307 "to play out a destiny" *NYT*, Apr. 2, 1992

307 "a lot of ambition" *New York Post* meeting, Apr. 2, 1992

308 "We influence, we shape" *LAT*, Jun. 3, 1992

310 "I admire his guts" *LAT*, Jul. 16, 1992

310 "My father, Pat Brown!" "Gov. Jerry Brown 1992 Convention Remarks," Jul.15, 1992 www.c-span.org/video/?27116-1/gov-jerry-brown-1992-convention -remarks

18: A Different Shade of Brown

Sources: "Crawford v. Los Angeles Unified School District," *University of Laverne Law Review*, Vol. 31; Field Poll; "Undocumented Immigration in California," PPIC; Census Data; Author interviews with Anne Gust Brown, Kathleen Brown, Kathleen Kelly, Myers, Reese, Rice, Sauter

311 "I am a proud Californian" "Democratic Issues," Woman's National Democratic Club, Apr. 9, 1992, www.c-span.org/video/?25457-1/democratic -issues

313 "a wonderful girl" Diary, Oct. 11, 1960, EGB, Vol. 26

313 "Kathy is Pat's favorite" *NYT*, May 25, 1992

314 "the highest calling" *LAT*, Dec. 19, 1974

314 "because my name is Brown" *LAT*, Mar. 10, 1975

315 **"standard of living"** *Reader's Digest*, March 1976

315 **"I'm twenty-nine and a half"** *LAT*, Jun. 2, 1975

315 **"a constitutional obligation"** *Crawford v. Board of Education*, Supreme Court of California, Jun. 28, 1976

316 **"here I sit"** Minutes of Mar. 3, 1977, LAUSD archives, Box 942, UCLA

316 **"honest differences"** *LAT*, Mar. 5, 1977

317 **more and more empty desks** *LAT*, Oct. 9, 1979; Nov. 30, 1979

318 **"chronic bedwetters"** *Sun Valley Guide*, Winter 2007

318 **"a matter of love"** *SFC*, Apr. 5, 1982

318 **"the house radical"** Ibid.

319 **"a Magellan Avenue kid"** *Washington Post*, Feb. 25, 1994

319 **"don't have time for newcomers"** "Letters Home," *LAT*, Dec. 29, 1985

320 **"you will be governor"** Pat to Kathleen, Jul. 27, 1988, EGB, Carton 27, Folder 12

320 **"everywhere I go"** *LAT*, Apr. 30, 1989

320 **"different shade of Brown"** *Sacramento Bee*, Feb. 1, 1979

320 **"Kathleen is more natural"** *NYT*, May 25, 1992

321 **"Everybody likes Kathy"** Ibid.

321 **"the best of both"** *LAT*, Mar. 13, 1989

321 **"on the national ticket"** *LAT*, Dec. 30, 1990

322 **"He never asked me"** *LAT*, Jan. 4, 1991

323 **"great day to be a girl"** *LAT*, Jun. 4, 1992

323 **"kind of scary"** *Vanity Fair*, June 1994

323 **"a fair princess"** *Economist*, Jan. 9, 1993

323 **"I am incredibly proud"** *LAT*, Jul.12, 1992

324 **"Family transcends politics"** Ibid.

324 **"Jerry's brilliant"** *NYT*, Apr. 30, 1994

324 **"He's my brother"** Ibid.

325 **"rooted in the values"** Jun. 21, 1994, calvoter.org/archive/94general/cand /governor/brow/browspeech5.html

325 **"you lack the courage"** Oct. 14, 1994, www.c-span.org/video/?60854-1 /california-gubernatorial-debate

326 **percentage of foreign-born residents** "Immigrants in California," PPIC, Jan. 2017; U.S. Census Bureau and American Community Survey

327 "Immigration and immigrants add immeasurable value" *LAT*, Sep. 30, 1993

328 remained disproportionately white Caroline J. Tolbert and Rodney E. Haro, "Race/Ethnicity and Direct Democracy: An Analysis of California's Illegal Immigration Initiative." *Journal of Politics* 58 (3):806–18

328 "going to reverberate" C-SPAN, Nov. 7, 1994

328 "a fight for California" *LAT*, Nov. 13, 1994

329 "remember who you represent" Ibid.

329 "a mystical feeling" *Vanity Fair*, June 1994

329 "There was pressure" *LAT*, Dec. 31, 1994

331 "touched so many lives" *TRIB*, Feb. 20, 1996

331 Kathleen Kelly recalled *SFC*, Feb. 22, 1996

331 "Expanding and building" Ibid.

19: Oakland Ecopolis

Sources: Beth Bagwell, *Oakland, The Story of a City* (Novato: Presidio Press, 1982); Self, *American Babylon*; Stephen Talbot, *The Celebrity and the City* (2001); Matthew Fox, *Confessions, Revised and Updated*; Author interviews with Damrell, Grell, Kathleen Kelly, Tagami, Tramutola

332 four-year-old Gertrude Stein moved to Oakland Lois Rather, *Gertrude Stein and California* (Oakland: Rather Press, 1974)

333 "promote better government" Incorporation, "We the People," CA Secretary of State

333 "take America back" *TRIB*, Oct. 8, 1993

333 "the diversity of America" *Terrain* magazine, February 1995

334 "some form of *common life*" *SFE*, Apr. 25, 1993

334 "we need cooperative caring" *NYT*, Aug. 10, 1995

334 "take apart the conventional wisdom" *California Journal*, April 1994

334 "an excellent opportunity" *SFC*, Jul. 1, 1995

335 With Gore Vidal "We the People," July 1996, "Gore Vidal on Jerry Brown," posted by quuzellmynxits, www.youtube.com/watch?v=-OMfg-JGaSQ

335 "what I know how to do" "Moving toward the abyss," *Salon*, Jun. 3, 1996

335 "I'm ready for community" ITA conference, Santa Clara, Jun. 10, 1995

336 "enjoy running for office" *California Journal*, April 1994

336 "softer, fuzzier version" *TRIB*, Aug. 29, 2003

336 "his time has passed" *TRIB*, Nov. 21, 1996

336 he contacted **Ernest J. Yanarella** Ernest J. Yanarella, "How Green Is Jerry Brown?" www.terrain.org/essays/9/yanarella.htm

337 "at stake right here" *TRIB*, Oct. 29, 1997

337 "a tight little club" *Horizon* magazine, Feb. 1998

339 "have some impact" April 1999, General Assembly of Bay Area Governments, in *Whole Earth Catalog*, Summer 1999

340 "people voted for change" *TRIB*, Jun. 3, 1998

340 "being down on the field" *Diablo* magazine, January 2001

340 "test of Democratic leadership" July 12, 1988, convention transcript, CA Labor Federation proceedings, UC Berkeley Institute for Research on Labor and Employment

340 "catalyst for change" Inaugural Address, Jan. 4, 1999

341 "gun put in their back" *The Celebrity and the City*, 2001

341 "a specific dead body" Mayor's Blog, Jun. 22, 2005

341 "be able to produce" *City Journal*, Autumn 1999

341 "make laws and unmake them" CA Labor Federation, Jul. 21, 1988

341 "focused on potholes" *Whole Earth Catalog*, Summer 1999

342 "Suburbs are cheaper, cleaner, safer" Ibid.

342 "They all want an autograph" *The Celebrity and the City*, 2001

342 "to shake things up" *SFC*, May 13, 2000

342 "Every single project" State of the City address, April 1999

343 "They'll call it gentrification" *The Celebrity and the City*, 2001

343 "what's wrong with that?" *Nation*, Mar. 18, 2002

343 his own divinity school Fox, *Confessions, Revised and Updated*

343 "take some risk" "The State of Our Cities," Milken Institute Global Conference, April 1, 2003

344 "he pelts questions at me" *San Francisco Business Times*, Nov. 20, 2005

344 "It was a big mistake" Ibid.

345 "It's a scandal" *LAT*, Aug. 4, 2003

345 "there is tension" "Making Government Work," Temple University, May 8, 2000

345 "deep intellectual exchange" Jerry to David Brower, Nov. 8, 1999, Brower Papers, BANC

345 **"in friendship pursuing truth"** *SFC*, Aug. 29, 2000

345 **"I find it interesting"** *NYT*, Sep. 17, 2000

346 **Jerry wrote in a eulogy** *Whole Earth Review*, Spring 2003, www.wtp.org

347 **"the inspiration to learn"** interview with Shane Goldmacher, *LAT*, Oct. 7, 2009

347 **"right was right"** "Jerry Brown Speaks to AFSCME 2620- Part 2," San Jose, Aug. 27, 2009, posted by 2620afscme, www.youtube.com/watch ?v=dJVlOVn_VCw

348 **"my most lasting achievement"** *TRIB*, Feb. 10, 2003

348 **half a million dollars** "We the People" Form 990, California Secretary of State

349 **"a tsunami coming at us"** *Hannity and Colmes*, Aug. 7, 2003

350 **"voter rebellion"** "Global Viewpoint," *New Perspectives Quarterly*, Oct. 8, 2003

351 **"the steady hand"** *TRIB*, May 11, 2002

351 **"she created the order"** *TRIB*, May 14, 2002

351 **"nothing in my past"** *The Celebrity and the City*, 2001

352 **"not everybody's favorite"** *East Bay Express*, Mar. 19, 2003

352 **"eight-year-old with an ant farm"** *TRIB*, Jul. 2, 2003

352 ***Oakland Tribune* columnist** *TRIB*, Nov. 1, 2000

353 **"for a good cause"** Mayor's Blog, Apr. 15, 2005

354 **"fourth day of marriage"** Mayor's Blog, Jun. 22, 2005

20: Son of Sacramento

Sources: Author interviews: Anne Gust Brown, Damrell, Matosantos, Nichols, Quinn, Starr, Tagami

355 **"my first glimpse"** "Jerry Brown Inaugural and Behind Scenes," Jan. 8, 2007, posted by NewWestNotes, www.youtube.com/watch?v=AO479saDweU

356 **"it's about tradition"** *LA Weekly*, Jan. 24, 2007

356 **"his vocation"** *LAT*, Jun. 6, 2012

357 **"It's been fascinating"** Ibid.

357 **"life that we're leading"** *LAT*, Oct. 22, 2010

357 **"pretty invaluable"** Jerry to CA Dept. of Justice employees, Dec. 2006

357 **"a broad title"** *East Bay Times*, Jan. 5, 2007

358 **"panoramic view"** *East Bay Times*, Apr. 20, 2016

358 **"global warming legislation"** Jerry to CA Dept. of Justice employees

359 **"the Party of California"** *LAT*, Nov. 16, 2003

360 **"totally unique threat"** *Sacramento Bee*, Aug. 23, 2007

362 **"crossed my mind"** *Sacramento Bee*, Aug. 23, 2007

362 **"the historic character"** Associated Press, April 9, 2009

363 **"a meat grinder"** AFSCME 2620, Aug. 27, 2009, in San Jose

363 **"drawn to the task"** "Jerry Brown Talks at Google," Mountain View, Apr. 9, 2010, www.youtube.com/watch?v=I-ndAoifYyE

364 **"civic engagement"** "Jerry Brown Speech at Green:Net 2010," Apr. 29, 2010, archive.org/details/JerryBrownSpeechatGreen-Net2010-sV-gbcSEvGQ

365 **"common sense"** *LAT*, Oct. 22, 2010

367 **"I cannot win"** Gubernatorial debate, CSU Fresno, Oct. 2, 2010

367 **"kick you out"** Ibid.

368 **"due to Anne"** *LAT*, Oct. 22, 2010

369 **"The new comes out of the random"** "Jerry Brown Talks at Google," Apr. 9, 2010

369 **"this beautiful Fox theater"** "Election Night!" Nov. 2, 2010, posted by Brown for Governor, www.youtube.com/watch?v=dMGsAdoedgc

21: Second Chances

Sources: Author interviews with Anne Gust Brown, Cummins, Diana Dooley, Matosantos, Quinn

372 **"those pillars"** "The California Report," KQED, May 2, 2014

374 **"I can be president"** Anthony York Q&A, *LAT*, Sep. 2012

374 **"a 'purer' view"** *Atlantic*, June 2013

374 **"I have a group of people"** York interview, Sep. 2012

375 **"an extra pair of hands"** KCRA, May 22, 2013

375 **"running on time"** *Capitol Weekly*, Nov. 24, 2010

375 **"corral him"** "She Shares" conversation, Jun. 5, 2013, posted by CalChannel, www.youtube.com/channel/UCkxI9dQAfQC8gpud5Iaiwwg

375 **"like a vacation"** Ibid.

376 **"a caste system"** "Gov Jerry Brown on UC Budget at UC Regents - 1/17/2013," Jan. 17, 2013, posted by L4NER619, www.youtube.com/watch?v=2R6UW2ri9Mc

376 **"chess game"** Google forum, Mountain View, April 9, 2010

379 "safety, fear, religion" *Sacramento Bee* editorial board, Sep. 12, 2016

380 "screw things up" California Prison Industry Authority forum, San Diego, Sep. 1, 2017

380 "souls in purgatory" California Legislative Black Caucus MLK Breakfast, Jan. 12, 2017

380 "a little humility" San Diego, Sep. 1, 2017

381 not "yeasty" enough Yale Law School reunion, "AW '14 Panel 2: Picking Judges," Oct. 25, 2014, vimeo.com/110354435

382 "send a message" "Gov. Jerry Brown Prop 30 Speech Highlights & Reactions at UCLA," Oct. 16, 2012, posted by UCLA Daily Bruin, www.youtube.com/watch?v=GBSYkyU6xqU

383 Latino share of the vote California Civic Engagement Project study, January 2016

383 graduation speech "Governor Jerry Brown's address to political science graduates," UC Berkeley, May 20, 2013, posted by thedailycal, www.youtube.com/watch?v=WJKaTFff1D0

22: Fiat Lux Redux

Sources: "University Eligibility for the Public High School Class of 2015," RTI International; "Improving College Pathways," PPIC, November 2017; "Higher Education in California," PPIC, September 2017; Transcripts, video, and minutes of Regents meetings; Author interviews with Dan Dooley, Johnson, Kirst, Myers, Taylor

385 "dream big" *SFC*, May 17, 2009

386 out of poverty Census Bureau report, Sept. 2017; PPIC Poverty Fact Sheet, 2017

386 $15-an-hour minimum wage "Gov. Jerry Brown Signs the $15-per-hour Minimum Wage Bill," Apr. 4, 2016, posted by Los Angeles Times, www.youtube.com/watch?v=CjduaZw_UeU

386 the poverty rate "Poverty in California," PPIC, Oct. 2017

386 with a bachelor's degree "Higher Education in California," PPIC, Sep. 2017

387 percentages of Latinos graduating "Statistical Picture of Latinos in California," CA Senate Office of Research, Jan. 2014

387 fewer than a third "Improving College Pathways in California," PPIC, Nov. 2017

387 "a little humility" Jerry to U.S. Education Secretary Arne Duncan, Aug. 28, 2009

388 "a good test" American Federation of Teachers conference, Jul. 11, 2014, posted by AFTHQ, www.youtube.com/watch?v=ydyVfFCnhS0&feature=em-subs_digest-vrecs

388 "districts might screw up" Berggruen Institute fifth anniversary, May 5, 2016, vimeo.com/165498026

389 had the requisite grades RTI International study, Jul. 2017

389 "engine of growth" Google forum, Apr. 9, 2010

390 "long-term game plan" Anthony York Q&A, *LAT*, Sep. 2012

390 "That left a scar" "Gov Jerry Brown on UC Budget at UC Regents - 1/17/2013," posted by L4NER619, www.youtube.com/watch?v=2R6UW2ri9Mc

391 "We're dealing with California" Ibid.

391 "Let's get real" "Gov Jerry Brown comments at UC Regents meeting 1-16-2013," posted by L4NER619, www.youtube.com/watch?v=KXq9cIhpROg

392 "the five percent" "California Gov. Brown Talks About Politics & Budget at UC Regents: Nov. 14, 2013," posted by danieljbmitchell, www.youtube.com/watch?v=VdiqL2ntJzU&t=1s

392 "I love learning" Regents meeting, Jan. 17, 2013

393 single largest increase Transcript of Regents meeting, Mar. 16, 2017

393 the greatest role in economic upward mobility "California's Upward-Mobility Machine," *NYT*, May 25, 2017, Sep. 16, 2015

393 "a very powerful university" Regents meeting, Jan. 17, 2013

23: Past as Prologue

394 On January 5, 2015, she took the microphone Governor's inauguration, "Gov Jerry Brown Inauguration 1-5-2015," posted by L4NER619, www.youtube.com/watch?v=MGgRDCYWKTQ

395 "a trendsetter" "Governor Jerry Brown Interviewed by UC Campus Newspapers," *Daily Californian*, Oct. 22, 2012, soundcloud.com/hardandsoft/jerry-brown-interview-with-uc

396 "taking in the laundry" Anthony York Q&A, *LAT*, Sep. 2012

396 "My father, I don't think" "Jerry Brown Speaks to AFSCME 2620-Part 2," Aug. 27, 2009, posted by 2620afscme, www.youtube.com/watch?v=dJVlOVn_VCw

398 **"attracted the bold"** "California Governor Visits JPL," Aug. 22, 2012, www.ustream.tv/recorded/24892144

398 **"The Gold Rush"** Commonwealth Club of SF, Nov. 1, 2012

399 **"my little ilk"** Dedication of Los Angeles State Historic Park, Apr. 22, 2017

400 **"While Washington waffles"** Bill signing, Oct. 5, 2013

400 **"alive and well"** Bill signing, Oct. 3, 2013

401 **"'fugitive democracy'"** "Governor Jerry Brown's Address to Political Science Graduates," UC Berkeley, May 20, 2013, posted by thedailycal, www.youtube.com/channel/UCooUV6rU2bPDbyB8NQl4ebQ

401 **"real leadership"** Probation officers conference, Sacramento, Oct. 20, 2017

402 **"moment for prophets"** Jerry Brown, "Johannesburg Summit on Environment and Development," Aug. 2002, webarchive.loc.gov/all/20020914063537/http://www.jerrybrown.org/my_opinion.htm

403 **"new set of players"** Bill signing, Los Angeles, Sep. 8, 2016

403 **"eat the dirtiest air"** Ibid.

403 **"some cockamamie legacy"** California Senate hearing, Jul. 13, 2017

404 **"That is a breakthrough"** C40 Cities, New York, Sep. 18, 2017

404 **"this is pretty great"** Cap and trade bill signing, San Francisco, Jul. 25, 2017

405 **"This is California"** State of the State address, Jan. 24, 2017

407 **"from a mere state"** Eastern Economic Forum, Vladivostok, Sep. 6, 2017

407 **"man of the moment"** World Economic Forum, New York, Sep. 22, 2017

407 **"on the chopping block"** Stuttgart, Nov. 8, 2017

407 **"not just a light rinse"** Pontifical Academy of Science, Vatican City, Nov. 4, 2017

408 **"stuff we do in politics"** Norwegian TV, Nov. 22, 2017, NRK TV, tv.nrk.no/serie/torp/NNFA52112217/22-11-2017

408 **"the oil, the cars"** Ibid.

408 **"the rules of nature"** Ibid.

409 **"fighting self all my life"** Asia Society, San Francisco, May 11, 2012, asiasociety.org/video/gov-jerry-brown-california-mend

409 **"growing up in the Catholic faith"** *Sacramento Bee*, Jul. 22, 2015

409 **"the crux of the matter"** Signing message, Oct. 5, 2015

409 "optimism of the will" Norwegian TV, Nov. 22, 2017

410 "I have a skeptical eye" Studs Terkel, *Hope Dies Last: Keeping the Faith in Troubled Times* (New York: The New Press, 2003), pp. 221–222

411 "you as truth tellers" "A Conversation with Jerry Brown," San Francisco, Dec. 14, 2016, posted by American Geophysical Union, www.youtube .com/watch?v=kWSgncpqWtE

The Mountain House

Sources: Kathleen Brown papers; Author interviews with Jerry Brown, Kathleen Brown, Schaad, Staple, Surber, Tagami

412 the crowd gathered "The Final Rally in Williams California," Nov. 1, 2014, posted by Brown for Governor, www.youtube.com/watch?v=GTtX2j vr5is&t=140s

415 "I went up to my land" Press conference, Sacramento, Nov. 9, 2012

415 "what the land was" Author interview, April 11, 2015

415 "a hostile environment" Ibid.

417 "Like Cincinnatus" Climate change conference, San Francisco, May 24, 2017

417 "People will come" Author interview, April 11, 2015

418 "It has a history" Ibid.

418 "When we think Hall of Fame" California Hall of Fame induction, Oct. 28, 2015

Index